Glossing Practice

Glossing Practice

Comparative Perspectives

Edited by
Franck Cinato, Aimée Lahaussois,
and John B. Whitman

LEXINGTON BOOKS
Lanham • Boulder • New York • London

Published by Lexington Books
An imprint of The Rowman & Littlefield Publishing Group, Inc.
4501 Forbes Boulevard, Suite 200, Lanham, Maryland 20706
www.rowman.com

86-90 Paul Street, London EC2A 4NE

Copyright © 2023 by The Rowman & Littlefield Publishing Group, Inc.

"The Vespasian Psalter" (London, British Library, Cotton MS Vespasian A I, f. 12v) Manuscript produced in the first quarter of the 8th century. Main text in Latin with interlinear translation in Old English written in the 9th century. https://www.bl.uk/manuscripts/FullDisplay.aspx?ref=Cotton_MS_Vespasian_A_I. © British Library Board: London, British Library, Cotton MS Vespasian A I, f. 12v

Domingo de Santo Tomás, Grammatica o Arte de la lengua general de los Indios de los Reynos del Peru (1560). Digital facsimile at the John Carter Brown Library. Printed text in Quetchuan with interlinear glosses in Spanish. https://archive.org/details/grammaticaoarted00domi/page/n3/mode/2up. Public Domain

Daibirushana-kyō sho 大毘盧遮那経疏: Kōzanji-bon manuscript (colophon date of Eiho 2, 1082). Photo taken by Teiji Kosukegawa.

All rights reserved. No part of this book may be reproduced in any form or by any electronic or mechanical means, including information storage and retrieval systems, without written permission from the publisher, except by a reviewer who may quote passages in a review.

British Library Cataloguing in Publication Information Available

Library of Congress Cataloging-in-Publication Data

Names: Cinato, Franck, editor. | Lahaussois, Aimée, editor. | Whitman, John, 1954- editor.
Title: Glossing practice : comparative perspectives / edited by Franck Cinato, Aimée Lahaussois and John B. Whitman.
Description: Lanham : Lexington Books, [2023] | Includes bibliographical references and index.
Identifiers: LCCN 2022046768 (print) | LCCN 2022046769 (ebook) | ISBN 9781793612809 (cloth; alk. paper) | ISBN 9781793612823 (paper; alk. paper) | ISBN 9781793612816 (ebook)
Subjects: LCSH: Language and languages—Glossaries, vocabularies, etc. | LCGFT: Essays.
Classification: LCC P331 .G56 2023 (print) | LCC P331 (ebook) | DDC 413.028—dc23/eng/20221031
LC record available at https://lccn.loc.gov/2022046768
LC ebook record available at https://lccn.loc.gov/2022046769

∞™ The paper used in this publication meets the minimum requirements of American National Standard for Information Sciences—Permanence of Paper for Printed Library Materials, ANSI/NISO Z39.48-1992.

Contents

List of Figures   vii

List of Tables   ix

Introduction   1

I. COMPARATIVE GLOSSING PRACTICE   7

1   Continuity and Discontinuity: Glossing as a Dynamic System   9
Franck Cinato, Aimée Lahaussois, and John B. Whitman

2   The Five Services of Sanskrit Commentaries and Diomedes' Grammar Program   27
Franck Cinato

II. GLOSSES AS TOOLS FOR ACCESS TO KNOWLEDGE   45

3   Glossing Glosses: Methods for Transcribing and Glossing Japanese *Kundoku* Texts   47
Matthew Zisk

4   Issues in Dictionaries Recording *Kunten* Glosses   83
Teiji Kosukegawa

5   Interconnecting Knowledge in Early Medieval Glosses   95
Sinéad O'Sullivan

6   *Auraicept na nÉces* and the *Art of Medicine*   113
Deborah Hayden

III. GLOSSES AND LINGUISTICS — 137

7 Dry-point Grammatical Glosses — 139
   Andreas Nievergelt

8 The Pragmatics of Paratextual Paraphernalia — 153
   David Cram and Alderik H. Blom

9 A Revised Typology for the St Gall Priscian Glosses — 197
   Pádraic Moran

10 Glossing Practices in 1850–1911 Descriptions of Languages with Complex Verbal Morphology — 223
   Aimée Lahaussois

Index — 249

Index of Manuscripts — 257

About the Editors — 259

About the Contributors — 261

List of Figures

Figure 3.1	Arrangement of Middle Chinese Tone Marks	56
Figure 3.2	Excerpt from Yoshizawa (1915)	58
Figure 3.3	Excerpt from Kasuga (1942)	60
Figure 3.4	Excerpt from Nakada (1954–1958/1979)	61
Figure 3.5	Excerpt from Tsukishima (1965–1967)	62
Figure 4.1	The Phrase dàn shǎoxǔ 啖少許 in the *Shìshuō xīnshū* 世説新書	84
Figure 4.2	The Phrase lìng bǐ qǔ 令彼取 or lìng bǐ dàn 令彼啖 in *Daibirushana-kyō sho* 大毘盧遮那経疏	85
Figure 4.3	The Character dàn 啖 in the Story No.2 in the *Shìshuō xīnshū* 世説新書, Tenth-Century Glossing in the Collection of the Kyoto National Museum Based on e-Museum	86
Figure 4.4	The Phrase jiào jiào kūn míng 噍噍昆鳴 in the *Hàn shū Yáng Xióng Zhuàn* 漢書楊雄伝, 948 kunten Glossing in the Collection of the Kyoto National Museum Based on e-Museum	87
Figure 4.5	The Relationship between the *kunten* Glossing *muragare* ムラガレ to the Character *kūn* 昆 and the Traditional Annotations or Matched Couplet in the *Hàn shū Yáng Xióng Zhuàn* 漢書楊雄伝 in the Collection of the Kyoto National Museum Based on e-Museum	88

viii   *List of Figures*

Figure 4.6	The White Ink Glossing *haki* ハキ to the Right of the Character tǔ 吐 in the *Hàn shū Yáng Xióng Zhuàn* 漢書楊雄伝 in the Collection of the Kyoto National Museum Based on e-Museum	89
Figure 8.1	The Relation Between Semantics and Pragmatics	166
Figure 8.2	The Expedition of Humphry Clinker	175
Figure 10.1	The Continuum from "Most Free" to "Least Free" Translation Types	228
Figure 10.2	Paradigm for the Present Tense of the Verb "Say"	230
Figure 10.3	Example of the Free Translation (with Archaic Pronouns) that Accompanies Verb Form Examples	231
Figure 10.4	First Paradigm with a Speech Act Participant Object	231
Figure 10.5	Imperative Paradigm Involving Speech Act Participant Objects	232
Figure 10.6	Present Indicative Paradigm for the Verb "See"	232
Figure 10.7	Inverse Present Indicative Paradigm for "See"	233
Figure 10.8	Imperative Paradigm of the Verb "See"	233
Figure 10.9	Paradigm for the Verb "Give"	234
Figure 10.10	A "Passive" Paradigm from Vayu	234
Figure 10.11	A Paradigm with First and Second Persons as Both Subject and Object	235
Figure 10.12	Number-Coded Verb Forms for Bahing	236
Figure 10.13	Paradigm with only Speech Act Participant Arguments	237
Figure 10.14	An Inverse Paradigm	238
Figure 10.15	An Inverse Paradigm with Non-Archaic Second Person Pronouns	238
Figure 10.16	Text Specimen from Vayu Sketch Grammar in the LSI	240
Figure 10.17	Text Specimen with Interlinear Translation	242

List of Tables

Table 2.1	Partial Overlap of the Grammarian Services/Tasks	31
Table 3.1	Representation of Middle Chinese Tone Marks	71
Table 3.2	Representation of Vowel Sequences by Period	72
Table 3.3	Consonant Phonemes of Pre–Mid-Twentieth-Century Japanese	73
Table 3.4	Representation of Initial and Intervocalic p by Period	73
Table 3.5	Representation of Onglide Moras by Period	74
Table 9.1	Count of Glosses in Hofman's Five Main Typological Groups	200
Table 9.2	Subtypes of Glosses on Prosody	202
Table 9.3	Subtypes of Lexical Glosses	203
Table 9.4	Subtypes of Glosses on Morphology/Grammatical Glosses	205
Table 9.5	Subtypes of Glosses on Nouns	205
Table 9.6	Subtypes of Glosses on Pronouns	206
Table 9.7	Subtypes of Glosses on Syntax	208
Table 9.8	Subtypes of Group 41 "Syntactical Glosses Using Symbols"	208
Table 9.9	Distribution of Symbols According to Gloss Type	211
Table 9.10	Subtypes of Group 42 "Syntactical Glosses Using Words"	214
Table 9.11	Subtypes of Explanatory Glosses	214
Table 9.12	Proposed Revised Typology for the St Gall Priscian Glosses	218

Introduction

This volume is the first book to focus specifically on the topic of comparative glossing.[1] It brings together new research on glossing practices from traditions in both the West and East Asia (with a focus on Japan). It also touches on the relationship between the current chronological extremes of the practice, spanning the medieval manuscript tradition and contemporary descriptive linguistics. The purpose of the book is to present a sample of the most recent studies on glossing as it is practiced across very different parts of the world, highlighting the many shared features found across space and time.

The book contains ten chapters which outline how comparison in glossing practice—between past and present, East and West—broadens our knowledge of the phenomenon of "glosses." It has been organized thematically into three parts: part I, *Comparative Glossing Practice*, provides an introduction to comparative approaches; part II, *Glosses as Tools for Access to Knowledge*, contains papers that discuss the relationship between glossing and other modes of knowledge formation; part III, *Glosses and Linguistics*, shifts the focus to glossing in modern linguistics, regarding grammatical analysis, theoretical issues related to glosses as paratextual material from the standpoint of linguistic pragmatics, typology, and current scientific glossing practices.

Glossing practice has become an increasingly central and formalized part of modern linguistic analysis. Few linguists would spontaneously accept the possibility of any sort of continuity between the glossing of linguistic data in contemporary linguistics and the type of textual glossing practiced in the medieval West and, as demonstrated elsewhere in this volume, particularly the East Asian Sinosphere. Yet in chapter 1, *Continuity and Discontinuity*, we argue for exactly such a continuity, including but not confined to a certain objectification of language (Sakai 1992), appropriation of an ambiguous space between translation and replication, the distancing effect of lexical and grammatical analysis, and the creation of new forms in the glossing language (Whitman and Cinato 2014; Moran and Whitman 2022).

Glosses take many forms and serve numerous functions according to when and where they are produced. They constitute a cross-cultural phenomenon anchored in language and are the manifestation of hermeneutic processes involved in the transfer of knowledge from one linguistic area to another. Glosses are an integral part of all the stages of this transfer, which is characterized by the necessity to decode and explain the message, encompassing basic grammatical commentary and wider exegetical discussions. The second chapter, *The Five Services of Sanskrit Commentaries and Diomedes' Grammar Program*, aims at comparing two independent traditions, namely Sanskrit and Latin, to identify theoretical lines of thought to better understand the notion of gloss. To compare the traditions, the chapter takes the perspective of the "commentator's program," which uses an analytical grid as a formal guide to the composition of commentaries. This forms a parallel between the five kinds of glosses needed for a Sanskrit commentary in the Pāṇinean grammatical tradition and for the program presented in Diomedes' *Ars grammatica* (second half of the fourth century AD). The comparison is possible because both traditions share the same point of view regarding the practical aspects of hermeneutic mechanisms: glosses are a minimal component of the processes devoted to explain work. Not only the external aspects but also the purpose and method are comparable, showing how readers shared similar needs and how grammarians developed similar strategies to fulfill their requests.

A comparative approach to glosses reveals that they can no longer be considered solely as bearing witness to the reactions of isolated readers or of networks of scholars in a center of learning; in addition to their documentary value, they embody universal methodologies. For example, the act of translation (Lat. *Interpretatio*) is one of the results of these transfer-related processes, and the Japanese practice of *kanbun kundoku* (vernacular reading of classical Sinitic texts) shows that a system of prescribed rules for a vernacular (i.e., Japanese) reading of Chinese texts can be passed down from generation to generation. Chapters 3 and 4 propose an up-to-date overview of practices in Japanese glossing. Chapter 3, *Glossing Glosses. Methods for Transcribing and Glossing Japanese Kundoku Texts*, gives a general presentation of what *kundoku* is and proposes a standard of transcription and glossing for scholars dealing with glosses, especially devoted to citing examples from Japanese glossed texts in English publications in a comparative perspective between Western and Eastern glossing. Chapter 4, *Issues in Dictionaries Recording Kunten Glosses*, discusses the practice of collecting and publishing *kunten* glosses recorded from the eleventh century to the present day. It presents scientific working tools used in this research field focusing on the different problems they raise and proposing solutions.

Glosses, glossaries, and modern dictionaries reflect an aspect of the historical phenomenon that pushes speakers to produce tool sets (in the sense of Auroux 1994) linked to the epistemological phenomenon of the "grammatization" of languages. In the cases of Japan and Korea, for example, the academic and technical vocabulary is largely Sinoxenic, that is, based on literate loans from Chinese read in Sino-Japanese and Sino-Korean. It has been well known since the seminal work of Yamada (1935) that the chief medium for this transmission was the practice of *kanbun kundoku* or vernacular reading of Chinese texts; the same is true in Korea (for an updated account of this process, see Zisk 2017). Less well known is the fact that the specific route for the adoption of Chinese loans in vernacular reading was based on *kunten* glossing (Alberizzi 2015).

In Europe, where Latin texts were glossed in Latin as well as in vernaculars, glosses were the place where debates occurred, sometimes displaying code-switching and creating neologisms based on new conceptions. Chapter 5, *Interconnecting Knowledge in Early Medieval Glosses*, shows how glosses act as a medium connecting various texts and broadly different kinds of knowledge, using word pairing and code-switching. The Irish grammatical tradition, for example, offers many cases of the first occurrences of vernacular words appearing in glosses. Chapter 6, *Auraicept na nÉces and the Art of Medicine*, in a similar perspective as chapter 5, examines some of the glosses inserted in an Irish grammatical text assembled over a long period of time that reflect elements of Aristotelian natural philosophy and finds parallels in the corpus of early Irish medical material. The chapter also considers the significance of such glosses for the dating of the *Auraicept's* later commentary, as well as their implications for our understanding of the text's use in scholarly circles during the medieval period.

In the third part, chapters 7 to 10 offer discussions on glossed material from a theoretical and linguistic point of view. Chapter 7, *Dry-point Grammatical Glosses*, examines dry-point glossing in the German language area (Glaser-Nievergelt 2009), and especially morphosyntactic glosses, which are almost always abbreviated without any mark of abridgment, some reduced to a simple grammatical ending (Henkel 2001; Ernst 2009). Since the phenomenon is well known in vernacular glosses such as Old High German and Old Saxon, it can hardly be claimed to be a coincidence, and the question therefore arises as to why this type of abridged grammatical glosses was so frequently written with a stylus. The chapter investigates the practical background that led to this phenomenon. Chapter 8, *The Pragmatics of Paratextual Paraphernalia*, argues that there is much that modern pragmatic theorists can learn from the theory and practice of glossing in various grammatical traditions, not just in the classical and vernacular traditions of Western Europe but also the equally complex and long-standing Sanskrit, Chinese, and Hebrew traditions.

It also argues that the insights provided by modern pragmatic theory into the working of contextual effects—often assumed to be primarily marked by paralinguistic features in spoken language—can very helpfully be deployed in the study of the paratextual paraphernalia associated with written texts. The basic thesis of the chapter is that if paratextual elements are to written texts as paralinguistic markers are to spoken utterances, then there are theoretical extrapolations to be made in both directions that have hitherto failed to attract the attention they deserve. Chapter 9, *A Revised Typology for the St Gall Priscian Glosses*, discusses the different scientific typologies that scholars propose in order to assess the overall profile of a collection of glosses. It offers insight based on previous typologies in both manuscripts and traditions, for Western and Eastern glossing systems, which are directly comparable at a structural level. Based on the assertion that to be valid, any comparative exploration to some extent stands or falls on the robustness of the common typology used for the comparison and that typology must be subjected to a detailed critical analysis. Chapter 10, *Glossing Practices in 1850–1911 Descriptions of Languages with Complex Verbal Morphology*, looks into the use of glosses for explicating the roles of verbal arguments in early descriptions of languages known to have polypersonal indexation in Kiranti (Nepal) and Algonquian (North America) languages. In earlier descriptions, there were no standardized grammatical glosses to facilitate the understanding of the arguments of a complex verb, leaving linguists to resort to lexical glosses and to the creative use of word order in order to convey the argument structure of the verbs they were describing. The chapter discusses glossing in descriptions written from 1850 to 1911, with an eye to seeing how authors expressed the person/number of argument roles on verbs with agent and patient marking.

The central object of study throughout this volume is glosses and glossing practices, which provides us with the opportunity to compare similar but historically independent practices, allowing us to reexamine these subjects with some distance, thereby amplifying our understanding.

NOTE

1. We would like to thank all our colleagues at HTL research group (https://htl.cnrs.fr/) for discussion and exchanges about glossing practices, and especially to its director, Anne Grondeux, and also to Pádraic Moran (University of Galway) for their insightful comments on the first chapter.

REFERENCES

Alberizzi, Valerio Luigi. 2015. "The Role of Kunten Materials in the Process of Sino-Japanese Hybridization." *Quaderni Di Linguistica E Studi Orientali*, *1*, 233–258.

Auroux, Sylvain. 1994. *La révolution technologique de la grammatisation. Introduction à l'histoire des sciences du langage*. Liège.

Ernst, Oliver. 2009. "Kürzung in volkssprachigen Glossen." In *Die althochdeutsche und altsächsische Glossographie. Ein Handbuch*, edited by Rolf Bergmann and Stefanie Stricker, 282–315. Berlin, New York: Walter de Gruyter.

Glaser, Elvira, and Andreas Nievergelt. 2009. "Griffelglossen." In *Die althochdeutsche und altsächsische Glossographie. Ein Handbuch*, edited by Rolf Bergmann and Stefanie Stricker, 202–229. Berlin, New York: Walter de Gruyter.

Henkel, Nikolaus. 2009. "Glossierung und Texterschliessung. Zur Funktion lateinischer und volkssprachiger Glossen im Schulunterricht." In *Die althochdeutsche und altsächsische Glossographie. Ein Handbuch*, edited by Rolf Bergmann and Stefanie Stricker, 468–496. Berlin, New York: Walter de Gruyter.

Moran, Pádraic, and John Whitman. 2022. "Glossing and Reading in Western Europe and East Asia: A Comparative Case Study." *Speculum*, *97*(1), 112–139.

Sakai, Naoki. 1992. *Voices of the Past: The Status of Language in Eighteenth-Century Japanese*. Ithaca: Cornell University Press.

Whitman, John, and Cinato, Franck (eds). 2014. *Lecture vernaculaire des textes classiques chinois/Reading Chinese Classical Texts in the Vernacular, Dossiers d'HEL 7*. Laboratoire Histoire des Théories Linguistiques, Université Paris Diderot. https://shesl.org/index.php/dossier7-lecture-vernaculaire/.

Yamada, Yoshio. 1935 *Kanbun no Kundoku ni Yorite Tutaeraretaru Gohō* [Word Usage Transmitted Through *kanbun kundoku*]. Tokyo: Hōbunkan.

Zisk, Matthew. 2017. "Middle Chinese Loan Translations and Loan Derivations in Japanese." *Japanese/Korean Linguistics*, *24*, 315–329.

I
COMPARATIVE GLOSSING PRACTICE

1

Continuity and Discontinuity

Glossing as a Dynamic System

Franck Cinato, Aimée Lahaussois, and John B. Whitman

Any consideration of glossing should be preceded by mapping out a clear distinction between two notions: on the one hand, glosses are a component of a hermeneutic process, and, on the other hand, they are the physical manifestation of an annotating practice. Glosses can be written directly into margins and between the lines of a text, in manuscripts or printed books, but all annotations cannot be considered to be glosses. This means that a gloss is defined by characteristics which point to specific functions (see the detailed discussion on a typology of glosses in Moran, chapter 9, this volume). Moreover, glosses are not exclusively transmitted as annotations, since many glosses have their own traditions as autonomous texts: Glosses can take the shape of glossaries, of author lexica, and even of commentaries (lemmatical or autonomous).[1] The oldest attestation of word lists with a resemblance to glossaries is found in bilingual Mesopotamian tablets around the third millennium BC (cf. Reiner 2000). Thus, the history of glosses is independent of the history of annotating practices; glosses are part of this history but have their own course. Since glosses exist in all (written) linguistic traditions around the world, the history of glosses must take into account more than just one tradition.

Glosses are a rich topic of study, raising many questions, and in this introductory chapter, we will discuss some of them, with a focus on one particular aspect, namely tracking glossing practices through the ages to reveal their disparities and commonalities and to address the question of continuity and discontinuity, both synchronically across different linguistic areas and diachronically across the Western tradition.

WHAT ARE GLOSSES?

Nowadays, the word "gloss" is used to designate a wide range of linguistic objects, studied in many subfields, perspectives, and across a considerable time range, from antiquity to the modern day. We propose to define glosses as "linguistic objects" rather than as "small bits of discontinuous texts" as suggested by the commonly used definition,[2] because glosses do not belong to the same level as a conventional "text." To a certain extent, glosses are metatext, especially when they deliver grammatical information. Originally, a "gloss" was a technical metalinguistic term created by Greek grammarians to designate a word that they considered obscure or difficult, for reasons related to its rarity or archaism. Grammarians felt the need to transmit and explain rare words, in their role as antiquarians of language, pairing them with synonyms more widely known to their contemporaries. This primary perspective relies on the notion of lexical substitution (Irvine 1994: 221; see also Blom 2017: 29–32), but this conception eventually took on a broader sense. The strong link that unites a difficult word and its (easier) synonym led to the pairing (difficult word/easy synonym) being seen as a whole, and in the transition from antiquity to the Middle Ages, the meaning of "gloss" moves from the former (difficult word) to the latter (its synonym), until a gloss designates the explanation provided for the rare word. Glosses are now conventionally the explanation for a lemma, as both are united more or less tightly according to textual context. The nature of this relationship (text vs. lemma/gloss) determines how durable the pairing is through time and space.

WHAT IS TEXTUAL GLOSSING?

To qualify as a gloss, the linguistic object must have a relation to/with a text, or at the very least this must be the case for the lemma which takes on this linking role. An insightful overview has been provided by Irvine (1994: 371–393), showing various examples of manuscripts transmitting glossed texts, which is, according to him, "a social and institutional event with a historically situated material form" (Irvine 1994: 371). Irvine concludes that "glossed books present the interpreter of medieval culture with a paradox: the frame of the marginal gloss is a representation of the attempt simultaneously to disclose and control the text" (*ibid.*: 392). As pointed out by Teeuwen,

> The margins show us a great range of activity: astonishing scholarly work, disapproval and criticism, quick jumps to completely unexpected new material, ingenious visualizations of abstract knowledge, and newly devised methods

to organize material and make it memorable or ready for quick consultation. (2017: 36)

In this respect, glosses are transmittable material. Studying Carolingian glosses on Priscian's *Ars grammatica*, Cinato has shown (2015: 210, 219, 417–418) that it is their specificity that defines how durable glosses are and to what extent they are reused across generations. Interestingly, the more specific information a gloss provides for a lemma, the less durable it is; conversely, the more general the gloss, the more likely it is to be conserved and copied for a considerable period of time and to be transferable to other contexts. Several examples of unstable glosses can be provided: a single-word vernacular gloss (which can be understood as a translation) is in a precarious position because it can be replaced by another word by the scribe (see Grondeux 2000); even though medieval practices are conservative and glosses may be added to using terms like *uel, siue, uel aliter*, and so on, a gloss discussing a doctrinal issue can be replaced by another (gloss's) discussion a single generation later, whereas a gloss giving an etymology or a brief definition may be preserved and transmitted through many centuries and may eventually be replicated regardless of the text it was produced for. Cinato explains this phenomenon by alluding to the specificity of the (metatextual) link connecting the lemma and its gloss to a given text. If the lemma is detached from its text, a gloss having a weak specific relation to the text or none at all can be reused easily in another context; if the gloss remains attached to the same text, it is not affected by changes in fashion or in doctrinal perspectives. On the other hand, when a strong and specific relation exists between the gloss-lemma pair and its text, it loses coherence and intelligibility when detached from the context. This idea of a relation based on specificity can help disentangle the two main levels in glossing: reading glosses (a type of substitution gloss or supplement gloss; see Moran, chapter 9, this volume), which are inseparable from their text, and explanatory glosses, which can be understood without textual support.

The type of reading gloss known in Japanese as *kun yomi* (vernacular reading or gloss reading; cf. Moran and Whitman 2022, and Zisk, chapter 3, this volume), while at first appearing to counterexemplify this link between specificity or context dependence and durability, in fact confirms it. *Kun yomi* are the source for the established Japanese readings of Chinese characters in the reading tradition known as *kanbun kundoku* (vernacular reading of Sinitic texts), thus achieving extreme durability. But virtually every Chinese character used in Japan has multiple *kun yomi*; those tied to specific contexts are less likely to survive as the dominant or standard reading. Thus, the character 訓 *kun* (Chinese *xùn*) has as its most common Japanese vernacular reading *yomu* "read"; the more obscure reading *osieru* "teach" is closer to the original Chinese meaning, but less well known because it is mainly tied to the glosses of specific classical Chinese texts.

This situation shows that glosses must be evaluated not on a single level, but on at least three: the quality of the relationship (weak or strong) to a text, the function of the lemma/gloss pairing, and the semantic content of the gloss.

It is therefore clear that within the same glossing tradition we see phenomena of continuity or discontinuity, as a result of the influence of a master, the environment for the glosses, and the needs of the times. The "linguistic objects" called "glosses" thus appear to constitute flexible and evolving material; from their origins to the present day they have been tools and can be considered to be much more than simple discontinuous bits of texts. Moreover, in the West, medieval glossing practices do not disappear in the Renaissance,[3] since aspects of glossing have been perpetuated in the commentary processes. The salient example of this continuity is the tradition of word-for-word glossing as practiced by linguists, which brings with it a long legacy of linguistic analysis. A major argument of this volume is that modern linguistic glossing practice can be directly linked to the premodern habitus of textual glossing. We will now examine this hermeneutical heritage.

"Glossing" is a polysemous term, which on the one hand refers to the entire process of putting in writing and analyzing linguistic data (in other words, the annotation of data) and, on the other hand, to the morphemic analysis of each element of the transcribed data. If the former, it usually consists of three tiers, or levels, conventionally termed together the trilinear gloss: a transcription tier (typically phonemic or orthographic, often containing segmentation of the material into words and into morphemes, the unit of analysis relevant for the tier immediately beneath the transcription tier; it is important to note that this tier, no matter how carefully and scientifically it is produced, is still an interpretation and thus an imperfect replica of the original "text"), a glossing tier (typically made up of lexical as well as, later, grammatical glosses corresponding to each segment of the transcription tier), and a translation tier (typically made up of a free translation, which can also be accompanied by a more literal translation; in a sense, when a literal translation accompanies a free translation, the former serves as a gloss of the latter, attempting to bridge the distance between glossing and translation tiers, something which is more important when the typological distance between the target and metalanguage is great; see Schultze-Berndt 2006). There are many points of similarity between the trilinear gloss in contemporary linguistics and medieval Western and East Asian glossing traditions. To name a few: the coexistence of sound glosses with morphological and syntactic glosses, the practice of alignment with units in the lemma, and the fact that the translation and even the glossing tier provide a complete reading of the source text in the glossator's language.

The last similarity is a point of contact with East Asian glossing/reading traditions such as Japanese *kanbun kundoku* or Korean *kugyŏl* and the rarer Western examples where reading glosses provide a vernacular reading for an extended text. The practice of interpreting or reading an extended text based on the glossing tier is referred to as "glossese" and is practiced by typologists and theoretical syntacticians alike.

WHY DOES ONE GLOSS?

Textual glossing in the early Middle Ages aims to help and support subsequent readers. The glosses are part of a multilevel reading process, through which a text is prepared and this preparation can be transferred. The preparation is performed by glossators, who are grammarians and masters. The resulting text provides a frame that aligns with the wider cultural context in which the text is received, as described by Cram and Blom (chapter 8, this volume) under the term "paratextual paraphernalia." Glosses are polymorphous tools capable of providing various types of information, as detailed by Moran (chapter 9, this volume). In the medieval West, glosses begin to gain more and more favor from the late antique period, reaching a peak from about the sixth century onward (see McNamee 2007), but it is the Carolingian masters who lend them a consistency which borders on the systematic. In Japan, *kunten* glossing emerges in the eighth century, roughly a half century after the beginning of state-sponsored Buddhism. For the first century, it is focused on Buddhist texts; glossing of secular Chinese classical texts appears later. The first Korean *kugyŏl* glossed texts date to the tenth century, but there is historical evidence that the Korean tradition is older and influenced the development of its Japanese counterpart.

Carolingians were collectors and transmitters and used glosses to collect and compile information that was considered relevant for the understanding of a given text, and beyond, gathering cultural knowledge from the Latin legacy (see O'Sullivan, chapter 5, this volume). Depending on the different environments (cultural, linguistic, textual, etc.) glosses did not deliver a uniform range of material, nor was the discussion they provided homogeneous. Generally, a set of glosses varies according to geography and the links between monastic institutions, since it results from the work of generations of materials compiled in different ways depending on the masters at every step in the chain and, to a lesser extent, on scribes as well.

The appearance of glosses depends on the nature or status of a text (or material): not all texts were glossed, even if they were in the same manuscript. Any text receiving glosses presents particularities in terms of its relevance and interest from a cultural perspective. Moreover, the language of the text also has an influence on its glossing (see Cinato, chapter 2, this volume, and Kosukegawa and Whitman 2018).

Status of Glossed Materials

Unlike the Middle Ages, where texts were glossed because they were of religious/cultural significance, the situation is rather different in descriptive linguistics.

In this field, the very act of glossing elevates the status of the data, because that material then becomes part of the reference corpus for that language. In the case of endangered languages, collecting materials is a challenging enterprise: it necessitates that a linguist engage with the language community, gain their trust, find speakers whose mastery is still sufficient for the production of viable natural data, and learn the language well enough to be able to gloss the material. The limited amount of glossed material that can be produced by a linguist (or small team of linguists) and the fact that this (nearly) closed dataset becomes the basis for the production of dictionaries and grammars gives the glossed data its value. In an era of rapid advances in typology, new data from undocumented languages are crucial in shaping our understanding of linguistic universals, and the glossed material which provides insight into previously undocumented linguistic features is prized accordingly. Interestingly, this does not necessarily reflect the social/cultural status of the materials: casual conversations between members of the community can constitute a precious source of information about a wealth of linguistic features, even though their inherent cultural value may be considered low by the community. In other words, it is the act of glossing that transforms the glossed material into the corpus that, for rare and endangered languages, is sometimes the sum total of what is known about the language, making the data highly valuable to linguists and sometimes to the community as well.

Even though the language continues (one hopes) to exist and evolve in its natural setting, a snapshot of it is captured by the corpus and becomes representative of the language (despite issues such as the limited number of speakers and varieties and materials that compose the corpus), as far as the wider world is concerned.

Because endangered languages, with their low speaker numbers, are often seen to change faster than languages spoken by large communities and equipped with written materials, and speakers sometimes have prescriptive attitudes about their language, recordings from older speakers (who are often recognized by voice by the community), considered more linguistically accurate, are accorded higher status. Thus, the glossed corpus, through its ability to capture and make available a particular linguistic variety, also has elevated status in the eyes of speakers.

The Role of Grammarians: The Scientific Nature of Glossing

In the Middle Ages, the distinction between a *grammatica practica* (i.e., grammar for learning) and a *grammatica speculativa* (i.e., containing scientific debates about the Latin language) does not exist until the thirteenth century (cf. Rosier 1998). Consequently, glossing reflects both aspects at the same level. From antiquity, grammatical discussion has had two orientations: prescriptive and descriptive, one imposing a standard and the other reflecting the usage of leading authors. Despite medieval glossing practices not being systematic or standardized, the glossator seems to follow tacit rules regarding the method and the nature of information delivered by glosses. These practices left space for improvisation and individuality, although most of the time the glosses were copied from an exemplar. But faced with a "new" text, glossators were forced to innovate, adapt, and interconnect knowledge (see O'Sullivan, chapter 5, this volume).

In Japan, grammatical analysis has its origin in *kunten* glossing. The term for postnominal particles and verbal suffixes in traditional Japanese grammar, *teni(w)oha*, is based on the sequence of morphological glosses or *(w)okototen* in the *Hakaseke-ten* glossing tradition. *(W)okototen* involve a system of dots, lines, and other symbols placed around the quadrant of a Chinese character to indicate the Japanese particle or suffix to be attached to the character in its vernacular reading (see Zisk, chapter 3, this volume). The high-frequency morphemes at each corner of the quadrant in the *Hakaseke-ten* system are *-te* (gerundive suffix), *=ni* (dative/locative particle), *=wo* (accusative particle), and *=ha* (< *=pa*, topic particle). It is telling that the glossing system that gave its name to these functional morphemes in general was the system of the *Hakaseke*, the families that provided the faculty for the imperial university or *Daigaku-ryō*. This faculty glossed the Chinese classics for vernacular reading; the process of systematizing this practice led to the first elements of a grammatical analysis of Japanese.

For glossing in descriptive linguistics, two aspects of its scientific nature are its *systematicity* and its *standardization*. The systematic glossing of every element of data is important: the number of segments (i.e., elements separated by segmentation marks) in each word of the transcription and glossing tiers is expected to match. It is the systematicity that makes it possible to read glosses in languages one does not know, ensuring that they can be used for purposes other than those set by the glosser-linguist, such as typological work on an emerging grammatical topic.

In a similar vein, again for typological glossing, its *standardization* has considerably evolved over the last half century. Where initially transcription was a somewhat ad hoc process, the efforts of Voegelin and Voegelin (1959) helped standardize the presentation of the transcribed data. From the 1980s on, there has been a concerted push to standardize morphemic glossing. The work of Lehmann (1982) was very influential in this area and was further formalized in the *Leipzig Glossing Rules*, which include recommended abbreviations for grammatical glosses as well as rules for segmentation and alignment across tiers. The *Leipzig Glossing Rules* have been adopted as the "industry" standard, with a number of journal editors recommending their use. The one tier which is not yet governed by attempts at standardization is the translation tier, which is associated with vague recommendations (most often, that it be "free"), the result of which is a great variety of practices (Lahaussois 2016; Lahaussois and Léon 2015), with potential consequences, such as difficulties of use for comparative purposes (Wälchli 2007).

It is important to remember that, despite being the result of a scientific process, glossing is not completely objective: because the analysis of linguistic data is necessarily grounded in theory, there is a subjective dimension to the practice which deflects from systematicity. One example of this is the question of segmentation of transcribed data into morphemes: depending on one's views on morphology, segmentation will be carried out differently (a proponent of Item-and-Arrangement may produce rather different glosses from a Word-and-Paradigm follower) (Blevins 2016). As a result, the process of glossing, when carried out by different linguists, will necessarily have different outcomes, reducing the possibility of adhering to the scientific objective of replicability.

WHAT HAPPENS WHEN A TEXT IS GLOSSED?

Creation of a Metalanguage

In Europe, as in east Asia, and especially Japan, glosses are the locus of a discussion of grammatical issues, but also etymologies, and semantic elucidations. In glossed manuscripts and commentaries on Latin texts, it is common to find metalinguistic comments from the late antique period and throughout the Middle Ages: explaining difficulties in texts was one of the roles of grammarians (see Cinato, chapter 2, this volume). For Celtic, the first occurrences of terminology in vernacular languages denoting a grammatical metalanguage were found in languages like Old Breton and Old Irish (see Lambert 1987, 1999; Hofman 1996). In Old High German, special strategies were developed without associated terminology but using abbreviated verbal forms, for example (see Nievergelt, chapter 7, this volume). The first attempt in Latin glossaries to indicate information such as the morphosyntactic word class (*partes orationis* or parts of speech) is found in a monolingual Latin glossary (*Abutere*) copied in northeastern France (in MS Leiden,

Bibliotheek der Rijksuniversiteit, BPL 67E, fol. 1ra-61va) at the beginning of the ninth century, where each explanation is preceded by a letter: mainly "n." (= *nomen*, a noun), "u." (= *uerbum*, a verb)'. In the eleventh century, the grammarian Papias composed a glossary titled *Elementarium doctrine rudimentum* based on the oldest *Liber glossarum*, at the beginning of which he announces a system indicating gender, declension, conjugation, but his enterprise was never achieved and the system was abandoned (see Grondeux forthcoming). Later, these kinds of indications (and many more) were systematically added to bilingual Latin/old French glossaries in about the thirteenth century, in the *Catholicon* and its descendants, such as *Aalma*, from the end of the fourteenth century (see Merrilees et al. 2019).

Because Japanese *kunten* and Korean *kugyŏl* glossings were applied to a target language with less morphological complexity than either, the glossing tradition in Sinoxenic East Asia did not lead directly to the development of specialized terminology, except in the case of Japanese *teni(w)oha* mentioned above, in most linguistic subdomains. The exception is phonology, where, for example, the Chinese terminology for tones and the standard positions for tone glosses were adopted in both Japan and Korea.

A salient aspect of contemporary glossing is the appearance, over the last 100 years, of grammatical glosses (Lahaussois, chapter 10, this volume; Lahaussois 2021). From a situation where the majority of glosses were lexical, we have arrived at one where glosses for grammatical morphemes (case markers, inflection markers, derivational material, etc.) have a different form from lexemes: they have their own recommended abbreviations (as per the *Leipzig Glossing Rules*) and typographical conventions. This in essence amounts to a new kind of metalanguage, specifically associated with the production of glosses.

Objectification of Language

When contemporary linguists produce glossed text, the goal is generally to make explicit linguistic features of the language, as well as the transmission of cultural materials. The goals of language documentation (see Himmelmann 1998; Sakai 1992) suggest that the collected/glossed materials should be able to be viably used by scholars from many fields, and in this sense, glossing should serve more widely than the needs of linguists interested in morphosyntax. That being the case, there is nonetheless a focus on language as an object of study, and, to this end, there is a trend, in oral archives where texts are presented outside the context of grammatical description, toward more literal translation tiers, reflecting the morphosyntax of the language, rather than more fluid translations, which are better at conveying content than structure (Lahaussois 2016; Lahaussois and Léon 2015).

Influence of the Material Nature of Text on the Form of Glosses

It is difficult to evaluate how Western glossing was affected by changes in types of books, with the replacement of papyrus scrolls (*volumina*) by parchment books (*codices*) around the third and fourth centuries. The *Antiqui* annotated their scrolls, like sheet music, in order to prepare the oral performance of the text, but preserved fragments show that this practice was less extensive than the medieval practice, with its heavily glossed manuscripts (see Holtz 1984). It is worth noting that, in the Sinosphere, scrolls never resulted in an impediment for glossing. *Kunten* glossing continued in Japan with the development of various bound book formats, while in Korea, where printing was developed very early, the vast majority of surviving *kugyŏl* glossed texts are xylographs. In the Sanskrit tradition, books were made of various materials (birch bark, palm leaf, etc.), often leaving no space around the text area and between the lines to allow glossing. Despite this, Sanskrit manuscripts were annotated with glosses but later and less densely than European manuscripts. Thus, the different types of material receiving text do not seem to have influenced the presence of glosses, but they create particular conditions which can influence the form given to glosses.

As for the description of oral languages, glossing, in its broader sense, involves creating a written form of the "text," including its transcription, for something which only exists in the form of sound waves. This means that in many cases, the only written version of the data is, in many cases, an abstraction produced by the linguist. Currently, the development of glossing software has made it possible to link the original audio files with the glossing, anchoring the annotation in the original material. At the same time, these types of software constrain the output of the glossing process, ensuring the systematicity of its physical layout. Both these features—the fact that one is glossing an oral event, and that modern technology in essence forces the glossing into a certain output—constitute a considerable departure from earlier traditions.

Exact Transmission of Material and the Creation of Space between Translation and Replication

The presence of glosses ensures *proper transmission*, in ancient practice as well as in current scientific glossing. This is very much the case for endangered language materials: without access to a native speaker, there is very little that can be done with unglossed (i.e., untranscribed and unanalyzed) sound files. This is a problem faced by certain archives, which contain reels of recorded materials with only minimal metadata; even with the name of the language, it is close to impossible to use the materials for any scientific purposes. It is the glossing that accompanies a sound file that renders it usable to a wider community of researchers and ensures its proper transmission.

The creation of a space between translation and replication is particularly interesting for contemporary glossing, due to the tiered nature of the data. As contemporary glossing generally consists of transcription, glossing, and translation tiers, it covers the full range of spaces inhabited by medieval text transmission practices: the transcription tier can be compared to the replication (or copying) of earlier texts, attempting to render, as closely as possible, the original sound event; the translation tier can be compared to the activity of translating medieval texts for transmission. The space between these two activities is the morphemic analysis of the language, the very same (physical) space which is situated between the two other tiers in the form of the glossing tier. In Japanese and Korean vernacular reading, morphological glosses such as Japanese *(w)okototen* and syntactic glosses such as inversion marks and other indicators of word order in the vernacular version correspond to the glossing tier; together they are expected to provide the expert reader enough information to produce a vernacular reading on her own, corresponding to the translation tier. An idea of the complexity of this approach is provided in chapter 3 by Zisk.

On the opposite end of the spectrum, medieval glossing transmission can be qualified as "fluid": glossators generally made their own selection within inherited sets of glosses (from one or several exemplars). They decided what was worth transmitting, as they had the authority to produce changes in the material. This process stands in opposition to the replication of the text bearing the glosses, which had to be kept identical to the model: in this sense, few glosses are as authoritative as the main text. The emblematic counterexample is the *Glossa ordinaria* on the Bible,[4] which was aggregated by theologians—especially Anselme of Laon († 1117) and Pierre Lombard († 1160)—who, piece by piece, recorded and built a canonical set of explanations, fixed and transmitted identically. Replication of the text bearing the glosses, canonically a religious text, was also a prime limiting factor in Japanese *kunten* glossing as well: the earliest *kunten* glosses were in white ink (*hakuten*), so as not to obscure the black ink of the lemmata, and drypoint or scratch glossing was widely used to avoid sullying the primary text.

CONCLUSION

There are a great many differences among the various glossing traditions and practices discussed in this volume. The phenomenon which the Greco-Latin tradition designated with the metalinguistic term "gloss" is a legacy from antiquity which was passed down through the Middle Ages with major changes. The medieval masters were recipients of this strategy, developed it further, and enhanced the process of glossing to such an extent that at the end of the Middle Ages, glosses were ubiquitous in textual hermeneutics and teaching. Glosses kept the texts under control, as stated by Irvine (*op. cit.*), or, as Cram and Blom propose with their metaphor of a text enclosed in scaffolding made of glosses (this volume), with the consequence of superimposing a prism between the text and the reader. The control exerted by glosses on texts has had its critics: before the end of the eleventh century, in Biblical studies, some masters started to complain about glosses (in particular those in the glossed Psalter) because they imposed a *lectio discontinuata* (disjointed reading). This allowed scholars to break away from the holds of glossing even before the end of the Middle Ages. Daniel of Lérins, in the preface to his commentary on the Psalms (written before 1102), writes the following to Eldebert, abbot of Lérins:

(. . .) *Tu vero mihi obiicis aciem luminum quorundam fratrum aetate provectorum, tamen ad hoc perlegendum unanimiter suspirantium, non posse rimando tueri marginalium cum interlinearibus diversitatem sententiarum et, ob hoc, necessarium esse ut continuata lectio, in nullo devians, duceret lectorem per tramitem directum.* (ed. Morard 2011: 437)

But you object to me that the visual acuity of certain brothers of an advanced age, although unanimously yearning to make of this work a *continuous reading*, does not allow them, while scrutinizing it, to embrace within their gaze *the dispersion of marginal sentences and interlinear material*, and that, for this reason, it is necessary that a continuous reading, without deviating in any way, leads the reader by a direct path. (Following the French translation by M. Morard, *ibid.*)

This quotation, which was ahead of its time, reveals that glosses had a real influence on the way texts were to be read and understood (on the difference between *lectio* and *enarratio*, see Cinato, chapter 2, this volume). In counterpoint, more than 50 years later, Pierre le Vénérable († 1156) provides an opposite opinion by praising the humility of a brother (Benedictus) who, confessing his difficulty in understanding certain subtleties in the reading of the Psalms, let himself be helped by the glosses:

Psalterium glosatum semper circumferebat, quoniam psalmos non perfunctorie, ut quibusdam moris est, set summa cum intentione atque deuotione cantabat. Vbi, si quid quod non intelligeret offendisset, ad glossas statim oculum conuertebat.[5]

He (Brother Benedict) always carried a glossed psalter with him, for he did not sing the psalms superficially, as some are used to do, but with the greatest attention and devotion. And there, if he was struck by something he did not understand, he immediately turned his eye to the glosses. (Following the French translation by A. Grondeux *ibid.*)

In the twelfth century, glosses had a bright future ahead of them, but the margins gradually emptied out, leading to the Renaissance and the first printed editions of ancient texts, even though printed books tried to imitate medieval manuscripts and glossed manuscripts. Glosses were then confined to the realm of philologists and lexicographers. It is first with the work of Bonaventure De Smet, under the pseudonym Vulcanius, who published his *Thesaurus utriusque linguae* (printed in 1600), then the *Glossarium* by Du Cange (seventeenth century), and later, the first real Latin dictionaries (like Forcellini's *Lexicon totius latinitatis*, 1771) that glosses were seen again as objects worthy of study by linguists and historians (cf. Gitner and Goldstein forthcoming). However, it was only at the end of the nineteenth and the beginning of the twentieth centuries that glosses regained their former glory, with the first actual edition of glosses and glossaries.

Looking for the Missing Links

In attempting to interrogate the precedents of a certain type of analytical activity and searching for a "horizon of retrospection" (Auroux 1987, 2006),[6] we must concede that modern glossing seems inspired by medieval practices. The continuity between these two points on the temporal scale is not historically linear, since there is a gap between the old practices and the new ones; there is, however, a clear link in terms of intellectual posture and of hermeneutical approach (see Lahaussois, chapter 10, this volume, on some aspects of glossing practices from the nineteenth century up to present). Perhaps the missing link, bridging the two traditions, is to be found in the missionary grammars of the Renaissance: these descriptions were produced by scholars well-versed in the classical languages and who applied the Extended Latin Grammatical model (Auroux 1994: 82–88) and the concept of Greek and Latin morphosyntactic units (*partes orationis*) to the languages they encountered. It is very possible that this period is an important pivot between a Latin-based philological tradition that includes glossing and the application of such annotational practices to the description of undescribed and exotic languages. According to Smith-Stark 2019, the current principles that a language's documentation should be made up of grammar, a dictionary, and a corpus (often referred to as the "Boasian trilogy") can be traced back to sixteenth-century missionary practices of providing languages with a catechistic trilogy of grammar, vocabulary, and doctrinal texts, with the latter serving as the corpus from which the former two were able to be elaborated. The doctrinal corpus often featured versions in both the indigenous and the (European) language of the missionary, and different configurations of these textual correspondences eventually led to an interlinear presentation. Zwartjes (2014: 19) presents Domingo de Santo Tomas's 1560 interlinearized Quechua as one of the earliest exemplars.

Significant ongoing work on missionary grammars should soon provide critical further insight into the possibility of descriptive grammars of unknown languages of this period being the bridge between medieval glossing practices and those found associated with current documentary work.

Another factor to consider is that glossing may represent a universal cognitive behavior in written cultures: the activity of glossing is a means of parsing and making sense of new materials, something which second-language learners appear to do intuitively (and without prior models) when faced with sentences in the language they are acquiring. This hermeneutic activity, the goal of which is to break down complicated material into more manageable units, may well be a link through the ages and across cultures.

NOTES

1. In grammatical field, see for example Fredborg 1973 who shows relationships between a lemmatical commentary and a grammatical sum; this sum (*summa*), mainly based on Priscian's grammar, represents a further—or deeper—evolution of a commentary toward an autonomous text discussing an authoritative text. See also Kneepkens 1995 for an overview.

2. The "commonly used definition" can be illustrated by the following two examples: in French "Annotation brève portée sur la même page que le texte, destinée à expliquer le sens d'un mot inintelligible ou difficile ou d'un passage obscur, et rédigée dans la même langue que le texte" (*TLFi*: Trésor de la langue Française informatisé, http://www.atilf.fr/tlfi, ATILF—CNRS & Université de Lorraine); or "a brief explanatory note or translation usually inserted in the margin or between lines of a text or manuscript" (*The American Heritage college dictionary*, third ed.).

3. In studies on Priscian, some Renaissance editions go so far as to imitate the layout of medieval manuscripts by printing a twelfth-century commentary in the margin (see Grondeux 2016).

4. Among a huge and rich bibliography, some useful references are: Smalley 1937; Wielockx 1982; Smalley 1983; Lobrichon 1984; Gibson 1992; Smith 2009.

5. Pierre le Vénérable, *De miraculis libri duo*, ed. Bouthillier, *CCCM* 83, Turnhout, 1988, 1, 20, 52, quoted and discussed by Grondeux 2000: 192–193, whom we warmly thank to have drawn our attention to this citation.

6. In this, we will follow the author's recommendations to avoid a teleological approach explaining the future of a practice by observations made in the past course of events; on the other hand, we will try to demonstrate that there is a causal link between the two practices.

REFERENCES

Auroux, Sylvain. 1987. "Histoire des sciences et entropie des systèmes scientifiques. Les horizons de rétrospection." In *Geschichte der Sprachtheorie 1 : Zur Theorie*

und Methode der Geschichtsschreibung der Linguistik, edited by Peter Schmitter, 20–42. Tübingen: Gunter Narr [1ère parution en 1986 dans *Archives et Documents de la SHESL*, 7, 1–26.]
———. 1994. *La révolution technologique de la grammatisation. Introduction à l'histoire des sciences du langage.* Liège.
———. 2006. "Les modes d'historicisation." *Histoire Épistémologie Langage* 28/1: 105–116.
Blevins, James. 2016. *Word and Paradigm Morphology.* Oxford: Oxford University Press.
Blom, Alderik H. 2017. *Glossing the Psalms: The Emergence of the Written Vernaculars in Western Europe From the Seventh to the Twelfth Centuries.* Berlin, Boston: Walter de Gruyter GmbH.
Bow, C., B. Hughes, and S. Bird. 2003. "Towards a General Model of Interlinear Text." In *Proceedings of EMELD Workshop*, 1–47. http://emeld.org/workshop/2003/bowbadenbird-paper.pdf.
Comrie, Bernard, and Norval Smith. 1977. "Lingua Descriptive Studies: Questionnaire." *Lingua* 42(1): 1–72.
Fredborg, K. M. 1973. "The Dependence of Petrus Helias' *Summa super Priscianum* on William of Conches' *Glose super Priscianum*," *Cahiers de l'Institut du Moyen Age Grec et Latin* 11: 1–57.
Gibson, Margaret T. 1992. "The Place of the 'Glossa Ordinaria' in Medieval Exegesis." In *Ad litteram: Authoritative Texts and their Medieval Readers*, edited by K. Emery, 5–27. Jordan, Notre Dame (Indiana), London.
Gitner, Adam, and David Goldstein. Forthcoming. "The Lexicography of Latin." In *International Handbook of Modern Lexis and Lexicography*, edited by P. Hanks and G.-M. de Schryver. Berlin, Heidelberg: Springer-Verlag.
Grondeux, Anne. 2000. *Le Graecismus d'Évrard de Béthune à travers ses gloses. Entre grammaire positive et grammaire spéculative du XIIIe au XVe siècle.* Turnhout.
———. 2016. "Reprise humaniste d'un commentaire médiéval. A propos de la première édition incunable des *Glosulae in Priscianum*." In *La rigueur et la passion. Mélanges en l'honneur de Pascale Bourgain*, edited by Cédric Giraud and Dominique Poirel, 797–812. Turnhout.
———. Forthcoming. "Comment définir un 'dictionnaire' latin." In *Aux racines des dictionnaires de l'hébreu. Traduire, Transcrire, Transmettre*, edited by J. Kogel.
Himmelmann, Nikolaus P. 1998. "Documentary and Descriptive Linguistics." *Linguistics* 36(1): 161–195.
Hofman, R. 1996. *The Sankt Gall Priscian commentary. Part 1.* (Studien und Texte zur Keltologie, Bd. 1) Münster.
Holtz, Louis. 1984. "Les manuscrits latins à gloses et à commentaires: de l'antiquité à l'époque carolingienne." In *Il Libro e il testo, Atti del convegno internazionale (Urbino, 20-23 settembre 1982)*, directed by C. Questa and R. Raffaelli, 139–167. Urbino.
Irvine, Martin. 1994. *The Making of Textual Culture: Grammatica and Literary Theory 350–1100.* Cambridge.

Kneepkens, C. H. 1995. "The Priscianic Tradition." In *Sprachtheorien in Spätantike und Mittelalter*, edited by S. Ebbesen, 239–264. Tübingen: Gunter Narr Verlag (Gesschichte der Sprachtheorie).

Kosukegawa, Teiji, and John Whitman. 2018. "On the Significance of the Glosses in Vietnamese Classical Chinese Texts." *Journal of Vietnamese Studies* 13(3): 28–49.

Lahaussois, Aimée. 2016. "The Translation Tier in Interlinear Glossed Text: Changing Practices in the Description of Endangered Languages." In *Translation as Innovation: Bridging the Sciences and the Humanities*, édité par Patricia M. Phillips-Batoma et Florence Xiangyun Zhang, 261–278. Victoria, TX: Dalkey Archive Press.

———. 2021. "Glossing in the Linguistic Survey of India: Some Insights into Early 20th Century Glossing Practices." *Historiographia Linguistica* 48(1): 25–59.

Lahaussois, Aimée, and Jacqueline Léon. 2015. "Transcription and Translation of Unwritten Languages in American Linguistics (1950s to 2000s)." In *La traduction dans l'histoire des idées linguistiques: représentations et pratiques*, édité par Emilie Aussant, 235–258. Paris: Geuthner.

Lambert, P.-Y. 1987. "Les gloses grammaticales brittoniques." *Études Celtiques* 24: 285–308.

———. 1999. "Gloses en vieil-irlandais: la glose grammaticale abrégée." In *Ildánach ildírech*, edited by J. Carey, et al, 81–96. Andover.

Lehmann, Christian. 1982. "Directions for Interlinear Morphemic Translations." *Folia Linguistica* 16: 199–224.

Lobrichon, Guy. 1984. "Une nouveauté : les Gloses de la Bible." In *Le Moyen Âge et la Bible*, edited by Pierre Riché and G. Lobrichon, 95–114. Paris: Bible de tous les temps.

McNamee, Kathleen. 2007. *Annotations in Greek and Latin Texts From Egypt*. American Studies in Papyrology, no. 45. New Haven, CT: American Society of Papyrologists.

Merrilees, B., W. Edwards, and Anne Grondeux. 2019. *Le dictionnaire Aalma. Les versions de Saint-Omer, BM 644, Exeter, Cath. Libr. 3517 et Paris, BnF, Lat. 13032*. Lexica Latina Medii Aevi 6. Turnhout.

Moran, Pádraic, and John Whitman. 2022. "Glossing and Reading in Western Europe and East Asia: A Comparative Case Study." *Speculum* 97(1): 112–139.

Morard, Martin 2011. "Daniel de Lérins et le Psautier glosé : un regard inédit sur la Glose à la fin du xie siècle." *Revue bénédictine* 121(2): 393–445.

Reiner, Erica. 2000. "The Sumerian and Akkadian Linguistic Tradition." In *Geschichte Der Sprachwissenschaften: Ein Internationales Handbuch Zur Entwicklung Der Sprachforschung von Den Anfängen Bis Zur Gegenwart*, edited by Sylvain Auroux, vol. 1, Handbücher Zur Sprach-Und Kommunikationswissenschaft 18, 1–5. Berlin, New York: W. de Gruyter.

Rosier, Irène. 1998. "La *grammatica practica* du ms. British Museum V A IV. Roger Bacon, les lexicographes et l'étymologie." *Lexique* 14 [*Actes de la table-ronde*: "*L'étymologie au Moyen Age*" (Strasbourg, Mai 1992), éd. par C. Buridant, 97–125.

Sakai, Naoki. 1992. *Voices of the Past: The Status of Language in Eighteenth-Century Japanese*. Ithaca.
Schultze-Berndt, Eva. 2006. "Linguistic Annotation." In *Essentials of Language Documentation*, édité par Jost Gippert, Nikolaus Himmelmann, et Ulrike Mosel. Berlin and New York: Mouton de Gruyter.
Smalley, Berryl. 1937. "La *Glossa ordinaria*. Quelques prédécesseurs d'Anselme de Laon." *Recherches de théologie ancienne et médiévale* 9: 365–400.
———. 1983. *The Study of the Bible in the Middle Ages* (4th ed.). Notre Dame, IN: University of Notre Dame Press.
Smith, Lesley. 2009. *The Glossa ordinaria: The Making of a Medieval Bible Commentary*. Leiden: Brill.
Smith-Stark, Thomas. 2009. La trilogía catequística: Artes, Vocabularios y Doctrinas en la Nueva España como instrumento de una política lingüística de normalización. In *Historia Sociolingüística de México. Vol. I: México prehispánico y colonial*, edited by Rebecca Barriga Villanueva and Pedro Martín Butragueño, 451–482. México D.F.: El Colegio de México.
Teeuwen, Mariken. 2017. "Voices From the Edge: Annotating Books in the Carolingian Period." In *The Annotated Book in the Early Middle Ages: Practices of Reading and Writing*, edited by Mariken Teeuwen and Irene van Renswoude, Utrecht studies in medieval literacy (USML) 38, 13–36. Turnhout, Belgium: Brepols.
Voegelin, Charles, and Florence Voegelin. 1959. "Guide for Transcribing Unwritten Languages in Field Work." *Antrhopological Linguistics* 1(6): 1–28.
Wälchli, Bernhard. 2007. "Advantages and Disadvantages of Using Parallel Texts in Typological Investigations." In *STUF - Language Typology and Universals (Special Theme Issue: Parallel Texts: Using Translational Equivalents in Linguistic Typology)*, edited by Michael Cysouw and Bernhard Wälchli 60(2): 118–134.
Wielockx, Richard. 1982. "Autour de la *Glossa ordinaria*." *Recherches de théologie ancienne et médiévale* 49: 222–228.
Zwartjes, Otto. 2014. "The Missionaries' Contribution to Translation Studies in the Spanish Colonial Period: The Mise en Page of Translated Texts and Its Functions in Foreign Language Teaching." In *Missionary Linguistics V/Lingüística V: Translation Theories and Practices. Selected Papers From the Seventh International Conference on Missionary Linguistics, Bremen, 28 February–2 March 2012*, edited by Otto Zwartjes, Klaus Zimmermann, and Martina Schrader-Kniffki, vol. 122, 1–50. John Benjamins.

2

The Five Services of Sanskrit Commentaries and Diomedes' Grammar Program

Franck Cinato

OVERVIEW

To what extent can two different grammatical traditions share some scholastic devices?[1] This is one among many questions that arise when one tries to compare manuscript annotations across linguistic areas. Comparative grammar has of course shown that some languages have genetic commonalities, some of them specific enough to delineate families. In the present case, both Sanskrit and Latin belong to the Indo-European family, but their writing systems are different, as are their grammars, and even their entire social and cultural contexts. From a historical perspective, the similarities between these two languages are so distant that only close linguistic examinations are able to demonstrate actual links dating back to a very early period, from a thousand years distance. Regarding their history of *grammatisation*, both traditions are considered to be entirely independent.[2]

In this chapter, the possible bridges between Sanskrit and Latin will be explored not in a strictly linguistic dimension, but from the hermeneutical methodology attached to grammatical practices. That is to say, how linguistico-grammatical knowledge was transmitted in each tradition through textual commentaries. To discuss the topic, this chapter takes as a point of departure the analytical grid defined by grammarians to explain a text or, more generally, a work, regardless of its transmission medium (writing or orality). For the Sanskrit tradition, a very concise list of devices which forms a formal guideline for the composition of commentaries will be presented. This list then will be compared with the program of the Latin grammarian that Varro defined as *officia* (services, duties, functions, etc.) in the second or first century BC, and which was transmitted by Diomedes in the second half of the fourth century AD to Medieval grammarians (see Kaster 1988).

The Sanskrit grammatical tradition is remarkable in many respects. In addition to its older time-depth (Pāṇini's grammar, fifth or fourth century BC?), it was much more developed than the Greco-Latin tradition (Auroux 1994, 34). In the Pāṇinian tradition, the glosses—used as scholastic devices—are ubiquitous among all kinds of commentaries in any field, and commentaries are key literary works in teaching. As Gary A. Tubb wrote:

> Works of commentary pervade the history of Sanskrit thought to a degree that is unparalleled in the writings of most other traditions: it is no exaggeration to say that all the expository works available in Sanskrit most are, at least in external form, commentaries. (Tubb & Boose 2007, 1)

From the point of view of generic composition, these Sanskrit commentaries are collections of glosses discussing several aspects of a work, with which they are interlaced. A commentary takes the shape of a text, called the root (the *mūla*), disrupted by glosses (*vṛtti*), which deliver comments covering a large range of themes:

> In a Sanskrit work the additional material is usually presented in a more continuous composition that relies on a large body of conventional terminology and special syntactical devices in fulfilling its role as a commentary on the original text. (Tubb & Boose 2007, 3)

The Sanskrit tradition comprises several kinds of commentaries, such as the *anvayamukhī* style, in which the *mūla* is reworded according to the "natural/normal" (*anvaya*) construction, or the *kathaṃbhūtinī* type, which introduces each word of the *mūla* by a question such as "what is the nature of . . . ?" and the *bhāṣya* style, which in a maieutical mode proposes a dialog more orientated toward the doctrinal content (but not exclusively). In all these cases, the textual segments which do not belong to the *mūla* are considered as glosses: they are either *vṛtti* which explain the text *ad litteram* or *vārttika* ("part/element of explanation") which more precisely discuss the dogma expressed in the text and propose changes—adding words or splitting—in order to clarify the doctrinal content of the *mūla*.

In this context, the glosses consist of a ruled system of services. These services or characteristics of a commentary have been transmitted as a mnemonic stance (*kārikā*) in the *Paraśārapurāṇa* (quoted in the *Nyāyakośa*). Here, quotation is made according to Tubb and Boose (2007) and (Grimal 2000):

> *Padacchedaḥ padārthoktir vigraho vākyayojanā /*
> *ākṣepeṣusamādhānaṃ vyākhyānaṃ pañcalakṣaṇam*

"The commentary (*vyākhyāna*) has five characteristics:
pada-ccheda (word-division),
padārthokti (*pada-artha-ukti*, stating the meaning of the word),
vigraha (analysis of grammatical complexes),
vākya-yojanā (construing the sentences),
ākṣepa-samādhāna (the answering of objections)."

According to Tubb and Boose (2007, 9): "The first four are services of glossing and deal directly with the words of a text, while the fifth is a service of discussion and is concerned more with the ideas expressed in that text." In the Latin grammatical tradition, focus will be done on the Varronian definition of grammar, as Diomedes presents it (Diomedis *ars*, in *GL* 1, 426.12-427.2 *de grammatica*). In short, grammar is a two-part science consisting of four services/offices:

(a) Grammatica est specialiter scientia exercitata lectionis et expositionis eorum quae apud poetas et scriptores dicuntur, apud poetas, ut ordo seruetur, apud scriptores, ut ordo careat uitiis.
(b) Grammaticae partes sunt duae, altera quae uocatur exegetice, altera horistice. exegetice est enarratiua, quae pertinet ad officia lectionis: horistice est finitiua, quae praecepta demonstrat, cuius species sunt hae, partes orationis uitia uirtutesque.
(c) Tota autem grammatica consistit praecipue intellectu poetarum et scriptorum et historiarum prompta expositione et in recte loquendi scribendique ratione.
(d) *Grammaticae officia, ut adserit Varro, constant in partibus quattuor, lectione enarratione emendatione iudicio.*
  (1) *Lectio* est artificialis interpretatio, uel uaria cuiusque scripti enuntiatio seruiens dignitati personarum exprimensque animi habitum cuiusque.
  (2) *Enarratio* est obscurorum sensuum quaestionumue explanatio, uel exquisitio per quam unius cuiusque rei qualitatem poeticis glossulis exsoluimus.
  (3) *Emendatio* est qua singula pro ut ipsa res postulat dirigimus aestimantes uniuersorum scriptorum diuersam sententiam, uel recorrectio errorum qui per scripturam dictionemue fiunt.
  (4) *Iudicium* est quo omnem orationem recte uel minus quam recte pronuntiatam specialiter iudicamus, uel aestimatio qua poema ceteraque scripta perpendimus.
"(a) *Grammatica* is particularly the practical knowledge of reading and explaining things said by poets and [prose] writers—by poets, so that style (*ordo*) may be preserved, by [prose] writers, so that style may lack faults.

(b) There are two divisions of *grammatica*: one is called exegetical, the other definitive. The exegetical part is interpretation, which pertains to the office of reading. The definitive part makes definitions which demonstrate precepts of this kind: the *partes orationis* and the faults and ornaments of style.
(c) But the whole of *grammatica* consists primarily in the understanding of the poets, [prose] writers, and histories by ready exposition, and in the principles of speaking and writing correctly.
(d) *The functions of grammatica, as Varro asserts, consist of four parts: reading, interpretation, emendation, criticism.*
   (1) *Reading* is an artful rendering, or the various recitation of each kind of writing, preserving the dignity of persons and expressing the character of each mind.
   (2) *Interpretation* is the explanation of obscure meaning or questions, or the close study by which we resolve the nature of each thing through poetic glosses.
   (3) *Emendation* is where we set in order individual matters as the subject (res) itself demands, judging the various meaning of all the writings, or the correction of errors that occur through writing and speaking.
   (4) *Criticism* is that by which we judge all expression to be stated correctly or less than correctly, or an assessment by which we weigh carefully poems and other writings." (Translated by Irvine 1994, 66–67; divisions are mine; Desbordes 2007b, 230)

Diomedes is part of a clearly prescriptive approach guided by respect for authors and standards (a, c). Grammar, therefore, has an explanatory and a prescriptive side (b). For our purposes, the exegetical side is directly interesting (d). In the following pages, the two grids will be compared, giving some remarks on the translation by Martin Irvine and discussing the European early medieval development of glossing practices related to Varro/Diomedes' program. In Marius Victorinus' grammar (see n. 3), likely composed during the fourth century, the four services are expressed with some differences (by verbs instead of nouns) but date back to Varro: *Ars grammatica (. . .) eius praecipua officia sunt quattuor, ut ipsis placet, scribere, legere intellegere, probare* ["The services of the grammar are mainly four, according to him: to write, read, understand, judge"]. It is remarkable that, despite a different order and vocabulary, the *officia* corresponding in Varro/Diomedes' program, the verb *scribere* put in place of *emendatio* confirms that "correction" is related to writing transmission.

COMPARISON

The five services of commentary in the Sanskrit tradition thus constitute what one might call the program of the commentator. In Varro's conception as relayed by Diomedes, the definition of grammar also describes several services (*officia*) requested of grammarians, which, from the exegetical perspective, also match those of the commentary services in the Sanskrit tradition. The comparison of the two programs shows a partial overlap in terms of function (table 2.1) since readers, despite particular contexts, have identical needs.

At the end of each program are reading and criticism. The case of "correction" in the Latin tradition is rather peculiar, thus I will not discuss it, but to some extent the notion of correction in the Sanskrit commentaries is present in discussions on variant readings (see below *iti* + *paṭha*). Criticism and correction will be left aside in order to concentrate on *lectio* and *enarratio*. While *lectio* in Latin covers a wider category than *padaccheda*, *enarratio* overlaps with three services of the Sanskrit tradition which clearly concern the three basic levels of linguistic analysis: semantics, morphology, and syntax.

Reading

In the Sanskrit tradition, the preparation for reading involves the resolution of *sandhis*, both internal and external, that is, the identification of euphonic links (*sandhi* literally means "union"). The primary function of the commentary consists in *padaccheda*: the division of words linked phonetically and graphically by the alphasyllabic scripts deriving from Brāhmī (Gupta, Sidham, Devanagari, etc.; historical information can be found in Verma 1971).[3] This type of writing is qualified as a continuous script (*scriptio continua*; a script without word division) where the only separations occur between a final vowel and an initial consonant. The reader must therefore first isolate the words (external *sandhi*) and recognize the compounds (internal *sandhi*).

To do so, several strategies can be applied, such as for example *padapāṭha* "reciting of words," but usually in the context of commentary, several autonymic processes (quotative markers) make it possible to quote a word (all examples are borrowed from Tubb & Boose's Handbook; see Aussant 2005,

Table 2.1 Partial Overlap of the Grammarian Services/Tasks

1) Identifying the word division	*padaccheda*	*lectio*
2) Stating the meaning of the word	*padārthokti*	*enarratio*
3) Analysis of grammatical complexes (compounds, derivation)	*vigraha*	
4) Construing the sentences, indicating the construction of the text	*vākyayojanā*	
—Correction	—	*emendatio*
5) Criticism (the answering of objections)	*ākṣepeṣusamādhānaṃ*	*iudicium*

especially pp. 78–84, for a comprehensive study of Sanskrit autonymic practices):

(a). alternation of words of the *mūla* and glosses (following the pattern: word + gloss, word + gloss, etc.)
(b). using a terminological process which identifies words in an autonymic position, for example, (x) + *iti*; or (x) + *śabda* "the word x"; (x) + *kara* "the phoneme x":
   vikriyanta iti karmani ["(the verb) *vikriyante* is passive"].
(c). or discussing variant readings indicated by the sequence "(x) *iti* + *pāṭha*" or another form of the verb *paṭhati* [he/she reads]:
   prārthayadhvam ity apapāṭhaḥ ["prārthayadhvam" is a bad reading].

In the Latin world, the theorizing that resulted in late-antique grammars (*artes grammaticae*)—and therefore that of *lectio*—was carried out in a context of *scriptio continua* as well, at least after the second century AD (Desbordes 2007a, 269; Wingo 1972).[4] From this period up to the seventh century (when usages changed), the string which forms the text must, to be understood, be divided into words and prepared for vocalization by the reader itself.

According to the definition given by Diomedes "Reading is an artful rendering, or the various recitation of each kind of writing, preserving the dignity of persons and expressing the character of each mind," as translated by M. Irvine (*op. cit.*), should be first modified somewhat, to stick closer to the Latin sentence: so, not "preserving" . . . but "in the service of dignity of persons and expressing each feeling" (*seruiens dignitati personarum exprimensque animi habitum cuiusque*). The definition is twofold, since *lectio* is an *artificialis interpretatio* [artful rendering] or an *enuntiatio* [performance], the particle "or" (*uel*) has copulative (and not disjunctive) meaning, since these form two aspects. Another definition can help to understand what *lectio* is for Latin readers: the definition of Terentius Scaurus, *floruit* under the Hadrian reign in the first half of the second century AD (Tempesti 1977; Zetzel 2018), has been quoted by Audax (*Audacis excerpta de Scauro et Palladio*, see Kaster 1988, no. 190) and by Maximus Victorinus (cf. Kaster 1988, no. 274)[5] and recalls the Varronian definition. Scaurus provided more information (the differences between both grammarians is given between brackets); some of them are also recalled by Diomedes elsewhere in his grammar:

Scaurus (quoted by Audax *GL* 7, 322.4–19 and Maximus Victorinus 6, 188.6–23):

Grammaticae officia quot sunt?—*Quattuor, id est lectio, enarratio, emendatio, iudicium. Lectio quid est?*—*Secundum accentus et sensuum necessitatem propria enuntiatio (pronuntiatio* Victorin.*). Enarratio quid est?*—*Secundum poetae*

uoluntatem uniuscuiusque descriptionis explanatio. (. . .) DE LECTIONE. Partes lectionis quot sunt?—Quattuor, id est (quae sunt? Victorin.) **accentus, discretio, pronuntiatio, modulatio***.*
Accentus quid est?—Vniuscuiusque syllabae in sono pronuntiandi qualitas. Discretio quid est?—Confusarum significationum perplana significatio.
(. . .)
[. . . What is *lectio*?—It is the proper utterance according to the need of the pitch (*accentus*) and meanings. What is *enarratio*?—It is the clarification of every scene according to the author's will. (. . .) ABOUT READING. How many divisions of *lectio* are there?—Four, i.e. pitch, distinction, recitation, modulation. What is pitch? It is the sounding value of every syllable to be pronounced. What is distinction? It is the bringing out of ambiguities of clear meaning. (. . .) (Translation is mine, inspired by Irvine, *op. cit.*, 69)]

To sum up, according to Scaurus, reading presents four aspects: three are related to the performance itself (*accentus*, *pronuntiatio*, and *modulatio*) and one requires actual linguistic skills (*discretio*). Overinterpreting the term *discretio*, Irvine has gone too far and committed an anachronism in translating this technical vocabulary with a periphrastic "distinguishing syntactic division" because for late-antique grammarians, punctuation was the result of a practice which originally marked the pauses in the oratory performance; punctuation subsequently took an even more logico-syntactic turn (Saenger 1997, esp. 71–74). This can be seen in the extended definition by Diomedes, who added details to Scaurus' *Discretio est confusarum significationum perplana significatio, quae ostenditur modis quinque, continuatione separatione distinctione subdistinctione vel mora* (ars 2, 436.24–26) ["distinction is (giving) a clear meaning by resolving ambiguities, which is produced according to five modes: continuation, separation, division, subdivision or pause"]. Here Diomedes, like Scaurus, describes reading from a performative point of view, which stresses the fact that, in a textual context, *discretio* is of course related to punctuation but has a more general significance which consists in selecting meaning when a phrase shows ambiguity (see Desbordes 2007a, 274–276 for the description of the main types of ambiguities). These definitions prove that the *discretio* as a component of the *lectio* deals with the same issue as *padaccheda*: thus, whatever the tradition, reading is claimed to be a decoding process in order to make the text understandable; in this process glosses possibly intervene to disambiguate the information.

Explaining

In the Sanskrit tradition, the commentators' services clearly distinguish the type of explanations according to the three linguistic levels, as said above, and with respect to this point, the Latin tradition seems more flexible.

Enarratio, after the reading, is the part of the hermeneutical process devoted to explaining all the remaining obscurities encountered. The definition by Diomedes is still twofold, because these explanations take the form of an *exquisitio*, a research aimed at revealing the meaning sometimes obscured by the poetic language. Diomedes writes: "Interpretation is the *explanation* (*explanatio*) of obscure meaning or questions, or the *close study* (*exquisitio*) by which we resolve the nature of each thing through poetic glosses" (Irvine); instead, I propose translating the end of the Latin sentence *unius cuiusque rei qualitatem poeticis glossulis exsoluimus* like this: "we release from the poetic language the value (*qualitas*) of each utterance (*res*)."[6]

In short, the broad term *enarratio* covers several technical concepts: commentators have all the freedom to remove ambiguities of any kind without having to conform to a rigid framework. Scrutinizing the content of the *enarratio*, all the aspects stressed by the list of Sanskrit services can be identified. In the following comparison, I will draw examples from commentaries by the grammarian Servius (fourth century AD), since his commentaries of Virgil's poems are a model for *enarratio* (Irvine 1994, 126), and he was a model to medieval grammarian.

Meaning

Padārthokti glosses are delivered by a large number of processes. The commentator can provide synonyms (see Aussant 2014 for an overview), definitions, and other methods related to the next service (*vigraha*) from a grammatical point of view, elucidating the composition or derivation. A common strategy is to indicate when a word is a proper noun: (x) + *nāma* = "(x) by name."

With common nouns, a useful way to attach a meaning is to indicate the species through a hyperonym: (x)- *viśeṣa* = "a species of (x)"; both processes are similar to the Latin glosses "*proprium (nomen)*" and "*genus (x)*" (*genus arboris, auis, piscis*, etc.) [kind of tree, bird, fish, etc.]. A good example of this synonymic strategy is provided by this passage, where Servius discusses the *significatio* of the verb *cano* using synonyms accompanied with quotations from Virgil:

> Servius, in Aen. 1, 1: *CANO polysemus sermo est. Tria enim significat: aliquando laudo, ut (Verg. Aen. 7, 698) "regemque canebant"; aliquando divino, ut (Verg. Aen. 6, 76) "ipsa canas oro"; aliquando canto, ut in hoc loco. Nam proprie canto significat, quia cantanda sunt carmina.*
>
> *Cano* is a polysemic word. It actually means three things: sometimes "*laudo*" [I praise], as "and they praised the king"; sometimes "*diuino*" [I predict], like "Sing thyself, I pray" (litt.:I pray you to make the oracle yourself); sometimes "*canto*" [I sing], like here, because it properly means "*canto*" [I sing], since the songs must be sung.

Grammatical Information

The third service of Sanskrit commentaries, *vigraha*, intervenes as a more technical extension of the previous one, since literally, it is a question of developing the meaning expressed by a word having a synthetic form (compound/derivative) through a phrase or sentence in more ordinary language. Therefore, this kind of gloss identifies stems, affixes, compounds, derivation, and so on according to a wide range of technical terms based on Pāṇinian grammar: "For each type and subtype of complex formation susceptible to analysis in ordinary language, there exists a basic formula . . ." (Tubb & Boose 2007: 35), for example:

> *yudhyanta iti yodhāḥ* "they fight, thus fighters"

The discussion of the word Amazon serves as a good illustration of this particular grammatical feature in the Latin tradition. Servius emphasizes the stylistic use of a derived word *Amazonidum* from Greek, instead of the standard Latin *Amazonarum*; then he turns on two competing etymologies and ends his explanation with the observation of their disappearance at his time.

> Servius *in Aen.* 1, 490,
> "*Amazonidum*" *autem derivatio est pro principalitate, sicut (Georg. 2, 170)* "*Scipiadas duros bello*" *pro Scipionibus. Sane Amazones dictae sunt vel quod simul vivant sine viris, quasi* ἅμα ζῶσαι, *vel quod unam mammam exustam habeant, quasi* ἄνευ μαζοῦ. *has autem iam non esse constat, utpote extinctas partim ab Hercule, partim ab Achille.*
>
> *Amazonidum* [of the Amazons] is a derivation instead of the primary word, like "The Scipians [*Scipiadas*] hardy at war" instead of "the Scipios" [*Scipiones*]. Presumably the Amazons are so called because they live together without husbands, as it were ἅμα ζῶσαι [to live together], or because they have a burned breast, as it were ἄνευ μαζοῦ [without/deprived of a breast]. It appears that they no longer exist today, because they have been destroyed partly by Hercules, partly by Achilles.

Thus, Servius, after describing the form as a result of derivation, tries to make clear the meaning of the Greek proper noun by providing two possible etymologies (by *scinderatio phonorum* "sound decomposition") from Greek words:

> Ἀμαζών = ἅμα-ζῶ(σαι) or ἄ(νευ)-μαζοῦ. [Amazōn = hama-zō(sai) or a(neu)-mazou]

Constructing Meaning

The processes associated with *vākyayojanā* are intended to reorder sentences. It can take two aspects, but in all cases, the added explanatory materials are superimposed (Tubb & Boose 2007, 149) in the framework of repetitions of the *mūla* words: "The standard prose word order... is characterized by subject, object, and verb, placing modifiers before what they modify." There are two kinds of reordering: *kathaṃbhūtinī*, which gives a basic "skeleton sentence," and *anvayamukhī*, which rearranges the words of the *mūla* and comments word by word.

In addition, these strategies also include many processes in order to connect the various explanatory elements to each other, but also to supplement information (supplying words and several devices for marking features of syntax) in order to complete the meaning (cf. Tubb & Boose 2007, 165).

In the Latin tradition, the example of two verses from the *Georgics* illustrates well how Servius clarifies the poetic constructions of Virgil by changing the order of words.

- Verg. *Georg.* 3, 146–47
  Est lucos Silari circa ilicibusque virentem /
  plurimus Alburnum volitans ...
  "Round wooded *Silarus* and the ilex-bowers /
  Of green *Alburnus* swarms a winged pest."
- Servius, *in Georg.* 3, 146–47
  Ordo talis est: circa lucos Silari, fluminis Lucaniae, et Alburnum, eiusdem montem, est plurimus volitans: ac si diceret, est multa musca.
  "The construction is so: "around the sacred woods of the *Silarus*," a river of Lucania, "and (around) the Alburnus," a mountain from the same place, "there are flying swarms," as if he would mean there are many flies."

Note that the reordering contains three inserted glosses: two which explain proper nouns with hyperonyms (river and mountain) and one which helps to resolve the meaning of *plurimus volitans*.

The following example is interesting because it confirms that the term "*ordo*" in Servius' commentary refers to syntactic relationships and not just to stylistics: the gloss makes it possible to correctly associate the plural genitive *Danaum* [*Danai* = The Greeks] with the noun *dona* [gifts], as a well-formed noun phrase.

Servius *in Aen.* 2, 44
(... *aut ulla putatis /*) *dona carere dolis Danaum? Ordo est "dona Danaum," non "dolis Danaum."*
"(Think ye) the gifts of Greeks can lack for guile?": The construction is "the gifts of the Greeks," not "the guile of the Greeks."

These few examples, selected among many others, demonstrate that the *enarratio* overlaps with the very same aspects as those described in the Sanskrit tradition under the heading of *padārthokti* for elucidating meaning; of *vigraha* for grammatical formation of words; of *vākyayojanā* for the syntax.

EPISTEMOLOGICAL PERSPECTIVE FOR COMPARISON

What conclusions can we draw from this convergence of practices? It is worth quoting S. Auroux again:

> Il n'y a aucune raison pour que des savoirs situés différemment dans l'espace-temps soient organisés de la même façon (. . .) la reconnaissance de ce fait constitue notre position résolument historiciste, en même temps qu'elle fournit l'intérêt heuristique de tout travail historique (Baratin/Desbordes 1981, 12) (. . .) Elle ne doit cependant pas conduire au mythe de l'incomparabilité de connaissances enfermées dans des paradigmes spécifiques. (. . .) C'est pourquoi on peut reconnaître, par-delà la diversité des analogies (. . .) des analogies affectant les situations cognitivo-phénoménales. (. . .) Dans des circonstances analogues des phénomènes analogues produisent des connaissances analogues. (1994, 16)

I think that glosses belong to this category of analogic phenomena, which results from a similar cognitive environment. I have only touched superficially on this topic and I am aware that it requires further investigation into the "six traditions of metalinguistic knowledge" (as defined by Auroux 1994, 26–32: Sumerian and Akkadian, Egyptians, Sanskrit, Greek and Latin, Chinese, and Arabic). As a result, the following are only some thoughts on what should be evaluated in other glossing traditions.

This chapter has mainly stressed two aspects: *lectio* and *enarratio*. Interestingly, in both traditions, reading shows two facets: an analytical aspect which aims to distinguish the components of the message (e.g., isolating parts of speech) and a performative aspect depending on the literary genre of the work (speech, poetry, etc.). In the Sanskrit tradition and in Latin as well, the context is the *scriptio continua*, that is to say, a graphical chain of characters which do not distinguish the meaningful units of words or morphemes or phrases. We must recall however that the glosses have not been generated by this particular writing context, since they find their origin in orality (because languages sometimes need to explain themselves), but the specific writing context may push exegesis toward a particular orientation.

In the Sanskrit tradition, it was not a character string, but a phonetic string, forming a continuous stream, that had to be transmitted. Because of the *sandhis*, in order to avoid transforming the message, something which would be disastrous in a ritual framework, it was necessary to isolate all the elements in order to understand their composition. In the Latin tradition, reading is also originally closely linked to a performance, in the sense that the act of oratory represents the ultimate culmination of the antique education.

In other words, in both traditions examined here, the first step of the hermeneutic program pursues the same goals: the validation of the accuracy of the message for its performance and the guarantee of its transmission in an invariable way. Therefore, it is reasonable to think that the comparison of both traditions allows us to observe several constants which emerge. The first of these is an answer to the question "why did one work generate glosses (and thus commentaries), but not another?" in other words, what is the trigger for glosses?

First, two things must be considered: (a) the work and its (state/status of the) language and (b) its historical context and significance. The work, which can be a written text or not, follows the same universal momentum as everything: birth, growth, and death, which, transposed to a work can be seen as its composition, diffusion/transmission, and eventually disappearance or denaturation. During this life cycle, the language in which the work was composed has evolved, causing a kind of diglossia (see, e.g., Adams 2003, 589–593; Boisson et al. 1991, 270).[7] This implies two things: either the work, which cannot be understood anymore, is forgotten and disappears, or it remains "in use" and acquires a special cultural status. The best example of this historical process is religious texts. In some ways, the gap between different states of the same language (causing a cultural diglossic situation) is a possible trigger for glosses, but this is not sufficient. In addition, the status of the language (which depends on linguistic and historical context) must be particular: consequently, a work particularly significant in a cultural context—that is, the usefulness of the work in a particular socio-cultural context—shares its status with the language in which it is transmitted. Because the Bible was transmitted in Hebrew, Greek, and Latin, these languages were considered by medieval peoples to be "sacred languages" (the *tres lingae sacrae*; cf. Bourgain 2019; Blom 2012).[8]

For this very reason (status and performative efficiency), it is necessary to transmit the work in its original languages: its transmission unchanged becomes an essential condition. In this context, reading is studying, because a gap widens between the state of language fixed at the time of the composition of the work and the various historical developments of this same language. From this moment, the language state in which the work is fixed (for Latin, it is based on socio-linguistic status/level) becomes a linguistic standard and assumes the role of cultural language: this status is a precondition for the *grammatisation* process. In this sense, the text becomes "foundational," as expressed by Auroux:

> "Ce n'est donc pas un hasard si l'on voit souvent débuter la réflexion linguistique après la constitution du texte caractéristique de la civilisation en question

(Homère, le Coran) et à son propos" (and he added n.1): "paradoxalement, ce rôle du texte demeure valable pour les Indes, quand bien même on admet qu'il n'ait existé à l'époque qui nous intéresse que sous forme oral." (Auroux 1994, 48)

In my reading, the gloss is therefore a necessary mechanism that comes to life at the very moment of the transmission of work with special status; the text must be read/studied in its original language, which is different from what is normally used in a given time and place.

The *padaccheda/lectio* forms the point of departure, which can be compared to a preliminary decoding. After reading, the explanatory processes are the nucleus of the hermeneutic program. In both traditions, the concerns are almost identical:

padārthokti	=	sensus / intellectus / significatio / interpretatio
vigraha	=	derivatio / compositio / etymologia
vākyayojanā	=	ordo / (ordinatio / constructio *according to Priscian*)

A commentary must therefore elucidate all the essential aspects of language obscurities: semantics, morphology, and syntax. Even though these aspects were not treated with the same systematicity in both traditions, several strong convergences can be noted:

i) The gloss, as the minimal discursive unit of a commentary, is a successful model and shows a kind of "scientifisation" in becoming a means of expression for grammarians. This is evidenced by the massive use of metalinguistic terminology in glosses, especially perceptible in Sanskrit tradition.
ii) The convergence of both "programs"—defined similarly as services—sheds light on the fact that glosses assume *universal hermeneutical functions*, through their role as a multi-functional tool.
iii) The metalinguistic nature of glosses goes beyond unique language considerations, and these glosses play a role in wider debates generated by the work. Glosses are also a medium for expressing opinions.

In the future, other aspects will be investigated, since the metalinguistic and functional purpose of glosses does not seem to be affected by cultural and linguistic differences. On the other hand, cultural differences seem to influence the form of glosses (superficially) and the nature of their content. Their form seems to be determined by several factors, the main ones of which are: the methods of its transmission—oral/written—and, when written, the material nature of the text, in terms of writing medium.

GLOSSING AND ANNOTATION

From the perspective of disambiguating information, I suggest that annotating the transmitted text directly with glosses—placed as close as possible to the word(s) requiring disambiguation—is a tradition inherited from late-antique practices related to *lectio*. This hypothesis is supported by the following statement by Françoise Desbordes:

> "L'usage des grammairiens—certainement adopté par les lecteurs ordinaires—était d'annoter les textes en vue de la lecture, comme on annote aujourd'hui une partition musicale" [The customs of grammarians—certainly adopted by ordinary readers—was to annotate the texts for reading, as we do now on a music sheet.] (Desbordes 2007a, 274)

In this view, glossed texts are the culmination or the synthesis of, on the one hand, the comments needed by some special works (the *ennaratio*) and, on the other hand, the practices attached to the *lectio*. This view needs to be extended and explored in six other grammatical traditions (Sumerian and Akkadian, Egyptians, Sanskrit, Greek and Latin, Chinese, and Arabic). Marginal and interlinear glosses do not appear to be a peculiarity of Medieval Europe or of the Near- and Far-East as, to a lesser extent, the Sanskrit tradition made use of this practice, at least within the Kashmirian Sanskrit tradition, as confirmed by Ratié (2018, 307), but in this area, it appears to be a limited and late practice compared to Western developments.

Medieval European glosses are a sort of culmination based on the late-antique grammatical tradition. Looking at the typology of medieval glosses, it becomes apparent that Varro's program of Latin grammar, as defined by Diomedes, is also in fact that of the medieval glossators. Unlike the Antique Latin and Sanskrit traditions that formalized glosses mostly as autonomous texts (the commentaries are works in and of themselves), medieval glossators favored a different orientation: direct annotation of the text. In this conception, glosses are embedded as close as possible to the word they explain; the commentary is intimately inserted in the blank spaces of the text. In this sense, the annotated glosses record a *lectio* at the same time as an *enarratio*. The distinction between the text and its comment is based on a codified logography (the layout): module and type of script; layout of the textual elements in the page.

This particular methodological orientation further confirms that the glossing phenomenon is independent of the written word and annotation practices, since all the annotations are not glossing, and glosses are not necessarily annotated. Therefore, in both Sanskrit and Latin traditions, the form and the content show similarities, as well as the numerous functions and diversity of types regarding their content. It appears that these similarities in glossing reflect commonalities in the history of textual practices, as recalled by S. Auroux (quoted above), "In similar circumstances analogous phenomena produce analogous knowledge"; we can assert the same regarding the strategies used to transfer knowledge. These glossing strategies result from the combination of several determining factors, and among them, three seem essential: (1) the particular status attached to a work (requiring its transmission) constitutes the catalyst for glossing; (2) the materiality of the text and its writing appear to have an impact on the external form of the glossing (commentary versus annotation, both composed of glosses); and (3) a diglossic heterogeneous linguistic context (in a broad sense) appears preeminent in influencing the content of glossing—that is, one finds an increasing number of grammatical, semantic, and syntactic information when the targeted readers are not "native" speakers.

In addition, the linguistic context can explain the ambivalence of glosses: between pedagogical and scientific functions, sometimes both levels are closely entangled in the same margins. However, the pedagogical function of glosses does not seem to predominate (of course this depends on the function of a given text and its environment) and appears rather as an amplification of its primary function, which is to transmit knowledge, regardless of the audience, pupil, or teacher.

Finally, the comparison proposed here highlights two points: (1) Glosses form a system whose ultimate goal is the transmission of work, including all its linguistic levels, from the letters to the meaning. (2) Differences and convergences seem to be linked to a particular material and cultural contexts whose study opens the way to a sociology of the text through the analysis of their glosses.

NOTES

1. I would like to thank warmly Émilie Aussant, who helped me with Sanskrit material and gave me a clear overview of the main issues regarding the Sanskrit grammatical tradition and its historical context she studies in HTL.

2. On this concept of *grammatisation* see Auroux (1994, especialy 9, 71–73, and chapters 3–5 in general).

3. See for example the *Pārameśvaratantra*, written in a script type called "Late Gupta" from the ninth century (828 CE) in the manuscript Cambridge, University Library, MS Add.1049.1 digitized online at https://cudl.lib.cam.ac.uk/view/MS-ADD-01049-00001/9.

4. See for example a fragment of *Institutiones* by Gaius, in a papyrus from the third century AD (?) in Oxford, Sackler Library, Papyrology Rooms P. Oxy. 2103 (*The Oxyrhynchus Papyri* vol. XVII no. 2103), digitized online http://www.papyrology.ox.ac.uk/POxy/VExhibition/scribes_scholars/gaius_institutiones.html

5. This Victorinus is not the author of the *Ars grammatica* ascribed to Marius Victorinus (ed. I. Mariotti, *Marii Victorini ars grammatica. Introduzione, testo critico e commento*, 1967, Firenze; *CGL* 6, 3–31, 16); see Petrilli 2009b; A. Garcea, "Ars grammatica, Victorinus," in *Corpus de textes linguistiques fondamentaux*, http://ctlf.ens-lyon.fr/n_fiche.asp?n=19; Kaster 1988, no. 273 "Victorinus grammaticus."

6. The translation proposed by Irvine is anachronic, and it wrongly renders the Latin meaning. The construction of the verb *exsolvo*, a ditransitive verb (or trivalent according to a generative grammar perspective) selects in addition to the (synthetic) subject, two complements (direct and indirect); thus, *exsolvo* + acc. + abl. "I release *aliquem aliqua re*": *exsoluimus qualitatem (ex) poeticis glossulis*. In Diomedes' time, the term *glossula* designates the obscure word itself, but not its explanation. This latter meaning will be common after a switch occurred from the early Middle Ages.

7. This diglossia can be caused, in the case of early Egyptian word lists described by Boisson, Kirtchuk, and Béjoint (1991), by the chronological distance between an archaic state of a given language and its later developments, creating a bilingualism inter-dialectal; but also according to Adams 2003, who discusses the diglossic situation of Latin and Greek in Egypt, the distinction between High (H) and Low (L) language regarding their use in a specific context allows him to deny the designation to this situation: "The old diglossic opposition H–L does not apply to the relationship between Latin and Greek in Egypt, because both languages were High in different senses (. . .) This ancient evidence ought to be added to the general critique of conventional diglossia that is now under way." (p. 637)

8. It is noteworthy to mention that, very early in the Latin tradition, some archaic texts were considered as sacred and needed to be explained, as for example the *Carmina Saliorum* about which Quintilian wrote (*Institutio oratoria* 1, 6, 40) "The chants of the Salii are hardly properly understood by their own priests; but their *religio* forbids them to be changed, and they must be used in their sanctified form" (translation quoted by Blom 2012, 133) and thus these *Carmina* were explained in detail by the Roman writer Aelius Stilo (circa 100 BC) in his *Explanatio Carminum Saliarium*, unfortunately lost.

REFERENCES

Adams, J. N. 2003. *Bilingualism and the Latin language*. Cambridge.
Auroux, S. 1994. *La révolution technologique de la grammatisation. Introduction à l'histoire des sciences du langage*. Liège.
Aussant, É. 2014. "Sanskrit Theories on Homonymy and Polysemy." *Bulletin d'Études Indiennes* 32: 13–36.
Aussant, Émilie. 2005. "L'autonymie dans la tradition grammaticale sanskrite paninéenne." *Histoire Épistémologie Langage* 27 (1): 73–92.
Baratin, Marc, et Françoise Desbordes, éd. 1981. *L'Analyse linguistique dans l'antiquité classique*. Horizons du langage. Paris: Klincksieck.

Blom, A. 2012. "Linguae sacrae in ancient and medieval sources. An anthropological approach to ritual language." In *Multilingualism in the Graeco-Roman Worlds*, édité par Mullen et P. James, 124–140. Cambridge.

Boisson, Cl., P. Kirtchuk, et H. Béjoint. 1991. "Aux origines de la lexicographie: les premiers dictionnaires monolingues et bilingues." *International Journal of Lexicography* 4 (4): 261–315.

Bourgain, P. 2019. "Le caractère sacré du latin au Moyen Âge." In *Hiéroglossie 1. Moyen Âge latin, Monde Ararbo-Persan, Tibet, Inde. Collège de France 16-17 juin 2015*, édité par J.-N. Robert, 79–96. Paris.

Desbordes, Françoise. 2007a. "Écriture et ambiguïté d'après les textes théoriques latins." In *Idées grecques et romaine sur le langage. Travaux d'histoire et d'épistémologie*, 259–281. Paris.

———. 2007b. "Sur les débuts de la grammaire à Rome." In *Idées grecques et romaine sur le langage. Travaux d'histoire et d'épistémologie*, 217–233. Paris.

GL = *Grammatici Latini*, ed. H. Keil, Leipzig, I-VIII, 1857–1880 (réimp. Hildesheim, 1961).

Grimal, F. 2000. "Pour décrire un commentaire traditionnel sur une œuvre littéraire sanskrite." *Bulletin de l'École française d'Extrême-Orient* 87 (2): 765–785.

Irvine, M. 1994. *The Making of Textual Culture: Grammatica and Literary Theory 350–1100*. Cambridge.

Kaster, R. A. 1988. *Guardians of Language: The Grammarian and Society in Late Antiquity*. Berkeley.

Ratié, I. 2018. "For an Indian Philology of Margins. The Case of Kasmirian Sanskrit Manuscripts." In *L'espace du sens. Approches de la philologie indienne*, édité par S. D'Intino et S. Pollock, 305–354. Paris.

Saenger, P. H. 1997. *Space Between Words: The Origins of Silent Reading*. Standford.

Tempesti, M. A. 1977. "Quinto Terentio Scauro grammatico adrianeo." *Studi e Ricerche dell'Istituto di Latino* 1: 175–220.

Tubb, G. A., et R. E. Boose. 2007. *Scholastic Sanskrit: A Manual for Student*. New York.

Verma, Thakur Prasad. 1971. *The Palaeography of brāhmī Script in North India (From c. 236 B.C. to c. 200 A.D.)*. Varanasi.

Wingo, E. O. 1972. *Latin Punctuation in the Classical Ages*. The Hague, Paris.

Zetzel, J. E. G. 2018. "Scaurus." In *Critics, Compilers, and Commentators: An Introduction to Roman Philology, 200 BCE–800 CE*, 318–319. Oxford.

II

GLOSSES AS TOOLS FOR ACCESS TO KNOWLEDGE

3

Glossing Glosses

Methods for Transcribing and Glossing Japanese **Kundoku** *Texts*

Matthew Zisk

1. GLOSSING AS A CROSS-CULTURAL PHENOMENON

The practice of glossing, or adding interlinear or marginal notes to a written text, has been carried out for more than 1,500 years throughout numerous cultures ranging from Western Europe, through the Middle East, to Far East Asia. Until recently, most research on glossing was limited to a single tradition in a single region, with the bulk of the English literature focusing solely on the glossing traditions of medieval Europe. Over the past decade, however, a gradual shift toward comparative research aiming to clarify the universal characteristics, as well as regional idiosyncrasies, of glossing has been steadily underway. One major milestone in the promotion of comparative research has been the establishment of the Network for the Study of Glossing in 2015, an online register and mailing list of researchers from around the globe formed for the purpose of exchanging ideas and organizing workshops related to glossing across cultures. Since its establishment, members of the Network have hosted a number of glossing-related workshops and conferences throughout Europe and Japan, and much discussion has been held concerning the similarities between the Western and Eastern glossing traditions. Over the past decade, there have been a number of studies in English introducing East Asian glossing traditions. Frellesvig (2010), Lurie (2011), Steininger (2017), and Kornicki (2018) each contain chapters on the Japanese tradition, while King (2006, 2010, 2013) covers the Korean and Kosukegawa and Whitman (2018) the Vietnamese traditions. Sketches of all three of these traditions are given in Handel (2019), while the recently translated Kin (2021) provides what is perhaps the most in-depth coverage to date of the Japanese and Korean traditions. Studies on the universality of glossing, comparing Western and Eastern traditions, are still few and far between, however, being limited to Whitman (2011, 2020), Whitman and Cinato (2014), and Moran and Whitman (2022), as far as I am aware.

One major hindrance to further work being published on the subject of East Asian glossing in English is, of course, the language barrier. While the majority of glossed texts in Western Europe contain glosses in vernacular European languages on Latin, or to a lesser extent, Greek, in East Asia, the target language of the glosses is Literary Sinitic (henceforth LS), or Classical Chinese, with the glosses themselves being written in the East Asian vernaculars of the Sinosphere: primarily Japanese, Korean, and, to a lesser extent, Vietnamese. Perhaps the larger hindrance is, however, the lack of common terminology for the many specialized terms used in the description of East Asian glosses, as well as the lack of a standard for transcribing and glossing—in the modern descriptive sense of adding an interlinear morphemic gloss to a text—examples from East Asian glossed texts in English. In the case of Japanese, the East Asian language with the largest number by far of surviving premodern glossed texts, hundreds, if not thousands, of papers on glossing have been published over the past century in Japanese, with an entire academic society devoted to the subject of glossing (*Kuntengo gakkai* 訓點語學會 "The Society for Research in Kunten Language"). The number of papers published in English, on the other hand, is limited to roughly a dozen or so. The issue of a common terminology was tackled by Whitman et al. (2010), in which the authors proposed Korean, English, and Italian translations for 57 commonly used terms in Japanese glossing research. To this date, however, there have been no proposals concerning how to transcribe and morphemically gloss examples from Japanese glossed texts in English.

The purpose of this chapter is to propose a standard of transcription and glossing that will present researchers with an easy-to-follow method of citing examples from Japanese glossed texts in English publications, further promoting comparative research between Western and Eastern glossing traditions. This chapter will start out in §2 with an overview of the various types of glosses found in LS texts in Japan and an introduction to the method of reading an LS text word-by-word in Japanese following the glosses in the text known as *kanbun kundoku* 漢文訓読 (hereafter, simply "*kundoku*"). In §3, I will look at the various methods of transcription that Japanese linguists have used since the early twentieth century to describe *kundoku* texts in modern academic publications. I will then present my own glossing and phonemicization standard for citing examples from *kundoku* texts in English publications in §4. Finally, in §5, I will look at how the glossing standard presented for *kundoku* texts in the current study could be applied to the description of other East Asian glossing practices as well. An appendix containing a list of glossing labels for the most common functional morphemes found in *kundoku* is provided at the end of the chapter.

2. WHAT IS *KUNDOKU*, WHEN DID IT START, AND HOW DOES IT WORK?

The term *kanbun kundoku* 漢文訓讀 can be literally translated as "reading LS through interpretation," where *kanbun* 漢文 is Japanese for "LS," *kun* 訓 expresses a "vernacular interpretation or reading" of a Chinese character, and *doku* 讀 is the act of "reading" an LS text using such vernacular interpretations. *Kundoku* has been translated into English a number of ways, including "vernacular reading" (Whitman et al. 2010), "reading by gloss" (Lurie 2011), and "text transposition" (Zisk 2017). Each of these terms is more or less accurate, but they emphasize different aspects of the *kundoku* process. The term "vernacular reading" focuses on the result of the *kundoku* process: a vernacular (in this case, Japanese) rendition of an LS text. Meanwhile, "reading by gloss" and "text transposition" focus on the process itself. The former emphasizes the fact that glosses are typically used to give the readings of words in the text, while the latter emphasizes that rather than being a translation in the proper sense, *kundoku* is a direct word-by-word rendering, or "transposition," of the LS text into Japanese with little room for translational license.

When reading an LS text through the *kundoku* method, apart from a small number of words expressing functional morphemes with no direct equivalent in Japanese, the reader—or, more accurately, the interpreter—either translates or reads in Sino-Japanese (SJ) every word of the LS text verbatim, creating a nearly exact "transposition" of the text into Japanese on the spot. A number of strategies, namely the supplementation of Japanese functional morphemes such as verbal suffixes and particles not present in the original LS text and the rearrangement of word order to match that of Japanese, are carried out to make the text grammatically coherent. The individual words, expressions, and phrasing, however, remain largely unaltered by the interpreter. Each Chinese character is given a prescribed Japanese reading, or *kun*, for each of its major usages and while these can differ slightly depending on the period or reading tradition (religious sect, school of thought, etc.), they remain largely consistent between texts. For example, the character 書, which can be used as a verb to express the meaning "write" or as a noun to express the meaning "book," "letter," or "script," is (apart from cases in which it is rendered in SJ as *syo*) regularly read as *kak-u* "write" when used as a verb and *pumi* "book, letter" when used as a noun. In this sense, *kundoku* differs from translation proper, in which a polysemous word such as that expressed by 書 could be translated in a myriad of ways including but not limited to "write, record, transcribe, writing, record, book, letter, script, character," depending on context. Due to the high systematicity and lack of license allowed in *kundoku*, when provided with the same LS text, two interpreters will typically produce strikingly similar renditions, a feat which is not nearly as common when speaking of translation in the traditional sense. Glosses are often added to an LS text to aid with the *kundoku* process. These glosses may be added by the interpreter him or herself, added by a student or acolyte recording the transmitted reading of his or her teacher, or copied literatim from another earlier MS. Glosses are not a requirement for *kundoku*, though, and skilled scholars and monks could have produced a *kundoku* reading of an LS text simply from knowledge of the various conventions alone.

When exactly the practice of *kundoku* started in Japan is not entirely clear. There are records that early Japanese histories, such as *Kojiki* "Account of ancient matters" (712) and *Nihon shoki* "Chronicles of Japan" (720), written in (pseudo-)LS were read in Japanese through *kundoku*.[1] The earliest surviving glossed MSS of *Kojiki* and *Nihon shoki* only date to the tenth century, though, and are far from complete copies, leaving much of the original interpretation up to speculation. A late eighth-century MS of *Kegon kanjōki* "Huìyuǎn's Commentary on the Avataṃsaka sūtra," held by Daitōkyū Kinen Bunko (hereafter, "DKB"), is generally held to be the earliest surviving *kundoku* gloss of an LS text bearing a dated colophon. According to its colophon, the MS was collated with a Sillan MS in 783 and then again with a Tang MS in 788. It is assumed that the glosses were added during one of the collations, although it is not clear which one. The glosses found in *Kegon kanjōki*, DKB MS are highly simplistic compared to later glossed texts, consisting solely of punctuation marks and Chinese numerals used to indicate Japanese word order (word order inversion glosses). While *Kegon kanjōki*, DKB MS is the only eighth-century glossed text to bear a dated colophon, Tōdaiji temple in Nara holds several other MSS of *Kegon-gyō* "Avataṃsaka sutra" and related texts containing lexical glosses in kana that can be dated to roughly the same period or slightly later. Given the dominance of Kegon (Japanese for "Avataṃsaka") sources among early glossed texts, it seems likely that *kundoku* found its beginnings among the monks of the Kegon sect of Buddhism sometime in the mid to late eighth century.[2]

Entering the ninth century, both the number of surviving glossed texts and the variation of the glosses themselves increase dramatically, with roughly 100 glossed texts surviving from the ninth century and over 4,000 glossed texts reported for the entirety of Early Middle Japanese (EMJ: ninth to twelfth centuries) (Ishizuka 2001). Glossed texts for both Buddhist and secular works survive, although the former both predate and exponentially outnumber the latter (Kosukegawa 2001). While the earliest glossed texts, such as *Kegon kanjōki*, DKB MS are comparatively simplistic in nature, providing little information other than word order inversion and scattered Japanese readings, glossed texts from the early ninth century onward contain a comprehensive system of glosses, allowing a reader to transpose the entire original LS text into Japanese using the *kundoku* method.

Below, I will look at the different reading strategies, followed by the various types of glosses, used in *kundoku* in order to transpose an LS text into Japanese. Each of these reading strategies and gloss types will need to be taken into consideration when producing an accurate transcription of a *kundoku* text. Unless stated otherwise, all examples in this chapter are given in EMJ.

Reading Strategies

(a) Word order inversion (*hendoku* 返讀)

LS being a primarily subject-verb-object (SVO) and Japanese a primarily subject-object-verb (SOV) language, most sentences cannot be read in the exact same word order when transposing a text. To produce a more natural Japanese word order, the words of an LS text are typically rearranged into SOV word order as part of the *kundoku* process: for example, 枕ₐ石ᵦ漱ᴄ流ᴅ → *isi=ni*ᵦ *makura+si*ₐ *nagare=ni*ᴅ *kutisusug-u*ᴄ "rest one's head on a rock and rinse one's mouth in the stream" (Cao Cao, Song of Qui Hu I). Other common inversions include the rearrangement of particles expressing polarity, voice, tense, aspect, modality, and so on, which typically precede a verb in LS, into verbal suffixes or auxiliary verbs in Japanese: for example, 不ₐ知ᵦ → *sir*ᵦ-*azu*ₐ "don't know," 不ₐ能ᵦ知ᴄ → *sir-u koto*ᴄ *atap*ᵦ-*azu*ₐ "can't know." This reordering may be aided by the addition of word order inversion glosses to a text, but many glossed texts only partially employ inversion glosses or omit them altogether, leaving the reordering of the text to the discretion of the reader. Word order inversion is one of the oldest reading strategies, with examples of word order inversion glosses being found in the earliest surviving glossed texts from the late eighth century (see also (c) "Unread characters" below).

(b) Iterated readings (*saidoku* 再讀)

A reading strategy similar to word order inversion is iterated readings. When transposing an LS text, while in most cases, word order discrepancies are dealt with through simple inversion, a small number of preverbal particles are read twice, once preceding the verb as an adverb and a second time following the verb as a verbal suffix. For example, the particle 當, expressing that an action or occurrence is necessary or preferable, is first read using the adverb *masani* "truly, certainly" in its original preverbal position, and then again with the verbal suffix -*(r)ube-si* (necessitive) following the verb in *kundoku*: for example, 及ₐ時ᵦ當ᴄ勉励ᴅ → *toki=ni*ᵦ *oyob-ite*ₐ *masani*ᴄ BENREI+*s*ᴅ-*ube-si*ᴄ "seize every opportunity and <u>be sure to</u> endeavor in all things" (Tao Yuanming, Miscellaneous Poem I). Another common example is the particle 未, expressing that an action or occurrence is yet to be realized, which is first read with the adverb *imada* "yet" and then with the negative verbal suffix -*(a)zu*: 未ₐ知ᵦ生ᴄ, 焉ᴅ知ₑ死f

→ _imada_$_a$ SEI=wo$_b$ sir$_c$-_azu_$_a$, idukunzo$_d$ SI=wo$_f$ sir-am-u$_e$ "how am I to know death if I still do not know life?" (Confucius, *The Analects*)

(c) Unread characters (*fudokuji* 不讀字 or *okiji* 置き字)

While the goal of *kundoku* is to produce a vernacular reading as close as possible to the original LS text, not all characters can be easily rendered into Japanese. It is thus not uncommon for certain grammatical particles with no Japanese equivalent to be left unread in a transposed text. The sentence-final particle 矣, expressing affirmation or supposition, for example, is commonly left untranslated in *kundoku*: 我$_a$欲$_b$仁$_c$, 斯$_d$仁$_e$至$_f$矣$_g$ → _ware_$_a$ ZIN=wo$_c$ poqsu-reba$_b$, koko=ni$_d$ ZIN$_e$ itar-u$_f$ ∅$_g$ "If I yearn for virtue, then virtue shall be upon me" (*The Analects*). A similar phenomenon occurs with characters such as the particle 而, which links two verbs in a serial verb construction. While 而 can generally be translated using the sequential converb -*(i)te* in Japanese, it is more often than not left unglossed, with -*(i)te* being added to the preceding verb instead. In the famous opening line to *The Analects*, 學$_a$而$_b$時$_c$習$_d$之$_e$ → _manab_$_a$-_ite_$_b$ toki=ni$_c$ kore=wo$_e$ narap-u$_d$ "study, and in time you shall acquire," for example, while -*(i)te* appears to be a translation of 而, in nearly all glossed MSS and printed texts of *The Analects*, _manab-ite_ is added as a whole to 學, with 而 left unglossed. As -*(i)te* may be added to verbs in *kundoku* with or without the presence of 而, it is impossible to discern whether -*(i)te* is being used as a translation for 而 or simply supplemented for context and thus it is standard practice in *kundoku* studies to also treat characters such as 而 as unread.

(d) Supplemented readings (*hodoku* 補讀)

Similar to how not all characters in an LS text can be translated into Japanese, there are cases in which additional words or morphemes must be added to a text in order to render an accurate Japanese reading. In the broadest sense, supplemented readings include all particles and verbal suffixes added to a vernacular reading that are not present in the original LS text. Elements such as case-marker particles and verbal inflections, for example, must be added to the Japanese text in order to make it grammatically licit. In the narrower sense, supplemented readings refer specifically to words or morphemes added to a text simply to aid comprehension, which are not required for grammatical coherence. In the following passage from *Konkōmyō saishōō-kyō* "Golden light sutra," Saidaji MS (glossed in the early ninth century), the complementizer particle *to* and verb *ip-u* "say" are added after the subject of each clause.

往時$_a$薩埵$_b$者$_c$。即$_d$我$_e$牟尼$_f$是$_g$。勿$_h$生$_i$於$_j$異念$_k$。王$_l$是$_m$父$_n$淨飯$_o$。后$_p$是$_q$母$_r$摩耶$_s$。

WAU=no toki=ni$_a$ SAQTA$_b$=_to ip-isi_=pa, sunapati$_d$ ware$_e$ MUNI$_f$ kore=nar-i$_g$. INEN=wo$_k$ SYAU+zu-ru koto$_i$ na-kar-e$_h$. WAU$_l$=_to ip-u_=pa kore$_m$ titi$_n$ ZYAUBON=nar-i$_o$. KOU$_p$=_to ip-u_=pa kore$_q$ papa$_r$ MAYA=nar-i$_s$.

"He who was <u>called</u> bodhisattva in the past is I, Shakyamuni. Do not think otherwise. He who is <u>called</u> the king is my father, Śuddhodana, and she who is <u>called</u> the queen is my mother, Māyā." (vol. 10)

While particles such as *pa* (topic), *no* (genitive), and *ni* (dative) or the copula *nar-i* are added out of grammatical necessity, were *to ip-isi* "was called" and *to ip-u* "is called" to be omitted, the passage would still be grammatically licit. This is apparent in the English translation as well, in which the verb *called* could just as well be omitted without rendering the passage grammatically illicit.

(e) Alternate readings (*idoku* 異讀)

One final reading strategy that must be taken into consideration when transcribing glossed texts is alternate readings. It is often the case that multiple glosses, yielding more than one possible reading, are given to a character or string of characters in a text. This can, of course, simply be the result of multiple hands glossing the same MS, in which case it is desirable to only transcribe one hand at a time; however, it is just as common for a single hand to provide multiple readings. In this case, each possible reading must be provided if aiming for an accurate transcription. Take the following passage from *Konkōmyō saishōō-kyō*, Saidaiji MS.

於$_a$一切$_b$時$_c$失$_d$正慧$_e$, 故$_f$我$_g$説$_h$彼$_i$爲$_j$無明$_k$.
IQSAI=no$_b$ *toki=ni*$_c$ *SYAUWE=wo*$_e$ [1. *usinap-er-i*$_d$] [2. *usinap-u=wo mot-ite*$_d$], *yuwe=ni*$_f$ *ware*$_g$ *kare=wo*$_i$ *tok-ite*$_h$ *MUMYAU=to ip-u*$_k$.
"In all times, the true knowledge [1. has been lost.] [2. being lost,] therefore, I preach of this and call it Avidyā (ignorance)." (vol. 5)

In this passage, the reading *(usina)p-er-i* "has been lost" is added to the right side of the character 失 "lose," while the alternate reading *(usina)p-u=wo mot-ite* "being lost" is added to the left. Both readings produce a grammatically licit result in Japanese: the former renders the initial clause as an independent sentence, while the latter renders it as a subordinate clause.

Gloss Types

(a) *Kana-ten* (假名點)

Man'yōgana (Chinese character phonograms), katakana, or hiragana glosses added to the right or left side of a Chinese character or characters to give the Japanese or SJ reading of the character(s) or add functional morphemes, such as verbal suffixes or particles, not present in the original LS text but necessary for comprehending the text in Japanese. Man'yōgana glosses are observed from around the end of the eighth century, with katakana and hiragana glosses appearing in the early ninth century. At first, there was no hard distinction between katakana and hiragana, with both syllabaries often mixed together within the same glossed text. Entering the tenth century, man'yōgana and, eventually, hiragana gradually fell out of usage in glosses, with katakana becoming the dominant phonographic script (Tsukishima 1981: 158). At first, there was a large amount of variation among the individual katakana letters, with many letters possessing multiple forms, often within the same text. The katakana script was gradually standardized, however, with most letters more or less resembling their modern form by the late twelfth century (*ibid.*).

(b) *Wokoto-ten* (ヲコト點)

Dots, lines, and other symbols added around the edges (or sometimes in the middle) of a Chinese character to indicate a single or multiple Japanese (C)V mora(s), mark word order inversion, or add punctuation. The majority of *wokoto-ten* are used to add functional morphemes, giving rise to the translation "morphosyntactic gloss" (Whitman et al. 2010; Whitman 2011) or "morphosyntactic dot gloss" (Zisk 2017) in the English literature; however, this translation is not entirely accurate as *wokoto-ten* may also be used to indicate the Japanese reading of a character or characters similar to *kana-ten*. Thus, with the exception of inversion glosses and punctuation, *wokoto-ten* should be viewed as an economical alternative to *kana-ten*, rather than an abstract representation of functional morphemes (Osterkamp 2019). *Wokoto-ten* first appear at the turn of the ninth century and are heavily used throughout the entirety of EMJ but gradually fall out of use in Late Middle Japanese (LMJ: thirteenth to sixteenth centuries). The term "*wokoto-ten*" comes from the accusative case-marker particle *wo* and the nominalizer *koto* "lit. thing," both of which are commonly expressed via *wokoto-ten*. *Wokoto-ten* vary greatly depending on the period, religious sect, or school of thought.

(c) Inversion glosses (*kaeri-ten* 返り點)

Chinese numerals or symbols used to indicate the inversion of the LS word order to match that of the Japanese. There are two main types of inversion glosses: simple inversions, which switch the order of two adjacent characters or character compounds, and complex inversions, which reorder an entire clause or sentence. The earliest inversion glosses are of the second category and consist of Chinese numerals (一, 二, 三, etc.), such as those found in *Kegon kanjōki*, DKB MS. The evolution of inversion glosses is complicated, and space precludes me from going into detail, but, simply put, numeral inversion glosses were supplemented with *wokoto-ten* inversion glosses and various other symbols, such as an upward crescent (♩), from the ninth century (Kobayashi 1974). In most cases, *wokoto-ten* and symbol inversion glosses only mark the starting point of inversion and not the end point. Therefore, in a string of characters ABCD, where A is to be read after D, an inversion gloss will be added to D, but not to A. This is remedied in later texts by adding an end point inversion gloss in the form of an additional *wokoto-ten* or a downward crescent (♩), but as this only allows for the inversion of two characters, this method is gradually replaced with numeral inversion glosses and, later, other methods of numeration using Chinese characters (*ibid.*). These include the characters 上, 中, 下 "top, middle, bottom" from the ninth century and 甲, 乙, 丙, and so on (the signs of the "heavenly stems," a set of ancient Chinese ordinals) from the fourteenth century (*ibid.*). One of the most common types of inversion glosses in later texts is the *re-ten* (ᐯ), a marker of simple inversion that takes its name from its resemblance to the katakana letter レ <re>. A *re-ten* is placed at the bottom left of a character, indicating that it is to be switched with the following character. *Re-ten* proper do not appear until roughly the sixteenth century; however, a predecessor, known as *karigane-ten* "flying wild goose mark," resembling the spread wings of a flying bird (⌒) positioned directly beneath the inverted character, can be found from the late twelfth century (*ibid.*).

(d) Tone marks (*shōten* 聲點)

Dots, hollowed circles, or lines placed around the corners of Chinese characters to indicate their tone in Middle Chinese (MC: fifth to twelfth centuries). The use of tone marks can be traced back to seventh-century China, with ample examples found among the Dunhuang MSS (Ishizuka 1993). Tone marks in Japanese glossed texts begin to appear in the late ninth century. Early on, many Japanese sources distinguished between six tones: *píngshēng-zhòng* 平聲重 "heavy level tone," *píngshēng-qīng* 平聲輕 "light level tone," *shǎngshēng* 上聲 "rising tone," *qùshēng* 去聲 "departing tone," *rùshēng-zhòng* 入聲重 "heavy entering tone," and *rùshēng-qīng* 入聲輕 "light entering tone." The distinction between heavy and light tones gradually fell out of use from the thirteenth century, resulting in a four-tone system becoming mainstream. Tones were added in a clockwise fashion from the bottom left of a character to the bottom right in the order of *píng* (bottom left), *shǎng* (top left), *qù* (top right), and *rù* (bottom right). In glosses following a six-tone system, the heavy tones were placed in the bottom corners of a character with the light tones positioned slightly above them (figure 3.1).

(e) Punctuation

Dots, lines, and other symbols used to mark logical breaks in a text, draw focus to a specific word or section of a text, and mark compoundhood or carry out any other function not directly related

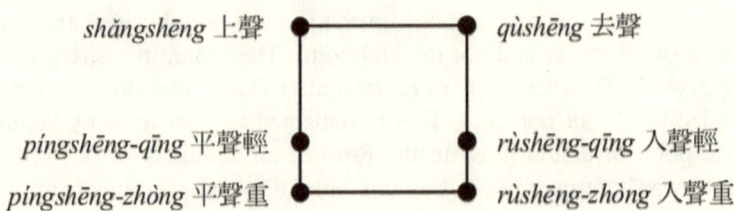

Figure 3.1 Arrangement of Middle Chinese Tone Marks.

to the actual translation of the text. The most common forms of punctuation include *kuten* 句點 "commas," *tōten* 讀點 "full stops," *kadanten* 科段點 "paragraph marks," and *gōfu* 合符 "compound bars." *Kuten* and *tōten* function similarly to their Western counterparts, the former marking a break between clauses, with the latter marking the end of a sentence. This distinction is not always clear, however, and especially in texts prior to the tenth century, it is common for a single mark to be used for all breaks (Kosukegawa 2011). *Kadanten* take the form of large dots or hollowed circles at the top center of a character and mark the start of a new paragraph. Similar to tone marks, the origin of *kuten*, *tōten*, and *kadanten* can be traced back to Chinese glossing practices, with each type of mark being observed in the Dunhuang MSS. *Gōfu* are short vertical bars, or "bridges," that are placed between two (or more) characters to mark compoundhood. *Gōfu* first appeared in the early ninth century and are seemingly unique to Japanese glossing (*ibid.*).[3] Some texts make a distinction between SJ and native Japanese compounds, using a *gōfu* to the right or in the middle of the line to represent the former (*on-gōfu*) and a *gōfu* to the left of the line to represent the latter (*kun-gōfu*). In addition to *gōfu*, a vertical bar on the right or left side of a character may be used to simply indicate an SJ reading (*on-yomi*) or native reading (*kun-yomi*), respectively, regardless of compoundhood.

(f) Literary Sinitic annotations

Interlinear annotations in LS used to add context to a Chinese character, character compound, or phrase. Such annotations are by no means limited to Japanese glossing and are widely observed throughout the Sinosphere. They may consist of Chinese character readings, either through the use of homophonous/near-homophonous characters or *fǎnqiè* 反切 spellings,[4] notes describing the meaning or usage of a character or compound or any other comment adding extra context to the text. While many annotations have no direct connection to the *kundoku* process, homophonous/near-homophonous characters and *fǎnqiè* spellings may be used in place of (or alongside) kana to express an SJ reading and such examples could be viewed as a form of lexical gloss.

3. METHODS FOR TRANSCRIBING *KUNDOKU* TEXTS BY JAPANESE SCHOLARS IN THE TWENTIETH AND TWENTY-FIRST CENTURIES

In Japan, various methods for transcribing *kundoku* texts in modern academic publications, each taking into account the various reading strategies and gloss types outlined in the previous section, have been practiced by Japanese scholars since the inception of the field of *kuntengogaku* 訓點語學 "gloss linguistics" in the early to mid-twentieth century. Over the past century, these methods have been gradually refined, resulting in a widely adopted standard for transcribing *kundoku* texts, known as the *yakubun* 譯文 "lit. translated text," which presents a full transcription of the transposition, or vernacular reading, of a glossed text, while at the same time allowing for a relatively accurate reconstruction of the original glossed text through a series of orthographical conventions and symbols.

The earliest scholar in Japan to cite examples from *kundoku* texts in a modern linguistic study was Ōya Tōru (1851–1928). Ōya was hired by the Japanese government in 1902 to serve as a member of the newly formed National Language Investigation Committee and tasked with surveying the historical development of the kana script. As the vast majority of early sources of kana letters are found among Japanese glosses of LS texts, the bulk of Ōya's research consisted of surveying glosses and copying down portions of text to show the different forms each kana letter took in each MS. Ōya's earliest work on the subject, *Kanazukai oyobi kana jitai enkaku shiryō* "Historical materials on the development of kana usage and kana glyphs" (1909), featured summaries of 50 historical sources, 47 of which were glossed LS texts. Each source contained a short facsimile of a few lines from the MS along with examples of *kana-ten* and a chart of all the forms of kana letters appearing in the MS. None of the examples were transposed into Japanese word order and were simply direct reproductions of the glossed text. Between 1920 and 1922, Ōya published three short studies on ninth-century glossed texts, this time including short excerpts from the texts. Once again, Ōya did not rearrange the text into Japanese word order, but he did transliterate all the *wokoto-ten* into kana, making these studies an early attempt at using modern orthographic conventions to transcribe *kundoku* texts.

The Kyoto University professor and linguist Yoshizawa Yoshinori (1876–1954), who is widely regarded as the founding father of the field of *kuntengogaku*, also published a number of studies on *kundoku* in the early twentieth century, starting with his transcription and study of *Daitō sanzō hōshi hyōkei* "Manifest of Tripitaka Master Xuanzang of the great land of Tang," Chionin MS (Yoshizawa 1915). In his transcription, Yoshizawa preserved the original LS word order of the LS text, similar to Ōya (1920, 1922), but employed a number of orthographic conventions to increase readability of the text.

Namely, he transliterated all the *wokoto-ten* into hiragana, while leaving all *kana-ten* in katakana, thus making a crucial distinction between the two, while adding his own reconstructions of unglossed portions of the text in

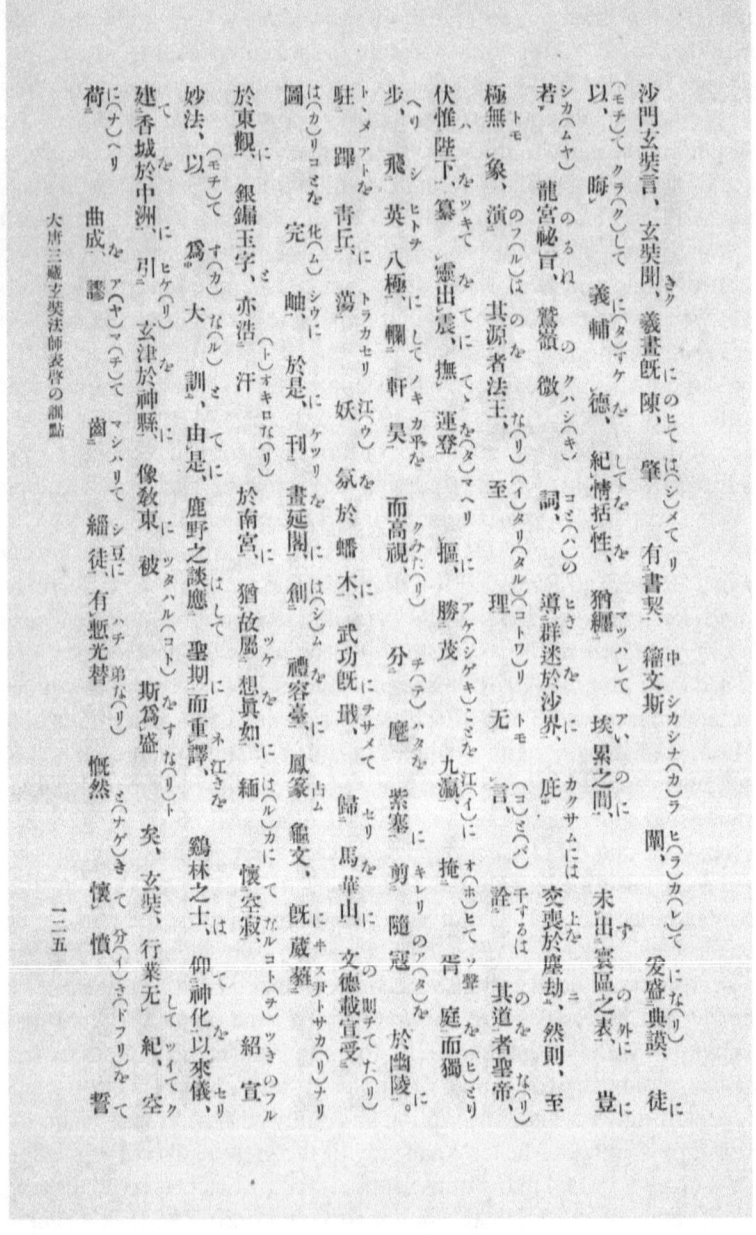

Figure 3.2   Excerpt from Yoshizawa (1915).

rounded brackets (figure 3.2). Yoshizawa used the same method in later transcriptions of other glossed texts as well. While not transpositions in the strict sense, as they preserved the original LS word order, Yoshizawa's transcriptions were influential to the field of *kuntengogaku*, providing the first attempt at producing reader-friendly representations of *kundoku* texts. Furthermore, his method of using hiragana for *wokoto-ten* and katakana for *kana-ten*, while placing reconstructions in rounded brackets, would go on to become the standard among scholars in the field.

While Ōya and Yoshizawa were both clearly influential in the development of transcription methods, the scholar to truly revolutionize the description of *kundoku* texts—and the field of gloss linguistics as a whole—was Kyushu University professor and linguist Kasuga Masaji (1878–1962). In 1942, Kasuga published his magnum opus, *Saidaijibon konkōmyō saishōō-kyō koten no kokugogakuteki kenkyū* "A Japanese linguistic study of the early glossed text of the *Golden light sutra*, Saidaiji MS." The study comprised three volumes: a monochrome facsimile of the text accompanied by a full typeset transcription, a concordance of words found in the glosses of the text and a linguistic study of the language used in the glosses. Unlike his predecessors, Kasuga's transcription was a transposition in the proper sense, presenting a full reconstruction of how the text would have been read vernacularly according to the glosses. In addition to following the standard set forth by Yoshizawa, using hiragana for *wokoto-ten*, katakana for *kana-ten*, and placing reconstructed readings in rounded brackets, Kasuga rearranged the text into Japanese word order, following the word order inversion glosses of the text and placed certain elements such as verbal suffixes and particles in-line with the main text, rather than in-between the lines as his predecessors had, creating a highly readable reproduction of the transposed text (figure 3.3). Kasuga employed a number of additional conventions such as placing unread characters in tortoiseshell brackets at their original position in the text (e.g., 〔而〕, 〔也〕) and alternate readings in tortoiseshell brackets with a small katakana イ (shorthand for *idoku*) at the beginning (e.g., 〔イ失フヲモチテ、〕).

Kasuga's method of transcribing *kundoku* texts quickly became a standard among scholars in the field of *kuntengogaku* and over the past 70 years, well over 100 transcriptions of *kundoku* texts following Kasuga's standard have been published in academic journals, with no less than two dozen book-length transcriptions currently available. Two examples of book-length transcriptions are Nakada (1954–1958/1979: figure 3.4) and Tsukishima (1965–1967: figure 3.5), both of which, while also employing conventions of their own, follow the basic framework laid out by Kasuga (1942). The adoption of Kasuga's standard played a major role not only in the field of *kuntengogaku* but Japanese linguistics as a whole, as having a reader-friendly format for transcribing (and transposing) *kundoku* texts helped introduce these crucial sources to linguists of a variety of backgrounds, not necessarily possessing the highly specialized knowledge

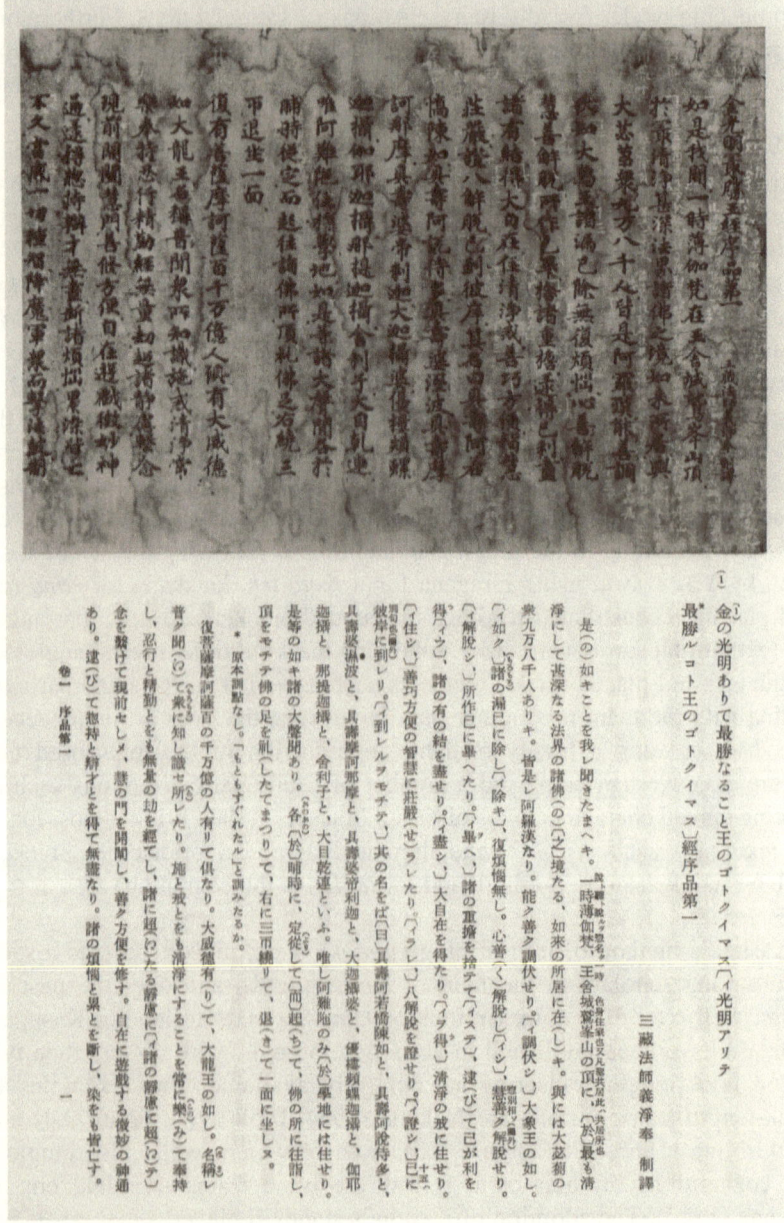

Figure 3.3   Excerpt from Kasuga (1942).

required to interpret *kundoku* texts. In this sense, Kasuga's standard continues to be an indispensable tool to Japanese linguists to this day.

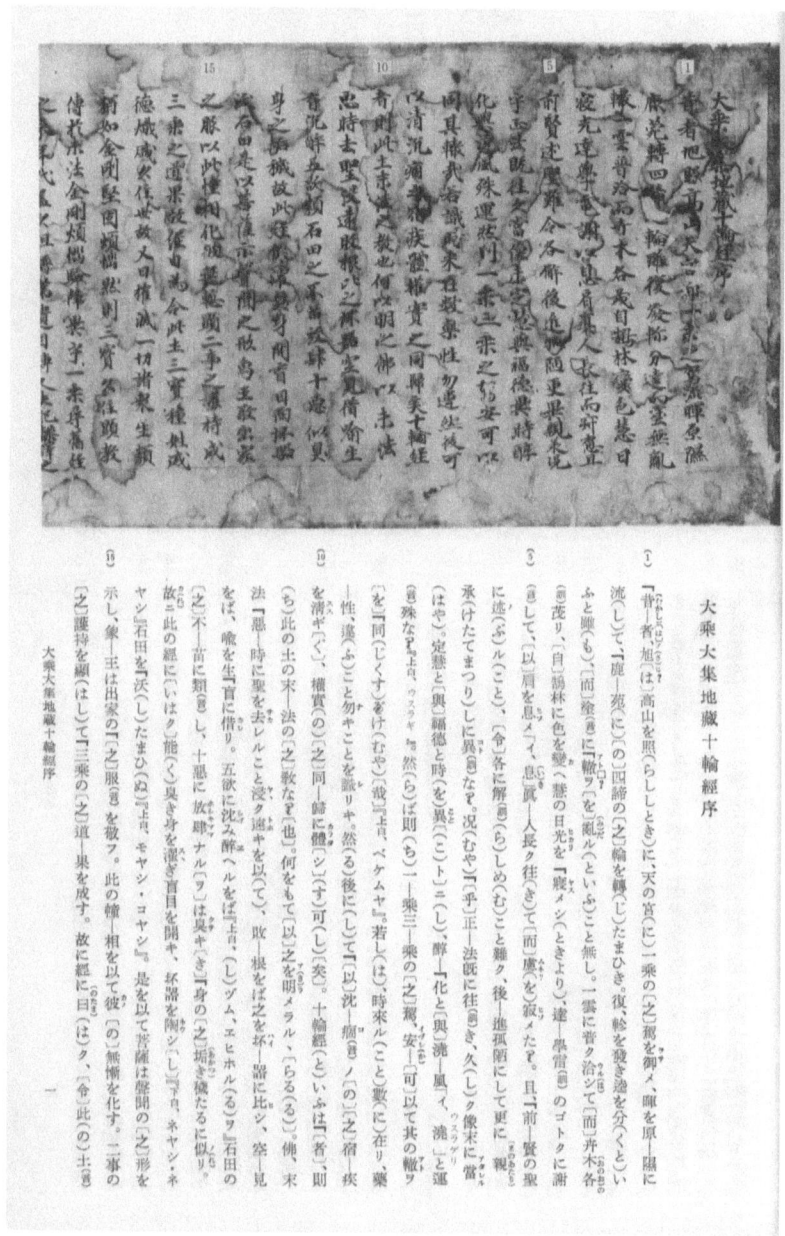

Figure 3.4   Excerpt from Nakada (1954–1958/1979).

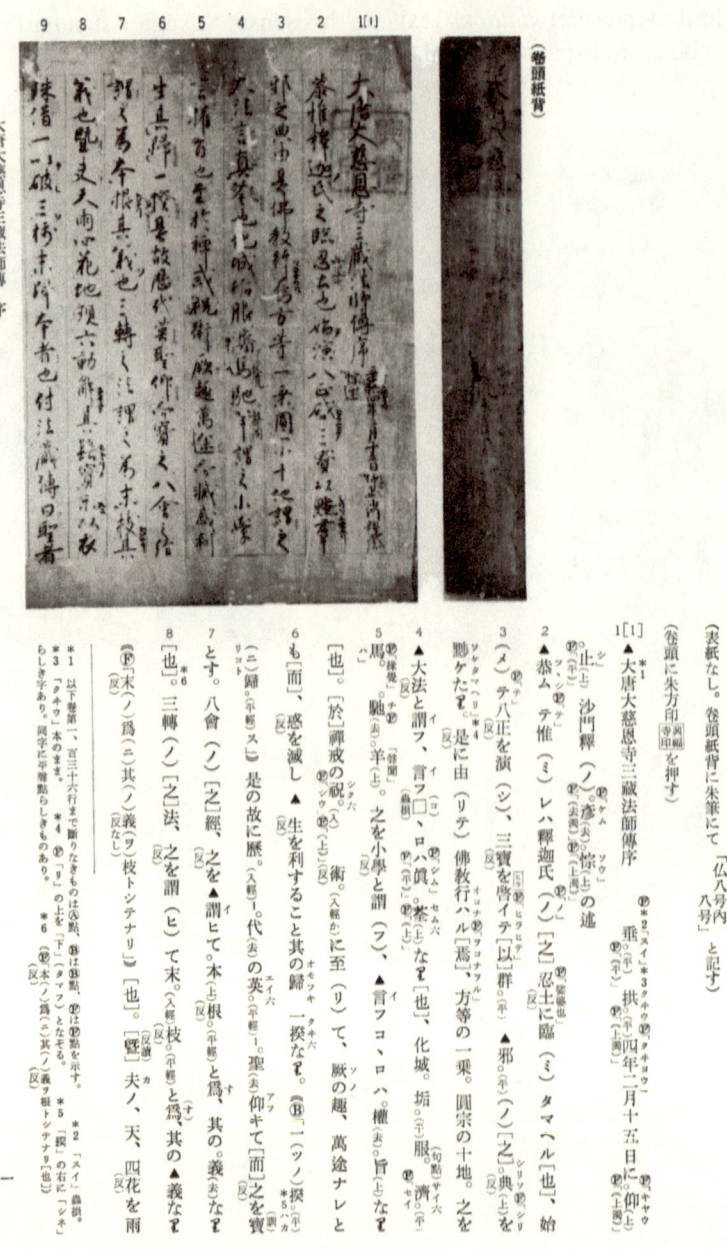

Figure 3.5   Excerpt from Tsukishima (1965–1967).

4. STANDARD FOR TRANSCRIBING AND GLOSSING *KUNDOKU* TEXTS IN ENGLISH PUBLICATIONS

While Kasuga's method of transcribing *kundoku* texts using modern orthographic conventions has been the standard in Japan for well over half a century now, there still exists no such standard for transcribing *kundoku* texts in English publications. Although there has been a recent surge in interest in *kundoku* among Western scholars (see §1), the lack of a transcription and glossing standard for *kundoku* texts had greatly impeded further discussion on the topic in the English-speaking world. The following is a set of transcription and glossing rules for use when citing examples from *kundoku* texts in English publications. These rules follow the format laid out by the *Leipzig Glossing Rules*[5] established by the Max Planck Institute for Evolutionary Anthropology with a number of modifications added to more accurately describe *kundoku* texts. While the rules have been designed with *kundoku* texts in mind, many of these rules could be applied to transcriptions and glosses of classical (or even contemporary) Japanese sources in general.

I. Glossing Tiers

As *kundoku* produces a direct word-by-word translation of an LS text, it is desirable to provide a transcription and gloss of the original LS text along with its transposition in order to give an accurate portrayal of the transposition process. This results in a maximum of seven glossing tiers, with three devoted to the original LS text, another three to its transposition, and a final tier provided for the English translation and source. Tiers 1, 3, 5, 6, and 7 are mandatory, while Tiers 2 and 4 are optional.

Tier 1: Transcription of original LS text using Chinese characters
Tier 2: Phonemicization of original LS text using Roman alphabet
Tier 3: Morphemic gloss of original LS text
Tier 4: Transcription of Japanese transposition following Kasuga's standard
Tier 5: Phonemicization of Japanese transposition using Roman alphabet
Tier 6: Morphemic gloss of Japanese transposition
Tier 7: English translation and source

In most cases, Tier 2 may be omitted as the pronunciation of the original LS text will vary from period to period and region to region and, in many cases, only exist as a reconstruction. Tier 4 may also be omitted when space is at a premium. While this runs the risk of obfuscating the link between each character and its vernacular reading, most of this information can be inferred by comparing Tiers 3 and 6. See the following section for an example of a seven-tier gloss. In all of the examples below, Tier 2 (when provided) follows the MC phonemicization of Baxter and Sagart (2014).

Seven-Tier Gloss

1 舍利弗	汝等	當IT 一RE 心	信解2	受持3	佛語1	
2 *syaeXlijHpjut*	*nyoX-tongX*	*tang 'jit sim*	*sinHheaX*	*dzyuwXdri*	*bjutngjoX*	
3 Śāriputra	you-PLU	must unite heart	believe	retain	Buddha's.teachings	

4 舍利弗	汝	當IT.1	心(ヲ)	一(ニ)	シ)テRE
5 *SYARIPOTU*	*NANDI)-ra*	*(masani*	*kokoro=wo*	*pitotu=ni*	*si)-te*
6 Śāriputra	you-PLU	truly	heart=ACC	one=DAT	do-SEQ

4 佛語を1	信解し2	受持(ス)3ベシIT.2と	(マウス)
5 *(BUTUGO)=wo*	*(SINGE)+si*	*(ZYUDI+s-u)be-si=to*	*(maus-u)*
6 Buddha's.teachings=ACC	believe+do.ADV	retain+do-NEC-CCL=CMP	speak-CCL

7 "Śāriputra said, 'You must truly put your hearts together as one to believe and retain the teachings of Buddha.'"

    Myōhō renge-kyō "Lotus sutra," Yamada MS (mid-ninth century), ln. 146 (Kobayashi 2012: 182) (inversion glosses added by Kobayashi)

II. Overall Format

Each tier of the gloss is to be formatted according to the following rules. Rules (a)–(d) are adapted from the *Leipzig Glossing Rules* with (e) added by the author.

(a) *Word-by-word alignment*
  Left-align the corresponding words of each tier, treating affixes and clitics as part of a larger word, so that they line up vertically on the page. This can be achieved in Microsoft Word or similar software by setting custom tab stops.

  For example,

子	曰く	學びで	時に	之を	習ふRE
si	*ip-aku*	*manab-ite*	*toki=ni*	*kore=wo*	*narap-u*
Confucius	say-NML	study-SEQ	time=DAT	this=ACC	learn-CCL

              (Confucius, *The Analects*)

(b) *Morpheme-to-morpheme correspondence*

When adding segmentation (further below) be sure to add the same segmentation to both the phonemicization and morphemic gloss tiers. No segmentation is needed in the original LS or Japanese transcription tiers. While interpretations of morpheme boundaries will vary from author to author, avoid over-simplification of boundaries such as in the last example below.

For example,

ar-iker-i	OR	*ari-ker-i*	OR	*ar-i-ker-i*
exist-HPS-CCL		exist-HPS-CCL		exist-THM-HPS-CCL (THM = thematic suffix)

NOT	*ar-iker-i*	OR	*arikeri*	OR	*ari-keri*
	existed		exist-HPS-CCL		exist-HPS

(c) *Glossing labels*

Functional morphemes and grammatical functions associated with a lexical morpheme, such as honorific meaning, are to be marked with glossing labels (a three-letter abbreviation of the main grammatical function of the morpheme; also referred to as "category labels") in the morphemic gloss using small caps (see the appendix at the end of this chapter for examples).

For example,
kore=wo ("this" + accusative → this=ACC)
ip-u ("say" + conclusive → say-CCL)
tok-i+tamap-u ("preach" + adverbial + respectful auxiliary + conclusive → preach-ADV+RSP-CCL)

(d) *One-to-many correspondences*

When a single morpheme embeds multiple meanings (lexical, grammatical, or both) that cannot be broken down into further morphemes or an affix is morphologically null, a glossing label for each meaning is to be added and separated by a period. The same rule applies to cases in which two or more English words are used to gloss a single LS or Japanese word.

For example,
maus-u → speak.HUM-CCL (*maus-u* is a humble variant of the verb "speak")
ayum-azu → walk-NEG.CCL (the suffix *-(a)zu* doubles as a negative and conclusive suffix and cannot be broken down any further)
ake → open.ADV (the adverbial suffix is null after vowel-stem verbs)
buqten → Buddhist.scripture (two English words to one Japanese word)

(e) *Form over function*

It is common in Old and Middle Japanese (as well as in the modern language) for one morpheme to express various grammatical functions depending on context. Perhaps the most notorious example of this is the case-marker particle *ni*, which can express the dative, locative, allative, temporal, translative, agentive, comparative, causal, or purposive case (Irwin and Zisk 2019: 82). While marking each instance of *ni* with a gloss related to its specific case marking may be useful in a study of case-marker particles, in the majority of cases, this will simply lead to unnecessary complication. Thus, when possible, it is preferable to place form over function and keep the number of glossing labels at a minimum. The exception to this rule is when the various meanings of a form are so far separated that they cannot be inferred from a single glossing label. For example, *ni* can also be used as a derivational particle to form an adverb (*siduka=ni aruk-u* "walk silently"; Irwin and Zisk 2019: 88). Thus, while a single label DAT (dative) should be used for all case markings expressed by *ni*, this gloss is not optimal for *ni* used as a derivational particle and a different label, such as AVZ (adverbializer), should be used instead.

III. Segmentation

Morpheme boundaries in the phonemicization and morphemic gloss tiers are to be marked using the following conventions.

(a) Affix boundaries

Boundaries between a stem and an affix or between two or more affixes are to be marked with a hyphen (-). For morphologically null affixes, use a period (.) in the morphemic gloss (see Rule IId).

For example,
tanosim-u → enjoy-CCL (one affix)
naduke-rare-tar-u → name-PAS-STA-ADN (multiple affixes)
ip-iki → say-EPS.CCL (morphologically null affix)

(b) Clitic boundaries

Boundaries between a stem or affix and a clitic, or between two or more clitics, are to be marked with an equal sign (=). While which forms are to be classified as clitics as opposed to words or affixes is an issue of major debate in Japanese linguistics, for the sake of convenience, here I treat all particles and copulas as clitics.

For example,
potoke=no → Buddha=GEN (one particle)
su-ru=nomi=ni=pa → do-ADN=RST=DAT=TOP (multiple particles)
tokoro=nar-i → place=COP-CCL (copula)

(c) Compound boundaries

Boundaries between stems within a compound are to be marked with a plus sign (+). This includes auxiliary verbs such as *tamap-u* (respectful auxiliary) and *s-u* "do" following an SJ noun to form a nominal verb. For commonly occurring or exocentric (semantically opaque) compounds, the plus sign may be omitted.

For example,
pikar-i+kakayak-u → shine-ADV+glisten-CCL (compound verb)
kik-i+tamap-u → listen-ADV+RSP-CCL (lexical verb + auxiliary)
SYUGYAU+s-u → training+do-CCL (SJ noun + *s-u*)
kare+kore → that+this

OR

karekore → this.and.that (exocentric compound)

IV. Rules Specific to *Kundoku* Texts

The following rules deal with orthographic conventions specific to *kundoku* texts. By following these rules, it is possible for the reader to more or less accurately reconstruct the original glossed LS text from the contemporary transcription and gloss in a similar fashion to the transcription standard set forth by Kasuga (1942), widely adopted in Japanese publications (see §3).

(a) Word order inversion

Word order inversion is to be marked using the following labels in both the original LS text (Tier 1) and the Japanese transposition (Tier 4; when omitting Tier 4, add the labels to Tier 5, the phonemicization tier, instead).

IN.1, IN.2	*wokoto-ten* or symbol inversion gloss (use IN.1 for starting point and IN.2 for ending point)
1, 2, 3, ...	Chinese numeral inversion gloss (simply replace the Chinese numerals with Arabic numerals)
TOP, MID, BTM	上 "top," 中 "middle," 下 "bottom" inversion gloss
KŌ, OTSU, HEI, ...	Heavenly stem ordinal (甲, 乙, 丙, ...) inversion gloss
RE	*re-ten* or *karigane-ten*

When word inversion glosses are absent from the original MS, use Arabic numerals for complex inversions and RE for simple inversions. When doing so, be sure to either place all inversion glosses added by the author in rounded brackets or to add a note explaining that the glosses are not original (this applies to secondary sources in which inversion glosses are added by the author as well; see Rule I for an example of this). For *wokoto-ten* or symbol inversion glosses with only a starting point and no ending point marked in the original MS, place IN.2 in rounded brackets. In the case that multiple sets of inversions overlap with one another, add an apostrophe next to the second set of labels (i.e., IN.1', IN.2', 1', 2', 3', etc.; see §5 for an example of this).

For example, Simple inversion

Tier 1:	枕RE	石		漱RE	流
...					
Tier 4:	石に	枕しRE		流れに	漱ぐRE

OR (if omitting Tier 4)

Tier 5:	*isi=ni*	*makura+si* RE	*nagare=ni*	*kutisusug-u* RE

Complex inversion

Tier 1:	不3	能2	知1
...			
Tier 4:	知る	こと1	能は2ず3

OR (if omitting Tier 4)

Tier 5:	*sir-u*	*koto*1	*atap*2*-azu*3

(b) Iterated characters

For iterated characters, place the label IT next to the iterated character in the original LS text (Tier 1) and the label IT.1 next to the first iteration and IT.2 the second iteration in the Japanese transposition (Tier 4; or Tier 5 if omitting Tier 4). As there is no gloss to specifically mark iteration (the first and second readings are simply added to the right and left side of a character, respectively), one may optionally place IT, IT.1, and IT.2 in rounded brackets to indicate that they do not represent glosses from the original MS.

For example,

Tier 1:	及2	時1	當IT	勉励
...				
Tier 4:	時に1	及びて2	當にIT.1	勉励すべしIT.2

OR (if omitting Tier 4)

Tier 5:	*toki=ni*1	*oyob-ite*2	*masani* IT.1	*BENREI+s-ube-si* IT.2

(c) Unread characters

Unread characters and any phonemicizations and glosses thereof are to be placed in square brackets in the original LS portion of the transcription and gloss (Tiers 1–3) and ignored in the Japanese portion (Tiers 4–6).

For example,

Tier 1: 子	曰	學	[而]	時	習RE	之
Tier 2: *tsiX*	*hjwo*	*thaewk*	[*nyi*]	*dzyi*	*zip*	*tsyi*
Tier 3: Confucius	say	study	[and.then]	time	learn	this

(d) Alternate readings

When two or more readings are given for a single character, compound, or phrase, first give the default reading (typically the reading added to the right side of the character(s)), followed by any alternate readings (typically any readings added to the left side of the character(s)) in curly brackets. When there are two or more alternate readings, add an Arabic numeral 1, 2, 3, and so on at the start of each set of curly brackets. In the case that the *kana-ten* and *wokoto-ten* provide alternate or overlapping readings to a portion of the text, give the reading constructed from the *wokoto-ten* first, followed by that of the *kana-ten*. When multiple layers of glosses from different hands are present within a single MS, only one hand needs to be provided in any given example; however, if desired, one may provide the glosses from alternate hands in curly brackets as well. In this case, place a capital letter A, B, C, and so on at the start of each set of curly brackets. In the example below from *Konkōmyō saishōō-kyō*, Saidaiji MS, the default reading is provided by *wokoto-ten* and *kana-ten* in-line with the text, with alternate readings given on both the right and left side of the text.

For example,

六賊	依止	不(2)	相	知(1)
six.thieves	depend	NEG	together	know

六賊は   依止(し)タレども   {1六賊ノ
(ROKUZOKU)=pa   *(EZI+si)-tar-edomo*   {1 *(ROKUZOKU)=no*
six.thieves=TOP   depend+do-STA-HCO   { I six.thieves=GEN

依止セルイハ}
(EZI)+se-ru=i=pa}
depend+do-ADN=NOM=TOP}

{2六賊ノ　　　依止ノミシテハ}　　　相ひ知ラ(1)ず(2)。
(ROKUZOKU)=no　(EZI)=nomi+si-te=pa}　(a)pi+sir-azu
six.thieves=GEN　depend=RST+do-SEQ=TOP}　REC+know-NEG.CCL

"Even if the six thieves (the six sensual organs (the eyes, ears, nose, tongue, skin, and mind) that cause affliction) depend on each other {1 The six thieves, depending on each other,}{2 The six thieves depend only on each other and} do not know each other."

Konkōmyō saishōō-kyō, Saidaiji MS, vol. 5
(Sōhonzan Saidaiji 2013: v. 1, p. 138; Kasuga 1942: 86)

(e) Distinguishing between gloss types and lexical strata

In MSS where both *kana-ten* and *wokoto-ten* are used, *kana-ten* are to be indicated by regular font with *wokoto-ten* in bold. Any portions of the reading supplemented by the author for coherency are to be placed in rounded brackets. Additionally, SJ and native words or morphemes may be distinguished by the use of capital letters for the former and lowercase letters for the latter, as is done throughout this chapter.

(f) Punctuation

Mark any punctuation present in the original MS in Tier 1 (original LS text) of the transcription using the characters and conventions below. Punctuation may optionally be added to the Japanese transposition (Tier 4; or Tier 5 if omitting Tier 4) as well, but in most cases is not necessary. If adding punctuation of your own for readability or citing from a secondary source in which punctuation is added by the author, be sure to indicate that the punctuation is not original either through the addition of a note or rounded brackets around all author-added punctuation.

kuten:	comma (,)
tōten:	full stop (.)
kadanten:	white circle (○)
gōfu:	en dash (東–西); *do not confuse with a hyphen (-), which marks a morpheme boundary
on *gōfu*:	overscore or macron (東⁻西)
kun-gōfu:	underscore (東_西)
on-yomi:	single overline(東) or double underline (東)
kun-yomi:	single underline (西)

(g) Other glosses and conventions

Other glosses such as MC tone marks or annotations not directly related to the vernacular reading of the text are to be given in angle brackets next to the glossed character(s) when deemed necessary by the author. Use the labels given in Table 3.1 in the original LS text (Tier 1) and the morphemic gloss thereof (Tier 3) to represent tone marks.

Glossing Glosses

Table 3.1 Representation of Middle Chinese Tone Marks

Tone Name	Tier 1	Tier 3
píngshēng	<平>	PING
píngshēng-zhòng	<平重>	PING.Z
píngshēng-qīng	<平輕>	PING.Q
shǎngshēng	<上>	SHANG
qùshēng	<去>	QU
rùshēng	<入>	RU
rùshēng-zhòng	<入重>	RU.Z
rùshēng-qīng	<入輕>	RU.Q

For Chinese character readings provided through homophonous/near-homophonous characters or *fǎnqiè* spelling guides, provide the annotation in Tier 1 with the MC reading indicated by the annotation in Tier 3.

For example,

Tier 1: 鳴<音明>
Tier 3: cry<mjaeng> (pronunciation indicated by homophone)
Tier 1: 東<德紅切>
Tier 3: east<tuwng> (pronunciation indicated by *fǎnqiè* spelling guide: tok + huwng)

Two-lines-in-one annotations (*warichū* 割注) may be marked by double angle brackets with a vertical bar (|) to mark a line break.

For example, Original MS: 有子曰 孔曰弟子有若

Tier 1: 有子　　曰　<<孔　　　曰　弟 | 子　有若>>
Tier 3: Youruo　say　<<Confucius　say　disciple　Youruo>> ...
Tier 7: "Youruo says <<Confucius says, 'Youruo is a disciple'>> ..."

(*Lúnyǔ jíjiě* "Collected commentaries on *The Analects*")

V. Phonemicization of Japanese by period

The following is a set of guidelines to adhere to when adding the phonemic transcription (Tier 4) to an example. Phonemicizations for Japanese vary considerably from scholar to scholar and period to period and the following guidelines are to be taken merely as suggestions and not rules. What is perhaps more important than the phonemicization itself is that the author is consistent in his or her transcriptions. The following rules focus primarily on Old and Middle Japanese. See the author's website (https://tohoku.academia.edu/MatthewZisk/) for a more detailed set of guidelines including conventions for later stages of the language.[6]

(a) Vowels
   (1) The Old Japanese (OJ: eighth century) *kō-otsu* 甲乙 distinction, where present, is to be indicated by means of index notation, that is, using a subscript number 1 or 2 next to the mora in question.

   For example, 時 (等伎) *to₂ki₁*   心 (許己呂) *ko₂ko₂ro₂*   霍公鳥 (保等登藝須) *poto₂to₂gi₁su*

   (2) Long *a*, *i*, *u*, and *o* are to be indicated by writing the same vowel twice, not by using a macron or circumflex.

   For example, ああ *kakaa*   飯田 *iida* (←EMJ *ipida*)   内宮 *naiguu*   東海 *tookai* (← EMJ *toukai*)

   (3) Long *e* is to be written as *ei* for SJ vocabulary and *ei* or *ee* for native vocabulary depending on the kana spelling.

   For example, 傾城 *keisei*   おとなしくせい *otonasi-ku se-i*   おめへ *omee*   くだらねえ *kudaranee*

   (4) EMJ vowel sequences that underwent monophthongization in LMJ are to be indicated as follows according to period. The so-called "open" long *o* (*kaichōon* 開長音), transcribed as <ŏ> by the Portuguese-speaking Jesuits, is to be indicated by *åå* (cf. Irwin and Narrog 2012). This long vowel merged with *oo* in the early seventeenth century.

(b) Consonants
   (1) The following 17 phonemic consonants can be posited for Japanese prior to the mid-twentieth century, with *f* arising sometime during Early or LMJ from lenition of *p* (except after mora consonants) and *h* from the subsequent lenition of *f* sometime around the early seventeenth century. A phonemic distinction between syllable-final *n* and *m* is present in EMJ, with both of the nasal codas merging as the mora nasal ɴ in LMJ.

Table 3.2 Representation of Vowel Sequences by Period

	舊記 "chronicle"	遷宮 "shrine relocation"	教義 "doctrine"	公案 "koan"	高座 "high chair"
9–12C	kiuki	senguu	keugi	kouan	kauza
13–14C	↓	seɴguu	↓	kouaɴ	↓
15–16C	kyuuki	↓	kyoogi	kooaɴ	kååza
17C–	↓	↓	↓	↓	kooza

Table 3.3 Consonant Phonemes of Pre–Mid-Twentieth-Century Japanese

	labial	alveolar	palatal	velar	glottal	moraic
plosive	p b	t d		k g		q
fricative	→ f	s z			→ h	
nasal	m	n				→ n
tap		r				
glide			y	w		

(2) The phonetic value of present-day Japanese *h* in Old and Middle Japanese is highly controversial, with no consensus on when *p* fully weakened to *f*. These guidelines follow Kiyose (1985), using *p* for OJ and EMJ with *f* for LMJ. The further lenition of *f* to *h* through debuccalization is less controversial, widely held to have occurred starting in the early to mid-seventeenth century. Here, I uniformly use *h* for the entirety of Modern Japanese (NJ: seventeenth century–present). While the merger of intervocalic *p* with *w* is said to have occurred gradually starting in the late tenth century, for the sake of simplicity, intervocalic *p* should be indicated by *p* throughout EMJ, but as *wa*, *wi*, *u*, *we*, and *wo* when spelled so in a primary source. For LMJ onward, follow table 3.4 which takes the mergers in (3) into account as well.

(3) The mergers of the moras *i* ~ *wi*, *e* ~ *ye* ~ *we*, and *o* ~ *wo* are both complex and controversial. The general consensus is that *e* ~ *ye* merged as *ye* in the mid-tenth century, with *o* ~ *wo* merging as *wo* in the early eleventh century, and *i* ~ *wi* as *i*, *ye* ~ *we* as *ye* in the thirteenth and fourteenth centuries. As a general rule of thumb, distinguish between these moras when the distinction is present in a primary source and follow table 3.5 when no distinction is made and from LMJ onward, where any distinction between *o* and *wo* is merely orthographical.

(4) Postconsonantal *y*-glides (*kaiyōon* 開拗音) and *w*-glides (*gōyōon* 合拗音) are to be indicated by *y* and *w* respectively throughout all

Table 3.4 Representation of Initial and Intervocalic *p* by Period

	かは "river"	はひ "ash"	あふ "meet"	はへ "fly"	かほ "face"
9–10C	kapa	papi	apu	pape	kapo
11–12C	kawa	pawi	au	pawe	kawo
13–16C	↓	fai	↓	faye	↓
17–18C	↓	hai	↓	haye	↓
19C	↓	↓	↓	↓	kao
20C–	↓	↓	↓	hae	↓

Table 3.5 Representation of Onglide Moras by Period

	えみし "barbarian"	えだ "branch"	ゑみ "smile"	いろ "color"	ゐなか "countryside"	おと "sound"	をとこ "man"
9–10C	emisi	yeda	wemi	iro	winaka	oto	wotoko
11–12C	yemisi	↓	↓	↓	↓	woto	↓
13–18C	↓	↓	yemi	↓	inaka	↓	↓
19C	↓	↓	↓	↓	↓	oto	otoko
20C–	emisi	eda	emi	↓	↓	↓	↓

periods; only indicate *w*-glides in moras other than *kwa* and *gwa* when the kana spelling specifically indicates its presence.

For example, 釋迦 *syaka*   觀音 *kwannon* 日月ジツグヱツ *jitugwetu* OR *jitgwet* (see (7) below)

(5) Nasal codas and mora nasals (*hatsuon* 撥音) are to be indicated by *n* for alveolar nasals and *m* for bilabial nasals in EMJ and universally as a small caps ɴ in LMJ and NJ after their merger into a single mora consonant. For sources that distinguish SJ velar nasals on the orthographic level, velar nasals may be indicated by *ũ*, *ĩ*, or *ng* depending on the kana spelling, although since views as to whether or not this phone was distinctive are contested, this final convention is optional.

For example, 聞 EMJ *ken* → LMJ *keɴ*   侵 EMJ *sim* → LMJ *sɪɴ* 經 *kyau* OR *kyaũ* OR *kyang*   靈 *rei* OR *reĩ* OR *reng*

(6) Mora obstruents (*sokuon* 促音) are to be indicated by a small caps ǫ across all periods.

For example, 欲ホンス *hoǫ-u*   因ヨテ *yoǫ-te*   以モツテ *moǫ-te*

(7) Multiple sources confirm that SJ *t*-codas (*zetsunai nisshōon* 舌内入聲音) spelled as ツ <tu> (but not チ <ti>) were realized as closed syllables in LMJ, although whether or not this was the case in EMJ is unclear. For the sake of simplicity, I suggest simply following the kana spelling when transcribing *t*-codas, although *t* may be used for accuracy when transcribing SJ *t*-codas spelled as ツ in LMJ, especially when a closed syllable realization is apparent from a primary source such as *Vocabulario da Lingoa de Iapam* (*Nippo jisho*).

For example, 刹那 LMJ *setuna* OR *setna*   發熱 LMJ *fotunetu* OR *fotnet*

5. FINAL THOUGHTS

While the examples given in this chapter focus solely on Japanese, a similar method of description could also be used for other countries in the Sinosphere in which vernacular reading was historically practiced, such as Korea and Vietnam. For example, the *gugyeol* 口訣 system of rendering an LS text in Korean, used during the Goryeo and Joseon dynasties in Korea, utilizes similar types of glosses and reading strategies to *kundoku* in Japan. *Gugyeol* texts contain abbreviated Chinese character glosses (*jato* 字吐), dot glosses (*jeomto* 點吐), and inversion glosses (*yeokdokjeom* 逆讀點). Most *jato* act as phonograms, carrying out a function identical to *kanaten* in *kundoku*, while *jeomto* are used in the same fashion as *wokoto-ten* and *yeokdokjeom*, the same fashion as Japanese inversion glosses. A small number of *jato* act as semantograms, representing a semantically equivalent Korean word, similar to Japanese *kun* reading. The gloss ᄼ , an abbreviated form of 爲 "do," for example, is used to indicate the stem of the verb *hʌ*- "do." Taking these similarities into account, a seven-tier gloss, similar to that presented in §4, could be used to transcribe examples from Korean *gugyeol* texts as well. An example from a thirteenth-century MS is provided below, with phonogram glosses transcribed in regular lowercase and semantogram glosses representing Korean morphemes in bold (this particular MS lacks dot glosses). Sino-Korean is transcribed using MC readings minus any tones, as Sino-Korean from this period is yet to be accurately reconstructed.

Seven-Tier Gloss (*gugyeol* text)

```
1 復        有(IN.2) 五道      一切    衆生IN.1         復     有(IN.2)
2 bjuwH hjuwX   nguXdawX 'jittshet tsyuwngHsraeng  bjuwH  hjuwX
3 also   exist  five.paths all   sentient.beings   also   exist
```

```
1 他方      不(IN.3')  可IN.2'    量IN.1'   衆IN.1
2 thapjang  pjuw       khaX       ljang     tsyuwngH
3 elsewhere NEG        possible   measure   people
```

```
4 復ᄼ ㄱ         五道ㅌ              一切       衆生ㅣIN.1
5 (sto)hʌn      (NGUDAW)=s          ('JITTSHET  TSYUWNGSRAENG)=i
6 also          five.paths=GEN      all         sentient.beings=NOM

  有ㅌㅏㄱ(IN.2)
  (i)s-kjə-mjə
  exist-CNT-SIM
```

4	復ツヿ	他方セ	量ノ㆑IN.1'	可セツリIN.2'
5	*(sto)hʌn*	*(THAPJANG)=s*	*(LJANG)+ho-m*	*(ci)s+hʌ-n*
6	also	elsewhere=GEN	measure+do-NMZ	possible+do-NMZ

4	不矢リヒセ(IN.3')	衆IN.1	有セナ㆑(IN.2)
5	*(an)ti=i-nʌ=s*	*(TSYUWNG)*	*(i)s-kjə-mjə*
6	NEG=COP-NMZ=GEN	people	exist-CNT-SIM

7 "In addition to all the sentient beings of the five paths, there exist people of uncountable numbers in other realms, and . . ."

Guyeog inwang-gyeong "Benevolent king sutra" fragment, Sudeoksa (early thirteenth century), ln. 1–2 (CNT = continuous)

(Gugyeol Hakoe 1997)[7]

Interest in glossing as a cross-cultural phenomenon is steadily increasing, and the need for a universal standard for the description of glossed texts, similar to the widely adopted *Leipzig Glossing Rules* for the description of languages, has never been stronger. It is my hope that the transcription and glossing standard presented in this chapter will help scholars working on *kundoku* texts to introduce their research to a broader audience and at the same time promote a discussion on transcription and glossing practices for glossed texts in general.

APPENDIX: LIST OF GLOSSING LABELS FOR FUNCTIONAL MORPHEMES IN EARLY MIDDLE JAPANESE

Provided below is a list of glossing abbreviations for some of the most common functional morphemes in EMJ. This list is by no means limited to the language of *kundoku* texts and could be used for glossing examples from other sources as well. See the author's profile at Academia.edu (https://tohoku.academia.edu/MatthewZisk/) for a more exhaustive and up-to-date list of functional morphemes including later stages of the language.

KEY

rounded brackets (. . .)	union vowel/consonant[8]
square brackets [ ]	omissible

hyphen (-)		affix boundary
equal sign (=)		clitic boundary
plus sign (+)		auxiliary (compound stem) boundary
tilde (~)		allomorph
ellipsis (…)		stem surrounded by prefix and suffix (circumfix)
zero sign (∅)		null morpheme, that is, having no phonetic realization

Function	Label	Corresponding forms
ablative	ABL	=kara, =yori
accusative	ACC	=wo
adnominal	ADN	-(r)u, -ki
adverbial	ADV	-(i)∅, -ku
adverbializer	AVZ	=ni
allative	ALL	=pe
analogical	ANL	=dani, =sape, =sura ~ =sora
causative	CAU	-(s)ase- ~ -(a)sime-
classifier	CLF	-ka, -piki, -nin, -tai, -do, etc.
comitative	COM	=to
complementizer	CMP	=to
concessive	CON	=mo, =monowo ~ =monono ~ =monokara
conclusive	CCL	-(r)u ~ -i, -si ~ -∅
confirmative	CNF	=kasi
conjectural	CJT	-(a)m-, -(r)uram-
copula	COP	=nar-, =tar-
counterfactual	CFT	-(a)masi ~ (a)mase-
dative	DAT	=ni
desiderative	DES	-(a)baya, -(i)sika, -(a)mapo-, -(i)ta-
emphatic	EMP	=i, =si
empirical past	EPS	-(i)ki ~ -(i)ke- ~ -(i)si ~ -(i)se-
evidential	EVD	-(r)urasi
exclamatory	XCL	=ka[mo ~ na], =na, =nomi, =pa, =wo, =ya, =yo
exempletive	EXE	=nado ~ =nando
fixed concessive	XCO	-(r)uto[mo] ~ -(i)to[mo], -ku[to]mo
fixed conditional	FCD	-(r)eba, -kereba
focus	FOC	=koso, =namu ~ =nan, =so ~ =zo
focused accusative	FAC	=woba
genitive	GEN	=ga, =no
hearsay evidential	HEV	-(r)unar-
hearsay past	HPS	-(i)ker-

humble	HUM	+kikoye-, +mawos- ~ +maus-, +paber-, +saburap- ~ +samurap- ~ +saurap-, +tamape-, +tatematur-
hypothetical concessive	HCO	-(r)edo[mo], -keredo[mo]
hypothetical conditional	HCD	-(a)ba, -kupa
imperative	IMP	-e ~ -yo ~ -ø
inclusive topic	ITO	=mo
instrumental	INS	=site
interrogative	INT	=ka, =ya
iterative	ITR	-(i)tutu
locative	LOC	=nite
necessitive	NEC	-(r)ube-
negative	NEG	-(a)n- ~ -(a)zu, -(a)zar-
negative conjectural	NCJ	-(a)zi
negative necessitive	NNE	-(r)umazi
negative sequential	NSE	-(a)de
nominal	NML	-(r)aku, -keku
nominalizer	NMZ	-(i)ø, -mi, -sa, =no
nominative	NOM	=i
non-volitional perfect	NPR	-(i)n-
optative	OPT	-(a)namu, =gana, =gani, =moga[mo ~ na]
ordinal	ORD	dai-
passive	PAS	-(r)are- ~ -(r)aye-
past conjectural	PCJ	-(i)kem-, -kem-
plural	PLU	-domo, -gata, -ra, -tati
prohibitive	PRH	-(r)una, na- ... -(i)so
realis	RLS	-(r)e, -kere
reciprocal	REC	api-
respectful	RSP	+asobas-, +tamap-, +wopase-, go- ~ gyo-, mi-, wopomi- ~ wopom- ~ wom- ~ wo-
restrictive	RST	=bakari, =nomi
sequential	SEQ	-(i)te, -kute
sequential complementizer	SCM	=tote
simultaneous	SIM	-(i)nagara, -nagara, =nagara
stative	STA	-(e)r-, -(i)tar-
tendential	TND	-gati, -ge
terminative	TER	=made
topic	TOP	=pa
verbalizer	VBZ	-kar-
visual evidential	VEV	-(r)umer-
volitional perfect	VPR	-(i)te-

ABBREVIATIONS

EMJ   Early Middle Japanese (ninth to twelfth century)
LMJ   Late Middle Japanese (thirteenth to sixteenth century)
LS   Literary Sinitic
MC   Middle Chinese (fifth to twelfth century)
NJ   Modern Japanese (seventeenth century to present)
MS   manuscript
MSS   manuscripts
OJ   Old Japanese (eighth century)
SJ   Sino-Japanese

NOTES

1. The compiler of *Kojiki*, Ō no Yasumaro, talks about the difficulty of expressing Japanese using solely Chinese characters in the preface, indicating that *Kojiki* was to be read in Japanese, not MC, and the thirteenth-century commentary on *Nihon shoki*, *Shaku nihongi* "Interpreting *Nihon shoki*" records that lectures on the proper Japanese reading of *Nihon shoki* were conducted regularly, starting in 721, just one year after its completion.

2. If the word order inversion glosses in *Kegon kanjōki*, DKB MS were copied from the Sillan MS, it is possible that they represent Old Korean, rather than OJ word order. In addition to *Kegon kanjōki* DKB MS, various forms of stylus glosses in several early to mid-eighth-century MSS of the *Avataṃsaka sūtra* and related texts have been reported by Kobayashi Yoshinori in recent years (Kobayashi 2004–2005, 2017). More important, perhaps, is Kobayashi's claim that at least three of these stylus glossed texts represent Old Korean (in particular, the Sillan variety), indicating a direct link of transmission of glossing traditions from Korea to Japan in the eighth century (*ibid.*). While Kobayashi's findings are yet to be verified by the academic community at large, if true, they could provide a much needed missing link between the Korean *gugyeol* (see §5) and Japanese *kundoku* traditions.

3. Kobayashi (2004–2005, 2017) reports the use of *gōfu* in stylus glosses added to Sillan and Japanese MSS from the eighth century. If true, then *gōfu* are most likely a borrowed rather than indigenous innovation; however, similar to his reports on eighth-century stylus glosses in general, these findings are yet to be verified by the larger academic community and must be taken with caution.

4. *Fǎnqiè* spellings are a common technique used from the late Han dynasty (second to third century) to express the pronunciation of a character by combining the initial from one character with the final (rime) of another. For example, the pronunciation of the character 東 "east" (MC *tuwng*) may be indicated as follows 德紅反 or 德紅切, where the character 德 "virtue" (MC *tok*) indicates the initial *t-* and 紅 "crimson" (MC *huwng*) the final *-uwng* of 東, with 反 *fǎn* or 切 *qiè* indicating that the annotation is a *fǎnqiè* spelling.

5. See Lahaussois' chapter in this volume for an overview of the *Leipzig Glossing Rules*.

6. The following guidelines were heavily inspired by the phonemicization guidelines provided by Mark Irwin (Yamagata University) for a joint volume coedited with the author (Irwin & Zisk forthcoming). I would like to thank Mark for his many suggestions when creating these guidelines. It goes without saying that any errors are my own.

7. I would like to thank Inyeong Heo of Korea University for assisting me in the interpretation of this example. Again, it goes without saying that any errors are my own.

8. For ease of description, I treat the vowels and consonants found between the stem of a verb and its suffix as "union segments" belonging to the suffix, following Kiyose (1995). Whether to treat these segments as part of the stem, part of the suffix, or as independent morphemes (thematic suffixes) is a matter of debate with no consensus among scholars. See Shimoji (2017) for a discussion of the merits and demerits of each view, albeit in relation to Ryukyuan.

This work was supported by JSPS KAKENHI Grant number 19H01265.

REFERENCES

Baxter, William H., and Laurent Sagart. 2014. *Old Chinese: A New Reconstruction.* New York: Oxford University Press.

Frellesvig. 2010. *A History of the Japanese Language.* Cambridge: Cambridge University Press.

Gugyeol Hakoe 'Gugyeol Society'. 1997. Jaryo yeongin *Guyeog inwang-gyeong* sang 'Facsimile of the *Benevolent king sutra*, upper volume'. *Gugyeol yeongu* 'Studies in Gugyeol' 2: 11.

Handel, Zev. 2019. *Sinography: The Borrowing and Adaptation of the Chinese Script.* Leiden: Brill.

Irwin, Mark, and Heiko Narrog. 2012. "Late Middle Japanese." In *The Languages of Korea and Japan*, edited by Nicolas Tranter, 246–267. London: Routledge.

Irwin, Mark, and Matthew Zisk. 2019. *Japanese Linguistics.* Tokyo: Asakura Publishing.

———. Forthcoming. *Japanese Sociohistorical Linguistics.* Berlin: De Gruyter Mouton.

Ishizuka, Harumichi. 1993. "The Origins of the ssŭ-shêng Marks." *ACTA ASIATICA* 65: 30–50.

———. 2001. "Heian jidai shoki" 'Early Heian period'. In Yoshida et al., 2001, pp. 28–32.

Kasuga, Masaji. 1942. *Saidaiji-bon konkōmyō saishōō-kyō no kokugogaku-teki kenkyū* 'A Japanese Linguistic Study of the Early Glossed Text of the *Golden light sutra*, Saidaiji MS'. Tokyo: Shidō Bunko.

Kin, Bunkyō (ed. King, Ross; trans. King, Ross & Burge, Marjorie & Park, Si Nae & Lushchenko, Alexey & Hattori, Mina). 2021. *Literary Sinitic and East Asia: A Cultural Sphere of Vernacular Reading.* Leiden: Brill.

King, Ross. 2006. "Connecting Dialects and Kwukyel." In *Hanmun dokbeopgwa dong-asia ui munja* 'Hanmun Reading Techniques and Writing in East Asia', edited by Gugyeol Hakhoe 'Gugyeol Society'. Seoul: Taehaksa, pp. 291–320.

———. 2010. "Pre-Imjin kugyŏl Sources in North American Library Collections: A Preliminary Survey." *Gugyeol yeongu* 'Gugyeol Studies' 25: 217–282.

———. 2013. "The kugyŏl Glosses in the Asami Collection Copy of the *Ch'ŏllo kŭmgang kyŏng* 川老金剛經." *Acta Koreana* 16(1): 199–233.

Kiyose, Gisaburō Norikura. 1985. "Heianchō ha-gyō siin *p* onron" 'Evidence That Modern Japanese *h*- Was *p*- in the Heian Period'. *Study of Sounds* 21: 73–87.

———. 1995. *Japanese Grammar: A New Approach.* Kyoto: Kyoto University Press.

Kobayashi, Yoshinori. 1974. "Kaeriten no enkaku" 'Development of the Inversion Gloss'. *Kuntengo to kuntenshiryō* 'Diacritical Language and Diacritical Materials' 54: 86–111.

———. 2004–2005. *Kakuhitsu bunken kenkyū dōron* 'Introduction to Research on Stylus Glossed Texts', Vols. 1–3. Tokyo: Kyūko Shoin.

———. 2012. *Heian jidai no bussho ni motozuku kanbun kundoku-shi no kenkyū III: Shoki kuntengo taikei* 'Studies in the History of *kanbun kundoku* Based on Buddhist Texts of the Heian Period III: The Lexicon of 9th Century Glossed Texts'. Tokyo: Kyūko Shoin.

———. 2017. *Heian jidai no bussho ni motozuku kanbun kundoku-shi no kenkyū II: Kunten no kigen* 'Studies in the History of *kanbun kundoku* Based on Buddhist Texts of the Heian Period II: The Origin of *kundoku* Glosses'. Tokyo: Kyūko Shoin.

Kornicki, Peter Francis. 2018. *Languages, Scripts, and Chinese Texts in East Asia.* Oxford: Oxford University Press.

Kosukegawa, Teiji. 2001. "Kanseki" 'Chinese Classics'. In Yoshida et al. 2001, pp. 90–100.

———. 2011. "Kutōten no kinō kara mita higashi ajia kanbun kundoku-shi" 'The History of *kundoku* in East Asia Viewed From the Function of Punctuation Marks'. *Kuntengo to kuntenshiryō* 'Diacritical Language and Diacritical Materials' 127: 1–10.

Kosukegawa, Teiji, and John Whitman. 2018. "On the Significance of the Glosses in Vietnamese Classical Chinese Texts." *Journal of Vietnamese Studies* 13(3): 29–50.

Lurie, David B. 2011. *Realms of Literacy: Early Japan and the History of Writing.* Cambridge, MA: Harvard University Asia Center.

Moran, Pádraic, and John Whitman. 2022. "Glossing and Reading in Western Europe and East Asia: A Comparative Case Study." *Speculum* 97: 112–139.

Nakada, Norio. 1954–1958. *Kotenbon no kokugogakuteki kenkyū* 'Japanese Linguistic Study of Early Glossed Texts'. Tokyo: Dainihon Yūbenkai Kōdansha. (Revised Edition From Benseisha, 1979).

Osterkamp, Sven. 2019. "Translation Glosses in Japan: Typological and Terminological Issues." Paper Presented at Glossing From a Comparative Perspective, Philipps-Universität Marburg, June 6–7, 2019.

Ōya, Tōru. 1909. *Kanazukai oyobi kana jitai enkaku shiryō* 'Historical Materials on the Development of Kana Usage and Kana Glyphs'. Tokyo: Kokutei kyōkasho kyōdō hanbaijo.

Shimoji, Michinori. 2017. *A Grammar of Irabu, a Southern Ryukyuan Language*. Fukuoka: Kyushu University Press.

Sōhonzan Saidaiji, ed. 2013. *Kokuhō saidaiji-bon konkōmyō saishōō-kyō tenpyōhōji rokunen kudara no toyomushi gankyō* 'Golden light sutra, Saidaiji MS, National Treasure, Transcribed by Kudara no Toyomushi in 762'. Tokyo: Bensei Shuppan.

Steininger, Brian. 2017. *Chinese Literary Forms in Heian Japan: Poetics and Practice*. Cambridge, MA: Harvard University Asia Center.

Tsukishima Hiroshi. 1965–1967. *Kōfukuji-bon daijionji sanzō hōshiden no kokugogakuteki kenkyū* 'Japanese Linguistic Study of *The Biography of the Tripitaka Master of Dacien Temple*, Kōfukuji MS'. Tokyo: University of Tokyo Press.

———. 1981. *Nihongo no sekai 5: Kana* 'The World of Japanese 5: Kana'. Tokyo: Chūōkōronsha.

Whitman, John. 2011. "The Ubiquity of the Gloss." *Scripta* 3: 95–121.

———. 2020. "Gloss to Lexicon East and West: A Comparison of the Relationship Between Glossing and Lexicography in Medieval East Asia and Europe, With a Translation of the Preface to the *Shinsen jikyō* 新撰字鏡 (898–901)." In *Trends in Eastern and Western Literature, Medieval and Modern*, edited by Yoko Wada, 43–72. Osaka: Junius.

Whitman, John, and Franck Cinato, eds. 2014. *Lecture vernaculaire des textes classiques chinois/Reading Classical Texts in the Vernacular (Dossiers Histoire Épistémologie Langage* 7). http//dossierhel.hypotheses.org/dossiers-hel7-sommaire; accessed 2021.01.13.

Whitman, John, Miyoung Oh, Jinho Park, Valerio Luigi Alberizzi, Masayuki Tsukimoto, Teiji Kosukegawa, and Takada Tomokazu. 2010. "Toward an International Vocabulary for Research on Vernacular Readings of Chinese Texts (漢文訓讀 Hanwen xundu)." *Scripta* 2: 61–85.

Yoshida, Kanehiko, Hiroshi Tsukishima, Harumichi Ishizuka, and Masayuki Tukimoto. 2001. *Kuntengo jiten* 'Dictionary of Gloss Linguistics'. Tokyo: Tōkyōdō Shuppan.

Yoshizawa, Yoshinori. 1915. *Daitō sanzō hōshi hyōkei no kunten* 'Glosses in Manifest of Tripitaka Master Xuanzang of the Great Land of Tang'. Tokyo: Geibun.

Zisk, Matthew. 2017. "Middle Chinese Loan Translations and Derivations in Japanese." *Japanese/Korean Linguistics* 24: 315–329.

4

Issues in Dictionaries Recording *Kunten* Glosses

Teiji Kosukegawa

INTRODUCTION

In Japan, *kunten* glosses[1] originally added to Classical Chinese texts have been collected and recorded in dictionaries since the Early Middle Japanese (Heian) period. Particularly famous examples of this are the Zushoryō-bon *Ruiju myōgishō*[2] 図書寮本類聚名義抄 (Insei Period, end of the eleventh century) and its expanded and supplemented edition, the Kanchiin-bon *Ruiju myōgishō* 観智院本類聚名義抄, both of which include a large number of entries derived from *kunten* glosses. The practice of collecting and publishing *kunten* glosses has continued to the present day. A prime example is the nine-volume *Kunten goi shūsei* 訓点語彙集成 [Compendium of *kunten* vocabulary] (2007–2009, Kyūko shoin) compiled by Tsukishima Hiroshi (1925–2011). This compendium assembles an enormous amount of data from 600 *kunten*-glossed texts surveyed by Tsukishima, comprising some 200,000 examples; furthermore, for each of the *kunten* glosses recorded, it includes information about the source text and location of the gloss in the source text. It is thus a very useful compendium of glosses. However, in this recent compendium as in its predecessors, there are the following types of issues, each leading to the danger that if the compendium or dictionary is cited without reference to the original source, a misconception at variance with the original gloss may take on "a life of its own." This chapter classifies the issues into the three types listed below and exemplifies each with concrete examples. In doing so, it hopes to clarify what kinds of elements should be taken into account in future efforts to compile compendia of *kunten* materials.

CASES WHERE THE GLOSS RECORDED HAS BEEN MISTAKEN FOR ANOTHER GLOSS

The *Shìshuō xīnshū* 世説新書 "New Account of Tales of the World" (Japanese *Sesetsu shinsho*) is a collection of anecdotes about distinguished persons in China from the Later Han dynasty (25–220) until the Eastern Jin dynasty (317–419). It was compiled by Liú Yìqìng 劉義慶 (403–444) during the Song dynasty (420–479), one of the Southern dynasties of the Six Dynasties period (220–589), and later annotated by Liú Xiàobiāo 劉孝標 during the Liang dynasty (502–557). Fascicle 6 exists in Japan in the form of a manuscript copied between the latter half of the seventh century to the first half of the eighth century. Detailed *kunten* glosses were added to this manuscript in what is estimated to be the beginning of the tenth century.

The phrase *dàn shǎoxǔ* 噉少許 "eat a little" of the Jié Wù 捷悟 section no. 11 story no. 2, held in the collection of the Kyoto National Museum, is marked with vermillion *okototen* (morphosyntactic glosses), *kaeriten* (inversion marks), punctuation, and *katakana* (phonogram glosses, see figure 4.1a). These glosses can be interpreted as specifying 「少許を[X ト X]て、」 *shǎoxǔ=wo* [X=*to* X]-*te* "(read) *shǎoxǔ*" "a little as X-ly X-ing," but the *katakana* gloss ト *to* on *dàn* 噉 "eat" is hard to interpret. By way of reference, when we compare the Cabinet Library (Naikaku bunko) manuscript of this text in the collection of the National Archives glossed by the Edo period (seventeenth century) scholar Hayashi Gahō 林鵞峯, we find the *katakana* gloss フ *fu* for *dàn* 噉 "eat," indicating that Hayashi interpreted this character as the infinitive form クラフ *kurafu* "eat" (see figure 4.1b).

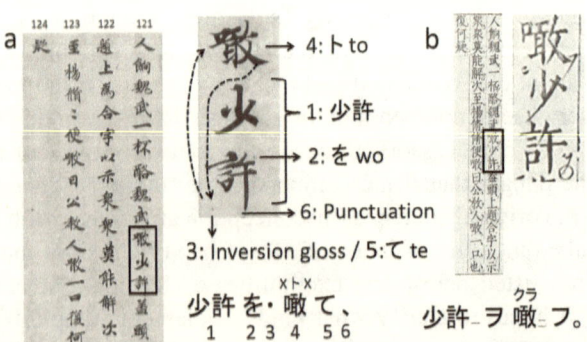

Figure 4.1 The Phrase *dàn shǎoxǔ* 噉少許 in the *Shìshuō xīnshū* 世説新書. (a) tenth-century glossing in the collection of the Kyoto National Museum based on e-Museum; (b) seventeenth-century glossing in the Cabinet Library (Naikaku bunko) manuscript based on National Archives Japan Digital Archive.

So how should we read *dàn* 噉 "eat" = *to* ト in the Kyoto National Museum manuscript? Examining the Kamakura period dictionary Kanchiin-bon *Ruiju Myōgishō*, or the authoritative modern Chinese character dictionary, Morohashi's *Dai Kanwa Jiten*, we find no reading of *dàn* 噉 "eat" containing the syllable *to* ト. However in volume 5 of Tsukishima's *Kunten goi shūsei*, the entry for *torafu* (捕) "take, capture" contains these characters: 促、俘、囚、取、噉、囮、圄、執、將、幽、扼、投、抱、拘、持、捉、捕、掠、接、掩、提、援、搦、摯、擒、攫、收、牛+句、獲、略、縛、繋、繫、虜、補、襲、調、鉤、鋼. Among these we find *dàn* 噉. The example is coded as 11200015⑨110, which designates the vermillion glosses dated Hoan 1 (1120) in the Tōji Kongōzō *Daibirushana-kyō sho*[3] 金剛蔵大毘盧遮那経疏. However, not only does the *Daibirushana-kyō sho* (better known as the *Dainichi-kyō sho* 大日経疏, Chinese *Dàri-jīng shū*) not contain the designated expression *lìng bǐ dàn* 令彼噉 "make him eat," but a search of the SAT *New Corrected Taishō Tripitaka* text database reveals no occurrence of this phrase in any text in the *Taishō Tripitaka*.[4] As the Tōji Kongōzō *Daibirushana-kyō sho* is not publicly available for verification, I checked for this or similar expressions in the Kōzanji-bon manuscript (colophon date of Eiho 2, 1082). Near the end of fascicle 9, we find *lìng bǐ qǔ* 令彼取 "make him take" (line 730), and right next to that (731) in the phrase *zhí bǐ qǔ* 執令彼 "take and order him," the character *zhí* 執 "take" is glossed *torafe* トラヘ "take," while at the end of line 730 we find the character *dàn* 噉 "eat" glossed as *kurafute* クラフテ "eating." There is a high probability here that the character 取 "take" has been mistaken for the very similar character *dàn* 噉 "eat" and that the gloss *torafe* トラヘ "take" for the character *zhí* 執 "take" on its immediate right has been mistakenly interpreted as the gloss

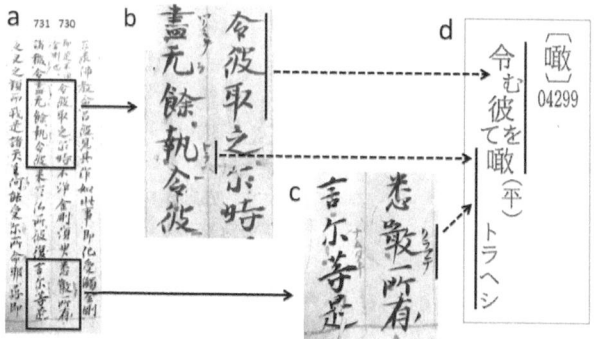

Figure 4.2 The Phrase lìng bǐ qǔ 令彼取 or lìng bǐ dàn 令彼噉 in *Daibirushana-kyō sho* 大毘盧遮那経疏. (a–c) Kōzanji-bon manuscript (colophon date of Eiho 2, 1082) based on photo taken by the author; (d) Tōji Kongōzō *Daibirushana-kyō sho* (glosses dated Hoan 1, 1120) based on Tsukishima's *Kunten goi shūsei*.

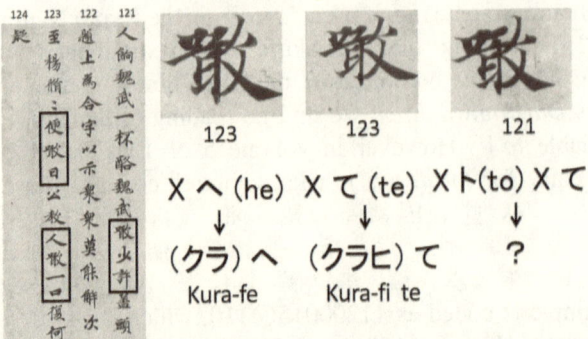

Figure 4.3 The Character *dàn* 噉 in the Story No.2 in the *Shìshuō xīnshū* 世説新書, Tenth-Century Glossing in the Collection of the Kyoto National Museum Based on e-Museum.

for *qǔ* 取, which has been misread as *dàn* 噉 (see figure 4.2). I am unable to confirm this with the Tōji Kongōzō *Daibirushana-kyō sho*, but given that, excluding this single example in Tsukishima's *Kunten goi shūsei*, there is no case of *dàn* 噉 "eat" being assigned the lexical meaning *torafe* トラヘ "take" nor is there any actual textual example of this form; it is highly likely that this example is the result of an error on the part of Tsukishima Hiroshi.

With this assumption, let us return to the issues of the vermillion kana gloss *to* ト added to *dàn* 噉 "eat" in the *Shìshuō xīnshū* 世説新書 (Japanese *Sesetsu shinsho*). In the story in this section (lines 121–124), the character *dàn* 噉 "eat" is used three times: *dàn shǎoxǔ* 噉少許 "eat a little" (line 121), *biàn dàn rì* 便噉曰 "then ate and said" (line 123), and *rén dàn yī kǒu* 人噉一口 "somebody eat one bite" (line 123) (see figure 4.3). The character *dàn* 噉 "eat" has the vermillion *kana* gloss *–fe* ヘ in the last example; this can be readily interpreted as the imperative ending *kura-fe* クラヘ "eat!" of the verb *kurafu* クラフ "eat." The second example has no *kana* gloss, but it does have a vermillion *okototen* morphosyntactic point gloss which marks the gerundive suffix *–te* テ. Since *–te* attaches to the infinitive (*ren'yōkei*), the character must have been read as infinitive form *kura-fi* クラヒ "eating" of *kurafu* クラフ "eat." In the context of this story, *dàn* 噉 "eat" allows no other interpretation but *kurafu* クラフ "eat." The gloss *to* ト in the first example remains unexplained.

CASES WHERE A GLOSS INTERPRETABLE ONLY ON THE BASIS OF A COMMENTARY TEXT IS RECORDED AS IS, WITHOUT PROVIDING THE RELEVANT BACKGROUND

The *Nihon kokugo daijiten* 日本国語大辞典 (first edition 1971–1976, 20 volumes; condensed edition 1979, 10 volumes; second edition 2000–2002, 14 volumes) is the largest dictionary of the Japanese language. Since 2007 it has been available in a convenient subscription-based online edition, through the site *JapanKnowledge Lib*. In the definitions for many entries, examples representing each historical period of the Japanese language are provided, but the date at which the source texts were compiled and the actual linguistic period are often confused. Moreover, examples are often taken third-hand from other reference sources, or the same textual material is attributed to multiple different sources, with the result that one hesitates to place too much faith in the examples. For example, there are extreme cases such as one where *kunten* glosses on a 1669 xylograph of the *Nihon shoki* 日本書紀 are assigned to 720, the date at which the original *Nihon shoki* was compiled, in other words almost a thousand years earlier. There are currently plans to partially revise the sections with such examples to fix issues of this kind.

The *Nihon kokugo daijiten* includes examples from *kunten* materials. The total number of examples cited is approximately 4300 from approximately 200 *kunten* sources. Considering, however, that the development of *kunten* was originally designed for the interpretation of texts in literary Chinese, there are cases where the *kunten* in the examples is not connected to the Chinese characters in the original text, as I will describe below. In such cases, some kind of explanation is required.

For instance, in the entry for *muragaru* "gather, swarm" (lemma Chinese characters群, 叢, 簇) the example *i i tosite muragare naku* 唯唯として昆（ムラガレ）鳴 "readily gather and make cries" is given, from the 948 *kunten* glosses to the *Hàn shū Yáng Xióng Zhuàn*漢書楊雄伝 [The Book of Han, Yáng Xióng Biography], but this example by itself does not establish the connection between the character *kūn* 昆 "swarm (noun), conglomerate" and the vernacular Japanese gloss *muragare* ムラガレ "swarming." In addition, 唯唯 is an incorrect quote for 噍噍 (see figure 4.4).

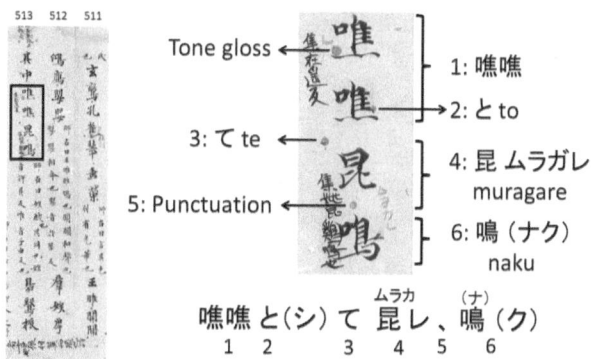

Figure 4.4 The Phrase jiào jiào kūn míng 噍噍昆鳴 in the *Hàn shū Yáng Xióng Zhuàn* 漢書楊雄伝, **948 kunten Glossing in the Collection of the Kyoto National Museum Based on e-Museum.**

In the original *Hàn shū Yáng Xióng Zhuàn* manuscript (copied in China, Tang period, seventh century, formerly in the Ueno family collection, now in the collection of the Kyoto National Museum) annotations from the *Hàn shū jí zhù* 漢書集注 (*Collected annotations on the Hàn shū*) by the Tang period scholar Yán Shīgǔ 顏師古 (581–645) are inserted as interlinear notes, in addition to annotations from the *Hàn shū gǔjīn jíyì* 漢書古今集義 (*Collected ancient and modern meanings in the Han shu*) compiled by Gù Yìn 顧胤 (ca. 650) and the *Hàn shū xūn zuǎn* 漢書訓纂 (*Compilation of glosses on the History of the Former Han*) by Yáo Chá 姚察 (533–606) in the margins and between the lines. When we examine how these references work on the *Hàn shū* interpret the character *kūn* 昆 in line 513, we find that Yán Shīgǔ annotates it as *Kūn tóng yě* 昆同也 "*Kūn* is *tóng* ('same')." The note from Yáo Chá (inserted on the left) says *Kūn jī míng yě* 昆鷄鳴也 "*Kūn* is the cry of a chicken." Neither of these interpretations fits with *muragaru* ムラガル "gather, swarm." Even when we consult the Kanchiin-bon *Ruiju Myōgishō*, or the *Dai Kanwa Jiten*, we do not find *muragaru* ムラガル "gather, swarm" given as a meaning for *kūn* 昆. The phrase *jiào jiào kūn míng* 噍噍昆鳴 forms a matched couplet, or was taken by contemporary glossators to form a matched couplet with the preceding phrase *qún xī hū qí zhōng* 羣嫉虖其中 "swarm and clamor, making cries in their midst." It is only when we juxtapose *qún xī* 羣嫉 "swarm and clamor" and *kūn míng* 昆鳴 "swarms make cries" that we understand the correlation of *kūn* 昆 "swarm" and *muragaru* ムラガル "gathering, swarming." The reason the *kunten* glossators did not follow the annotations is because whether we follow Yán Shīgǔ's note *Kūn tóng yě* 昆同也 "*Kūn* is *tóng* ('same')" and interpret the phrase as *jiào jiào tóng míng* 噍噍同鳴, or follow the *Hàn shū xūn zuǎn* note *Kūn jī míng yě*

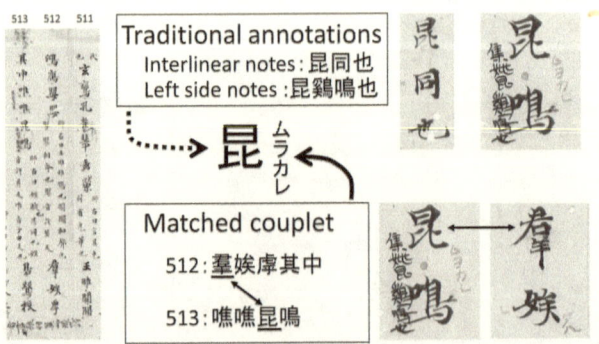

Figure 4.5 The Relationship between the *kunten* Glossing *muragare* ムラガレ to the Character *kūn* 昆 and the Traditional Annotations or Matched Couplet in the *Hàn shū Yáng Xióng Zhuàn* 漢書楊雄伝 in the Collection of the Kyoto National Museum Based on e-Museum.

昆鷄鳴也 "*Kūn* is the cry of a chicken" and interpret it as *jiào jiào jī míng* 噍噍鷄鳴, neither *tóng míng* "same cry" nor *jī míng* "chicken cry" makes sense in Japanese (see figure 4.5).

CASES WHERE A GLOSS HAS BEEN RECORDED WITHOUT CONSIDERATION OF TIGHTNESS OF THE RELATION BETWEEN THE GLOSS AND THE GLOSSED CHINESE CHARACTER

Here I would like to cite another case where the *Nihon kokugo daijiten* uses an example from the 948 *kunten* glosses on the *Hàn shū Yáng Xióng Zhuàn*. The phrase *tǔ huǒ shī biān* "spit fire, apply the whip" 吐火施鞭 (line 447) has the white ink gloss *haki* ハキ "spitting" to the right of the character *tǔ* 吐 "spit" (see figure 4.6).

The *Nihon kokugo daijiten* cites this as *gunreki hi o haki muchi o hodokosu* 群歴火を吐（ハキ）鞭を施す "spitting group fire apply the whip" (*gunreki* 群歴 here is a mistake for 霹歴 *pīlì* "thunder and lightning"). The character *tǔ* 吐 is a simple character, officially listed among the *Jōyō kanji* 常用漢字 (*Kanji* for everyday use) in Japan, as specified in the cabinet decree of November 30, 2010,[5] and the reading *haku* ハク "spit" is a standard reading for this character. From the standpoint that the relationship between the Chinese character and its Japanese reading is easy to understand, it is the exact opposite of the example in the previous section. The entry *haku* ハク (吐) "spit" in volume 6 of Tsukishima Hiroshi's *Kunten goi shūsei* provides 50 examples of *tǔ* 吐 "spit" glossed as *haku* ハク "spit," starting with the preceding example from the 948 *kunten* glosses to the *Hàn shū Yáng Xióng*

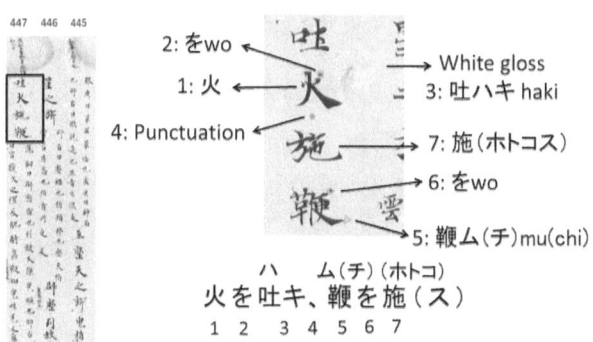

Figure 4.6 The White Ink Glossing *haki* ハキ to the Right of the Character *tǔ* 吐 in the *Hàn shū Yáng Xióng Zhuàn* 漢書楊雄伝 in the Collection of the Kyoto National Museum Based on e-Museum.

Zhuàn. From the standpoint of modern day *Jōyō kanji*—that is, the fact that this is an utterly common reading—the fact that Tsukishima lists so many excessively obvious examples seems a bit odd.

However, as examples older than the 948 *kunten* glosses to the *Hàn shū Yáng Xióng Zhuàn*, there exist only two white ink gloss examples below in the 883 *kunten* glosses to the *Dì zāng shí lún jīng* 地蔵十輪経 (Japanese *Jizō jūrin-kyō*).[6] The reason for the small number of examples is thought to be the fact that Tsukishima's *Kunten goi shūsei* is mainly based on *kunten* materials from 1001.

(1) *Ben wo faki* "spit, vomit" (*tǔbiàn* 吐辨) (Preface line 39, Tōdaiji library manuscript).
   Based on Nakada Norio 中田祝夫 1958. *Kotenpon no kokugogakuteki kenkyū, yakubun-hen*『古点本の国語学的研究（訳文篇）』.

(2) *Tsufaki wo fakite ifaku* "it is said for spitting saliva" (*tuò yán* 唾言) (Fascicle 7, line 26, Shōsōin manuscript).
   Based on Nakada Norio 中田祝夫 1980. *Shōsōin-bon Jizō jūrin-kyō kan go, shichi, Gangyō ten*『正倉院本地蔵十輪経巻五・七元慶点』.

The reading of *tǔ* 吐 "spit" as *haku* (Old Japanese *paku*, Middle Japanese *faku*) or *hakite* in the phrase "hang up a mirror and spit out pearls" 懸鏡吐珠 in the preface to the *Kojiki* 古事記 "Record of ancient things" (712) dates from the modern era. We have no idea how this was actually read in Japanese in 712, the date at which the *Kojiki* was promulgated.

According to Tsukishima (1963) *Heian jidai no kanbun kundokugo ni tsukite no kenkyū* 平安時代の漢文訓読語につきての研究 [Research on Heian period *kunten* language], the verb *faku* as a reading for the character *tǔ* 吐 "spit" is an expression exclusive to *kunten* materials, not used in *kana* literature of the period (p. 338). At the very least it does not appear in the main works of classical Japanese literature. In Old Japanese, the language of the Nara period in the eighth century, the verb *tuku* (衝) is used in the meaning of modern *haku* 吐 "spit." It is this verb that appears in the phonogrammatically transcribed *Kojiki song* (古事記歌謡) in the record of Emperor Ōjin:

(3) 美本杼理能　　　　　迦豆伎伊岐豆岐
   mipodori=no kaduk-i　　iki+duk-i　(Oxford Corpus of Old Japanese)
   grebe-GEN　　　　　　dive-ing breath+spit-ing
   "the diving and breathing (spitting out breath) of the grebe"

It also appears in volume 2 of *Man'yōshū* 万葉集 No. 210:

(4) 夜者裳 氣衝明之
   yworu=pa=mo iki+duki　　akasi
   night=to=even breath+spit　pass.until.dawn
   "(I) spend even the night breathing (sighing)"

Examples like this, involving the compound *iki+duku* from *iki* "breath" and *tuku* "spit, exhale," are common.

Let us now return to the 948 *kunten* glosses on the *Hàn shū Yáng Xióng Zhuàn*. There is a point here that demands our attention. Recall that the *kana* gloss indicating that tŭ 吐 "spit" is to be read *faki* (*haki*) is in white ink. As a tool for *kunten* glossing, white ink is not at all uncommon in *kunten* glosses on Buddhist texts. But in Chinese secular texts, there are no examples other than the 948 *kunten* glosses on the *Hàn shū Yáng Xióng Zhuàn*. When we examine this manuscript carefully, we discover the white ink glosses tend to show the following differences with the glosses in black or vermillion ink.

- Order of glossing: Vermillion -> black -> white (White glosses were added last).
- White ink glosses often generate a vernacular (Japanese) reading which synthesizes the readings specified by the sporadic vermillion and black glosses.
- White ink glosses specify common, everyday readings, to the point that one sometimes wonders why they were necessary.

Why then was white ink used rather than vermillion or black for the gloss *faku* "spit" on the character that tŭ 吐 "spit" in the 948 *kunten* glosses on the *Hàn shū Yáng Xióng Zhuàn*? If specifying the reading *faku* "spit" was absolutely indispensable, we might have expected a gloss in vermillion or black instead. On the contrary, if *faku* (*haku*) "spit" was the standard, everyday reading for this character as it is today, why make the special effort to gloss it in white ink, which is difficult to see? Was there some special intention in using white ink? I have not conducted a systematic investigation of the matter, but when we take into consideration the fact that examples of the character tŭ 吐 "spit" glossed as *faku* begin to appear only after the latter part of the ninth century, and that a different verb, *tuku*, was used with the meaning of "spit" in Old Japanese materials of the eighth century, it seems highly likely that the 948 *kunten* glosses of the *Hàn shū Yáng Xióng Zhuàn* had a different candidate gloss for this character.

SUMMARY AND CONCLUSIONS

Considering the issues outlined above, I would like to conclude by suggesting that to address such issues, and to improve the reliability of dictionaries or compendia based on glosses, three measures are indispensable:

(1) Not just textual information but a photographic image should be included in reference publications, to avoid misinterpretation.

(2) The "glossing process" by which the glossator interpreted the original Classical Chinese text and glossed it should be shown.
(3) The tightness of the relationship between gloss and glossed character should be indicated in the context of all examples of the character, so as to show whether the gloss in question is a standard gloss or one used only rarely, establishing an "index of standardness" for glosses.

NOTES

1. When reading Classical Chinese texts in Japanese, it has been a practice since the end of the eighth century to add small characters and codes that represent Japanese inversion marks that indicate differences in word order, punctuation marks, and so on (see Zisk, this volume) directly to the periphery of the Chinese characters. These characters and codes are collectively referred to as *kunten*, and the Chinese texts in which such *kunten* are written are called *kunten* materials. This method of reading in vernacular language can be found not only in Japanese, but also in Korean during the Goryeo and Joseon eras, Vietnamese during the Nguyen Dynasty, and also in the Dunhuang manuscripts of the Tang Dynasty.

2. *Ruiju myōgishō* is an old Japanese dictionary that explains the entry words of Chinese using Chinese and Japanese. There are two versions depending on the compilation time and content. Zushoryō-bon was compiled by a scholar of the Hosso sect at the end of the eleventh century, and the original source is clearly stated in the Chinese notes and Japanese *kunten* glosses used in the explanation. Kanchiin-bon was reorganized and supplemented by a Shingon Buddhist scholar in the middle of the thirteenth century, and although the *kunten* glosses of Japanese were greatly supplemented, there were almost no Chinese notes and the source was not displayed. Zushoryō is one of the departments of the Imperial Household Agency that manages documents and materials related to the imperial family and is the predecessor of Shoryōbu today. Kanchiin is the name of a small temple in Tōji Temple of the Shingon sect. The version of *Ruiju myōgishō* is called Zushoryō-bon and Kanchiin-bon, with the name of the original holding institution. Currently, Zushoryō-bon is in the Imperial Household Agency Shoryōbu and Kanchiin-bon is in the Tenri Library.

3. *Daibirushana-kyō sho* (better known as the *Dainichi-kyō sho* 大日経疏) is a commentary on the esoteric Buddhist scripture *Daibirushana-kyō* 大日経, compiled by Zen mui 善無畏 (637–735) in the Tang dynasty and his disciple Ichi gyo 一行 (683–727). There are many such kunten materials in Japan. Tōji Kongō is the name of the library of Tōji Kanchiin.

4. A complete collection of Chinese-translated Buddhist texts compiled over ten years from 1924 to 1934 by Takakusu Junjiro, Kaigyoku Watanabe, Ono Genmyo, and others. It is regarded as an international standard text when using the Chinese-translated Buddhist texts. The full digitized text has been opened on the internet by the SAT Daizōkyō Text Database Committee (SAT) since 2008.

5. Jōyō kanji is a guideline for the use of kanji when writing modern national languages in general social life such as laws and regulations, official books, newspapers, magazines, and broadcasting. It lists basic Sinoxenic reading and vernacular reading for 2,136 kinds of kanji. The Jōyō Kanji currently in operation is a revision of the Jōyō Kanji (1,945 kinds) notified in 1981.

6. A Buddhist scripture that describes Kṣitigarbha Bodhisattva 地蔵菩薩, who was the rescuer after the death of Śākya-muni Buddha 釈迦牟尼 until the appearance of the future Buddha, Maitreya Bodhisattva 弥勒菩薩.

ACKNOWLEDGMENTS

I would like to thank J. Whitman for translating the manuscript. This work was supported by JSPS KAKENHI Grant Number JP21K00544.

REFERENCES

Daibirushana-kyō sho 大毘盧遮那経疏: Kōzanji-bon manuscript, (colophon date of Eiho 2, 1082), Photo taken by the author.

Hàn shū Yáng Xióng Zhuàn 漢書楊雄伝 [The Book of Han, Yáng Xióng Biography]: the collection of the Kyoto National Museum, e-Museum, https://emuseum.nich.go.jp/ (accessed 2022-01-10).

JapanKnowledge Lib: https://japanknowledge.com/library/ (accessed 2022-01-10).

Kojiki 古事記 [Record of Ancient Matters]: Komima, N. ed., Ōfūsha, 1978, 255p.

Man'yōshū 万葉集 [Collection of Myriad Leaves]: Tsuru, H.; Moriyama, T., ed., Ōfūsha, 1972, 641p.

Morohashi, T. *Dai Kanwa Jiten* 大漢和辞典 [The Great Chinese-Japanese Dictionary]. 2nd ed., Taishūkan shoten, 1989–2000, 15 volumes.

Nakada, N. *Kotenpon no kokugogakuteki kenkyū: yakubun-hen* 古点本の国語学的研究（訳文篇）[Linguistic Studies on Early Chinese-Japanese Glosses: fascicle deciphered text]. Kōdansha, 1958, 770p.

Nakada, N. *Shōsōin-bon Jizō jūrin-kyō kan go shichi Gangyō ten* 正倉院本地蔵十輪経巻五・七元慶点 [Gangyō kunten glosses of volume 5 and 7 Jizō jūrin-kyō in the Shōsōin]. Benseisha, 1980, 275p.

Nihon kokugo daijiten 日本国語大辞典 [Shōgakukan Unabridged Dictionary of the Japanese Language]: first edition 1971–1976, 20 volumes; condensed edition 1979, 10 volumes; second edition 2000-2002, 14 volumes, Shōgakukan.

Ruiju myōgishō 類聚名義抄 [Classified Dictionary of Terms and Meanings]: Kanchiin-bon, Masamune, A. ed., Kazama shobō, 1978, 1332p.

Ruiju myōgishō 類聚名義抄 [Classified Dictionary of Terms and Meanings]: Zushoryō-bon, Ikejima, Y. ed., Benseisha, 1976, 346p.

Shìshuō xīnshū 世説新書 [New Account of Tales of the World]: The Collection of the Kyoto National Museum, e-Museum, https://emuseum.nich.go.jp/ (accessed 2022-01-10).

Shìshuō xīnshū 世説新書 [New Account of Tales of the World]: The Cabinet Library (Naikaku bunko) manuscript, National Archives Japan Digtal Archive, https://www.digital.archives.go.jp/index_e.html (accessed 2022-01-10).

The SAT Daizōkyō Text Database SAT大正新修大蔵経テキストデータベース: https://21dzk.l.u-tokyo.ac.jp/SAT/ (accessed 2022-01-10).

Tsukishima, H. *Heian jidai no kanbun kundokugo ni tsukite no kenkyū* 平安時代の漢文訓読語につきての研究 [Research on Heian Period Kunten Language]. University of Tōkyō Press, 1963, 1183p.

Tsukishima, H. *Kunten goi shūsei* 訓点語彙集成 [Compendium of kunten Vocabulary]. Kyūko shoin, 2007–2009, 9 volumes.

5

Interconnecting Knowledge in Early Medieval Glosses

Sinéad O'Sullivan

This chapter considers the practice of interconnecting knowledge in glosses in the Early Medieval Latin West.[1] It looks at specific instances of the practice such as word pairing and code switching in Martianus, Prudentius, and Virgil glosses. It argues that word pairing, for example across linguistic borders (Latin, Greek, Hebrew, and the vernacular), attests, among other things, to an interest in creating correspondences. Similarly, code switching bears witness not only to the integration of the vernacular into a Latin book culture but also to the establishment of cross-linguistic equivalence. Finally, I consider the contexts in which scholars interconnected knowledge, concentrating on important methods such as *collectio* and alignment.

WORD PAIRING

Word pairing was ubiquitous in early medieval intellectual culture. Individual Latin words were sometimes coupled with other Latin words or with words in the vernacular, Greek, or Hebrew, most notably in glosses and glossaries. Word pairing could function in various ways. For instance, it could provide synonyms or interpretations.[2] It was one of many devices used to achieve equivalence or near-equivalence by early medieval commentators and compilers. Glossators were especially fond of the synonym or near-synonym. Frequently, the choice of synonyms was not arbitrary. We regularly find the same lexical equivalents repeated across various works ranging from the grammatical to the encyclopedic. For example, the word pair *delibutus–unctus*, present in early medieval glosses on Prudentius' *Psychomachia*, occurs in numerous glossaries:[3]

Delibutus un<c>tus perfusus (*Abba, Glossae codicis Sangallensis 912*, CGL IV, 225); *Deliuotus* delicatus *unctus* perfusus (*Abstrusa-Abolita, Glossae codicis vaticani 3321*, CGL IV, 49); *Delibutus* perfusus uel bene *unctus* (*Abavus*, CGL IV, 328); *Delibatus* perfusus *perunctus* (*Affatim*, CGL IV, 503); *Delibutus perunctus* uel perfusus (*Amplonianum secundum*, CGL V, 283); *Delibutus perunctus* infusus (*Corpus*, CGL V, 405); *Delibatus unctus* contactus (*Liber Glossarum*).[4]

In Prudentius glosses, many such examples exist, as in the case of the gloss *prouocauit* annotating *lacessit* (ad *Psych.* 115).[5] These verbs are grouped together in Abstrusa/Abolita, Affatim, Abavus, Abba, Amplonian II, and the *Liber Glossarum*.[6] The appearance of standard word pairs suggests that words may have been learned in clusters. It also strongly indicates that, even at the level of the lexical gloss, knowledge was prescribed and uniform. Here, too, one may note the high degree of repetition of identical or near-identical information within the same gloss tradition, same family of glosses, different gloss traditions, glossaries, commentaries, encyclopedic works, and miscellanies.[7] Cross-linguistic word pairing follows a similar pattern, that is, the same bilingual equivalents appear in different sources. A good illustration is furnished by the Greek-Latin word pairs in early medieval glosses on the late-antique pagan text *De nuptiis Philologiae et Mercurii* of Martianus Capella. In the first and oldest of the gloss corpora on Martianus, that is, the tradition found in manuscripts dating from the second quarter of the ninth to the tenth century, considerable attention was paid by Carolingian glossators to the Greek words and phrases, loanwords from Greek and Greek mythology in *De nuptiis*. Glossators transcribed, highlighted, and annotated Martianus' Greek. The oldest gloss tradition on Martianus initially circulated in major Carolingian scriptoria in the Loire valley, northern and northeastern France, that is, in the heartland of the Carolingian world. When first I looked at the reception of Martianus' Greek by Continental commentators, I focused on how his Greek was not just elucidated as an arcane language but also created a sense of mystery. Indeed, Martianus' Greek seems, at times, to have been interpreted (and more Greek added) to obscure, reflecting thereby the wider strategy of concealment underpinning medieval hermeneutics. In this chapter, I will look at another aspect, namely the pairing of Greek and Latin words in early medieval glosses on Martianus Capella.

For their Greek-Latin word pairs, the early medieval commentators on *De nuptiis* needed lexicographical sources. These were readily available. Many bilingual and Latin materials carried the required information: glossaries, *Hermeneumata*, grammatical works, and *Graeca collecta*, as well as Late Latin and early medieval writings. Much of the Greek in the glosses on Martianus has analogues in these sources. Specific identification of the sources of the Greek in Martianus glosses is thus generally problematic as it could have been gleaned from different sources. The case of *palaestra* (παλαίστρα "a wrestling school") is illustrative: it was glossed with the Greek word πάλη ("wrestling") and Latin counterpart *luctatio* ("wrestling"), the sources of which could have been Servius, Isidore, glossaries, and *Hermeneumata*.[8] Similarly, for glosses on the loanword *Sibylla* (Σίβυλλα "a Sibyl"), analogues occur in Servius, Lactantius, the Mythographers, Isidore, *Hermeneumata*, glossaries, grammatical works, and the *Scholica Graecarum Glossarum*, as well as in the works of Hrabanus Maurus, Remigius of Auxerre, and John Scottus Eriugena.[9] For a great deal of the Greek in the Martianus glosses, standard Greek word-stock was deployed, as in glosses on *Galaxia* and *Galumnate* pointing to the same etymology, namely γάλα "milk."[10] In fact, many of the Greek or Greek-derived words in the Martianus glosses were commonplace and could have been gleaned from sources like Isidore of Seville's *Etymologiae*. The same is true for the deployment of Greek-Latin word pairs. For instance, annotators elucidating the Greek words in Martianus written in Latin letters such as *hemiolios* (ἡμιόλιος "containing one and a half") furnished word pairs that were well known:

HEMIOLIOS *emis* semis, *olon* totum[11]

In a similar vein, words such as *Pyrphlegethonta* in Martianus from the Greek Πυριφλεγέθων (Pyriphlegeton) were provided with the bilingual equivalents *pir ignis* ("fire") and *flox flamma* ("flame"), equivalents found in other sources:

PYRPHLEGETHONTA *pir* (πῦρ) ignis, *flox* (φλόξ) flamma[12]

Glossators also explained the loanwords from Greek in Martianus with the use of Greek-Latin word pairs that are attested elsewhere. This is the case with the annotation on *Tympanum* from τύμπανον ("a drum"), which they associated with Τῦφος ("conceit/vanity") and its Latin counterpart *inflatio* ("puffing up, insolence"), a pairing in Bede.[13] Similarly, Martianus glossators linked *condylus*, meaning "fist" (κόνδυλος "knuckle"), with the Latin word *colaphus* ("a blow with the fist"), a pairing in the pseudo-Cyrillus glossary.[14] Moreover, they made explicit the etymology of the word *hydraula* (ὕδραυλις or ὕδραυλος "a water organ"), itself a derivate of ὕδωρ ("water") through the use of word pairs. They offered the pairing ὕδωρ and *aqua*, which was ubiquitous, as well as the pairing *hydraula* and *organum*, which appears in the pseudo-Cyrillus glossary:

HYDRAVLARVM *Hydor* Grece, Latine aqua; *Hydraula* organum de aqua factum[15]

Annotators, likewise, introduced Greek words into their explanation of Latin words in Martianus. For instance, they glossed the words *longaevorum chori* with *macrobii*, drawn from μακρόβιος ("long lived"). They explained that *macrobii* was a compound of μακρός ("long") and βίος ("life"). Here Carolingian glossators not only introduced the word *macrobii* but supplied its constituent parts in Greek and Latin:

> LONGAEVORUM CHORI *Macrobii*, i. longe uiuentes. *Macron* longum, *bia* uita[16]

Another example is the gloss on *elementa* that includes the words *ilen* (ὕλη "matter") and *stochia* (στοιχεῖα "elements"). The words *ilen* and *stochia* are Greek words and had some circulation in medieval glossaries. Glossators connected these Greek terms with the Latin words *materies* and *elementa*, respectively:

> ELEMENTA *Ilen* Grece dicitur materies (sicut Isidorus dicit, quia *stochia* Grece, Latine elementa), unde inuisibilia cuncta procedunt.[17]

A high premium was evidently placed on interconnecting Greek and Latin in early medieval Martianus glosses. Greek-Latin word pairs attest to a fascination with Greek, their Latin equivalents, the origins of Greek words, their constituent parts, and their Latin counterparts. For the purposes of this chapter what is noteworthy is that the Greek-Latin word pairs in the Martianus glosses were rarely unique and were frequently an instrument of etymological investigation. Here it is useful to recall the importance of etymology as a scholarly method. Investigation of the origin of words, the cornerstone of Isidore's foundational encyclopedia, was no vain exercise. Words, for Isidore, had epistemic value. According to him, examination of the origin of words provided access to understanding: *Omnis enim rei inspectio etymologia cognita planior est* ("One's insight into anything is clearer when its etymology is known").[18] Etymology was much more than a "diachronic analysis of a lexeme" or a methodology.[19] For Isidore, it unlocked the *vis verbi vel nominis* ("sense/meaning of a verb or a noun").[20] As he says: *Nam dum videris unde ortum est nomen, citius vim eius intellegis* ("For when you have seen whence a word has originated, you understand its sense/meaning more quickly").[21] Word pairing was thus often part of a scholarly exercise motivated not so much by linguistic goals as a search for immanent meaning. That meaning could be unveiled through etymology is illustrated by glosses elucidating the names of classical gods and muses in Martianus glosses.[22] In the case of Nemesis, glossators associated the deity with the Greek word *nomos* (νόμος) and Latin equivalent *lex* ("law"), thus underscoring the connection of the goddess with retribution.

Moreover, the deployment of Greek-Latin equivalents to convey a message finds a counterpart in other scholarly endeavors, for instance in the areas of "cross-cultural translation" and "comparative mythology," where medieval scholars sought not only to highlight significant correlation but also to "transfer" the prestige and authority of one culture onto another.[23] Examples of such endeavors are furnished by Michael Clarke who underscores the sustained efforts made by the medieval Irish *literati* to establish equivalences between classical and Gaelic mythology. This is illustrated by the vernacular tale *Táin Bó Cúailnge* ("The Cattle Raid of Cooley") surviving in different recensions, where Allecto and the Morrígan are paired, that is one of the Furies from classical mythology and an Irish war goddess. Similarly, in the Middle Irish adaptation of Statius' *Thebaid*, the Irish phantom Badb appears analogous to Tisiphone, another one of the Furies.[24] In all such instances, establishing correspondences, whether across mythological or linguistic borders, was an important practice and one redolent with signification.

CODE SWITCHING

My second example used to illustrate the practice of interconnecting knowledge focuses on code switching between Latin and the vernacular in early medieval glosses, the precise function of which remains unclear, as Pádraic Moran has demonstrated for the Old Irish glosses in the St. Gall Priscian (St. Gallen, Stiftsbibliothek, Cod. Sang. 904, saec. IX^{med}, probably Ireland), where language instruction does not seem to fit the bill.[25] Among other things, cross-linguistic switching, that is, switching between one language and another, underscores an interest in forging connections. Early medieval glossators deployed both classical and vernacular languages to annotate texts, sometimes alternating between languages.[26]

An interesting case of code switching is found in a ninth-century Welsh manuscript that traveled to England by the mid-tenth century where it was supplemented and augmented. The manuscript is the Corpus Martianus Capella (Cambridge, Corpus Christi College, Ms. 153). CCCC 153 is the earliest surviving copy of Martianus Capella's *De nuptiis Philologiae et Mercurii* in Anglo-Saxon England transmitting all nine books. It has Old Welsh glosses, which were first discovered by Henry Bradshaw.[27] It also transmits an eclectic commentary on Martianus, known as the *Anonymus Cantabrigiensis*, a commentary which survives in only one other manuscript, namely in Cambridge, Corpus Christi College, Ms. 330, a late ninth-century continental manuscript. T. A. M. Bishop demonstrated that though the comments in the two manuscripts are very close, CCCC 153 is not a copy of CCCC 330, but both instead seem to have shared a common exemplar.[28] The exemplar behind this eclectic commentary probably originated in a German scriptorium, which fits with other evidence for well-known Anglo-German relations in the tenth century.[29] As a whole, CCCC 153 bears witness to the variety of continental gloss traditions on *De nuptiis* that made their way to Anglo-Saxon England, and the key role of Wales. The manuscript attests not only to the earliest reception of Martianus Capella in Wales but also to Welsh-Continental, Welsh-English, and English-Continental relations that underpinned the different stages of its composition. The original Welsh portion of CCCC 153 transmits Martianus Capella's *De nuptiis* and was written and glossed with marginal and interlinear Latin and Old Welsh annotations in Wales (s. IX² or s. X^in). The Latin glosses are from the oldest gloss tradition on Martianus, that is, from a continental gloss tradition. According to Bishop's palaeographical assessment, the Latin glosses were written by several scribes in a compressed pointed Insular minuscule dating to the second half of the ninth century. The vernacular glosses appear alongside the Latin glosses and are also written in a compressed pointed Insular minuscule of the same date.[30] Karianne Lemmen observes that nearly all of the Old Welsh glosses were entered into the parts of the text written by scribe A (the scribe responsible for the largest section of the main text in the original Welsh portion of the manuscript).[31] The Old Welsh glosses were copied not only at the same time as the Latin annotations but crucially, in places, by the same scribe or scribes. What is significant is that at least one of the hands writing Latin glosses seems to have entered vernacular annotations. Additionally, the Latin and Old Welsh glosses were clearly part of the same scholarly operation. This is evident in the glosses that deploy Latin and Old Welsh, as well as in the selection of words to be glossed in Old Welsh. Interestingly, Old Welsh and Latin words sometimes form a syntactic unit, as in the following annotation:

CELEBRAT *id est irgur hunnuid, i. Mercurius* ("CELEBRAT that is, that man, namely Mercury").[32]

Moreover, according to Paul Russell *irgur hunnuid* is probably a way of representing the Latin *ille* and very likely refers to the subject of the preceding sentence, namely Mercury. In Welsh, demonstratives like *hwn* "this" and *hwnnw* "that" (= Old Welsh *hunnuid*) are adjectival and cannot in the early language be used pronominally. Hence, you need to have a noun of some sort with them. Mercury is the subject of the preceding sentence. In the gloss, then, the annotator is very likely reminding the reader that Mercury is the subject, precisely where in Latin *ille* would have been used.[33]

Furthermore, the selection of words to be glossed in Old Welsh in CCCC 153 is noteworthy. It is clear that the annotators glossed words in the vernacular that are generally found glossed in Latin in manuscripts transmitting the oldest gloss tradition on Martianus. The choice of lemma, then, did not differ with respect to the Old Welsh and Latin glosses. Written at the same time as the Latin annotations and text by some of the same scribes, the Old Welsh annotations in CCCC 153 represent the expansion of a continental gloss tradition into the Brittonic-speaking world. In like manner, Moran noted that the occurrence of Irish in the St. Gall Priscian glosses "corresponds to Latin in equivalent glosses in other manuscripts."[34] In the case of CCCC 153, the vernacular was incorporated into an existing Latin continental gloss tradition. The glossators did not simply supplement the Latin glosses on *De nuptiis* with vernacular annotations. Rather they embedded their Old Welsh annotations into a Latin gloss tradition. As such, CCCC 153 provides an example of the scholarly practice of interconnecting knowledge across linguistic frontiers.

Another interesting case of code switching appears in early medieval glosses on Prudentius' *Psychomachia*. We find identical Latin and Old High German glosses in many manuscripts in the so-called Weitz tradition, a gloss tradition scattered throughout Alemannia, Bavaria, and the Rhineland, dating primarily to the tenth and eleventh centuries. The Weitz glosses span the late Carolingian and early Ottonian periods but are primarily rooted in the intellectual world of the Ottonians.[35] The glosses were largely copied in East Frankish monastic centers. Within the Weitz tradition, there are clusters of closely related manuscripts. An important group emanates from the Middle or Lower Rhine and is represented by the manuscripts Brussels, Bibliothèque Royale, lat. 9968–72 (saec. XI) and Cologne, Dombibliothek, Ms. 81 (saec. XI). The Latin and Old High German glosses in Brussels 9968–72 and Cologne 81 are a close match. In these two manuscripts, as in other Weitz manuscripts, identical Latin and Old High German glosses are found. Moreover, in some Weitz manuscripts, the Latin and Old High German glosses were entered by the same scribe.[36] Additionally, the Old High German glosses were, at times, part of the same syntactic unit.[37] Furthermore, like the Latin glosses, the Old High German glosses were, on occasion, written in secret script.[38] The Latin and Old High German glosses in the Weitz tradition clearly belonged to the same enterprise. What can be concluded? In CCCC 153, vernacular glosses were added to a continental Latin gloss tradition on Martianus Capella in Wales. In the Weitz tradition, by contrast, vernacular annotations were a constituent of a continental gloss tradition. Old High German glosses were copied together with the Latin glosses in Weitz manuscripts. Above all, early medieval glosses on Martianus and Prudentius attest to the efforts of glossators to establish links between Latin and the vernacular.

WORDS AND SYMBOLS

My third example used to demonstrate the practice of interconnecting knowledge comes from early medieval glosses on Virgil. The ninth and tenth centuries were an important period for the emergence of a flourishing tradition of glossing on Virgil. Silvia Ottaviano observes that the reception of Virgil surfaced in an initial "French" phase before the wider diffusion of his work throughout the Carolingian world and southern Italy. She notes the expansion of scholarly productivity in northeast France in the second half of the ninth century in the time of Charles the Bald.[39] One such Carolingian Virgil manuscript is Oxford, Bodleian Library, Auct. F. 2. 8 (saec. $IX^{2/4}$, Paris region). It not only provides insight into Carolingian scholarly engagement with Virgil but also has an especially striking feature—Tironian notes. In the Oxford Virgil, one of the gloss hands, dated by Robert Kaster to the ninth century, wrote in a mixture of Tironian notes and Caroline minuscule.[40] The glossator shifted not between two different languages, but between minuscule and a form of ancient stenography known as Tironian shorthand.[41] In several instances, the Tironian notes were decoded. The same hand that copied the glosses in a hybrid of Tironian notes and minuscule, or a very similar hand, appears sometimes to have decoded the symbols. Explanations were furnished in Latin and were recorded directly above the shorthand. The decoded forms appear to be an integral part of the scholarly exercise. Remarkably, even individual Latin words were copied in a mixture of Tironian notes and minuscule. In one instance, the compiler dissected a word and provided an equivalent in Tironian shorthand for a part of a Latin word.[42] In the Oxford manuscript, deciphering the notes may indicate the need for elucidation. Whatever their specific purpose, the notes, accompanied by their decoded forms, appear in place of Latin words in the glosses. Moreover, they were intertwined with Latin in the annotations. Additionally, the notes were correlated with their Latin equivalents. Even an individual component of a Latin word was equated with its Tironian counterpart. In the Oxford Virgil, then, we witness the sustained efforts of a compiler to correlate Latin and a system of shorthand current in the Carolingian world. That words and symbols could be part of the same scholarly enterprise is not unusual, as is illustrated by early medieval glossed Martianus manuscripts where we find repetition not only of identical glosses but also of identical *signes de renvoi*, that is, the symbols used to link annotations and text.[43] That words and symbols were interconnected is no surprise.[44]

INTERCONNECTING KNOWLEDGE AND ITS CONTEXTS

Even a cursory look at early medieval glosses indicates that a high premium was placed on interconnecting knowledge, that is, forging connections. We have seen this in various ways, for instance through word pairing and code switching. And the practice of establishing correspondences was not just limited to Greek and Latin or Latin and the vernacular, but also to words and symbols. Cumulatively, the examples discussed above strongly suggest an intellectual environment that valued interconnecting knowledge.

So, what can be said about the wider contexts underpinning the practices of interconnecting knowledge? The practices of interconnecting knowledge cohere with other methods, for example, with *collectio*, which focuses on excerpting, accumulating, and synthesizing materials. *Collectio* was an essential component of early medieval scholarly culture and of medieval *memoria*.[45] It was frequently at the heart of medieval glossing. In the case of Virgil glosses, for instance, glossators drew upon all the extant commentaries on Virgil. And glosses were not only often the products of excerption but were also themselves quarried as sources by compilers. For example, glosses were copied as running commentaries. We witness this in a ninth-century manuscript, Orléans, Médiathèque municipale, Ms. 191 (saec. IX^2, Fleury?), where annotations from the oldest gloss tradition on Martianus Capella's *De nuptiis* were transmitted as an independent text.[46] Glosses also became part of eclectic commentaries, as in Cambridge, Corpus Christi College, Ms. 153, Part II (saec. X$^{med.}$ or $^{3/4}$, England), where glosses from different gloss traditions on Martianus were blended.[47] Even specific glosses were assembled into running texts, for instance, notes on the gemstones at the end of Prudentius's *Psychomachia*, which surface both as annotations and as an independent text in early medieval manuscripts.[48] Similarly, we find unidentified comments on the legendary kings of Rome both as glosses and as independent texts in early medieval Virgil manuscripts.[49] In all such cases, glosses were excerpted by compilers and were part of the scholarly predilection for collecting and synthesizing, a predilection that coheres with the interest in interconnecting knowledge.

With regard to creating correspondences, the final context I wish briefly to consider is the practice of alignment, a profoundly influential practice inherited from antiquity and widely attested in the medieval Latin West. In broad strokes, this practice consisted of establishing connections through benchmarks or synchronistic hooks. Benchmarks were not just significant historical events or persons. They also served as coordinates around which historical narratives could be structured.[50] The practice chimes with the efforts of medieval glossators to create correspondences. It also accords with other scholarly enterprises and hermeneutical strategies. By way of illustration, we may note the scholarly projects that sought to establish links between the sacred and the profane. Such projects often connected peoples and events from the classical and biblical pasts. We see this in Eusebius' *Chronicon*.[51]

The practice likewise converged with biblical, patristic, and medieval hermeneutical strategies, especially with typology. Erich Auerbach, in his classic study of this form of figural interpretation, shows that typology was a kind of biblical allegory which

> establishes a connection between two events or persons, the first of which signifies not only itself but also the second, while the second encompasses or fulfills the first. The two poles of the figure are separate in time, but both, being real events or figures, are within time, within the stream of historical life. Only the understanding of the two persons or events is a spiritual act.[52]

Inherited from the writers of the Old and New Testaments and from biblical exegetes, typology had a profound effect on late antique and medieval historiography.[53]

Additionally, the interest in establishing correspondence is vividly attested by an important means of organizing knowledge, namely the tabular or columnar layout, which was deployed by Eusebius in his *Chronicon*. This layout was also used by Eusebius for his Canon Tables, which were developed to cross-reference information in the four gospels. Matthew Crawford argues that the Eusebian tables represent a milestone not only in the study of the gospels but also in the history of the book. Parallel columns or tables served many purposes.[54] On the one hand, they provided a means of "storage and retrieval," thus cohering with ancient and medieval concepts of *memoria*.[55] For this chapter, what is significant is that the columnar format allowed scholars to interconnect knowledge, whether that be across different versions of the Old Testament, across the canonical gospels, or across the histories of different peoples and events from the biblical and secular pasts. Cumulatively, the above-mentioned scholarly practices, strategies, and organizational systems are reminiscent of the endeavors of early medieval glossators who sought to establish equivalences, especially across linguistic borders.

CONCLUSION

This chapter has examined the practice of forging connections in early medieval glosses and suggested many contexts in which this practice may be considered. In short, interconnecting knowledge was pervasive in the Early Medieval Latin West. Above all, early medieval scholars conspicuously devoted considerable attention to collecting, excerpting, synthesizing, aligning, and constructing concurrence across manifold frontiers (e.g., historical, mythical, and linguistic) and varied media (e.g., words and symbols).

NOTES

1. I am extremely grateful to Franck Cinato for his detailed comments and suggestions.

2. Hebrew letters were often interpreted by early medieval scholars using Jerome's *Liber interpretationis hebraicorum nominum*. An example is found in the ninth-century glossed Psalter, St. Gallen, Stiftsbibliothek, Cod. Sang. 27, p. 502, where the following explanation occurs as a marginal gloss: DELETH *pauper vel tabul<a>e vel ianua* (de Lagarde 1975, 48, 15).

3. O'Sullivan 2004, 109.

4. Goetz et al. 1888–1923 [hereafter CGL]. For the *Liber glossarum*: Grondeux and Cinato 2016 (DE611 Delibatus).

5. O'Sullivan 2004, 193.

6. CGL 4:103, 253, 358, 532; Grondeux and Cinato 2016 (LA159 Lacessit).

7. O'Sullivan 2017, 9–10.

8. PALAESTRA Palestra dicta *apo tu palin*, hoc est rustica luctatione (ad *De nuptiis* I, 5; O'Sullivan 2010, 30, 31). O'Sullivan 2011a, 72. For *palaestra*, a loanword from Greek: Weise 1882, 48.

9. SIBYLLAM *SYOC* quasi *ZYOC, BYΛE* consilium, sybilla quasi dei consilium (ad *De nuptiis* I, 10; O'Sullivan 2010, 53, 30–31; ad *De nuptiis* II, 159; O'Sullivan 2010, 379, 13–18). O'Sullivan 2011a, 72; Lendinara 2011, 334. For the loanword *Sibylla*: Weise 1882, 35.

10. See glosses on *Galaxia* (ad *De nuptiis* I, 97; O'Sullivan 2010, 254, 9) and *Galumnate* (ad *De nuptiis* I, 67; O'Sullivan 2010, 194, 5); O'Sullivan 2011a, 75. For the loanword *Galaxia*: Weise 1882, 55.

11. Ad *De nuptiis* II, 107; O'Sullivan 2010, 271, 2. See also the pseudo-Cyrillus glossary, CGL 2, 382, 34 and Isidore, *Etymologiae* 6, 19, 35; 19, 22, 14. For similar information in the *Scholica Graecarum glossarum*: Laistner 1923, 436 and 440.

12. Ad *De nuptiis* II, 166; O'Sullivan 2010, 385, 4. The word pair *pir ignis* was ubiquitous. The word pair *flox flamma* is found in the pseudo-Cyrillus (Φλοξ flamma) and pseudo-Philoxenus glossaries (Flamma φλοξ): CGL 2, 72, 33; 472, 26. For *Pyriphlegethon*: Weise 1882, 44.

13. TYMPANVM *Typhos* inflatio (ad *De nuptiis* I, 67; O'Sullivan 2010, 198, 14). Bede comments on *uentus typhonicus* but does not mention the word *tympanum* in Laistner 1983, 93. Bede carries the Greek-Latin pairing (Τῦφως–inflatio) found in the Martianus gloss. For *tympanum*: Weise 1882, 61.

14. CONDYLOS *Condilizo* Grece colapho, i. Latine pugnis cedo. In condilos ergo, i. in colaphos, i. in plagas (ad *De nuptiis* I, 88; O'Sullivan 2010, 234, 41–42). Κονδυλος colafus (pseudo-Cyrillus, CGL 2, 353, 3). For *condylus*: Weise 1882, 390.

15. Ad *De nuptiis* II, 117; O'Sullivan 2010, 293, 6–9.

16. Ad *De nuptiis* II, 167; O'Sullivan 2010, 386, 7–8. See Grondeux and Cinato 2016 (MA59 Macrobii); pseudo-Cyrillus Glossary, CGL 2, 257, 43; 364, 19; pseudo-Philoxenus Glossary, CGL 2, 124, 25; 257, 43; *Hermeneumata Pseudodositheana*, CGL 3, 328, 17.

17. Ad *De nuptiis* I, 1; O'Sullivan 2010, 8, 6–8. For *ilen*, see Laistner 1923, 436 and 446; Grondeux and Cinato 2016 (YL3 Ylen). For *stochia*: the pseudo-Cyrillus

Glossary, CGL 2, 438, 15; pseudo-Philoxenus Glossary, CGL 2, 59, 20; *Hermeneumata Pseudodositheana*, CGL 3, 425, 3; 25, 28. See also Lendinara 2011, 344–345 and Stotz 2002, 549.

18. *Etymologiae* I.29.2. Barney et al. 2002, 55. For etymology and language as furnishing access to knowledge and the world, see Jacques Fontaine, Andy Merrills, and Mark Amsler. Jacques Fontaine states: *L'étymologie y est devenue la démarche essentielle de toute connaissance*. Fontaine 1959, vol. 1, 41. Andy Merrills maintains that for Isidore, "language offered a simulacrum of the world" and that Isidore saw etymology as a "strategy to uncover the deeper significance (*vis*) of words and hence as a means to understand better the world they represent." Merrills 2013, 303 and 307. Mark Amsler argues that for Isidore, "the etymologies of the names for things constitute epistemic access to things themselves." Amsler 1989, 12. Some qualification is furnished by Davide del Bello who takes issue with what he regards as Amsler's interpretation of language as the "all-embracing measure of reality," in which *res* (objects) is conflated with *voces* (verbal signs). Del Bello argues that language was "*allegorical*, the visible form of invisible meanings." Del Bello 2007, 97–102.

19. "The etymological study of a given word is for Isidore not just a diachronic analysis of a lexeme, but also a metaphysical investigation of a signified object." See Di Sciacca 2008, 14.

20. *Etymologiae* I.29.1; for the translation, I draw on Barney et al. 2002, 54. However, I render *vis* as "meaning." I am grateful to Franck Cinato for drawing my attention to the meaning of *vis* in this context.

21. Again, I draw on Barney et al. 2002, 55. However, I translate *vis* as "meaning." See Spevak 2020, 123–125: *En effet, quand on a vu d'où vient le nom, on comprend plus rapidement son sens.*

22. NEMESIN *Nomos* lex (ad *De nuptiis* I, 88; O'Sullivan 2010, 233, 23); MINERVA *Min* non, *erua* mors, immortalis (ad *De nuptiis* I, 42; O'Sullivan 2010, 168, 22); NEPTVNVS *Nepo* (νίπτω) lauo (ad *De nuptiis* I, 42; O'Sullivan 2010, 168, 30); HERCVLIS Quasi *eracleos* (ἔρα "earth," κλέος "fame," "glory") terrae gloria (ad *De nuptiis* II, 157; O'Sullivan 2010, 375, 13); PHRONESIS *Phrono* (φρονέω) sapio (ad *De nuptiis* II, 114; O'Sullivan 2010, 286, 6); ERIGONE *eris* (ἔρις) luctatio, *gone* (γυνή) mulier (ad *De nuptiis* II, 174; O'Sullivan 2010, 396, 15); VRANIE *Yranos* (οὐρανός) caelum (ad *De nuptiis* I, 28; O'Sullivan 2010, 124, 2).

23. Simultaneity and synchronization were used in constructions of historical narratives and universal histories to underscore the providential patterns underpinning history. See O'Sullivan 2021, 355.

24. Clarke 2014, 101–122.

25. For an interest in Greek in the Priscian manuscript: Ahlqvist 1988, 195–214.

26. For discussion of code switching: Bisagni and Warntjes 2007, 1–33; Bisagni 2014, 1–58; Clarke 2018, 1–31.

27. Bradshaw 1889, 282. See also Stokes 1873, 385–416. On the dating of the Old Welsh glosses by Bradshaw and Stokes: Jackson 1953, 53.

28. Bishop 1967, 267–271.

29. For the sources of the notes in the *Anonymus Cantabrigiensis*, see Bishop 1967, 257, fn. 1 and O'Sullivan 2011b, 33–56.

30. Bishop 1967, 264.

31. Lemmen 2006, 6.

32. *De nuptiis* 1.36; Cambridge, Corpus Christi College, Ms. 153, fol. 4va16.

33. I am very grateful to Paul Russell for explaining this to me. See also Lemmen 2006, 19. Russell also remarked that *gwr* (lit.) "man," but often better translated as "person," is often used to refer to God; for a good example, see the famous Juvencus manuscript, Cambridge, Cambridge University Library, MS Ff. 4.42. Here one finds in one of the Old Welsh poems commonly known as the "Juvencus Nine" the words *gur dicones*, which refers to God.

34. Moran 2015, 138. In his doctoral thesis, Franck Cinato 2010, vol. 1, 164, 186–187 and 190, drew attention to this phenomenon, noting the question of the vernacular in glosses. In particular, he drew attention to the complex relationship between vernacular and Latin glosses, as well as the function of the vernacular as an element of the interpretation.

35. The Weitz glosses comprise Latin and German annotations found in numerous manuscripts dating from the ninth to the thirteenth centuries. The tradition was named after Iohannes Weitz, a seventeenth-century scholar who based his edition of the annotations on two manuscripts, one in London and the other in Bern. Iohannes Weitz attributed his glosses to Iso but gave no reason for the attribution. The idea of Iso's authorship was based largely on one manuscript, Bern, Burgerbibliothek, Cod. 264, thought to emanate from St. Gall or its environs. See O'Sullivan 2004, 26.

36. The following gloss contains Latin and Old High German words written by the same hand: BUCCULAS genus uasorum uel rantboga (*Psych. Praef.* 31; Cologne, Dombibliothek, Ms. 81, fol. 67r2).

37. MAPALIA Magalia louba uel hxtta (*Psych. Praef.* 46; Cologne, Dombibliothek, Ms. 81, fol. 67v9); MILITE kemphen id est uirtute ule exercitu (*Psych.* 5; Cologne, Dombibliothek, Ms. 81, fol. 68v2).

38. MILITE kfmphfn (*lege* kemphen; *Psych.* 5; Bern, Burgerbibliothek Cod. 264, p. 68); UMBONIS rbntppgxn (*lege* rantbogen; *Psych.* 255; Bern, Burgerbibliothek Cod. 264, p. 87).

39. Ottaviano 2014.

40. The Oxford manuscript was compiled according to Bischoff in the second quarter of the ninth century in the Paris region, that is, in an area that became a hub of Virgilian scholarship. The Oxford Virgil, supplied early on with contemporary or near-contemporary annotations and emanating from a hub of Carolingian Virgilian scholarship, furnishes an illustrative case study for the reception of Virgil in the Carolingian age. Late antique commentaries on Virgil figure prominently in the marginal and interlinear glosses in the manuscript. Donatus' prose paraphrase of the *Aeneid*, that is, the *Interpretationes Vergilianae*, is mined for information, as are the *Explanationes in Bucolica Vergilii* of Iunius Philargyrius (extant in two recensions called I and II) and the closely related Bern scholia, which constitutes an important commentary tradition on Virgil surviving in many formats and contributing to the sizeable body of non-Servian materials on the poet.

41. O'Sullivan 2018a, 141–142.

42. In the following gloss, the first two letters of the word *abauus* (i.e., *ab*) in the final line of the annotation are copied in Tironian notes and the remaining letters of the word (i.e., *auus*) are written in minuscule. The gloss is written in a mixture of Tironian notes and minuscule: Qvartvs pater *id est abauus nec est contrarium illud, cui Pilumnus auus: potuit enim fieri ut et auus eius et* abauus *a Pilumno Pilumni nominarentur* (*Aeneid* 10.619; Oxford, Bodleian Library, Auct. F. 2. 8, fol. 188v; Thilo and Hagen 1881–1902, II: 454, 4–6).

43. O'Sullivan 2010, lxxxii.

44. For the circulation of Tironian notes in the Carolingian age: Ganz 2001. For the history of Tironian notes: Ganz 1990, 35–51. For their function and use: McCormick 1992; Hellmann 2000; Ganz 2023.

45. For studies of *memoria*: Yates 1966; Carruthers 1990; Carruthers and Ziolkowski 2002.

46. O'Sullivan 2010, lxxi–lxxvi.

47. O'Sullivan 2011b, 48–50.

48. See, for example, the comment on the sapphire copied as a gloss and as part of an independent text in O'Sullivan 2004, 332 and 341–342. See also the commentary on the 12 gemstones written as an independent text in London, British Library, MS. Add. 34248 (saec. XI, Southern Germany), fol. 203r.

49. Ottaviano 2013, 243; O'Sullivan 2018b, 171–172. Important was the discovery by Ottaviano of unknown glosses on the *Aeneid* in a Montpellier manuscript, some of which are also attested by a now fragmentary manuscript copied in the abbey of St Emmeram in Regensburg in the second third of the ninth century. This fragmentary manuscript, currently scattered across continental libraries, transmits glosses written by a contemporary hand and in a minuscule that manifests Insular traits. For the stemmatic relationship between the Montpellier Virgil manuscript and the St Emmeram manuscript, see Ottaviano 2013, 236. For the location and date of the fragments, see Bischoff 2004, Nr. 3353, 276. What is noteworthy about the shared glosses on the *Aeneid* in the Montpellier and St Emmeram manuscripts is that a number of them, heavily mythological in character, sometimes display, as Ottaviano demonstrates, similarities with the First Vatican Mythographer. See Ottaviano, 2013, 221 and 226.

50. For the origins of the practice of alignment, we need to look to ancient Greece, where Greek historians correlated key events in the different city states. For its evolution, Eusebius, with his innovative columnar format, was crucial: O'Sullivan 2021, 356–357.

51. In a similar vein, we find patristic and medieval exegetes assimilating the histories of different peoples in different times and places into a providential history of the universal church. Such exegesis is illumined by Jennifer O'Reilly in her study of Bede's use of the *topos* of Britain and Ireland as islands "at the ends of the earth," a *topos* that connects classical, patristic, and papal traditions. O'Reilly demonstrates that Bede, in his history of the English people, drew on classical geographical ideas that located these islands in the furthermost reaches of the habitable world, on patristic exegesis on preaching to all peoples "even to the uttermost part of the earth" and on papal writings on islands and idols as part of a continuing history of apostolic mission. See O'Reilly 2005.

52. Auerbach 1959, 53.
53. The "typological nature of medieval historical thought," as characterized by Gabrielle Spiegel, meant that the past was often regarded as redolent with prophetic undercurrents. See Spiegel 2002, 85.
54. Crawford 2019.
55. Grafton and Williams 2006, 135.

REFERENCES

Ahlqvist, Anders. 1988. "Notes on the Greek Materials in the St. Gall Priscian (Codex 904)." In *The Sacred Nectar of the Greeks: The Study of Greek in the West in the Early Middle Ages*, edited by Michael W. Herren in Collaboration With Shirley Ann Brown, 195–214. King's College London Medieval Studies 2. London: Boydell and Brewer.

Amsler, Mark. 1989. *Etymology and Grammatical Discourse in Late Antiquity and the Early Middle Ages*. Amsterdam Studies in the Theory and History of Linguistic Science 44. Amsterdam: John Benjamins Publishing.

Auerbach, Erich. 1959. "Figura." In *Scenes From the Drama of European Literature: Six Essays*, 11–78. New York: Meridian Books.

Barney, Stephen A., W. J. Lewis, Jennifer A. Beach, and Oliver Berghof, tr. 2002. *The 'Etymologies' of Isidore of Seville*. Cambridge: Cambridge University Press.

Bisagni, Jacopo. 2014. "Prolegomena to the Study of Code-Switching in the Old Irish Glosses." *Peritia* 24–25: 1–58.

Bisagni, Jacopo, and Immo Warntjes. 2007. "Latin and Old Irish in the Munich Computus: A Reassessment and Further Evidence." *Ériu* 57: 1–33.

Bischoff, Bernhard. 2004. *Katalog der festländischen Handschriften des neunten Jahrhunderts (mit Ausnahme der wisigotischen), vol. 2, Laon-Paderborn (aus dem Nachlaß herausgegeben von Birgit Ebersperger)*, Veröffentlichungen der Kommission für die Herausgabe der mittelalterlichen Bibliothekskataloge Deutschlands und der Schweiz. Wiesbaden: Harrassowitz.

Bishop, T. A. M. 1967. "The Corpus Martianus Capella." *Transactions of the Cambridge Bibliographical Society* 4: 257–275.

Bradshaw, Henry. 1889. "On the Oldest Written Remains of the Welsh Language." In *Collected Papers of Henry Bradshaw, Late University Librarian*, edited by Francis Jenkinson, 281–285. Cambridge: Cambridge University Press.

Carruthers, Mary. 1990. *The Book of Memory: A Study of Memory in Medieval Culture*, Cambridge Studies in Medieval Literature 10. Cambridge: Cambridge University Press.

Carruthers, Mary, and Jan M. Ziolkowski, eds. 2002. *The Medieval Craft of Memory: An Anthology of Texts and Pictures*. Philadelphia: University of Pennsylvania Press.

Cinato, Franck. 2010. "Glose de Prisciano: travaux de maîtres carolingiens sur L'*Ars de Priscien*: Gloses interlinéaires, marginales et collectées." PhD Dissertation, 2 vols. Paris: École pratique des hautes études.

Clarke, Michael. 2014. "Demonology, Allegory and Translation: The Furies and the Morrígan." In *Classical Literature and Learning in Medieval Irish Narrative*, edited by Ralph O'Connor, 101–122. Studies in Celtic History 34. Cambridge: D.S. Brewer.

Clarke, Michael. 2018. "Merger and Contrast Between Latin and Medieval Irish." In *Code-Switching in Medieval Ireland and England: Proceedings of a Workshop on Code-Switching in the Medieval Classroom, Utrecht 29th May, 2015*, edited by Mícheál Ó. Flaithearta, 1–31. Münchner Forschungen zur historischen Sprachwissenschaft 18. Bremen: Hempen Verlag.

Crawford, Matthew R. 2019. *The Eusebian Canon-Tables: Ordering Knowledge in Late Antiquity*, Oxford Early Christian Studies. Oxford: Oxford University Press.

De Lagarde, Paul, ed. 1975. *Hieronymus: Liber interpretationis hebraicorum nominum*, Corpus Christianorum Series Latina 72. Turnhout: Brepols.

Del Bello, Davide. 2007. *Forgotten Paths: Etymology and the Allegorical Mindset*. Washington D.C.: The Catholic University of America Press.

Di Sciacca, Claudia. 2008. *Finding the Right Words: Isidore's 'Synonyma' in Anglo-Saxon England*. Toronto: University of Toronto Press.

Fontaine, Jacques. 1959. *Isidore de Seville et la culture classique dans l'Espagne wisigothique*. 2 vols. Paris: Études Augustiniennes.

Ganz, David. 1990. "On the History of Tironian Notes." In *Tironische Noten*, edited by Peter Ganz, 35–51. Wolfenbütteler Mittelalter Studien 1. Wiesbaden: Harrassowitz.

Ganz, David. 2001. "Carolingian Manuscripts With Substantial Glosses in Tironian Notes." In *Mittelalterliche volkssprachige Glossen: internationale Fachkonferenz des Zentrums für Mittelalterstudien der Otto-Friedrich-Universität Bamberg, 2. bis 4. August 1999*, edited by Rolf Bergmann, Elvira Glaser, and Claudine Moulin-Fankhänel, 101–107. Germanistische Bibliothek 13. Heidelberg: C. Winter.

Ganz, David. 2023. "Latin Shorthand and Latin Learning." In *Crafting Knowledge in the Early Medieval Book: Practices of Collecting and Concealing in the Latin West*, edited by Sinéad O'Sullivan and Ciaran Arthur. Publications of the Journal of Medieval Latin 16. Turnhout: Brepols.

Goetz, Georg, Gustav Loewe, Gotthold Gundermann, and Paul Wessner, eds. 1888–1923. *Corpus Glossariorum Latinorum*. 7 vols. Leipzig: Teubner.

Grafton, Anthony, and Megan Williams. 2006. *Christianity and the Transformation of the Book: Origen, Eusebius, and the Library of Caesarea*. Cambridge, MA: Harvard University Press.

Grondeux, Anne, and Franck Cinato, eds. 2016. "Liber Glossarum Digital." Accessed November 21, 2021. http://liber-glossarum.huma-num.fr.

Hellmann, Martin. 2000. *Tironische Noten in der Karolingerzeit am Beispiel eines Persius-Kommentars aus der Schule von Tours*, MGH Studien und Texte 27. Hanover: Hahnsche Buchhandlung.

Jackson, Kenneth. 1953. *Language and History in Early Britain: A Chronological Survey of the Brittonic Languages First to Twelfth Century A.D.* Edinburgh: University Press.

Laistner, Max L. W. 1923. "Notes on Greek From the Lectures of a Ninth-Century Monastery Teacher." *Bulletin of the John Rylands Library* 7: 421–456.
Laistner, Max L. W., ed. 1983. *Bede: Expositio actuum apostolorum*, Corpus Christianorum Series Latina 121. Turnhout: Brepols.
Lemmen, Karianne. 2006. "The Old Welsh Glosses in Martianus Capella, Revised and Rearranged with Newly Found Glosses." M.A. Dissertation, Utrecht University.
Lendinara, Patrizia. 2011. "The *Scholica Graecarum Glossarum* and Martianus Capella." In *Carolingian Scholarship and Martianus Capella: Ninth-Century Commentary Traditions on "De Nuptiis" in Context*, edited by Mariken Teeuwen and Sinéad O'Sullivan, 301–361. Cultural Encounters in Late Antiquity and the Middle Ages 12. Turnhout: Brepols.
McCormick, Michael. 1992. *Five Hundred Unknown Glosses From the Palatine Virgil (The Vatican Library, MS. Pal. Lat. 1631)*. Studi e Testi 343. Vatican City: Biblioteca Apostolica Vaticana.
Merrills, Andy. 2013. "Isidore's *Etymologiae*: On Words and Things." In *Encyclopaedism From Antiquity to the Renaissance*, edited by Jason König and Greg Woolf, 301–324. Cambridge: Cambridge University Press.
Moran, Pádraic. 2015. "Language Interaction in the St. Gall Priscian Glosses." *Peritia* 26: 113–142.
O'Reilly, Jennifer. 2005. "Islands and Idols at the Ends of the Earth: Exegesis and Conversion in Bede's *Historia Ecclesiastica*." In *Bède le Vénérable: Entre tradition et postérité*, edited by Stéphane Lebecq, Michel Perrin, and Olivier Szerwiniack, 119–145. Histoire et littérature du Septentrion 34. Villeneuve d'Ascq: CEGES.
O'Sullivan, Sinéad. 2004. *Early Medieval Glosses on Prudentius' "Psychomachia:" The Weitz Tradition*. Mittellateinische Studien und Texte 31. Leiden: Brill.
O'Sullivan, Sinéad, ed. 2010. *Glossae Aevi Carolini in Libros I-II Martiani Capellae De Nuptiis Philologiae et Mercurii*. Corpus Christianorum Continuatio Mediaevalis 237. Turnhout: Brepols.
O'Sullivan, Sinéad. 2011a. "The Sacred and the Obscure: Greek and the Carolingian Reception of Martianus Capella." *The Journal of Medieval Latin* 21: 67–93.
O'Sullivan, Sinéad. 2011b. "The Corpus Martianus Capella: Continental Gloss Traditions on *De Nuptiis* in Wales and Anglo-Saxon England." *Cambrian Medieval Celtic Studies* 62 (Winter): 33–56.
O'Sullivan, Sinéad. 2017. "Text, Gloss and Tradition in the Early Medieval West: Expanding into a World of Learning." In *Teaching and Learning in Medieval Europe: Essays in Honour of Gernot R. Wieland*, edited by Greti Dinkova-Bruun and Tristan Major, 3–24. Publications of the Journal of Medieval Latin 11. Turnhout: Brepols.
O'Sullivan, Sinéad. 2018a. "Glossing Vergil and Pagan Learning in the Carolingian Age." *Speculum* 93 (1): 132–165.
O'Sullivan, Sinéad. 2018b. "*Scholia non serviana*, Lactantius Placidus, the Vatican Mythographers and Mythological Lore: A Case Study of Montpellier, Bibliothèque interuniversitaire, Section médecine, H 253." *Archivum latinitatis medii aevi* 76: 155–188.

O'Sullivan, Sinéad. 2021. "The Practice of 'Alignment' in Medieval Ireland." In *Litterarum Dulces Fructus: Studies in Early Medieval Latin Culture in Honour of Michael W. Herren for his 80th Birthday*, edited by Scott G. Bruce, 355–384. Instrumenta Patristica et Mediaevalia 85. Turnhout: Brepols.

Ottaviano, Silvia. 2013. "*Scholia non serviana* nei manoscritti carolingi di Virgilio: Prime notizie degli scavi." *Exemplaria Classica: Journal of Classical Philology* 17: 221–244.

Ottaviano, Silvia. 2014. "La tradizione delle opere di Virgilio tra IX e XI sec." PhD Dissertation. Pisa: Scuola Normale Superiore.

Spevak, Olga, tr. 2020. *Isidore de Séville, Etymologies, Livre 1: La grammaire*. Paris: Les Belles Lettres.

Spiegel, Gabrielle M. 2002. "Historical Thought in Medieval Europe." In *A Companion to Western Historical Thought*, edited by Lloyd Kramer and Sarah Maza, 78–98. Oxford: Blackwell Publishers.

Stokes, Whitley. 1873. "The Old-Welsh Glosses on Martianus Capella, With Some Notes on the Juvencus-Glosses." *Beiträge zur vergleichenden Sprachforschung* 7: 385–416.

Stotz, Peter. 2002. *Handbuch zur lateinischen Sprache des Mittelalters, Bd 1: Einleitung, Lexikologische Praxis, Wörter und Sachen, Lehnwortgut*. Munich: C.H. Beck Verlag.

Thilo, Georg, and Hermann Hagen, eds. 1881–1902. *Servii grammatici qui feruntur in Vergilii carmina commentarii*. 3 vols. Leipzig: Teubner.

Weise, Oscar. 1882. *Die griechischen Wörter im Latein*. Leipzig: Hirzel.

Yates, Frances A. 1966. *The Art of Memory*. London: Penguin Books.

6

Auraicept na nÉces and the *Art of Medicine*

Deborah Hayden

The medieval Irish grammatical compilation known as *Auraicept na nÉces* ("The Scholars' Primer") is a remarkably complex example of the early Irish exegetical tradition.[1] While parts of the text have been dated on linguistic grounds to the Old Irish period (*ca* 700–900 AD), the work only survives in late-medieval manuscripts that feature a substantial quantity of later glossing and commentary, amounting to nearly three thousand lines in the printed edition of the longest recension (Calder 1917, 171–257). Much of this commentary, which represents layers of scholia added to the text over the course of several centuries, is difficult to date with any precision and has received only limited attention from modern scholars. This contribution will consider some passages in the *Auraicept* that may reflect the involvement of medical scholars in the composition of the work. It will also seek to situate this material within the wider context of vernacular literary production and the activities of various learned families in Connacht, Ireland, during the later Middle Ages.

THE EARLIEST GRAMMAR OF THE IRISH LANGUAGE AND ITS PEDAGOGICAL CONTEXT

The numerous surviving witnesses to the text of *Auraicept na nÉces* present a convoluted accumulation of glossing and commentary dealing not just with elementary grammatical concepts such as letters, syllables, and grades of comparison, but also with matters pertaining more properly to the disciplines of rhetoric and dialectic. As a whole, therefore, the work has been argued (see, e.g., Poppe 1996; Burnyeat 2007) to constitute a vernacular reflex of the kind of scholarly activities subsumed under the medieval discipline of *grammatica,* broadly defined by Martin Irvine (1994, xiii) as "the gravitational center of several other institutions and practices—schools, libraries, scriptoria, commentaries, canonical texts and language." Much modern scholarly discussion concerning the history of language study in Ireland has tended to characterize the *Auraicept* as a distinctly early medieval text: a view framed in large part by Anders Ahlqvist's edition and analysis of its so-called "canonical core," which he dated to "a fairly early stage of the Old Irish period," partly on the basis of its preservation of some archaic linguistic forms (Ahlqvist 1983, 36). The very existence of such a core has not gone undisputed, however; thus Rijklof Hofman (2013, 197) has argued that the original compilers of the *Auraicept* may have "conceived their primer as a basic text accompanied by commentary from the outset," drawing on the model of contemporary Latin commentaries on the work of the famous late-antique grammarian Donatus.

In a similar vein, Erich Poppe (1996, 1999, 2002) has identified a number of parallels between some of the *Auraicept*'s scholia and the contents of a group of Hiberno-Latin commentaries on Donatus' *Ars maior* composed by Irish scholars working on the Continent during the ninth century, suggesting that some of the commentaries on the Irish text may date to around that period. Poppe also observed that several of the technical terms employed in the *Auraicept* to describe the properties of linguistic concepts, such as *cenél* ("genus"), *gné* ("species"), *coitchenn* ("common"), and *díles* ("proper"), indicate familiarity on the part of the text's scholiasts with elementary works on logic, such as Boethius' translation of Porphyry's *Isagoge* (or "Introduction" to Aristotle's *Categories*), a standard textbook in early medieval Europe that deals principally with the hierarchical classification of genera and species from substance in general down to individuals. For example, the meaning of the word *fidh* ("letter" or "vowel") is explained in the *Auriacept* as follows:

> *Fidh .i. fundamentum a bunad Laitne. [. . .] Ruidhles 7 diles 7 coitchend indiles do fedhaib .i. ruidhles do fhedhaibh aireghdhaibh, diles do forfhedhaib. Coitchend immorro do thaebomnaib acht huath. Indles do sen immorro, air ni taebomna etir, ut est: h non est litera sed nota aspirationis .i. nochon [fh]uil h co mbad litir acht ata conidh noit tinfidh.*
>
> Fid, letter, that is *fundamentum* its Latin root. [. . .] Peculiar, proper, common, and improper to vowels, i.e. peculiar to principal vowels, proper to diphthongs. Common, however, to consonants except h. Improper to it, however; for it is not a consonant at all, *ut est*: h *non est litera sed nota aspirationis*, h is not a letter but it is a mark of aspiration. (Calder 1917, 56–57, ll. 762–768; cited in Poppe 1996, 67)

This analytical framework, as Poppe pointed out, can be compared to Porphyry's explanation of the ontological category of *differentia* "difference":

> *Differentia vero communiter et proprie et magis proprie dicatur. Communiter quidem differre alterum altero dicitur quod alteritate quadam differt quocumque*

modo vel a se ipso vel ab alio; differt enim Socrates Platone alteritate et ipse a se vel puero vel iam viro vel faciente aliquid vel quiescente, et semper in aliquo modo habendi alteritatibus. Proprie autem differre alterum altero dicitur quando inseparabili accidenti altero differt; inseparabile vero accidens est ut nasi curvitas, caecitas oculorum, cicatrix cum ex vulnere obcalluerit. Magis proprie differre alterum altero dicitur quando specifica differentia disterit, quemadmodum homo ab equo specifica differentia differt rationali qualitate.

Let us say that difference has (1) a common meaning, (2) a proper meaning, and (3) a strict meaning. *Commonly* one thing is said to differ from another when by otherness it differs in any way at all either from itself or from another, for by otherness Socrates differs from Plato and, indeed, from himself: he was a child and became a man; he is doing something or he has stopped; and of course, he is always changing in qualitative degree. *Properly* two things are said to differ whenever they differ because of an inseparable accident, such as greyness of the eyes or a hooked quality of the nose or even a scar which has become hardened from a wound. *Strictly* two things are said to differ whenever they differ because of a specific difference, as a man differs from a horse because of a specific difference, the quality rational. (ed. and trans. Warren 1975, 42 and cited in Poppe 1996, 69)

Poppe's arguments regarding the intellectual background of the *Auraicept*'s early medieval commentators lend support to Ahlqvist's prior observations, in the preface to his edition of the so-called "canonical core" of the text, concerning the similarities in the exegetical approach adopted by both the scholiasts of the grammar and those responsible for copying and commenting on the surviving corpus of Old Irish legal material (Ahlqvist 1983, 11–14; for an overview of the medieval Irish legal commentary tradition, see Kelly 2002, especially 234–239).

There are indications, however, that the accretion of commentary and glossing in at least some copies of the *Auraicept* continued well into the later medieval period. On the basis of his tentative identification of some surnames of Irish scholars cited in the scholia to the text, Calder had suggested that the *Auraicept* in its extant form "was not completed before the middle of the tenth century, perhaps not till towards the end of the eleventh" (Calder 1917, xxxi). Ahlqvist (1983, 32) similarly indicated that the beginning of the twelfth century may have represented "more or less the end of a common tradition for the Auraicept commentaries" as we have them in the various extant manuscript copies, but also noted that 1100 did not necessarily represent the end of material being added to the text in some recensions. In keeping with this, I have recently argued that an encrypted stanza of poetry incorporated into the longest recension of the grammar, Calder's edition of which was based primarily on two sixteenth-century witnesses, may have originated in a marginal note found in another extant manuscript of the fourteenth century

(National Library of Ireland MS G3; see Hayden 2016a, 39–45). Other sources offer more indirect evidence to suggest that the *Auraicept* continued to be used well into the late-medieval period. For example, the text is cited as a source in the opening section of one of the early modern Irish bardic grammatical tracts (Mac Cárthaigh 2014, 50–51, 163–164), and a work referred to as the "Uraiceapt," along with other tracts transmitted alongside *Auraicept na nÉces* in several manuscript copies, are said to have been studied by the poet Fear Feasa Ó'n Cháinte in bardic verse dating to as late as the seventeenth century (McManus 2004, 104).

These indications that the *Auraicept* was used as a grammatical manual by late-medieval bardic poets call to mind Calder's description of the text in the introduction to his edition, where he states that the titular word *éices*, variously rendered into English as "scholar, learned man, sage, poet," is "often equivalent" to the word *fili* (Calder 1917, xix). While the term *fili* is conventionally translated as "poet," it is important to note that the Irish word had quite a broad application in the medieval period. As Breatnach (1996, 65) has observed, "the variety of material in verse form in Old and Middle Irish is nearly as extensive as that in prose"; the medieval Irish *fili* did not only compose professional panegyric and elegies for specific patrons but might also produce works pertaining to "the whole field of poetry, romance, history, biography, geography, grammar, antiquities, and law" (Calder 1917, xix; on this theme, see also Boyle 2017). In turn, the abstract noun *filidecht* could refer to a "general theoretical knowledge about the content, metrics and language of poetry," and thus stood in contrast to the word *dán*, which more properly denoted the composition of professional verse (Simms 2007, 122). The sum of the evidence, therefore, indicates that *Auraicept na nÉces* can best be understood as a text that served as a propaedeutic for students pursuing a range of different scholarly vocations, not merely that of the professional praise-poet.

MEDICAL LEARNING AND LINGUISTIC THOUGHT IN THE *AURAICEPT*

The learned discipline that is notably absent from the various poetic genres listed by Calder in the introduction to his edition of the *Auraicept* is that of medicine. This is perhaps unsurprising, since substantive evidence for medical practice in Ireland during the first millennium—the period during which most of the *Auraicept*'s commentary and glossing appears to have taken shape—is all but non-existent. Of the handful of medical texts that have thus far been edited from the extant Irish-language medical manuscripts, all belong to the later medieval period and very clearly show the influence of continental trends in medical learning that followed the recovery of numerous Greek medical and philosophical works from the twelfth century onwards, many of which were translated into Latin from Arabic versions (Shaw 1940, 1961; Nic Dhonnchadha 2000).

Some passages of commentary in the *Auraicept* may, however, offer tantalizing clues regarding the relationship between grammatical and medical learning in medieval Ireland. At a fundamental level, the approach taken by the text's scholiasts to analyzing linguistic concepts points to a continuation of the long-standing tradition, extending back to Antiquity, of discussing language in organic terms, as a biological phenomenon. One outcome of this was the tendency for many classical texts on metrical theory to describe meter using words such as "feet" (*podes*) or "finger" (*dactyl*) (Sluiter 2010, 30). A similar metaphorical framework is manifested in an extended passage of commentary in the *Auraicept* that provides medieval etymologies for terms denoting different metrical units, where the number of syllables in a given unit is compared to various parts of the human body.[2] Thus the word *luibenchossach*, designating a hexasyllabic line of verse, is explained in the commentary as *in choss cona luibnibh .i. na coic meoir 7 in traigh in sessed* ("the foot with its digits, the five toes; the foot being the sixth"). The term *claidemnas*, referring to a heptasyllabic line of verse, is then etymologized as a compound of Irish *claideb* "sword" and Latin *manus* "hand," that is, *claidebh-manus .i. manus lamh 7 claidebh na laimi in slindean: 7 is e in sechtmad dialt* ("sword-*manus*, to wit, *manus*, hand, and the sword of the hand is the shoulder-blade: and it is the seventh syllable") (Calder 1917, 110–111, ll. 1424–1427; Hayden 2014, 34). In the second of these two examples, the scholiast has attempted to explain the concept of a heptasyllabic metrical unit by comparing it to the part of the body that extends from the hand to the shoulder blade, perhaps because this anatomical section spans seven distinct joints; the triangular shape of the scapula, moreover, may have been understood to resemble the hilt of a sword. The etymology is presumably premised on the double meaning of the Irish word *alt* as either "joint of the body" or "division between the syllables of words."[3]

While the two etymologies just cited might be considered little more than fanciful elaborations on the *podes* and *dactyl* of the classical grammarians, it is nonetheless noteworthy that the *Auraicept*'s scholiasts elsewhere take the theoretical framework of anatomical metaphor to an extreme that has no obvious direct parallel in Latin grammatical sources. For example, one section of the Irish text includes declensional paradigms for nouns of the masculine, feminine, and neuter genders, the first two categories of which are represented by the words *fer* "man" and *ben* "woman." At some point in the development of the compilation, a scholiast expanded on these paradigms by detailing the various properties associated with the male and female anatomy. Thus the commentary on the word *fer* begins as follows:

> *Ceand cridi fulang a dhe* [recte *ad hē*] *demi tebidhi in fhir. Suil 7 fiacail lanamain in chind. Srebann 7 cru lanamain* [. . .] *in cridi. Lurgu 7 traigh lanamain ind fhulaing. Gene d*[*a*]*no na lanamnaide deme .i. ebrachtur* [. . .] *7 malu, lanamain (no gene) na sula. Bun 7 lethet lanamain (no gene) na fiacal. Croiceann 7 feich lanamain (no gene) na lurgan. Lith* [cf. l. 5004: *lethor*] *7 tond lanamain (.i. gene) na traiged.*
>
> Head, heart, [and] supporting [=legs?], those are the man's neuter selected attributes. Eye and tooth the couple of the head. Membrane and gore the couple [. . .] of the heart. Shin and foot the couple of supporting. A pair, too, of the correlated neuter, that is, eyelashes and eyebrow [. . .] a couple or pair of the eye. Root and breadth, a couple or pair of the teeth. Skin and sinew the couple or pair of the shins. Activity [*recte* skin?] and surface, the couple or pair of the feet (Calder 1917, 138–141, ll. 1808–1816, with some adjustments to the translation; for commentary on some of the problems with Calder's edition and translation of this passage, see Hayden 2014, 44–45 n 62).

Immediately following this passage, similar anatomical imagery is invoked in an analysis of different types of "accents" that are said to mark syllabic quantity, ending with the following example:

> *Arnin amal roghabh cnaim mullaich 7 leicni 7 cnuicc 7 find, 7 na hai nad genat lasin duine fochetoir, uair fo cosmaillius alta duini doniter alta huadh. Ni taidbet dno int airnin lasin focul fochetoir forsa tochradar co mbi fo deoidh arding in focul.*
>
> *Arnin* ("accent of middle quantity"), such as *cnáim mullaich* top bone, *leicni* jaw-bones, *cnuicc* knuckles, and *find* hair, and those that do not originate with man at first, for under the likeness of a man's limbs are the limbs of science[4] made. Now the *arnin* does not at once appear with the word on which it falls so that it is at the end that it compresses the word (Calder 1917, 140–141, ll. 1824–1828).

Although the above analogy is subtle, it would appear to represent an attempt to visualize the concept that Irish syllables with "middle quantity" are characterized by the pronunciation of a heavy consonant that stands at the end of the syllable rather than at the beginning. Since a listener would not perceive this heavy consonant at the inception of the syllable's pronunciation, it can therefore be compared to parts of the body that are not present at birth but only appear at a later point in human development. Syllables of middle quantity can thus be contrasted with those that have the short quantity, the pronunciation of which the commentator compares to the flesh and blood of a human because it "permeates the word from beginning to end without stretching it" (*co ngaib lasin focul o thosuch gu dereadh gan urgabail gan airditin*) (Hayden 2014, 58; on middle quantity in Irish syllabic verse, see Greene 1952).

It is unclear whether such highly obscure and apparently idiosyncratic analogies merely constitute an imaginative development of the Latin grammarians' approach to describing linguistic phenomena in corporeal terms, or whether there is in fact something else at play here. Could these very specific comparisons reflect the involvement of medical scribes and students in the composition of some of the *Auraicept*'s commentary? Some evidence to support such a hypothesis can be found by turning to the extant corpus of Irish-language medical texts. We might consider, for example, the following triad found in a compilation of questions and answers on rudimentary anatomical matters, now preserved in a sixteenth-century manuscript in the National Library of Scotland:

Cā līn cnāimh a corp duine gineas ar na geineamhain 7 na geineann reime? nī ansa. a trī, et ōn land bathaisi 7 fiacail 7 faircli glūine.

How many bones are formed in the body of a person after birth, and are not formed before it? Not difficult. Three, that is, the fontanelle (lit. "the plate of baptism"), the tooth and the kneecap. (National Library of Scotland, Advocates' MS 72. 1. 2, fol. 62r10–13; for further discussion of the text in which this passage occurs, see Hayden 2016b).

This triad recalls the aforementioned commentary from the *Auraicept* concerning the four body parts that "do not originate with man at first," invoked to explain a category of syllabic quantity. That the formula may have originated in a medical context is suggested, however, by the occurrence of a very similar passage in a Welsh medical text (Hayden 2014, 59–60; Luft 2020, 74–75). It is possible that such elementary medical precepts may have formed part of a common store of knowledge that circulated among members of various learned professions in early medieval Ireland and neighboring regions. The inclusion of the formula in the *Auraicept* as part of a lengthy excursus on the anatomical ontology of declensional paradigm words suggests, however, that the scholarly preoccupations of at least one of the grammar's scholiasts may have been distinctly medical in nature.

A GRAMMATICAL GLOSS ON "ESSENCE" AND IRISH MEDICO-PHILOSOPHICAL TEXTS

The evidence adduced above to suggest that students of medicine may have contributed to the accreted commentary to *Auraicept na nÉces* can be strengthened by analysis of one further passage of commentary that occurs only in the longest recension of the grammar. Calder's edition of this version was based primarily on two sixteenth-century witnesses that now form part of the manuscripts now known as the Yellow Book of Lecan (TCD MS 1318 [H 2. 16]) and British Library MS Egerton 88. These copies are textually very close, and indeed William O'Sullivan (1999, 285 and 290) argued that they were produced within a year of each other in the mid-1560s by scholars associated with the Mac Aodhagáin law school at Park, near Tuam, Co. Galway. The longer recension of the *Auraicept* was not translated by Calder and consequently has received rather less attention from modern scholars than his translated "short version" of the text; however, it does contain some interesting commentary not found in the shorter version, including the aforementioned gloss that seems to have originated in a marginal note to a fourteenth-century manuscript in the National Library of Ireland (on which see above, pp. 115–16).

The passage in question forms part of a longer discussion concerning the meaning of the Irish term *etargaire*, a word that denotes something like "separating" or "distinguishing." *Etargaire* is cited elsewhere in the *Auraicept* as one of the seven things "according to which the Irish language is measured" or "analyzed" (*seachta frisa toimsiter Gaedhelg*), along with concepts such as "letter" (*fid*), "verse-foot" (*deach*), "declension" (*réim*), "accent" (*forbaidh*), "syllable" (*alt*), and "gender" (*indsce*) (Calder 1917, 54–55, ll. 739–40). While Calder translates *etargaire* simply as "inflection," the term appears to have a fairly wide application throughout the text, ranging from different types of morphological inflection (such as declension or comparison) to semantic distinctions, including the kind of analysis involved in differentiating between, for example, *genus* and *species* (Lambert 2003). Most recently, Paul Russell (2020: 66–67) has interpreted it as "something closer to the 'base-form' [of various grammatical features] which can be further distinguished by the addition of further suffixes, pronouns, or particles."

In keeping with the exegetical approach taken elsewhere in grammar, a commentator on this section attempted to define the "essence" of each of the seven grammatical concepts listed, including that of the word *etargaire*. In medieval philosophical discourse, "essence" designated the attribute or set of attributes that make an entity or substance what it fundamentally is, and without which it loses its identity. Both the longer and shorter recensions of the grammar edited by Calder (1917, 68–69, ll. 913–916 and 218–219, ll. 3796–3797) define the essence of *etargaire* as *int athfegadh mete no laiget no inde no incho[i]sc no edardeifrighi no etardelighti no edarderscaigthe rodealbh Dia eter duilib* ("the consideration of size, smallness, quality, denotation, difference, variety, or distinction which God hath fashioned among created things"). In the longer recension of the *Auraicept*, however, the passage is expanded as follows:

> *Eisi .i. go mbeith esse d'ecensia .i. mar roinnius rann 7 uilidhecht .i. mar ta crand 7 a geuga 7 a cousmailius. Ese cruthoigti 7 eisi adbarrda: iss ed is eisi adbarrda and .i. mac do geineimain on athair 7 a cosmailius. Is ed is eisi cruthoighti and mar ata mac aga foghlaim [o] oidi no maigistir; 7 fiagfraidh int ugdar cie ai [i]s uaisle, eisi cruthoighthi na eisi adbarda, 7 ader gu rab uaisli eisi cruthoighthi: 7 is he a adpert sin nach bfil acht damna arna geinemain and no go gcruthoigther he o fhoglaim, ut dixit Plato.*
>
> *Eisi* "essence," i.e. that it be *esse* "essence" from *ecensia* (leg. *essentia*), i.e. as one separates *rann* "part" and *uilidhecht* "whole, universality," i.e. as is a tree and its branches and such like. Creative essence and material essence: material essence is i.e. a son born from the father and such like. Creative essence is as a son learning from a teacher or a master; and the authority asks which of them is more noble, creative essence or material essence, and he says that creative essence was more noble: and he who says that, what he said is that there is only primal matter at birth and that he is created from learning, *as Plato said*. (Calder 1917, 218–219, ll. 3795–3807; my translation)

Despite the attribution to Plato here, which may have been inspired by the concluding reference to "primal matter" (*damna*), this passage as a whole is distinctly Aristotelian in nature. Calder himself was evidently aware of this, since he cited, as a footnote to his edition of it, a reference to the text known as the *Lives and Opinions of Eminent Philosophers* by the third-century biographer Diogenes Laertius, who had credited Aristotle with the statement that "teachers who educated children deserved [. . .] more honour than parents who merely gave them birth; for bare life is furnished by the one, the other ensures a good life" (Calder 1917, 219 n; for the text, see Hicks 1959, 462–463). This sentiment concerning the superiority of teacher over parent seems to have established itself in learned discussions on grammar well before the time of Diogenes Laertius, however, since Diodorus of Sicily, who flourished in the first century BC, concluded a lengthy account of the benefits of acquiring literacy by stating that "while it is true that nature is the cause of life, the cause of the good life is the education which is based upon letters" (Irvine 1994, 12). A similar idea may be reflected in the glossing of an eleventh-century copy of the Old Irish text known as *Amrae Coluimb Chille*, when the word *fithir* "teacher" is etymologized as *feth-athair* "knowledge-father" (Russell 2014, 78–79; for the most recent edition and discussion of the text of *Amrae Coluimb Chille*, see Bisagni 2019).

In light of the fact that the Aristotelian maxim concerning the benefits of education seems to have become embedded in learned grammatical discourse from such an early stage, it is perhaps not surprising to see it surface in the medieval commentary to the *Auraicept*. It is also noteworthy, however, that the Irish scholiast added something to the maxim that does not occur in the earlier classical sources cited above: namely, a contrast between "material" essence (*eisi adbarrda*) and "creative" essence (*ese cruthoigti*), the latter of which is said to be more noble than the former because it can be compared to a "son learning from a teacher or master" (*mar atā mac aga foghlaim [ō] oidi nō maigistir*). This distinction echoes terminology used in a short tract found in two sixteenth-century Irish medical manuscripts, British Library Arundel MS 333 (fol. 9b) and National Library of Scotland, Advocates' MS 72. 1. 2 (fol. 33v15–z), which Standish O'Grady described as "Aristotelian excerpts":

> Adeir Aristotul go bhfuilit cheithri hérnuile ar in ngenemuin .i. gné cruthaigthech ocus gné adburda ocus gné dealbtach ocus gné truailligthech. Genemain cruthaigthech ymorro mar atá cruthugud na hyle ocus na naingeal ocus an anma résúnta ocus is leisan céd fheallsam sin d'iaruigh nó dho leanmhuin. Genemain adburda imorro mar atá genemain na corp ndúileta .i. duine ó duine ocus leomhan ó leomhan ocus gach uile ní ag techt óna cosmailis do réir náturae ocus is leisan liaigh nádúrdha sin do tuicsin. [. . .]
>
> Aristotle says that Generation has four species: a creative, a material, a formal, and a corrupt. Creative: as the creation of "*materia prima*," of the angels, of the rational soul; the seeking out and investigation of which generation belong to the "proto-philosopher" [metaphysician]. Material: as of created bodies, such as man of man, lion of lion, and all other [creatures] proceeding, according to nature, each from its like; the understanding of which mode of generation belongs to the "natural" physician. [. . .] (O'Grady 1926, 235–236)

The categories of generation outlined in this passage from two late-medieval medical manuscripts reflect Aristotle's teaching on causality, which attempted to explain why natural bodies are subject to change or movement. The philosopher identified four key factors in his explanation of the natural change, namely "matter," "form," "that which produces the change" (the "efficient cause"), and "the end of this change" ("the final cause"), all of which may contribute to the explanation of something (Falcon 2015). In *Metaphysics* V 2 Aristotle argued, for example, that "material cause"—which is presumably what is being translated using the adjective *adbarda* in the Irish texts—explains the material from which a thing comes into being, for example, the bronze of a statue or the silver of a cup. Conversely, he illustrated the "efficient cause," which is probably what is intended by the reference to *eisi cruthoigti* "creative essence" in the *Auraicept*, by explaining that "the father is the cause of the child" (Tredennick 1933, 210–211).

The description of material and efficient causes that is presented in Aristotle's *Metaphysics* thus corresponds only imperfectly to the distinction between "creative" and "material" generation in the two Irish texts cited above, where the generation of a son from a father is considered to belong to the category of "material" rather than "efficient" or "creative" cause. It is probable, however, that the distinction made in both of these texts between the adjectives *adbarda* "material" and *cruthoigti* (or *cruthaigthech*) "creative" does ultimately derive from Aristotelian metaphysical teaching. Such terminology would likely have been known in the medical milieu that produced the two manuscripts in which the passage on the four types of generation has been preserved, given that other texts in those manuscripts illustrate the confluence of medical and philosophical material in Irish tradition (Shaw 1940). In the case of the passage on "essence" found in the longest recension of the *Auraicept*, however, the binary distinction between "creative" and "material" varieties of the ontological category of "essence" has also been grafted onto a separate Aristotelian maxim concerning the value of literacy in providing individuals with not merely life itself but also a good quality of life—a sentiment which would no doubt have had considerable resonance in the specific context of grammatical learning that was the central objective of that compilation.

The classical background to this teaching naturally raises the question of precisely when the references to "creative" and "material" essence might have made their way into the *Auraicept*'s commentary. Aristotle's paradigm of four causes does not form part of the small corpus of logical works that were known in the early medieval period, such as Boethius' Latin translation of Porphyry's *Isagoge*, which, as noted above, may have been the source for some of the analytical terminology found throughout the scholia to the *Auraicept*. Rather, Aristotle gives his general account of the four causes in the second book of his *Physics* and the fifth book of his *Metaphysics*, both of which are first known to have been translated into Latin only in the twelfth century by figures such as James of Venice and Gerard of Cremona, the latter of whom was well known as a prolific translator of medical and scientific books from Arabic (Minio-Pauluello 1952, 265; Thorndike 1923–1958, ii, 89–90). On this basis, one might hypothesize that the addition of the commentary on "creative" and "material essence" in the *Auraicept* occurred at a period somewhat later than that in which most of the commentary to the grammar took shape, when texts like the *Physics* and *Metaphysics* had entered the general academic discourse in European centers of learning. If it is the case that Calder's so-called "Short" and "Long" recensions of the *Auraicept* diverged around the beginning of the twelfth century, this might explain why the additional commentary on "essence" only occurs in the longer version of the compilation, which, as noted above, seems to have still been acquiring scholia well into the late fourteenth century at least.

In addition to the "Aristotelian excerpts" from two Irish medical manuscripts cited already, one other even closer parallel for the *Auraicept*'s gloss on creative and material essence can be identified that likewise points to the origin of this teaching in a medical milieu. This occurs in a collection of medical *Aphorisms* commonly attributed to the eighth-century Syrian scholar John of Damascus, but which are in fact the work of the Arabic physician and medical author John Mesue (Yūhannū ibn Māsawayh), who practiced and taught in Baghdad in the ninth century (O'Boyle 1998, 114; Jacquart and Troupeau 1980, 7–8). After they were translated into Latin in the late-eleventh or early-twelfth century, Mesue's collection of *Aphorisms* enjoyed remarkable dissemination in Europe and eventually came to form as part of a group of thirteenth-century supplements to the *Ars medicine* ("Art of Medicine"), a collection of short medical tracts of Greek and Arabic origin that formed the "first and most propaedeutic sequence of texts to be used in university medical teaching" in Europe throughout the later Middle Ages (O'Boyle 1998, 7). From the end of the thirteenth century onwards, Mesue's *Aphorisms* sometimes appear together with a commentary attributed to a certain Isidore. That this commentary was composed no earlier than the second quarter of the thirteenth century has been suggested on the basis of its sources, which include a number of Aristotelian works known in Europe only in the later medieval period. Mesue's *Aphorisms*, both with and without the commentary by Isidore, enjoyed particular success in Ireland, where they were supplemented by additional glosses and commentary in Irish: a feature that is seemingly unparalleled in other vernacular written traditions (Jacquart and Troupeau 1980, 18–20).

The Irish commentary to Mesue's *Aphorisms* analyses the very first line of the text's prologue, which consists of a dedication to Mesue's disciple beginning *Liberet te Deus fili amantissime a devio [h]erroris* "God liberate thee, beloved son, from the deviation of error," by invoking the same Aristotelian maxim that we find in the *Auraicept* concerning the relative nobility of teacher versus father in "forming" or "creating" a son. In addition, however, the Irish commentator on the medical text links this idea, as does the scholiast of the *Auraicept*, to the bipartite distinction between "material" and "creative" essence:

> [. . .] *curuib uime sin adubert Iohanes Damasenus co saera Dīa tū á mic cartanaig ō aninmfis an tseacráin, 7 as ē mac tochuis se (?) and sin, .i. in deiscibal, ōir adeir Isidurus isin glūais sō Damasenus curub mō dligis an desicibal grād don magisidir nā dliges an mac grād don atuir, ōir ni tabair an t-atair acht eisi adburda dō 7 do-beir an maigisdir eisi cruthaigthe dō, oir is ūaisle in eisi cruthaigthe nā an eisi adburda, ōir is ī do-beir mogh laburta do neach 7 hegna 7 bēsa inmolta* [. . .]

So that is why Johannus Damascenus says "God liberate thee, beloved son, from the ignorance of error," and he is a son of qualification (?) there, i.e. the disciple, for Isidore says in this gloss from Damascenus that the disciple owes more love to the master than the son owes love to the father, for the father only gives him material being (*eisi adburda*) and the master gives him created being (*eisi cruthaigthe*), for created being is more noble than material being, for it is that which gives a person fitting speech and wisdom and praiseworthy habits. [. . .] (my edition and translation from NLS MS 72. 1. 13, fol. 1ra27–37)

The presence of a nearly identical passage of commentary in both the *Auraicept* and the commentary to Mesue's medical *Aphorisms* need not necessarily indicate direct borrowing from one source to the other; as demonstrated above, the proverb on which it is based appears to have been well known in learned grammatical discourse from the classical period. However, the specific linking of this proverb with the Aristotelian paradigm of the four causes, which is here attributed to the late-medieval commentary on the *Aphorisms* of Mesue composed by one "Isidore," is more striking and could point to a common background and exegetical training for the authors of both the Irish grammatical and medical commentaries in question. It is worth noting, in this regard, that commentaries on collections of medical aphorisms fulfilled a similar function to that served by the accreted scholia of the *Auraicept*: namely, to make a foundational text of the educational curriculum more accessible to students by explaining difficult points using various exegetical strategies. As Aoibheann Nic Dhonnchadha (2000, 218) has observed, one of the earliest datable Irish translations of a Latin medical text, and one of the most widely disseminated in the manuscripts, is a commentary on the *Aphorisms* of Hippocrates completed in 1403. In the absence of any clear indications regarding the scribes and circulation of the surviving witnesses of the Irish commentary on Mesue's *Aphorisms*, however, it is difficult to determine with any certainty whether the authors of that commentary, who were presumably medical scribes or students, might have also been responsible for adding the commentary on "creative" and "material essence" to the longest recension of the *Auraicept*.

GRAMMATICAL LEARNING AND THE EVIDENCE OF IRISH MEDICAL VERSE

The final part of this discussion will attempt to set the examples of "medico-grammatical scholia" considered above in the broader scholarly context of the transmission of *Auraicept na nÉces* among learned families active in Connacht during the later medieval period. Previous studies of the *Auraicept* have chiefly focused on its use by scholars specializing in law, history, and praise-poetry: an emphasis that is unsurprising, given that several copies of the grammar were produced by scribes associated with the influential Mac Aodhagáin legal family based at various locations in what are now Counties Tipperary and Galway (Ahlqvist 1983, 22–28; Kelly 1998, 253), while others can be traced to scholars linked to the school of Seán Ó Dubhagáin, a "noted and prolific historian-poet" from the region of Galway and Roscommon (Ahlqvist, 1983; Ó Muraíle 2018, 222; Hayden 2016a, 2022). As indicated above, students of law, history, and genealogy would have had good cause to avail of a primer that taught the rudiments of both basic grammar and metrics, since knowledge of the latter was useful for composing didactic verse. One might consider, for example, the work of the renowned fourteenth-century Connacht legal scholar, Giolla na Naomh Mac Duinnshléibhe Mac Aodhagáin, whose extant writings include a versified address to a student of law (Nic Dhonnchadha 1989) and a 78-stanza poem on the main principles of distraint (Kelly 2001, 2020). While medical writing in Irish has hitherto largely been associated with the medium of prose, some evidence for Irish-language medical verse does survive in two manuscripts produced by a family of practicing physicians who were closely connected to the Connacht-based scholars of law and history responsible for copying many of the extant witnesses of the *Auraicept*. It is possible that the authors of these didactic medical poems likewise used the grammar to acquire the rudiments of metrical composition and added glosses and commentary to the text as they did so.

The corpus of verse in question is found in a compilation of over 920 remedies and charms for various ailments that are now preserved in two distinct, composite manuscripts in the Royal Irish Academy library in Dublin, namely, RIA MSS 24 B 3 and 23 N 29.[5] The principal scribe of this treatise was Conla Mac an Leagha (*fl.* 1496–1512), who is known from several manuscript sources of the fifteenth and sixteenth centuries to have belonged to the hereditary family of medical practitioners of that name active primarily in the region of north Connacht (Roscommon and Sligo) during the late-medieval period. Although most of the cures in Conla's remedy book take the standard terse prose form typical of medieval *receptaria*, the collection also includes some 43 metrical passages, most of them versified remedies (for editions and translations of some of these, see Hayden 2018, 2019a, 2019b, 2021a). These medical poems are, like the aforementioned verse compositions of the Connacht legal scholar Giolla na Naomh Mac Dúinnshléibhe Mac Aodhagáin, invariably didactic in nature and usually feature some or all of the elements one would expect in a typical prose recipe, that is, the indication and ingredients, followed by some basic instructions for preparation and application (Hunt 1990, 16–22; Carroll 2004). It is possible that Conla Mac an Leagha was not himself the author of all (or even any) of the poems and merely copied them from an earlier source, although stanzas in two poems from the collection invoke the authority of one "Conn Mac an Leagha," who may have been either a living relative or an ancestor (Hayden 2018, 114–115).

The Connacht provenance of this prosimetrical remedy book can be established on the basis of notes added to the text by its principal scribe. Thus in one instance, Conla Mac an Leagha observed that he had copied part of the text while located in the parish of Killaraght in south Sligo, on the border of the medieval kingdom of Magh Luirg in Roscommon (Walsh 1947a, 215–216). Elsewhere, he claims to have been working as a practicing physician in the service of the nearby Mac Diarmada lords (Nic Dhonnchadha 2000, 220, 2019). It has been suggested that Conla's own home may have been located in the barony of Boyle, Co. Roscommon, perhaps in the townland of Greaghnageeragh (Murray 2018, 192; Nic Dhonnchadha 2019). Other marginalia in a separate medical manuscript now in the Kings Inns Library indicate, moreover, that Conla was the brother of Máel Eachlainn Mac an Leagha, who was employed as *ollamh* in medicine to the two Mac Donnchaidh lords in neighboring Ballymote and Tirerill, Co. Sligo (Walsh 1947a, 210) and apparently helped his brother to copy parts of his remedy collection (Nic Dhonnchadha 2019).

The significance of the geographical locale of Conla and Máel Eachlainn Mac an Leagha becomes clear when considered in light of other features of the prosimetrical remedy book that indicate familiarity with the literary training and activities of other learned families active in the region of north Connacht. For example, many of the medicinal cures in the collection are attributed to members of the legendary race of Irish settlers known as the "Túatha Dé," whose activities are well attested in Irish narrative tradition throughout the early medieval period (Hayden 2019a). Mícheál Hoyne (2013) has argued that the principal Irish narrative text in which the Túatha Dé play in a central role, *Cath Maige Tuired*, was re-worked for propagandistic purposes at the end of the fourteenth century by members of the Uí Dhuibhgeannáin family of poet-historians, who were variously based in Castlefore in the parish of Fenagh, Co. Leitrim; in south Sligo; and in the parish of Kilronan in north Roscommon (Murray 2018, 192). Like Conla Mac an Leagha, several members of the Uí Dhuibhgeannáin learned family worked under the patronage of the Mac Diarmada lords of Magh Luirg in Roscommon. For example, the so-called "Annals of Loch Cé" were compiled by Pilib Ballach Ó Duibhgeannáin for Brian Mac Diarmada, chieftain of Maigh Luirg who died in 1592 (Ó Muraíle 2018, 215).

In light of these connections between the medical writings of the Mac an Leagha medical scribes of north Connacht and texts produced by members of other learned families in that same region, it is no doubt significant to note that many of the surviving witnesses of *Auraicept na nÉces* were copied by scribes who were either working under the patronage of lords in that area or for learned families based somewhat further afield who can be shown to have maintained connections with scholarly activities in north Connacht. One of the scribes who contributed to the copying of the most famous extant witness of the grammar, which was found in the fourteenth-century manuscript known as the Book of Ballymote (Royal Irish Academy MS 23 P 12), was Magnus Ó Duibhgeannáin, a member of the aforementioned family of poet-historians associated with nearby Magh Luirg (Walsh 1947a, 1947b). Maghnus appears to have traveled to Ormond either for study or to copy manuscripts in the house of one of the renowned Mac Aodhagáin jurists who were active in the late fourteenth and early fifteenth centuries (Ó hUiginn 2018, 202–203). He also seems to have been in the employ of the Mac Donnchaidh lords in Sligo when the Book of Ballymote was copied for them in the late fourteenth century (Ó hUiginn 2018, 201–204). As noted above, Conla Mac an Leagha's brother Máel Eachlainn served as *ollamh* in medicine to these same Mac Donnchaidh lords about a century later, and therefore may well have been familiar with the contents of their library.

The two main witnesses of the *Auraicept* that were used by Calder for his edition of the longest recension of the grammar—that containing the passage on "creative" and "material" essence—are found in manuscripts copied by scribes associated with the Mac Aodhagáin law school at Park, near Tuam, Co. Galway during the mid-1560s. One of those witnesses forms part of British Library Egerton MS 88, which was written primarily by Domhnall Ó Dubhdábhoireann, an important member of the O'Davoren law school located in the townland of Cahermacnaghten, Co. Clare, in the medieval kingdom of Thomond (Murray 2018, 204; O'Sullivan 1999). Kevin Murray has recently drawn attention to the connections between certain literary texts in the Egerton 88 manuscript and material preserved in the famous north Connacht manuscript now known as Royal Irish Academy 23 N 10, which was written in 1575 in the house of Seán Ó Maol Chonaire in the townland of Ballycummin, north Roscommon (Murray 2018, 195, 203–205). Murray suggested that the Roscommon material from the 23 N 10 manuscript may have been drawn into the ambit of the Mac Aodhagáin legal family at Park in Galway—and therefore the Egerton 88 codex—through the long-standing contacts that existed between the Mac Aodhagáin scholars and a branch of the Ó Maol Chonaire learned family based in Ardchoill (townland of Ardkyle), Co. Clare (Murray 2018, 209 n 56, citing Ó Dálaigh 2008–2009, 59–60). The Uí Mhaoil Chonaire were among the most distinguished learned families of medieval Ireland and had resided chiefly in Roscommon, where "from the twelfth century they provided historians, chroniclers and master poets to the O'Conors, the McDermots [= Meic Dhiarmada, probable patrons of Conla Mac an Leagha] and other leading families of Connacht."

It is thus clear that the Mac an Leagha medical scribes who worked primarily in north Connacht during the late fifteenth and early sixteenth centuries were closely connected to other learned families from that region who were involved in producing copies of the *Auraicept*, including the two main witnesses to the longest recension of the text. Although it is not possible to determine precisely at what point the anatomically themed scholia and the medico-philosophical passage on creative and material essence made their way into the grammar's accreted commentary, the survival of a substantial quantity of medical verse composed and copied by members of the Mac an Leagha family suggest that those scribes would have had good reason to use a text like the *Auraicept* in the course of their elementary training in literacy and metrics. While it is tempting to suggest that this was where the scholia in question originated, it should however also be noted that there is other evidence pointing to the convergence of Irish medical writing with the manuscript transmission of the *Auraicept* outside the immediate remit of the Mac an Leagha scribal family. For example, TCD MS E 3. 3 (1432), a manuscript written in the fifteenth or sixteenth century by Diarmuid Ó Dubhugáin, contains copies of both *Auraicept na nÉces* and the Irish translation of the *Rosa Anglica*, a medical work completed by the Oxford physician John of Gaddesden in the first decade of the fourteenth century (Hayden 2022; on the manuscripts of the Irish *Rosa Anglica*, see Wulff 1929 and Nic Dhonnchadha 2016). Similarly, of the three extant copies of a short, anonymous commentary on the Latin word *magister* that I have recently identified, one is written on a pair of vellum slips preserved within a copy of the *Auraicept* in TCD MS H 4. 22 (1363), while the other two are found in manuscripts that are otherwise almost entirely medical in content but have no obvious connection to the Mac an Leagha family (Hayden 2017). While the precise origins of the grammatical scholia discussed in this first half of this contribution remain elusive, therefore, it can nonetheless be argued that the extant manuscript record of the *Auraicept* points more broadly to the inclusion of medical scholars in the later transmission of the text.

This article has aimed to set out some evidence to suggest that Irish medical scribes of later medieval Ireland, like historians or lawyers, may have used *Auraicept na nÉces* as part of their rudimentary training in literacy and metrics and contributed to its accreted commentary. Close examination of this scholia reveals features that not only challenge the relatively established perception of the work as a strictly early medieval text but also indicate a degree of continuity with commentaries on works belonging to the realm of late-medieval medicine, such as the collection of *Aphorisms* attributed to John Mesue. Much modern scholarship on the medieval Irish medical manuscripts has tended, with good reason, to emphasize the indebtedness of

Irish medical scribes to continental sources and educational trends (see, e.g., Shaw 1961; Binchy 1966, 5). Several more recent contributions to the subject have, however, also begun to paint a more nuanced picture of Irish scholars' reception and adaptation of these sources on a local level (see, e.g., Ní Shéaghdha 1984; Nic Dhonnchadha 2006, 2016; Harris 2016; Hayden 2019a, 2021b). These studies have important implications for how we understand the educational background of Irish medical scribes, who evidently could receive quite a good education at home. One might think, for example, of the sixteenth-century Ossory physician and prolific translator Donnchadh Óg Ó Conchubhair, who is described in one medical manuscript as "the best of the doctors of Ireland in his own time," though "he never left Ireland to study" (Nic Dhonnchadha 2000, 217). It can be argued that much more detail regarding the nature of the education that figures like Donnchadh Óg or members of the Mac an Leagha medical kindred might have received within Ireland can still be uncovered, not only by exploring some of the as-yet unpublished medical texts but also by re-visiting the contents of better-known works from a different genre, such as the grammatical compilation *Auraicept na nÉces*.

NOTES

1. Previous versions of this chapter were delivered as part of the Fourteenth International Congress on the History of the Language Sciences at the Université Sorbonne-Nouvelle—Paris 3 on August 31, 2017, and the annual Tionól of the Dublin Institute for Advanced Studies on November 2, 2018. I am grateful to members of the audiences at those events for their helpful feedback and to Paul Russell for reading a draft of the written version; I alone am responsible for any errors or shortcomings that may remain. I wish to dedicate this chapter to the memory of Professor Anders Ahlqvist, who was present in body at ICHoLS XIV and in spirit at the 2018 DIAS Tionól: unbeknownst to me on the former occasion, the subject-matter of this paper was to be among the last of many conversations we had about the *Auraicept* over the course of the nine years that preceded his unexpected death in August 2018. Professor Ahlqvist was a chief inspiration for my long-standing interest in the medieval Irish grammatical tradition and an unfailingly generous mentor and colleague to whom my work owes a great debt.

2. On the rationale underlying the medieval etymological method used in the *Auraicept* and related texts, see, e.g., Moran 2020.

3. See www.dil.ie, s.v. 1 *alt* (dil.ie/3016, last accessed November 3, 2021) and Hayden 2014.

4. Calder translates the word *uadh* (the genitive singular form of Ir. *aí*) as "science," but a better rendering might be "poetic inspiration, learning; metrical composition": see www.dil.ie, s.v. 2 *aí* (dil.ie/715, last accessed November 9, 2021).

5. Nic Dhonnchadha (2019) has demonstrated that some of the leaves of this treatise became separated from their original codex at an unknown point in its

transmission, with the result that the 32 vellum leaves comprising the majority of the text are still found in their original location (RIA MS 24 B 3 [445], pp. 33–[90], 90a, 90b and 91–3), while a further eight paper leaves are now bound up as part of a second, composite codex, namely R.I.A., MS 23 N 29 (467), ff 1–4 and 6–9. She established the correct collation of these leaves as follows: RIA MS 24 B 3 (445), pp. 33–70 + RIA MS 23 N 29 (467), ff. 1–4 + RIA MS 24 B 3 (445), pp. 71–4 + RIA MS 23 N 29 (467), ff. 6–9 + RIA MS 24 B 3 (445), pp. 75–93. For an edition and translation of one full chapter of this remedy book, see Hayden (2021b).

REFERENCES

Ahlqvist, Anders. 1983. *The Early Irish Linguist: An Edition of the Canonical Part of the Auraicept na n-Éces, With Introduction, Commentary and Indices*. Commentationes Humanarum Litterarum 73. Helsinki: Societas Scientiarum Fennica.

Binchy, Daniel. 1966. "Bretha Déin Chécht." *Ériu* 20: 1–66.

Bisagni, Jacopo. 2019. *Amrae Coluimb Chille: A Critical Edition*. Dublin: Dublin Institute for Advanced Studies.

Boyle, Elizabeth. 2017. "The Forms and Functions of Medieval Irish Poetry and the Limitations of Modern Aesthetics." In *Translating Early Medieval Poetry for the Twenty-First Century: Transformation, Reception, Interpretation*, edited by Tom Birkett and Kirsty March Lyons, 92–108. Woodbridge: Boydell and Brewer.

Breatnach, Liam. 1996. "Poets and Poetry." In *Progress in Medieval Irish Studies*, edited by Kim McCone and Katherine Simms, 65–77. Maynooth: Department of Old Irish, St. Patrick's College.

Burnyeat, Abigail. 2007. "The Early Irish *Grammaticus*?" *Aiste* 1: 181–217.

Calder, George. 1917. *Auraicept na nÉces: The Scholars' Primer*. Edinburgh: John Grant.

Carroll, Ruth. 2004. "Middle English Recipes: Vernacularisation of a Text-Type." In *Medical and Scientific Writing in Late Medieval English*, edited by Irma Taavitsainen and Päivi Pahta, 174–191. Cambridge: Cambridge University Press.

Falcon, Andrea. 2015. "Aristotle on Causality." In *The Stanford Encyclopedia of Philosophy* (Spring 2015 Edition), edited by Edward N. Zalta. Accessed 18 February 2019. https://plato.stanford.edu/archives/spr2015/entries/aristotle-causality/.

Greene, David. 1952. "Middle Quantity in Irish." *Ériu* 16: 212–218.

Harris, Jason. 2016. "Latin Learning and Irish Physicians, *c.* 1350—*c.* 1610." In *Rosa Anglica: Reassessments*, edited by Liam P. Ó Murchú. Irish Texts Society Subsidiary Series 28, 1–25. London: Irish Texts Society.

Hayden, Deborah. 2014. "Anatomical Metaphor in *Auraicept na nÉces*." In *Authorities and Adaptations: The Reworking and Transmission of Textual Sources in Medieval Ireland*, edited by Elizabeth Boyle and Deborah Hayden, 23–61. Dublin: Dublin Institute for Advanced Studies.

Hayden, Deborah. 2016a. "Cryptography and the Alphabet in the 'Book of Ádhamh Ó Cianáin'." In *Grammatica, Gramadach and Gramadeg: Vernacular Grammar and Grammarians in Medieval Ireland and Wales*, edited by Deborah Hayden and

Paul Russell. Studies in the History of the Language Sciences 125, 35–64. Amsterdam/Philadelphia: John Benjamins.

Hayden, Deborah. 2016b. "Observations on the 'Doors of Death' in a Medieval Irish Medical Catechism." In *Rosa Anglica: Reassessments*, edited by Liam P. Ó Murchú. Irish Texts Society Subsidiary Series 28, 26–56. London: Irish Texts Society.

Hayden, Deborah. 2017. "A Medieval Irish Commentary on the *Magister*." *Celtica* 29: 90–108.

Hayden, Deborah. 2018. "Three Versified Medical Recipes Invoking Dían Cécht." In *Fír Fesso: A Festschrift for Neil McLeod,* edited by Anders Ahlqvist and Pamela O'Neill. Sydney Series in Celtic Studies 17, 107–123. Sydney: Celtic Studies Foundation, University of Sydney.

Hayden, Deborah. 2019a. "Attribution and Authority in a Medieval Irish Medical Compendium." *Studia Hibernica* 45: 19–51.

Hayden, Deborah. 2019b. "A Versified Cure for Headache and Some Lexicographical Notes." *Keltische Forschungen* 8: 7–22.

Hayden, Deborah. 2021a. "Medieval Irish Medical Verse in the Nineteenth Century: Some Evidence From Material Culture." *Irish Historical Studies* 45(168): 1–19.

Hayden, Deborah. 2021b. "A Sixteenth-Century Irish Collection of Cures for Ailments of the Male Reproductive Organs." *Celtica* 33: 248–276.

Hayden, Deborah 2022. "*Auraicept na nÉces* and the Study of Language in the Book of Uí Mhaine: Textual Transmission and Scribal Context." In *The Book of Uí Mhaine/Leabhar Uí Mhaine,* edited by Elizabeth Boyle and Ruairí Ó hUiginn. Dublin: Royal Irish Academy.

Hicks, R. D. 1959. *Diogenes Laertius. Lives of Eminent Philosophers, Volume 1 (Books 1–5)*. Cambridge, MA: Harvard University Press.

Hofman, Rijcklof. 2013. "Latin Grammars and the Structure of the Vernacular Old Irish *Auraicept na nÉces*." In *Spoken and Written Language: Relations Between Latin and the Vernacular Languages in the Earlier Middle Ages,* edited by Mary Garrison, Arpad P. Orbán, and Marco Mostert. Utrecht Studies in Medieval Literacy 24, 185–198. Turnhout: Brepols.

Hoyne, Mícheál. 2013. "The Political Context of *Cath Muighe Tuireadh*, the Early Modern Irish Version of the Second Battle of Magh Tuireadh." *Ériu* 63: 91–116.

Hunt, Tony. 1990. *Popular Medicine in Thirteenth-Century England*. Cambridge: D. S. Brewer.

Irvine, Martin. 1994. *The Making of Textual Culture. 'Grammatica' and Literary Theory 350–1100*. Cambridge: Cambridge University Press.

Jacquart, Danielle, and Gérard Troupeau. 1980. *Le livre des axiomes médicaux (Aphorismi), Yūhannā ibn Māsawayh [Jean Mesue]: Édition du texte arabe et des versions latines avec traduction française et lexique*. Hautes études orientales 14. Genève: Droz.

Kelly, Fergus. 1998. *A Guide to Early Irish Law*. Early Irish Law Series 3. Dublin: Dublin Institute for Advanced Studies.

Kelly, Fergus. 2001. "Giolla na Naomh Mac Aodhagáin: a Thirteenth-century Legal Innovator." In *Mysteries and Solutions in Irish Legal History,* edited by D. S. Greer and N. M. Dawson, 1–14. Dublin: Four Courts Press.

Kelly, Fergus. 2002. "Texts and Transmissions: The Law-Texts." In *Ireland and Europe in the Early Middle Ages: Texts and Transmission*, edited by Próinséas Ní Chatháin and Michael Richter, 230–242. Dublin: Four Courts Press.

Kelly, Fergus. 2020. *The MacEgan Legal Treatise*. Dublin: Dublin Institute for Advanced Studies.

Lambert, Pierre-Yves. 2003. "Les *differentiae* dans la littérature irlandaise ancienne." In *La tradition vive: mélanges d'histoire des textes en l'honneur de Louis Holtz*, edited by Pierre Lardet. *Bibliologia* 20, 107–118. Turnhout: Brepols.

Luft, Diana, ed. 2020. *Medieval Welsh Medical Texts Volume I. The Recipes*. Cardiff: University of Wales Press.

Mac Cárthaigh, Eoin. 2014. *The Art of Bardic Poetry: A New Edition of Irish Grammatical Tracts I*. Dublin: Dublin Institute for Advanced Studies.

McManus, Damian. 2004. "The Bardic Poet as Teacher, Student and Critic: A Context for the Grammatical Tracts." In *Unity and Diversity*, edited by Cathal G. Ó hAinle and Donald E. Meek. Léann na Tríonóide/Trinity Irish Studies 1, 97–123. Dublin: The School of Irish, Trinity College Dublin.

Minio-Paluello, L. 1952. "Iacobus Veneticus Grecus: Canonist and Translator of Aristotle." *Traditio* 8: 265–304.

Moran, Pádraic. 2020. "Comparative Linguistics in Seventh-Century Ireland: *De origine scoticae linguae*." *Language & History* 63(1): 3–23.

Murray, Kevin. 2018. "The Late Medieval Irish-Language Manuscript Tradition in North Roscommon: The Case of Royal Irish Academy MS 23 N 10." In *Roscommon History and Society: Interdisciplinary Essays on the History of an Irish County*, edited by Richie Farrell, Kiaran O'Conor, and Matthew Potter, 191–209. Dublin: Geography Publications.

Ní Dhonnchadha, Máirín. 1989. "An Address to a Student of Law." In *Sages, Saints and Storytellers: Celtic Studies in Honour of Professor James Carney*, edited by Donnchadh Ó Corráin, Liam Breatnach, and Kim McCone. Maynooth Monographs 2, 159–177. Maynooth: An Sagart.

Ní Shéaghdha, Nessa. 1984. "Translations and Adaptations into Irish." *Celtica* 16: 107–124.

Nic Dhonnchadha, Aoibheann. 2000. "Medical Writing in Irish." *Irish Journal of Medical Science* 169(3): 217–220.

Nic Dhonnchadha, Aoibheann. 2006. "The Medical School of Aghmacart, Queen's County." *Ossory, Laois and Leinster* 2: 11–43.

Nic Dhonnchadha, Aoibheann. 2016. "The Irish *Rosa Anglica*: Manuscripts and Structure." In *Rosa Anglica: Reassessments*, edited by Liam P. Ó Murchú. Irish Texts Society Subsidiary Series 28, 114–197. London: Irish Texts Society.

Nic Dhonnchadha, Aoibheann. 2019. "An Irish Medical Treatise on Vellum and Paper From the 16th Century." In *Paper and the Paper Manuscript: A Context for the Transmission of Gaelic Literature*, edited by Pádraig Ó Macháin, 111–125. Cork: Cló Torna.

O'Boyle, Cornelius. 1998. *The Art of Medicine. Medical Teaching at the University of Paris, 1250–1400*. Leiden: Brill.

Ó Dálaigh, Brian. 2008–2009. "The Uí Mhaolchonaire of Thomond." *Studia Hibernica* 35: 45–68.

O'Grady, S. H. 1926. *Catalogue of Irish Manuscripts in the British Library [Formerly British Museum], Volume 1*. London: British Museum. Reprinted Dublin: Dublin Institute for Advanced Studies, 1992.

Ó hUiginn, Ruairí. 2018. "The Book of Ballymote: Scholars, Sources and Patrons." In *Book of Ballymote*, edited by Ruairí Ó hUiginn, Codices Hibernenses Eximii 2, 191–220. Dublin: Royal Irish Academy.

Ó Muraíle, Nollaig. 2018. "The Gaelic Heritage of County Roscommon." In *Roscommon History and Society: Interdisciplinary Essays on the History of an Irish County*, edited by Richie Farrell, Kieran O'Conor, and Matthew Potter, 211–239. Dublin: Geography Publications.

O'Sullivan, William. 1999. "The Book of Domhnall Ó Duibhdábhoireann, Provenance and Codicology." *Celtica* 23: 276–299.

Poppe, Erich. 1996. "Die mittelalterliche irische Abhandlung *Auraicept na nÉces* und ihr geistesgeschichtlicher Standort." In *Theoirie und Rekonstruktion. Trierer Studien zur Geschichte der Linguistik*, edited by K. D. Dutz and H.-J. Niederehe, 55–74. Munster: Nodus.

Poppe, Erich. 1999. "Latinate Terminology in *Auraicept na n-Eces*." In *History of Linguistics 1996, Volume 1: Traditions in Linguistics Worldwide*, edited by David Cram, Andrew Linn, and Elke Nowak, 191–201. Amsterdam/Philadelphia: John Benjamins.

Poppe, Erich. 2002. "The Latin Quotations in *Auraicept na nÉces*: Microtexts and Their Transmission." In *Ireland and Europe in the Early Middle Ages. Texts and Transmission*, edited by Próinséas Ní Chatháin and Michael Richter, 296–312. Dublin: Four Courts Press.

Russell, Paul. 2014. "*In aliis libris*: Adaptation, Re-Working and Transmission in the Commentaries to *Amra Choluim Chille*." In *Authorities and Adaptations: The Reworking and Transmission of Textual Sources in Medieval Ireland*, edited by Elizabeth Boyle and Deborah Hayden, 63–93. Dublin: Dublin Institute for Advanced Studies.

Russell, Paul. 2020. "Distinctions, Foundations and Steps: The Metaphors of the Grades of Comparison in Medieval Latin, Irish and Welsh Grammatical Texts." *Language and History* 63(1): 47–72.

Shaw, Francis. 1940. "Medieval Medico-Philosophical Treatises in the Irish Language." In *Essays and Studies Presented to Professor Eoin MacNeill*, edited by John Ryan, 144–157. Dublin: Sign of the Three Candles.

Shaw, Francis. 1961. "Irish Medical Men and Philosophers." In *Seven Centuries of Irish Learning, 1000–1700*, edited by Brian Ó Cuív, 75–86. Dublin: Stationery Office.

Simms, Katherine. 2007. "The Poetic Brehon Lawyers of Early Sixteenth-Century Ireland." *Ériu* 57: 121–132.

Sluiter, Ineke. 2010. "Textual Therapy: On the Relationship Between Medicine and Grammar in Galen." In *Hippocrates and Medical Education. Selected Papers Read at the XIIth International Hippocrates Colloquium, Universiteit Leiden, 24–26 August 2005*, edited by H. F. J. Horstmanshoff, 25–52. Leiden: Brill.

Thorndike, Lynn. 1923–1958. *A History of Magic and Experimental Science During the First Thirteen Centuries of Our Era*, 8 vols. New York and London: Columbia University Press.
Tredennick, H. 1933. *Aristotle: The Metaphysics, Books I–IX*. Loeb Classical Library 271. London: William Heinemann.
Walsh, Paul. 1947a. "An Irish Medical Family—Mac an Leagha." In *Irish Men of Learning*, edited by Colm Ó Lochlainn, 206–218. Dublin: Sign of the Three Candles.
Walsh, Paul. 1947b. "The Books of the O Duigenans." In *Irish Men of Learning*, edited by Colm Ó Lochlainn, 13–24. Dublin: Sign of the Three Candles.
Warren, E. W. 1975. *Porphyry the Phoenician. Isagoge*. Toronto: The Pontifical Institute of Mediaeval Studies.
Wulff, Winifred, ed. 1929. *Rosa Anglica seu Rosa Medicinae Johannis Anglici: An Early Modern Irish Translation of a Section of the Mediaeval Medical Text-Book of John of Gaddesden*. Irish Texts Society 25. London: Simpkin, Marshall Ltd.

III

GLOSSES AND LINGUISTICS

7
Dry-point Grammatical Glosses
Andreas Nievergelt

INTRODUCTION

This chapter deals with a special subset of medieval glosses, dry-point grammatical glosses, which are grammatical glosses not inscribed with pen and ink but instead scratched on the document with colorless instruments using dry-point technique. Grammatical dry-point glosses are thus characterized on the one hand by a certain glossing function and on the other by a certain inscriptional technique. From a theoretical perspective, they share with grammatical ink glosses the problem of definition: What actually is a grammatical gloss? However, they deserve special attention because they show some peculiarities due to the abbreviatory methods they exhibit. The still unresolved functional questions concerning the practice of dry-point writing—the motivation for a technique with such a low readability—are not specific to grammatical glossing.

In the following, I will highlight those peculiarities which distinguish dry-point grammatical glosses both from grammatical ink glosses and from non-grammatical dry-point glosses. What is of special interest here is the question of whether particular frameworks of medieval engagement with grammar become visible in this corpus of glosses. The prospects for this are very poor, because a comprehensive answer cannot be achieved based on current research. As it stands now—apart from the research on dry-point glosses in East Asia—grammatical dry-point glosses as a separate type have so far only been recognized within research on Old High German glossed materials. In other European philological traditions, research is lacking. As far as Europe is concerned, I will therefore try to outline the current state of research. To this end, I will first briefly introduce the phenomenon of grammatical glosses in the following section, then the phenomenon of medieval dry-point glossing.

Following, I will provide an overview of the relevant gloss material, discuss the differences between grammatical dry-point glosses and grammatical ink glosses, and deal with pragmatic backgrounds which the dry-point grammatical glosses might refer to. All instances which I later consider in detail concern Old High German glosses.

THE PHENOMENON OF GRAMMATICAL GLOSSES

The term *grammatical gloss* has been developed in functional gloss research. In functional terms, grammatical glosses are glosses explaining grammatical features of the glossed word, the *lemma*. The questions and issues of terminology and the latter's history have been previously dealt with in an article on the Old High German grammatical glosses (Nievergelt 2021). In this section, I would like to review the key points from the above-mentioned article.

There are different views among researchers as to what can be described as a grammatical gloss, such as whether non-verbal grammatical explanations are to be classified (or identified) as grammatical glosses. Another point of discussion is whether grammatical (read morphological) glosses can be separated from syntactic glosses. The different points of view are based on the use of different definitions of *gloss*. In research on monolingual glossing, the term *gloss* is usually broader than in bilingual material and sometimes extends to a very general concept of annotation. This has resulted in different typological classifications.[1]

Typologies developed in medieval Latin philology cannot be easily applied to bilingual vernacular glossing.[2] In the earliest research on Old High German glosses, the glossing type currently considered to be grammatical glosses was not initially characterized as such (Glaser 1994, 189). However, as soon as scholarship recognized that the vernacular practice could only be understood on the basis of the Latin practice, that view changed (Stricker 2009, 21–22, with further literature). As a result, the notion of a *grammatical gloss* was also introduced into research on vernacular glosses (Henkel 2009, 483; Nievergelt 2021, 94). The difficulty in separating grammatical from syntactic glosses is often overcome by using the collective term *morphosyntactic* glosses (Cinato 2015, 217, 229; Glaser 2003, 10–11).

The idea of a purely grammatical gloss turned out to be impractical in the case of the Old High German material. As word forms, glosses convey multiple types of information simultaneously and can be used both lexically and morphosyntactically. As for their intention, this leaves them open to different interpretations (Ernst 2007, 554). If one wants to adhere to a systematic use of the term *grammatical gloss*, a *purely* grammatical gloss must be exclusively metalinguistic and must not result from a translation.

Western medieval grammatical glosses do not differ externally from glosses assuming other functions, but they differ strikingly from grammatical notation systems used in the early Japanese and Korean glossing practices.[3] The Old Irish commentary glosses do not have counterparts among the Old High German glosses, nor do we find symbols marking parts of speech or terms for metalinguistic explanation. The most typical grammatical glosses are shortened glosses, which consist of word endings (Nievergelt 2016, 230, inter alia). Occasionally, in research on glosses, the term "grammatical glosses" has been—wrongly—applied to this type (cf. Voetz 1987).[4]

Forms of Grammatical Glossing

Grammatical information can be rendered by means of metalinguistic terms. In Latin glosses, we find information on case, part of speech, grammatical gender, and so on, for example, *ablativus* (also abbreviated as *abl.*), *adverbium*, *femininum*, and so on (Wieland 1983, 49–50; Schiegg 2015, 101). As far as the vernacular languages are concerned, comparable terms were developed in Old Irish.[5] In his Old English-Latin *Grammatica anglicę*, Ælfric coined Old English grammatical terms, but I am unaware of a manuscript that exemplifies the use of Ælfric's terms in Old English grammatical glosses. In the Old High German tradition, a single list of grammatical terms has survived, but these are most likely translations of corresponding Latin metalinguistic terms used for explanatory purposes, rather than reflecting actual Old High German terminology (Nievergelt 2013, 110–111, inter alia). This is suggested by the fact that these terms were never used for Old High German grammatical glossing.

A common form for grammatical glossing is detached inflectional morphemes: verbal endings such as Latin *bat* or Old High German *ta* used to indicate the past tense (Ernst 2009, 303–305, 310–315). Similarly, mode, gender, and so on are rendered by inflectional morphemes. When these are interpreted not as shortened word forms but as merographs, they explicitly function as grammatical glosses. A core stock is formed from unambiguous endings such as Latin *bat*, *bant*, or OHG *ta*, also in opposition to OHG *ti* for the subjunctive. See for example the glosses *perterruit—ta*, *deberet—ti* (Mayer 1974, 59, 64; Nievergelt 2016, 223; Nievergelt 2017, 290, n. 17. Cf. also Nievergelt 2021, 100–101). In Old High German, these endings are taken from the unambiguous weak verb inflections. The same method can be seen in *nt* (or *t*) and *n* used to indicate the mode of the third pl. present. For OHG masculine and neuter nouns, the endings of the genitive singular (*-s*) and plural (*-o*) are quite clear, as in the glosses *demonice* (= *daemoniacae*)—*s*, *trium—o* (Mayer 1974, 59).[6]

Other types of incomplete words can be interpreted as grammatical glosses with less certainty, such as prefixes or suffixes like Latin *con*, OHG *gi*, OE *for*, and so on. It is controversial whether they are used to really explain word formation or rather to clarify the syllable structure of Latin words, that is, using a gloss *gi* over *co-* of the lemma *coaevus* to explain that *co* forms a syllable. Glosses that consist of prepositions, pronouns, or interjections ("supplement glosses" in the typology of Blom 2017, 32–34) cannot be clearly classified as grammatical, either. Prepositions such as OHG *mit* can point to case, and pronouns to gender, person, case, or number.[7] Glossing with (definite) articles seems to be typically vernacular, while glossing with Latin demonstrative pronouns needs to be further investigated as to whether it fulfilled a similar function. However, as vernacular phrases can be behind the use of definite articles, it is difficult to define such glosses as grammatical (Glaser 2000, 198–200). Prepositions can also be shortened phrases: Compare for example the gloss *post dies tres—after drim tagum* (StSG 1,736,45) with the gloss *ordine—after* (StSG 2,630,23).[8]

Grammatical incongruence between the Latin word in the text (*lemma*) and its gloss (*interpretamentum*) may serve as an indication of the grammatical nature of a gloss; such incongruence is not rare in a bilingual situation (Glaser 2009, passim; Nievergelt 2021, 106–107. See for example the gloss *adimitur—noman* (Nievergelt 2019, 185), where a change in glossing strategy must have been obligatory because the language of the gloss did not have the corresponding grammatical category, that is, the Latin synthetic passive form.[9]

THE PHENOMENON OF DRY-POINT GLOSSES

Glosses are constituent parts of a commentary and, like commentaries generally, create secondary texts and are to be contrasted with primary texts. Different types and sizes of script create this contrast, but also the writing technique, and sometimes the use of cryptography.

The fact that the writing of the glosses shows so much formal and technical variation and modification plays a major role in the study of historical vernacular languages. In the entire history of the German language, none of the source genres has shown such a variety in the design of writing as the Old High German glosses. According to this diversity, writing is relevant to historical German linguistics on several levels. The material promises not only answers to questions of scripting but also answers to functional questions where research has so far been in the dark for lack of contextual knowledge and meta-information.

The practical aspects of writing in general have not been studied sufficiently, as can be seen in the field of writing techniques. Quill and ink were used for writing the main text, and the script and writing were defined by the objective of creating a fair copy, usually made from exemplars. Most of the ink glosses too originate from templates; that is, like the main text, they were copied. There was, however, also an alternative to quill and ink for writing on parchment: writing with a stylus,[10] tracing back, in Europe, to writing on wax tablets. The technique is called "dry-point," and the glosses written in this technique subsequently "dry-point glosses."[11] Another technique was writing with mineral pigments. Application of color resulted from abrasion of the coloring material, and one speaks of colored pencils, named for their color: "black pencil" or "brown pencil."[12]

Compared to research into ink glosses, research on stylus glosses and pencil glosses is recent. Old Japanese stylus glosses have been studied in a systematic way for more than 50 years, and ancient Korean stylus glosses for 20 years.[13] In contrast to the Far East, stylus glosses in Western Europe have been known for a long time, resulting in a strong imbalance in the acquisition of materials and in their evaluation.

In Europe, the most advanced research has been in the field of Old High German and Old Saxon. Early research on dry-point glosses in Old English also exists but has been declining in recent years. Research on Old Celtic dry-point glossing offers an unclear picture: The oldest medieval vernacular dry-point gloss is actually an Old Irish one, scratched onto a manuscript from the seventh century (Bischoff 1966, 211. For the manuscript and the glosses, see Ó Neill 1998). Although some other Old Irish dry-point glosses have been mentioned in research, they have been rejected on closer inspection (Bronner 2015, passim). As a result, only a single Old Irish dry-point gloss is confirmed (cf. Ó Cróinín 1995, 193; the gloss is not an explicitly grammatical one), and from the eighth century onwards no others have been detected. Breton examples have not been reported so far (Bronner 2015, 3, n. 6; Studer-Joho 2017, 243–244). Another picture is provided by the likewise sparse Old Slavic tradition, with four isolated manuscripts containing Old Slavic dry-point glosses (none of them explicitly grammatical). Dry-point glosses in Romance Languages have been found only very sporadically. For Old French dry-point glosses, see Porter (1999).

Why were alternative techniques used? What determined the choice of a particular technique? In the production process of a manuscript, alternative techniques had the function of preparing for fair copywriting with a quill and ink (page layout, delineation of text area, ruling were done with a stylus). When a manuscript was used by readers, correctors, scholars, and so on, all three techniques were applied as well: corrections of spelling, text-critical changes, and glosses were added with a colored pencil, a stylus, or a quill. In this process, the stylus and the colored pencil once again were preliminary means before quill writing: in certain scriptoria (e.g., St Gall; see Nievergelt

2013, 62–63) text revision was often carried out using a stylus and only later copied with ink. However, the techniques are also employed independently from each other. This was true in particular for reading aids, punctuation, and prosodic marks—accentuation, word separation, and sentence separation, *litterae significativae* (signs indicating interpretive chant), neumes (musical notation)—which were entered with a stylus. The alternative techniques were used in an autonomous way for glosses. Most of the stylus glosses and colored pencil glosses have nothing to do with the ink glosses of the same manuscript. To which aim a certain technique was chosen is an important question for determining specificities of grammatical dry-point glossing.

GRAMMATICAL DRY-POINT GLOSSES

A comprehensive survey of grammatical glosses written with a stylus is not feasible in the current status of research. On the one hand, dry-point glosses are still generally under-researched, as has been shown in the previous section. On the other hand, they have not been studied to the same extent for each language. There is, for instance, no knowledge of grammatical dry-point glosses in Latin.[14]

Considering the above we may conclude that—apart from Japanese and Korean—grammatical dry-point glosses can be examined only in Old High German, Old Saxon, and Old English. Here, too, the investigation has to be carried out in individual cases. Due to this situation, the following information is based on separate discrete observations and does not present an extensive overview.

THE EXAMPLE OF OLD HIGH GERMAN

The final part of this chapter is based on the study of Old High German glossing. Old High German grammatical dry-point glosses can be divided into two main groups according to their form. The glosses in the first group are conceptually integrated into the complex of merographic or shortened glosses which are, in turn, part of the glossing systems used in the so-called *interlinear versions* (Cf. Voetz 2009, 921). The second group involves complex explanatory techniques and is less explicitly grammatical. Generally, Old High German grammatical dry-point glosses are not to be defined as a group in formal terms, but certain forms occur with conspicuous frequency and in a particularly elaborate layout. Shortening to express a grammatical function is comparatively common. In ink glosses, glossing using definite articles is also quite frequent; however, this only appears in certain manuscripts.[15]

Grammatical incongruence between the Latin *lemma* and the gloss is observed repeatedly in dry-point glosses (Ernst and Nievergelt and Schiegg 2019, 210–214, 440–441, 704). However, glosses in their entirety are far from fully analyzed in this respect.

With regard to abbreviation, a radical reduction is specific to dry-point glosses (Nievergelt 2016, 239). The reduction of inflectional endings, function words, or auxiliary verbs to single letters is found almost exclusively in dry-point glosses. However, radical reduction in dry-point glosses does not only apply to grammatical glosses.[16]

Another remarkable characteristic of grammatical dry-point glosses is the fact that relevant corpora are sometimes systematically grammatical. For example, the Old High German dry-point glosses in Munich, BSB Clm 4542, have clear grammatical characteristics (*BStK online* [Nr. 477], inter alia). Among the abbreviated glosses, dry-point glosses are the most pronouncedly grammatical ones. Some abbreviations reached a sort of conventional status: In the manuscript Munich, BSB Clm 4542, passive forms were systematically designated *uu* or *u*, representing the lexically shortened OHG auxiliary *werdan*. In a similar way, regularity can be observed regarding the formal incongruence between *lemma* and gloss. An example of this is the distinction made between Latin deponent verbs and verbs in the passive by means of glosses based on different types of Old High German passive paraphrases. Compare the gloss *questus es–sochenti uuari* with the gloss *foedaretur–vvari katokan* (Ernst et al. 2019, 109, 113. However, in manuscripts this distinction is not consistent.)

Some word formation suffixes such as OHG *-lîhho* occur as glosses for Latin adverbs, such as glosses like *diuinitus–liho, studiose–liho* (Ernst 2007, 448–449; Mayer 1974, 58). These kinds of glosses are mostly added with a stylus. They have been interpreted as determining the part of speech and thus as grammatical, even though this cannot be proven with certainty.

To get a clearer functional profile, we can compare Old High German dry-point glosses with ink glosses in general, the former being more difficult to discern and to decipher. Examination of dry-point material requires a great deal of time and patience, and many readings remain problematic due to the difficulty in identifying and interpreting them. At first glance, they are often almost invisible, and it is hard to imagine that they could be used by a person other than the glossator. In fact, it appears that dry-point glosses in general were only used by the people who wrote them by themselves. The radical abbreviations mentioned above found only in dry-point glosses may be a sign of their personal use. Such non-standard abbreviations were most probably inaccessible to other readers.

Dry-point glosses could be written almost anywhere. The stylus is a mobile tool, and whereas ink glosses need a fixed and equipped workplace, dry-point entries could be written outside of the scriptorium. While some ink glosses are the work of inexperienced writers, in the case of dry-point glosses, there are no indications that the scribes had any technical problems and it is obvious that no beginners were at work. Furthermore, for dry-point glosses, there is no support for the view that schoolboys or students might have scribbled with a stylus in the manuscripts. There are sometimes errors in ink glosses, which can be explained by the fact that scribes at work copied without understanding, whereas obvious scribes' mistakes, like swapped letters or confusions in the placement of glosses, hardly ever occur in dry-point glosses.

Another feature of dry-point glosses suggests that scribes worked methodically and on their own. Ink glosses usually were copied over from manuscript to manuscript. Using the example of the Weitz glosses, O'Sullivan (2004, 84) shows that even basic Latin grammatical glosses are found repeated in several manuscripts. Dry-point glosses, however, are not part of this tradition of copying glosses, and the overwhelming majority of them do not take part in the circulation of copied glosses. The widely ramified gloss traditions are made up of ink glosses.

All this suggests that dry-point entries represent a separate field alongside the textual production by scribes in the scriptorium. They provide insight into the early scholarly world, the study process of an individual seeking to understand what he is studying and trying to explain it in his own words. We can conclude that the people who inscribed dry-point glosses were most likely not scribes working in the scriptorium copying manuscripts, and certainly not beginners or students. They were instead *literati*—scholars—and their writing reflects their theological, philological, and scientific activity, not primarily communicative and didactic in its character but rather personal, aiming at acquisition, reflection, and verification of knowledge. The study of grammar was obviously an integral part of personal textual study.

Assuming that our interpretation of the occurrence of dry-point glosses is correct, we can be quite sure that the glosses represent ad-hoc recordings of the spoken language: see, for example, the syncopated vowels in prefixes of glosses such as *glassannem, knoz, pfe*, and so on (for standardized *gilazzanem, ginoz, bife*, etc.) in dry-point glosses from Freising (Ernst and Glaser 2009, 1017–1018). Such linguistic material is extremely valuable for historical linguistics. All this leads us to believe that such glosses represent erudite work, written by someone with a scholarly background and therefore with a deliberately developed orthography. In dry-point glosses, we recognize the work of contemporary scholars and their engagement with grammatical questions.

I conclude by formulating a few more observations in this context—at least for Old High German glosses—which still require substantiation through further investigation. Dry-point grammatical glosses—at least in individual manuscripts—show more abstract, systematic, and consistent forms of grammatical glossing than Old High German ink glosses. The abstract formal systems of the grammatical dry-point glosses in Berlin, SBPK Ham. 542, Munich BSB Clm 4542, and Munich BSB Clm 4614—for example, *o* to indicate the genitive plural, or *u* to indicate the passive, or *it* vs. *ti* to distinguish between the indicative and the subjunctive (see above and Nievergelt 2021, 100–101)—have no equivalents in Old High German ink glosses. As far as can be observed, dry-point grammatical glosses are mostly vernacular glossing, suggesting that scholars used them to make personal notes in their own language. Furthermore, it also shows that they developed systems for doing so. Such systems might have been even passed on through instruction.

There is considerable evidence that dry-point grammatical glosses reflect the active study of grammar by scholars. They did not just take occasional notes but tried to develop a notation system for grammatical categories. Perhaps we see direct reflexes of this in the Old High German and Old English *interlinear versions*,[17] otherwise, only sporadic impacts can be seen in ink glosses. Much more will certainly be discovered about this tradition once dry-point glosses have been systematically collected and a comparison with the Latin-Latin tradition of the time and those of other vernacular languages has become possible.

NOTES

1. The basis for typology was formed by the classification of Wieland 1987, 96–97, enlarged and renewed by Stork (1990, 40); Cinato (2009, 432); Cinato (2015, 217, 242–253); and others. Cf. also Schiegg (2015, 104).

2. For the difficulties to adopt the scheme for Old English continuous interlinear versions, see Kornexl (1995, 120).

3. The Old Japanese morphosyntactic glosses (*wokototen*) were marked with a complex system of dots and other similar keys placed around a character. Nakata (1954) arranged the *wokototen* in eight categories. See also Kosukegawa (2012, 2014), Alberizzi (2014, 28–42), inter alia.

4. In Henkel (2001), however, the term "grammatical glossing" is not applied to incomplete words.

5. See, for example, the detailed classification of the Old Irish glosses transmitted by the manuscript St Gall Abbey Library 904 in *St Gall Priscian Glosses v2.0*.

6. Cf. Henkel (2009, 489–490) for the use of the Latin ending gen. pl. *orum* to clarify ambiguous forms. For certain restrictions see Nievergelt 2021, 100–102.

7. See Latin examples in Hellgardt (2009, 410). Old English examples can be seen in Rusche (1994), for example, 205, 209 the gloss *gurgustio—æt*. For relative pronouns see Nievergelt (2008, 78).

8. For interjections, see Nievergelt 2021, 104–105.

9. Cf. the various Old High German passive paraphrases to render the Latin synthetic passive forms or the use of the Dative case for the Latin Ablative. Motivation for such changes in strategy could be compared to the motivation for Japanese inversion glosses (*kaeriten*). For other strategies in the *kundoku* practices in Asia, see Alberizzi (2014) and Zisk contribution in this volume.

10. A selective bibliography: For the stylus technique and dry-point glosses, see Bischoff 1966; Glaser 1996, 49–79; Nievergelt 2007, 41–92; Studer-Joho 2017, 22–61. For the Old High German dry-point glosses see Glaser and Nievergelt (2009), for the Old English dry-point glosses Studer-Joho (2017), for the Old Celtic dry-point glosses Bronner (2015), Studer-Joho (2017, 58–59); for the Japanese dry-point glosses Kobayashi (1989), each citing additional literature.

11. English dry-point is a term derived from printmaking; it is a calque of French *pointe sèche*. In the research literature on Old High German, Old English and Old Irish glosses, the spelling *dry-point* or *dry point* is common. The term "stylus glosses" from the German term "Griffelglossen" now appears also in recent English research literature. It is assumed that the glosses were entered with a stylus. In reality, however, we mostly don't know the concrete tools used. The traces on parchment look quite different, which is why we can presume that completely different types of tools might have been used.

12. We know some individual types according to their materials—for instance the "red chalk" or "sanguine" or other chalks and crayons. But only very seldom do we know what the concrete tools looked like. See Nievergelt (2009, 231).

13. Stylus writing was first studied in Japan by Yoshinori Kobayashi. Stylus writing in Korea was discovered, also by Kobayashi, in 2000 (see Kobayashi 2004; Nam 2006).

14. The Latin dry-point glosses have only been evaluated by experts in a few cases (e.g., McCormick 1992). Those Latin dry-point glosses which are known to us in the majority of cases were edited by the linguists, who investigated vernacular glosses and sought to present the glossing integrally. See, for example, Mayer (1982, 161–163).

15. For the use of definite articles in Old High German glosses, see Glaser (2000) and Ernst (2007, 559–564).

16. They can be found also in the Old High German *interlinear versions*.

17. The so-called "Interlinearversionen" differ from interlinear glosses in that they gloss a text word by word without gaps and play a conceptual role in the layout of the text. Cf. Voetz (2009, 918–926).

REFERENCES

Alberizzi, Valerio. 2012. "Il Kanbun Kundoku nel giappone dall' VIII all' XI secolo." In *La figlia occidentale di Edo. Scritti in memoria di Giuliana Stramigioli*, edited by Andrea Maurizi and Teresa Ciapparoni La Rocca, 25–42. Milano: FrancoAngeli.

Alberizzi, Valerio. 2014. "An Introduction to kunten Glossed Texts and Their Study in Japan." *Les Dossiers d'HEL* 7, supplément électronique à la revue Histoire Epistémologie Langage, Paris, SHESL, 2014, n°7, accessed November 5, 2019.

http://shesl.org/index.php/dossier7-lecture-vernaculaire/intro-kunten-gloss/ [mise en ligne 25/11/2014].

Bischoff, Bernhard. 1966. "Über Einritzungen in Handschriften des frühen Mittelalters." In *Mittelalterliche Studien* I, edited by Bernhard Bischoff, 88–92. Stuttgart: Anton Hiersemann.

Blom, Alderik H. 2017. *Glossing the Psalms. The Emergence of the Written Vernaculars in Western Europe From the Seventh to the Twelfth Centuries.* Berlin/Boston: De Gruyter.

Bronner, Dagmar. 2015. "Dry-Point Glosses in Irish Manuscripts." In *Gloses bibliques et para-bibliques du haut Moyen Âge - Gloses à l'encre et gloses à la pointe sèche*, October 2014, Université Paris Sorbonne, France. halshs-01137740, accessed November 5, 2019. <https://halshs.archives-ouvertes.fr/halshs-01137740>. Submitted 2015.

BStK Online. Bergmann, Rolf and Stefanie Stricker. Datenbank der althochdeutschen und altsächsischen Glossenhandschriften, accessed November 5, 2019. https://glossen.germ-ling.uni-bamberg.de.

Cinato, Franck. 2009. "Les gloses carolingiennes à *l'Ars Prisciani* : méthode d'analyse." In *Priscien. Transmission et refondation de la grammaire de l'antiquité aux modernes*, edited by Marc Baratin, et al., 429–444. Turnhout: Brepols.

Cinato, Franck. 2015. *Priscien glosé. L'Ars grammatica de Priscien vue à travers les gloses carolingiennes.* Turnhout: Brepols.

Ernst, Oliver. 2007. *Die Griffelglossierung in Freisinger Handschriften des frühen 9. Jahrhunderts.* Heidelberg: Winter.

Ernst, Oliver. 2009. "Kürzung in volkssprachigen Glossen." In *Die althochdeutsche und altsächsische Glossographie. Ein Handbuch*, edited by Rolf Bergmann and Stefanie Stricker, 282–315. Berlin, New York: Walter de Gruyter.

Ernst, Oliver, Andreas Nievergelt, and Markus Schiegg. 2019. *Althochdeutsche Griffel-, Feder- und Farbstiftglossen aus Freising. Clm 6293, Clm 6308, Clm 6383, Clm 21525.* Berlin, Boston: Walter de Gruyter.

Glaser, Elvira. 1994. "Glossierungsverfahren früher Freisinger Textglossierung." In *Teoria e pratica della traduzione nel medioevo germanico*, edited by Maria Vittoria Molinari, 181–205. Padova: Unipress.

Glaser, Elvira. 1996. *Frühe Griffelglossierung aus Freising. Ein Beitrag zu den Anfängen althochdeutscher Schriftlichkeit.* Göttingen: Vandenhoeck & Ruprecht.

Glaser, Elvira. 2000. "Der bestimmte Artikel in den althochdeutschen Glossen." In *Zur Geschichte der Nominalgruppe im älteren Deutsch*, edited by Yvon Desportes, 187–213. Heidelberg: Winter.

Glaser, Elvira. 2003. "Typen und Funktionen volkssprachiger (althochdeutscher) Eintragungen im lateinischen Kontext." *Sprachwissenschaft* 28: 1–27.

Glaser, Elvira. 2009. "Formales Verhältnis von Lemma und Interpretament: Formenkongruenz und funktionale Adäquatheit." In *Die althochdeutsche und altsächsische Glossographie. Ein Handbuch*, edited by Rolf Bergmann and Stefanie Stricker, 372–386. Berlin, New York: Walter de Gruyter.

Glaser, Elvira, and Andreas Nievergelt. 2009. "Griffelglossen." In *Die althochdeutsche und altsächsische Glossographie. Ein Handbuch*, edited by Rolf Bergmann and Stefanie Stricker, 202–229. Berlin, New York: Walter de Gruyter.

Hellgardt, Ernst. 2009. "Exemplarische Analyse und Auswertung der lateinischen und althochdeutschen Glossen des Clm 18059 aus Tegernsee (Buch II, Vers 328–377). Oder: Wie man im deutschen Frühmittelalter Vergils Aeneis las." In *Die althochdeutsche und altsächsische Glossographie. Ein Handbuch*, edited by Rolf Bergmann and Stefanie Stricker, 398–467. Berlin, New York: Walter de Gruyter.

Henkel, Nikolaus. 2001. "Verkürzte Glossen. Technik und Funktion innerhalb der Glossierungspraxis des frühen und hohen Mittelalters." In *Mittelalterliche volkssprachige Glossen*, edited by Rolf Bergmann, Elvira Glaser, and Claudine Moulin-Fankhänel, 429–452. Heidelberg, Winter.

Henkel, Nikolaus. 2009. "Glossierung und Texterschliessung. Zur Funktion lateinischer und volkssprachiger Glossen im Schulunterricht." In *Die althochdeutsche und altsächsische Glossographie. Ein Handbuch*, edited by Rolf Bergmann and Stefanie Stricker, 468–496. Berlin, New York: Walter de Gruyter.

Kobayashi, Yoshinori. 1989. "Search of World of Kakuhitsu" (in Japanese). *Sinica* 9: 60.

Kobayashi, Yoshinori. 2004. *Kakuhitsu bunken kenkyūdōron, chūkan. Nihon kokunaihen (jō)* [Introduction to Research on Dry-Point Materials (1), Japanese Materials]. Tokyo.

Kornexl, Lucia. 1995. "The *Regularis Concordia* and Its Old English Gloss." *Anglo-Saxon England* 24: 95–130.

Kosukegawa, Teiji. 2012. *A Conceptual Structure for an Historical Outline of KANBUN KUNDOKU* (漢文訓読)." 富山大学人文学部紀要, 56号. Toyama University: Bulletin Paper, pp. 109–121.

Kosukegawa, Teiji. 2014. "Explaining kundoku in the premodern sinosphere." *Les Dossiers d'HEL* 7, accessed November 5, 2019. <http://shesl.org/index.php/dossier7-lecture-vernaculaire/explaining-kundoku/>.

Mayer, Hartwig. 1974. *Althochdeutsche Glossen: Nachträge—Old High German Glosses: A Supplement*. Toronto, Buffalo: University of Toronto Press.

Mayer, Hartwig. 1982. *Die althochdeutschen Griffelglossen der Handschrift Ottob. Lat. 3295 (Biblioteca Vaticana). Edition und Untersuchung*. Bern, Frankfurt a. M.: Lang.

McCormick, Michael. 1992. *Five Hundred Unknown Glosses From the Palatine Virgil (The Vatican Library, MS. Pal. lat. 1631)*. Città del Vaticano: Biblioteca Apostolica Vaticana.

Nakata Norio. 1954. *Kotenpon no kokugogakuteki kenkyū 1* [Linguistic Research on Old kunten Materials 1]. Tokyo: Kodansha.

Nam, Pung-hyun. 2006. "Hankul ŭi kodae kugyŏl charyo wa kŭ pyŏonch'ŏn e tae hayĕ [On kugyŏl Materials in Early Korean and Its Development]." In *Kukŏsa yŏngu ŏdikkaji wa issnŭon'ga [How Far Has Research on the History of Korean Come?]*, edited by Im Yonggi and Hong Yunp'yo, 615–638. Seoul.

Nievergelt, Andreas. 2007. *Die Glossierung der Handschrift Clm 18547b. Ein Beitrag zur Funktionalität der mittelalterlichen Griffelglosssierung*. Heidelberg: Winter.

Nievergelt, Andreas. 2008. "Relativpronomen in den althochdeutschen Glossen." In: *Historische Syntax und Semantik vom Althochdeutschen bis zum Neuhochdeutschen*, edited by Michel Lefèvre and Franz Simmler, 75–97. Berlin: Weidler.

Nievergelt, Andreas. 2009. "Farbstiftglossen (Rötel-, Braun- und Schwarzstiftglossen)." In *Die althochdeutsche und altsächsische Glossographie. Ein Handbuch*, edited by Rolf Bergmann and Stefanie Stricker, 230–239. Berlin, New York: Walter de Gruyter.

Nievergelt, Andreas. 2013. "St. Galler Schularbeit." In *Althochdeutsche und altsächsische Literatur*, edited by Rolf Bergmann, 106–113. Berlin, Boston: Walter de Gruyter.

Nievergelt, Andreas. 2016. "Kürzungen im Althochdeutschen." In *Variation Within and Among Writing Systems. Concepts and Methods in the Analysis of Ancient Written Documents*, edited by Paola Cotticelli-Kurras and Alfredo Rizza, 223–243. Wiesbaden: Reichert.

Nievergelt, Andreas. 2017. "Glossen aus einem einzigen Buchstaben." In *The Annotated Book in the Early Middle Ages: Practices of Reading and Writing*, edited by Mariken Teeuwen and Irene van Renswoude, 285–304. Turnhout: Brepols.

Nievergelt, Andreas. 2019. *Althochdeutsch in Runenschrift. Geheimschriftliche volkssprachige Griffelglossen. 2., aktualisierte und erweiterte Auflage*. Stuttgart: Hirzel.

Nievergelt, Andreas. 2021. "Die althochdeutschen grammatischen Glossen." In *Indica & Germanica - Beiträge zur Indogermanistik gestern und heute in Jena*, edited by Bettina Bock and Cassandra Freiberg, 93–112. Hamburg: Kovač.

Ó Cróinín, Dháibhí. 1995. *Early Medieval Ireland. 400–1200*. London: Longman.

Ó Neill, Pádraig P. 1998. "The Earliest Dry-Point Glosses in Codex Usserianus Primus." In *A Miracle of Learning*, edited by Toby Barnard, Dáibhí Ó Cróinín, and Katharine Simms, 1–28. Aldershot: Ashgate.

O Sullivan, Sinéad. 2004. *Early Medieval Glosses on Prudentius' "Psychomachia": The Weitz Tradition*. Leiden: Brill.

Porter, David. 1999. "The Earliest Texts With English and French." *Anglo-Saxon England* 28: 87–110.

Rusche, Philip G. 1994. "Dry-Point Glosses to Aldhelm's De Laudibus Virginitatis in Beinecke 401." *Anglo-Saxon England* 23: 195–213.

Schiegg, Markus. 2015. *Frühmittelalterliche Glossen. Ein Beitrag zur Funktionalität und Kontextualität mittelalterlicher Schriftlichkeit*. Heidelberg: Winter.

St Gall Priscian Glosses v2.0, Edited by Bernhard Bauer, Rijcklof Hofman and Pádraic Moran, accessed November 5, 2019. <http://www.stgallpriscian.ie>.

Stork, Nancy Porter. 1990. *Through a Gloss Darkly. Aldhelm's Riddles in the British Library MS Royal 12.C.XXIII*. Toronto: Pontifical Institute of Mediaeval Studies.

Stricker, Stefanie. 2009. "Definitorische Vorklärungen." In *Die althochdeutsche und altsächsische Glossographie. Ein Handbuch*, edited by Rolf Bergmann and Stefanie Stricker, 20–32. Berlin, New York: Walter de Gruyter.

Studer-Joho, Dieter. 2017. *A Catalogue of Manuscripts Known to Contain Old English Dry-Point Glosses*. Tübingen: Narr Francke Attempto.

Voetz, Lothar. 1987. "Formen der Kürzung in einigen alemannischen Denkmälern des achten und neunten Jahrhunderts." *Sprachwissenschaft* 12: 166–179.

Voetz, Lothar. 2009. "Durchgehende Textglossierung oder Übersetzungstext: Die Interlinearversionen." In *Die althochdeutsche und altsächsische Glossographie. Ein Handbuch*, edited by Rolf Bergmann and Stefanie Stricker, 886–926. Berlin, New York: Walter de Gruyter.

Wieland, Gernot Rudolf. 1983. *The Latin Glosses on Arator and Prudentius in Cambridge University Library, MS GG.5.35*. Toronto: Pontifical Institute of Mediaeval Studies.

8

The Pragmatics of Paratextual Paraphernalia

David Cram and Alderik H. Blom

In recent decades, there has been a blossoming of work on the gloss, which has served to establish the pivotal role that glossing has played in the transmission of texts of various sorts both in the Western tradition and elsewhere. This applies most notably in the case of religious texts, where glossing covers a spectrum ranging from an individual lexical gloss to a free-standing discursive commentary. In the Christian West these annotational practices were built on earlier Hebrew ones, also informed by Graeco-Roman grammar and rhetoric.[1] Glossing played a similar role in the transmission of primary texts other than biblical ones, notably legal and medical texts. In the Western legal tradition, there developed large bodies of literature dealing with the wording of statutes themselves on the one hand, and on the other hand the conditions governing their interpretation for judicial application in particular cases—a relation that is broadly parallel to that between biblical text and commentary.[2] Similar processes of accretion and commentary can be seen in the transmission of medical texts, a category embracing the alchemical and pharmaceutical traditions.[3]

The reason for here stressing the importance of hermeneutic scholarship at the level of the three higher disciplines of Theology, Law, and Medicine is that there is a feature of the Western European literary tradition which can deflect attention onto the lower level of the *artes sermonicales* of grammar, logic, and rhetoric. In the Middle Ages, the hermeneutic process of glossing and commentary was primarily conducted within the bounds of one single language, the *lingua franca* of Latin, but, as the various national languages gained scholarly ascendancy in the early modern period,[4] glossing and commentary came to be associated more strongly with the process of translation between Latin and the various European vernaculars. This focus on the European vernaculars has served to foster a large number of academic projects to gather and edit corpora of vernacular glosses, the form in which the earliest records of the modern Indo-European languages are most often preserved, as in the exemplary case of Old Irish.[5] Work on the collective glossaries emerging from individual texts further intersects with research into the various national dictionary traditions (Sauer 2009; Considine 2008, 2017) and also connects with an on-going thread of research into the pedagogy of teaching both Latin and the vernaculars in medieval times (Grafton 1981; Hunt 1991; Wieland 1985).[6] These factors have colluded to focus scholarly attention on the *trivium* at the expense of the larger context of the higher disciplines.

Two further things have enlivened and guided recent work on glossing. One is an academic shift away from studying written records as abstract textual objects and toward studying the manuscript and the book as physical objects in their own right—a perspective that sharpens focus on the graphic relation on the page between text and gloss. The *mise-en-page* of glosses (their interlinear or marginal positioning, their differentiating script and ductus, etc.) is one significant dimension, among others, on the basis of which a typology of glosses can be constructed.[7] It is probably not coincidental that this shift in codicological perspective has been accompanied by another broader shift toward a comparative approach in the study of glossing. This involves comparing and contrasting glossing practices not just within the European vernacular traditions but also between the European traditions and glossing practices elsewhere in the world. For example, the relationship between Latin and the European vernaculars, and its effect on glossing practices, has been thrown into new light by comparison with the parallel relation between Sanskrit as a scholarly *lingua franca* (or "cosmopolitan" language, Pollock 2000) and the various Prakrit vernaculars which are reflexes of it—a dynamic relation which in both cases has given rise to an associated grammatical and hermeneutic tradition (Pollock 2006; Tubb and Boose 2007; Formigatti 2015). A strikingly different type of relation between text and gloss can be documented in cases where a Chinese text written in a logographic script is read off in a typologically quite different language such as Japanese or Korean. This process has given rise to types of glossing devices (e.g., diacritic marks that indicate syntactic as well as lexical-semantic features) which do not neatly coincide with the received Western European categories (Whitman and Cinato 2014; Moran and Whitman forthcoming).[8] In short, the specificity of each of these different glossing traditions has started to emerge more clearly and distinctly as we have come to gain a better global understanding of the underlying hermeneutic processes involved—insights that would not have been accessible without recognition of what Whitman has famously characterized as the "ubiquity" of the gloss (Whitman 2011).

AIMS AND OUTLINE OF THE CHAPTER

The purpose of the present chapter[9] is to suggest that, emerging from the extensive range of descriptive and analytic work on the history of glossing, there are some valuable theoretical points about the linguistic status of the gloss in relation to the text with which it is associated that have hitherto not been explicitly identified and explored. In this first section, we will attempt to formulate some of these ideas with reference to the work of Jean Genette and his notion of "paratext," a framework that has proved to be a fertile one in the context of modern literary theory.[10] It is an odd fact that, in his study of the paratextual elements which surround a text and guide a reader as to how it should be read (such as titles, forewords, epigraphs, and footnotes), Genette does not specifically include the term "gloss."[11] This lacuna is evidence that modern literary theory is not always adequately informed about the longer history of hermeneutic thought of which it is part. Conversely, it also offers one possible reason why those engaged in the study of glossing in the earlier period have not taken full advantage of a modernist notion that is potentially a relevant and useful one.

The notion of paratext has been widely taken up by modern literary commentators, and in that context has proved productive in stimulating new avenues of thinking and new areas of research. One such project is the pioneering two-volume edition of *Paratexts in English printed drama to 1642* by Berger and Massai (2014). We single out this laudable work for comment, however, in order to distance ourselves from one assumption which has crept into the literary consensus, at least in Anglophone circles. In their introduction to the edition, Berger and Massai assert that there was no early modern counterpart to the term "paratext" and that when it is applied to the make-up of early modern books it is used anachronistically. More specifically, they affirm that "[w]hile the names and specific functions of different types of paratexts were already well established, early modern authors and stationers had no term to refer to these texts collectively" (Berger and Massai 2014, xi.) This assertion is not strictly incorrect: indeed there is at this period no *single-word* counterpart to Genette's term "paratext." But it is simply wrong to say that early modern thinkers had no form of words to refer to paratextual paraphernalia collectively. Early modern thinkers were garrulously obsessed with the divide between "naked text" on the one hand and "gloss or comment" on the other, as a few minutes' search using *Early English Books Online* will show.[12] The most frequent usages are in law and theology, where it is important to distinguish between the authoritative text (scriptural or legal) and the gloss or comment which gives the interpretation of an individual word or expression, but discussion extends to commentary and interpretation of all sorts. It can be clearly documented that the collective notion of what we are calling "paratextual paraphernalia" is quite clearly and explicitly expressed in contexts where the notion of what constitutes the "naked" text itself is being explicated: the paratextual paraphernalia are what is removed in order to make the text itself "naked."[13]

One important distinction that Genette draws, and which we think worthy of further elaboration in connection with the gloss, is between what he calls "*peri*-text" and "*epi*-text."[14] These together comprise the context which is relevant for a reader to gain an understanding of an author's intended meaning. But while some of these elements (the *peri*-text) are part of the immediate and manifest context of reading, there may be further *epi*-textual elements that are part of the general cultural background which frames the author's meaning but which are not immediately accessible to a reader from a different cultural context. Thus both the outer boundary of what counts as *epi*-text and also the internal borderline between *peri*- and *epi*-text will depend on the relation between author and reader: modern readers of an ancient Greek epic will need to avail themselves of a wider-ranging paratextual apparatus than an early modern reader would need, and both would need more than an ancient Greek contemporary reader would have done. At first glance, it might seem that the gloss belongs in, or at least is clearly anchored in, Genette's category of *peri*-text, given that it is an immediate part of the physical object of the page (albeit marginal) rather than being a more peripheral and abstract feature of the author's cultural background. But since the function of the gloss is precisely to act as a bridge between a reader's context and that of the author or originator of the text, the gloss does not, on closer inspection, belong *exclusively* to either of Genette's categories. Or, put more strongly, the distinction between *peri*-text and *epi*-text is not part of a well-formed taxonomy in which the gloss has its unique defining place.[15] But this does not mean that the distinction should be abandoned. It means that it must be rethought and redeployed in a way that enables us to target it more precisely if it is to help clarify the status and function of the gloss.

If the gloss is to be assigned a place in Genette's list of paratextual elements,[16] it fits most comfortably under the category of "marginal note." But this only defines it negatively with respect to the text that the margin frames. Although all paratextual elements are essentially marginal, not everything that is written in the margin of a text is paratextual. For example, there may be marginal notes in a book recording the date on which the book was loaned to a reader, or other notes which, even if they are penned by the author of the text, are not relevant to the reader's interpretation of it.[17] To qualify as paratext, a marginal element must "belong" to the text in some sense that is relevant to the interpretation of it: it must be hermeneutically relevant. The notion of "relevance" can be developed in a precise and sophisticated way in the framework of modern pragmatic theory, as we shall see, but the idea is readily accessible in the robust everyday sense of the word.

We have deployed the term "paraphernalia" as a handy general label for the larger set of paratextual elements in which the gloss is included, using the word in its common sense of the variegated set of things associated with a particular area of human activity. As it happens, the etymology of this term includes a technical legal sense which is apposite in the present context. Paraphernalia were historically "articles of personal property, especially clothing and ornaments, which (exceptionally at common law) did not automatically transfer from the property of the wife to the husband by virtue of the marriage" (OED). In other words, the category of paraphernalia covered items which "properly" belonged to a woman, as distinct from her dowry, which became the property of her husband upon marriage and which did not revert to being the property of the widow in the event of her husband's death.[18] We suggest that the legal differentiation between *paraphernalia* and *dowry* offers a useful metaphor for the distinction we are aiming to draw between paratextual paraphernalia on the one hand—the set of explanatory elements that "properly" belong to the hermeneutics of a given text (*scriptura*; a feminine noun, appropriately enough in the context of "paraphernalia")—and on the other hand the open-ended network of inter-textual links that are part of the general cultural backdrop that informs our reading of the text but are not immediately relevant to the process of textual hermeneutics. The metaphor thus offers a conceptual starting point for our reconstruction of Genette's distinction between *peri*-text and *epi*-text, understood in terms of degrees of *relevance* to the text in question.

In our reflections on the gloss as a paratextual element, we aim to avoid projecting modernist ideas anachronistically into areas where they do not comfortably belong. Our purpose is to build up a pragmatic framework to articulate insights emerging from the historical tradition, by comparing medieval perspectives on glossing with those which become dominant in the early modern period. A central point concerns the directionality of the relation between gloss and text, which functions in both directions. On the one hand, the gloss is essentially marginal in the sense that it is not part of the text itself, which is (to use the early modern term) seen as "self-interpreting"; on the other hand, the gloss has the paratextual function of being a doorway or threshold (a *seuil* in Genette's terminology) by means of which readers are guided and informed in their approach to the text. The key point in our analysis is that these two aspects of the gloss (and of paratextual elements more generally) are sides of one and the same coin. The nature of this bi-directionality is the very essence of what makes an element paratextual to a text. From an author's point of view, the defining feature of paratext is that it is peripheral or marginal (in both senses of the word) to the text; from the reader's point of view, however, it is the paratext that commands our reading of the text, rather than vice versa. We hope to supply an analysis that explains how and why the tail wags the dog in this way.

Drawing these various ideas together, we suggest that the pragmatics of paratextual paraphernalia can be explored as follows. In the first part of our analysis, the fundamental features of the relation between text and paratext are identified, using a combination of a medieval perspective (following section), which focuses on the marginality of paratext and its parasitic relation to text, and an early modern perspective (third section), which focuses (paradoxically) on the role of paratextual tools in authorizing the reading of text which is deemed to be "self-interpreting." Text and paratext thus emerge as correlative categories, in such a way that, from a hermeneutic perspective, a primary text (be it theological, legal, medical, or literary) carries with it the assumption that an informed (and/or appropriately catechized) reader will be able to supply a relevant range of glosses or commentary. This dynamic relation between text and paratext is a recursive one, in that sets of paratextual items (commentaries, glossaries) can themselves form independent texts which in turn may generate their own paratextual paraphernalia, as manifested by the "nested" *mise-en-page* of religious and legal texts in both the Latin and Hebrew traditions.[19]

Our hope is that the analysis in the first three sections of the chapter will adequately identify and exemplify the features of paratext that are more formally articulated in the fourth section in terms of the modern pragmatic theory. A fifth section looks more closely at the use of punctuation in legal texts and in the marking of direct quotations. In a brief concluding sixth section, we return to the idea of margins and thresholds and explore these in relation to the notion of the cognitive *frame*, drawing on insights about the cognitive effects of frames and framing that are available from the art-historical tradition.

PARATEXT AS PARASITIC ON TEXT:
A MEDIEVAL VIEWPOINT

The objective of this and the following section is to extrapolate general features of glossing which emerge from the detailed analysis of glossing practices of the sort briefly surveyed above. We believe that some valuable insights can be derived from a comparison of the medieval and the early modern periods in Western Europe, paying particular attention to the underpinning ideas about the *relation* between paratext and text. The relation between gloss and text is a dynamic one and prompts us to think about glosses, and indeed paratext more generally, as a process rather than a static product.

In contrasting a medieval perspective with an early modern one, we are fully aware that we are presenting two idealized constructs which are limiting cases at the end of a nuanced spectrum. But we hope these constructs are built on observations explicitly articulated by the scholars working in the relevant areas. What the two perspectives have in common is the central idea of paratext as marginal to the text to which it belongs. They differ in how that marginality is understood, in ways that might appear to be contradictory but are in fact complementary.

Key to medieval views of the relation between the gloss and the text to which it belongs is that the one is wholly dependent on the other, a notion that can be clarified and elaborated in a number of ways but is crisply articulated by Louis Holtz in an often-quoted formula: "Il existe entre le *texte* . . . et le *commentaire* . . . une hiérarchie naturelle; le second est subordonné au premier, n'existe que par le premier" (Holtz 1977, 257). There is, he says, an essential hierarchy between text and commentary, since the very *raison d'être* of the commentary is the text which it explains. The subordinate status of the gloss can be elaborated in terms of *mise en page*: "La glose va donc se placer *là où l'espace n'est pas rempli*: ce peut être entre les lignes, ou bien en face des lignes, à gauche ou à droite du corps principal du texte, ou encore en haut ou en bas" (Holtz 1977, 258). In other words, the gloss is marginal in the quite literal sense that it is written in places on the page which are empty of text, at either side of the block of text, or above and below it. Glosses can of course also be positioned within the text-block proper, and indeed the interlinear note which gives a vernacular equivalent of a single Latin word is perhaps the paradigm example of the "marginal" note. It was not uncommon for Latin texts to be made with enlarged interlinear spacing already prepared for the insertion of glosses, or a running translation to be inserted by a second hand. But where gloss and text overlap (and where paratextual elements fuse with textual elements, as with the rubrication of initials, functioning as a finding aid), the difference in status is typically marked by a contrast in ink, script, or ductus. It is important that the distinction between gloss and text is thus bidirectional, or as Cinato puts it, in a gloss on Holtz's discussion, there is a double contrast between them.

> Lorsque nous regardons un manuscrit portant des annotations [. . .] nous constatons immédiatement que deux familles d'éléments graphiques coexistent. D'un côté, se trouve un texte littéraire, de l'autre le "péritexte" qui l'accompagne et lui vaut son appellation de "manuscrit glosé." Ces éléments voisins du texte se différencient tant par leur graphie que par leur situation dans la mise en page. Ils provoquent ce "double contraste" décrit par Louis Holtz [1977, 258] qui évite toute ambiguïté entre les deux niveaux. (Cinato 2015, 188)

This double dissociation applies to what one might call the inner boundary which separates paratext from text, and text from paratext—one which needs to be constantly policed as paratextual elements are transmitted by copying alongside the text itself and are in danger of being incorporated into it.[20] But glosses and other paratextual elements also have an outer boundary. As already observed above, the category of marginalia can include various kinds of items not directly relating to the text, being written there simply because the manuscript or book happened to be the nearest thing to hand on which to make a note, or a memorable place to do so. Marginalia of this larger sort may have all sorts of interest relevant to authorship, readership, and literacy, but it is important to distinguish *paratextual* marginalia—elements properly and directly relevant to the interpretation of the text—as a proper subset of marginalia more generally. There can, one should note, be cases where an element straddles the boundary between marginalia in general and paratextual paraphernalia proper but, as with borderline cases more generally, these serve as test cases for the theoretical distinction rather than as rebuttal or negation of it.[21]

Having thus identified an outer limit to paratext—one that distinguishes glosses proper from non-paratextual marginalia—it must also be emphasized that what can count as directly relevant for the explication of a text is in principle open-ended. This is partly because it is contextual, depending on how much the author and reader have in common, and partly because the relation between text and paratext is potentially a recursive one. A paratextual note which makes an obscure text less so for one generation of readers may itself become obscure for a following generation; in this way paratext can itself invite subsequent paratextual glossing, the initial gloss in effect being category-shifted into having itself the status of text.[22] The recursive nature of the relation between text and paratext is made manifest in the Western tradition by the *mise en page* in cases where both religious and legal texts are multiply framed by commentaries in the manner of Russian dolls or Chinese boxes. It is likewise manifest in the Hebrew tradition. It is moreover of theoretical interest that the recursive framing of text with paratext—commentaries themselves generating further comment—can be independently documented in the Sanskrit tradition (Tubb and Boose 2007), and in other traditions in the Far East (Whitman 2011).

For the most part, the various parameters which together constitute what we are characterizing as the medieval view of paratext will also hold true of the early modern view. But there is one thing that marks a watershed between the two, emerging as a defining feature in the late medieval doctrine of biblical commentary exemplified by the Wycliffite tradition.[23] The point is a simple one, and best put in the words of an expert who has done extensive empirical work on glossing in this tradition:[24]

> Monks, friars and secular clergy during the Middle Ages did not consider the Scriptures as auto-exegetical. Indeed they regarded them as replete with both

small and large difficulties. [. . .] The divine text could not stand on its own. It required critical study, by way of commentators. (Kuczynski 2019, xlv).

The Wycliffite approach to textual interpretation and glossing is of course highly distinctive, and there are many ways in which it is unrepresentative of the longer medieval tradition. But as a limiting case with respect to the necessity of paratextual commentary, it is instructive to juxtapose it with a converse early modern view, to which we now turn.

TEXT AND PARATEXT AS CORRELATIVE TERMS: AN EARLY MODERN VIEWPOINT

The early modern view that we seek here to characterize shares the fundamental features of the Western European medieval view. It is distinctive in a way which complements rather than contradicts the earlier view. To use a visual image, where the medieval margin is typically *full*, the early modern margin is typically (or by default) *empty*. There is a stark visual contrast between a Wycliffite bible, with each block of sacred text surrounded by columns of paratextual glossing forming a frame around it on the page, and the early modern "self-explicating" bible, to be typified in a later century by the classic John Brown bible, which explicitly styles itself thus on its title page. But the contrast between these two examples is a nuanced one; both belong in the same longer-term tradition and are closely related variants of a doctrinal principle of "sola scriptura," the idea that the word of God as manifest in the sacred scriptures is fully sufficient for the salvation of the believer. Both viewpoints assume that paratextual work will also be necessary in this process, but there is a limiting case at each end of this spectrum. The medieval text comes with a margin already containing the necessary glosses, which are themselves transcribed when the primary text is transcribed. The early modern self-explicating text, by contrast, comes with a margin that is essentially blank, ready for the current reader's annotations.

A useful analogy here is to visualize paratext as scaffolding erected around a grand building. The status of the scaffolding is twofold. On the one hand, it is necessary for the purposes of inspection and for gaining access to areas of the building otherwise inaccessible; that is its most obvious defining function. On the other hand, the whole point of scaffolding is that it is not a proper part of the building itself; it is made to be taken down, and our view of the architecture is cluttered, or wholly occluded, until it is dismantled. Paratext is in effect textual scaffolding. The medieval view of it focuses on its functional necessity, the early modern view focuses on its essential dismantlability.

The nuances of the early modern view can usefully be pointed up by considering glossing on legal texts, rather than religious ones. In the Western legal tradition, there is an institutional division between the drafting of statutes and their implementation in particular cases.[25] The details of the relevant institutions differ considerably of course between civil and ecclesiastical (canon) law (Maclean 1992). The transition between the medieval and early modern periods marks fundamental changes in the overall structure of civil law, particularly in the way that common law develops in relation to statutory regulation (Plucknett 1922, 1956, 328–336). But the broad parallels between the way legal and religious texts are interpreted nevertheless provide perspectives for the history of glossing which warrant detailed investigation, since the institutional framework for legal proceedings requires explicit formulation of the rules for the interpretation of statutory texts.

These various considerations serve to highlight the fact that central to the early modern view is the idea that text and paratext are *correlative* categories.[26] The definition of the term "text" in the first edition of the *Encyclopaedia Britannica* makes this early modern usage quite explicit. "TEXT, a relative term, contradistinguished to gloss or commentary, and signifying an original discourse exclusive of any note or interpretation" (*Encyclopaedia Britannica* 1771, vol III, 894). From a lexical-semantic perspective, it is not surprising that the unmarked pole is referred to by a single-word term, and the marked pole by a phrasal element, typically in the scope of a negative of some sort (e.g., "without gloss or comment").

In this connection it is worth noting that the term "textbook" did not in the early modern period have its modern sense of a basic introductory study manual for a particular subject area.[27] "Textbook" at that time meant a teaching volume containing the bare text of a prescribed author with margins and interlinear spaces specifically emptied for paratextual annotation by the student. Bailey's English dictionary (1730) thus defines "text" and "textbook" as follows:

> Text, an original Discourse, exclusive of any Note or Interpretation.
> Text-*Book* [in *Universities*] is a Classick Author written very wide by the Students, to give Room for an Interpretation dictated by the Master &c, to be inserted in the Interlines. (Bailey, *Dictionarium Britannicum*, 1730)

Locally printed textbooks of this sort were in widespread use in Germany in the sixteenth century. That this format was not restricted to school usage is indicated by a contemporary account of the printing by Luther of editions to be used by those attending his sermons. These were close readings of biblical texts ("lectures" in the etymological sense of the word), and the response he expected from his congregation was that they should *gloss* them, as a contemporary diarist, Johannes Oldecop (aka Oldekop), reports.

> In the year 1515, on the Monday after Whitsun . . . I Johannes Oldecop came to Wittenberg. . . . And around that time Doctor Martin Luther began to lecture on Paul's Epistles to the Romans. For these purposes the Doctor had arranged with the book-printer Johannes Grunenberg to have Paul's epistle[s] printed, with each line widely-spaced from the next to allow for glossing.[28]

Although some copies of this booklet have indeed been preserved with contemporary annotations,[29] it is in the nature of such locally printed works, produced with inter-lining for the purposes of school use, that they survive either in very small numbers or not at all. Furthermore, like almanacs and other ephemera, there is quite often no record, or only an incomplete one, of their publication. Since the work was commissioned by schools and university teachers for the use of pupils in their charge, the printing was commonly done in-house.[30] Extensive work by scholars on educational "textbooks" of this sort from the sixteenth century onward has however provided a clear enough picture of their widespread usage.[31]

In England, the use of glossing in an educational context can be tracked in connection with the use of shorthand for such purposes. English shorthand systems, which were enormously popular from the late sixteenth century onward, were often marketed with opportunity for note-taking in the margin (or "margent") as a primary advantage of their use. Thus Peter Bales promises his readers that: "you may hereby note in the margent of your booke, more then is conteined in the page: And you may write as much in one day by this briefe Arte, as in a whole weeke by other writing" (Bales 1597, sig. B1 verso).[32] Visitors from the continent report their surprise at the widespread use of shorthand in England, not just in schools but also for the purpose of taking notes during church sermons; one such system published in the early eighteenth century has a frontispiece depicting a church service with members of the congregation taking notes.[33] Charles Darwin's grandfather Erasmus learned shorthand in his first year of study at Cambridge for the purpose of taking notes during lectures and was enthusiastic enough to compose a poem in praise of the system he used, one devised by Thomas Gurney (the elder).[34]

In an educational context, it is also worth mentioning that glossing with inter-lining (German *Durchschuss*), which is pervasive in the medieval manuscript tradition, becomes established in the seventeenth century as a standard method for foreign language learning. John Locke, in his *Thoughts Concerning Education*, describes this procedure as follows:

> INTER-LINING [*as a method for learning Latin, viz.*:] by taking some easie and pleasant Book, such as Æsop's Fables, and writing the English Translation (made as literal as it can be) in one Line, and the Latin Words which answer each of them, just over it in another. These let him read every Day over and over again, till he perfectly understands the Latin. (Locke 1693, 158–159)

This approach subsequently gave rise to any number of varieties of the method, which in the nineteenth century became firmly associated with the name of James Hamilton (1769–1829).[35]

One of the larger developments between the medieval and the early modern period is the gradual emergence and differentiation of a variety of paratextual tools. The commentary and the concordance are well established medieval genres, but some paratextual tools that seem self-evidently distinct categories to the modern reader in fact emerged slowly over several centuries. A case at point is that of the term (and concept) of a "title," in the sense of a unique identifier of a text, as Richard Sharpe has pointed out in an empirical and detailed study designed to alert both academics and library cataloguers to the methodological problems this poses (Sharpe 2005). "Titulus" (and vernacular translations of it) is an early modern term, emerging gradually from the amorphous variety of ways by which a text could be identified and referred to, including "incipits" (first lines) and colophons at the end of a work, giving various types of information about its authorship, transcription, dating, and so on. Before the early modern period, one could not guarantee that any way of referring to a text was a unique identifier; the methodological problem is that catalogues of books cannot be useful and reliable unless texts are systematically assigned names (or some equivalent designator). The emergence of the concept of the "title" is thus an instructive case study demonstrating the interplay between text and paratext, and their correlative status.[36]

What applies in the case of the "title" holds also for other paratextual tools: collections of *distinctiones* (lists of contrasting expressions both lexical and grammatical, see Cram 2003), *catechisms* (as a pedagogical tool for rehearsing paratextual commentary), and a range of study aids employing alphabetical ordering as forms of *index* (Rouse and Rouse 1990). Other tools which are most immediately pertinent to glossing can be broadly grouped together as belonging to the dictionary tradition, which explains the meaning of individual words. To start from an early modern source, Nathaniel Bailey's dictionary (1730) defines the three terms commentary, glossary, and dictionary as follows:[37]

> Commentary [*commentarium*, L.] a continued interpretation or gloss on the obscure and difficult passages in an author to render them more intelligible.
> Glossary [*glossarium*, L.] a Dictionary explaining the hard, obscure or barbarous Words of a Language.
> Dictionary [*dictionarium*, L.] a collection of all the words in a language, or of the terms of art in any science explained and commonly digested in an alphabetical order.

A commentary, in the sense here intended, first arises as a collection of glosses (or *scholia*) on a particular text, but then develops as a separate genre (a kind of text in its own right). It is initially not arranged in alphabetical order, but, by default, in the same order as that of the text. In an early modern context, both the Glossary and the Dictionary are subsequently assumed to be arranged, by default, in alphabetical order. The essential distinction between Glossary and Dictionary is, for Bailey, that the former is restricted in scope to the "hard words" in a given text, and, more specifically, to hard words pertaining to some particular art or science. The Dictionary is differentiated from the Glossary by its scope of coverage: in principle it includes all the words in a given language.

There is a further difference between Glossary and Dictionary for Bailey, one which is immediately relevant for present purposes since it has a bearing on the way individual entries are constructed. A Glossary, for him, gives explanations for each word in context, that is, the specific subsense of that word relevant to the art or science in question, while a Dictionary, by virtue of its global coverage, must necessarily group together the various subsenses of a polysemous word under a single alphabetical entry. The distinction can seem both obvious and trivial but has theoretical ramifications that will be further explored in the following section.

PARATEXTUAL PARAPHERNALIA: A RADICAL PRAGMATIC VIEWPOINT

In the previous sections we have looked at approaches to glossing in the Western European tradition using actors' categories, that is to say, using the terminology employed by the practitioners themselves rather than technical terminology deriving from modern usage. In this and the following sections, we aim to sketch out how these approaches can be usefully rearticulated in the terminology of modern pragmatic theory.

There are various theoretical approaches to pragmatics currently in play. Two of the leading ones are Neo-Gricean Theory, based on the work of the philosopher Paul Grice, and Relevance Theory, developed by Dan Sperber and Deirdre Wilson, an anthropologist and linguist. For present purposes, it is not inappropriate to see both frameworks as alterative developments of Grice's pioneering work in the 1960s, in which he developed a set of four pragmatic maxims (*Quantity*, *Quality*, *Relation*, and *Manner*) that guide the way we understand the meaning of sentences in context. Sperber and Wilson subsequently unified and refined these in terms of a single principle of *Relevance*.[38] These two frameworks give significantly different accounts of how semantic and pragmatic principles interact with each other,[39] but on many foundational issues the two approaches overlap and make the same central assumptions.

Pragmatic theory rests on a fundamental distinction between *sentence-meaning* and *speaker-meaning*, a distinction which is key to what the theory has to say about the function of paratextual paraphernalia. Sentence-meaning—the primary target of semantics—is what a string of words means when considered in isolation; speaker-meaning—the primary target of pragmatics—is what a speaker intends the hearer to understand by a sentence when uttered in some specific context. The way that this division of labor works within the larger scope of linguistic theory can be diagrammed as in figure 8.1.[40]

If human beings were robots, there would be no difference between what a sentence means and what is communicated by uttering it. But in human speech, there can be mismatches in both directions. Speakers can get a message across quite efficiently by saying something other than what they clearly mean, as when they use a word in a metaphorical sense. Conversely, they do so by meaning something other than what they actually say, as when they say something ironically and mean the exact opposite. How people can communicate in these indirect and oblique ways, with full confidence in the ability

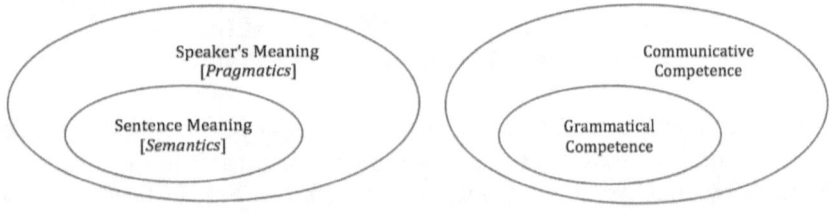

Sentence-meaning vs. Speaker-meaning   Grammatical vs. Communicative Competence

Figure 8.1 The Relation Between Semantics and Pragmatics.

of their addressees to understand their intended meaning, is what the theory of pragmatics seeks to explain.

The same sort of mismatches occur with written language as with spoken language, and there is a clear parallel between the way pragmatic principles account for such mismatches in speech and the way glosses are deployed to explain them in writing. Furthermore, the relation between an author and a reader is seldom an immediate "here and now," as it is in spoken language. It is typically displaced both in space and time, and the greater the displacement between the immediate context of the writer and the immediate context of the reader, the greater the possibility of misunderstanding and the greater the need for glossing.

There are useful classificatory ways in which a pragmatic approach can be applied in the analysis of written glosses. Thus, Markus Schiegg (2016) has produced an exemplary study of medieval glosses, using the framework of Speech Act Theory.[41] Schiegg's analysis identifies cases where a string of words in the text (a "locutionary act" in written form) is explained by a medieval gloss as having a functional meaning (an "illocutionary" force) over and above what the words literally mean, in ways that can be classified using the set of speech act categories developed by John Searle (1969). This is precisely the sort of study to which pragmatic theory opens the way and which can bring new classificatory applications in its train. However, there are ways in which more recent pragmatic thinking has moved beyond Speech Act Theory in a general direction sometimes labeled as "radical pragmatics," which we think is of particular relevance to the process of glossing. Speech Act Theory generally assumes the product of the locutionary act to be a string of words with its own "literal" meaning, which can be characterized in semantic terms independently of pragmatic (or functional) principles. Radical pragmatics, by contrast, sees the utterance (the production of a sentence-in-context) as the result of the *interaction* between syntactic and pragmatic principles.[42] This conception of pragmatics is most vigorously highlighted by proponents of Relevance Theory[43] but is arguably compatible with other approaches, including an appropriately extended version of Speech Act Theory, and can be readily formulated in robustly every day terms. Rather than dwell here on the theoretical issues involved, we will focus on a concrete example of the liturgical formula "Hoc est corpus meum." We believe that this case study highlights a fundamental difference between the hermeneutic perspectives in the medieval and early modern periods, as outlined above, and illustrates the usefulness of a pragmatic analysis.

The interpretation of the Eucharistic formula "this is my body" has been grounds for intense theological controversy in the Western tradition over many centuries. In the early modern period, the interpretation of these words came to be viewed as a focal point defining the larger-scale doctrinal differences between Catholic and Protestant thinkers following the Reformation. Indeed it further served as a defining point for finer-grained differentiation both within the Protestant camp and, to some degree, within anti-reformation theology. Central to the debate is how the words for "bread" and "wine" are to be understood in relation to the words for the "body" and the "blood," as used in the sacrament of the Eucharist. Thus the doctrine of the "Real Presence" as promulgated at the Council of Trent in 1551 is asserted by explicit reference to the counter-doctrine "that Christ is present in the Sacrament only as in a *sign* or *figure*," as later espoused by Calvin, Zwingli, and other Protestant theologians:[44]

> If any one denieth, that, in the sacrament of the most holy Eucharist, are contained truly, really, and substantially, the body and blood together with the soul and divinity of our Lord Jesus Christ, and consequently the whole Christ; but saith that He is only therein as in a sign, or in figure, or virtue; let him be anathema.

These differences of theological interpretation are precisely the sort of issue which prompts the accretion of a gloss on a liturgical text, either to assert a doctrinally orthodox reading of the words used or to anticipate and anathematize a doctrinally incorrect one. Alternatively, within both Catholic and Protestant traditions, a catechism that implants the relevant gloss in the catechumen's memory precludes the need for a gloss in the *mise-en-page* of the text. However, despite the bitterly divergent theological issues at stake, from a linguistic perspective there is remarkable agreement that the focus of attention in the formula "Hoc est corpus meum"—the textual anchor for the appropriate gloss—is the predicate of the sentence, that is, the noun phrase "my body." Both sides start out from an assumption that the literal meaning of this phrase is grammatically unproblematic; the locus of the dispute is whether and how the expression should, if at all, be contextually modulated, for example, taken metaphorically rather than literally. And this modulation does not involve grammar, but one of the tropes deriving from the adjacent discipline of rhetoric. In brief, the shared grammatical assumptions in this early modern debate amount to something very similar to the "code" model which is under attack from Relevance Theory.

Medieval discussions of the Eucharistic formula differ fundamentally from the early modern one just outlined, since the focus is not on the lexical item in the predicate, "body," but on the deictic expression in subject position, "this." From this perspective, our starting point is not to understand what the word "body" means, but rather what the demonstrative "this" is pointing to. As with the early modern approach we have just been looking at, this medieval perspective is one which has its own theoretical underpinnings. This is most elaborately developed in what is known as "speculative grammar," speculative in the sense of the Latin *speculum* (mirror), because language was held to "reflect" the structures of reality and the mind.[45] The way in which such grammars were applied in liturgical contexts, hinging on the key term "suppositio" in the explanation both of deixis and of reference more generally, has been investigated in a series of studies by Irène Rosier-Catach, most notably in the pioneering work *La parole efficace: Signe, rituel, sacré* (2004). More recently Frédéric Goubier has both helped consolidate this avenue of research (Goubier and Rosier-Catach 2020) and has also further explored the technical parallels between late medieval hermeneutics and modern pragmatic theory.[46] Of particular relevance for our purposes is the thirteenth-century debate concerning the distinction between interpretation *de virtute sermonis* and *secundum usum*.[47] This resonates strongly with the current debate regarding the interface between semantics and pragmatics (Goubier 2013a).

This brings us back to the issue of a mismatch between what a sentence literally means and what the speaker means by uttering it in a given context. Relevance Theory reverses the way the process of understanding utterances is thought to work. From the point of view of traditional grammar and rhetoric, we start by working out the literal meaning of what has been said and then apply rhetorical tropes to derive a meaning appropriate to the context if the literal meaning does not fit. From a pragmatic point of view, by contrast, it is assumed that we have an expectation (a pragmatic maxim) that the speaker will have a contextually appropriate meaning in mind, and we look for this. The odd thing that emerges from this theoretical approach is that the focus of the pragmatic component is not, as one might expect, on the stylistic tropes such as metaphor, sarcasm, and so on, with which traditional rhetoric primarily occupies itself, and which are in fact relatively well understood.[48] Modern pragmatic theories are in fact as much preoccupied with explaining how we work out the literal meaning of a sentence-in-context as with traditional rhetorical tropes—a position strongly articulated by François Recanati.[49]

It is of substantial interest that the notion of literal meaning has in fact been recognized as a problematic and complex one in the history of Western hermeneutics, the term "literal" here having two quite different senses within the tradition.

LITERAL1 = the non-metaphorical and non-oblique meaning of a word.
LITERAL2 = the clear and unambiguous meaning of a word, as intended by the author in the present context (where the intended meaning may in fact be a metaphorical or oblique one).

In the medieval sermon tradition, the term "literal" contrasts in meaning with a set of four senses of interpretation for preaching purposes: the Literal (dealing with what has happened), the Allegorical (involving typological parallels between Old and New Testament), the Moral (drawing inferences as to how we should act), and the Anagogical (dealing with eschatological matters). In such specific contexts, the term "literal" will carry the sense of literal$_2$ rather than literal$_1$. Indeed a case can be made that, more generally in the study of medieval hermeneutic matters, an advisable strategy is to assume that the literal$_2$ sense of the term is the "unmarked" case, and literal$_1$ (which has become the default modern reading) is the "marked" sense.[50]

It is worth noting that Chaucer illustrates how a fourteenth-century writer could rely on his readers appreciating the critical importance of distinguishing between what someone says and what they really mean, and to relish the trickiness this sometimes involves. Part of the plot of the *Friar's Tale* hinges on precisely this issue. A Summoner is out observing the world with an eye to identifying miscreants that he can summon to a final reckoning, and he is accompanied by the Devil. They overhear an angry Carter, who is cursing his horse and shouting that he "wishes the devil to take him." The Summoner turns to the Devil, assuming that, by dint of these very words both the horse and the Carter are his to carry away. But the Devil knows better, and he corrects the Summoner (Chaucer, *Friar's Tale*, Frag. III, 1568–1569):

Heere may ye se, myn owene deere brother,
The carl spak oo thing, but he thoughte another.

In other words: "The chap has said one thing but thought another." What the Carter really *meant* is something other than what he actually *said*, and it is what is *meant* that really counts, as is apparent from what follows in Chaucer's text.[51]

Pulling together the various threads of discussion, it is useful to distinguish three different layers at which a gloss (and paratextual paraphernalia more generally) can be said, from a pragmatic perspective, to function. At the layer closest to the primary text, in the case of a gloss providing a vernacular translation of a Latin text, the gloss will aim to spell out explicitly what the primary text literally means, bridging any mismatch between sentence-meaning and author-meaning. Taking the author-meaning as the target to be established, the interpretation must tread a fine line between under-interpretation and over-interpretation, to use the robust pragmatic terms developed by Umberto Eco (1992, 2003). Under-interpretation occurs when a reader misses a speaker-meaning by failing to respond to the trigger of a Conversational Implicature and thereby making an over-literal reading of the utterance. Over-interpretation occurs where a reader "reads more between the lines" than the author intended.

Beyond the first level, at which the speaker-meaning is made optimally explicit, glossing may have the rather different function of anticipating and forestalling possible *misreadings* of the primary text. This category is open-ended in more than one dimension, since it relates to bridges built between the cultural and linguistic contexts of the author, the glossator, and the targeted reader. When literary traditions develop paratextual tools that are not linked to particular primary texts (e.g., alphabetically arranged glossaries and dictionaries for general use), the likelihood of misreading a word in context is (paradoxically) increased by dictionaries that group together a full set of subsenses under a single heading; for example, the general lexeme KEY could have key_1 (a door key), key_2 (a musical key), and key_3 (a keyboard button). Glossaries for one specific text and for texts in one specific register (e.g., glossaries for one specific legal text, or for legal texts in general) will of course already single out the subsenses of words relevant to the register. The strategies for the glossing of individual words will thus be connected directly or indirectly with the larger set of paratextual tools which the glossator has available, and which it might be assumed the reader also has to hand. Work in this area has been greatly enriched by the recent emphasis on comparative approaches to glossing: careful comparison between the Western traditions and those of the Far East has served to highlight not just radical differences but also some fundamental similarities which would otherwise have lain unobserved (Whitman and Cinato 2014; Moran and Whitman 2022).

In the development of paratextual tools in the Western tradition there is a striking differentiation according to what is linguistically known as "register." The dictionary tradition in the English language emerges in the form of an alphabetical listing of "hard words" (i.e., words requiring explanation for the non-specialist reader). These are sometimes provided as separate glossaries of the technical terms in particular trades and professions but are typically gathered together in a single alphabetical volume, often with lists of these special areas on the title pages (Considine 2008, 2017). One of the earliest types of semantic marker used in English dictionaries is that of the specialist register to which the term belongs (e.g., *bot*[any]; *math*[ematics], etc.), which either identifies a word as being used exclusively as a technical term, or else marks the technical subsense of a word which is also in common currency in a looser sense.

These first two "layers" of glossing involve pragmatic principles which are assumed in Relevance Theory to apply to human communication and cognition generally, albeit with modulations that are culture- and language-specific. The first layer focusses on speaker/author-meaning, which is glossed in ways that make explicit what is said obliquely or implied indirectly, on the basis of pragmatic assumptions that an interlocutor brings with them. The second layer focuses on the possible displaced relation between the context that the author takes as given and the context of the glossator and of the reader of the gloss. In everyday conversational settings, a context can be displaced where the hearer is an eavesdropper on the author of the primary text, rather than a participant in the primary conversation between author and reader. In the written equivalent of such cases, the gloss may need to give an explanation of things which a reader contemporary with the author would not need, and, conversely, to forestall possible "wrong" readings which a contemporary would not entertain.

A third layer to glossing deserving separate mention is one that is more directly culture-specific than the first two. This is where the process of glossing is to some degree institutionalized, as in Western legal tradition where, as already mentioned above, the application of a statute in specific contexts by a judge is institutionally separate from the drafting of the statutes themselves. In cultures elsewhere, the interpretation of primary texts of various sorts, legal, religious, literary, and so on, is organized on different lines. Thus, for example, the roles of priest and grammarian are combined in the Sanskrit tradition (Pollock 2006; Tubbs and Boose 2007); the role of law-transmitter is combined with that of poet-grammarian in the Old Irish tradition (Ahlquist 1983; Moran 2019); and other configurations are to be found in cultures in the near and far East (Whitman 2011; King 2015).

Of particular interest with respect to glossing practice are cases where there is a documentary record as to how inductees are trained and initiated into subcultures which involve the interpretation of texts—the Old Irish poetic tradition being a spectacularly well-documented example (O'Cuív 1965, 1973; Breatnach 1978). The catechism is a special case within this general category, meaning, in the Western tradition, a question-and-answer routine where a trainee is versed in how elements of a text such as the Christian creed are glossed and explicated. Training in the catechism fits here with a notion of glossing as scaffolding, either appearing on the page alongside the text or of the sort that readers can supply for themselves in a blank margin. In many cultures, there is a prohibition on translating sacred scriptures (as with the Koran), but there may nevertheless be pedagogical traditions to instruct initiates how religious scriptures (or legal texts) are to be interpreted which are functionally equivalent to the Western catechistic method. Catechisms, and the larger genre of conversation, offer an avenue of research into glossing which may serve to reveal as yet underexplored dimensions of the dynamic relations between text and paratext.[52]

PRIMARY TEXT, PARATEXT, AND PUNCTUATION

With works of a religious, legal, and literary nature in the Western European tradition, it is usually possible to draw a clear distinction between an autonomous primary text and the paraphernalia of glosses, annotations, and commentaries which are parasitic on it (Cinato 2015, 188). But, as we have seen in the previous section, text and paratext turn out to be interdigitated in complex and theoretically interesting ways. In this section, we will turn to consider punctuation, which of all the paratextual elements would seem to be the one closest to the primary text, both in terms of *mise-en-page* and linguistic function. The two case studies which we will here examine—punctuation in legal texts and the punctuation of direct quotation—reveal a seemingly contradictory tension between text and paratext which we believe can usefully inform our understanding of the pragmatics of paratextual paraphernalia.

The contrast between the two case studies can be put simply in terms of *mise-en-page*. In the development of Western legal texts one finds a broad sweep of punctuation out of the primary text and into the margin; in the development of marking for direct quotation, there is a movement of markers out of the margin and into the primary text.

The punctuation of legal texts is usefully revealing for our present purposes, given the institutional division of labor between those who formulate the statutes and those who formulate the judicial wording of how a statute applies (or fails to apply) in particular cases.[53] And the familiar interplay between text and paratext is likewise legally implemented, so that a judicial ruling on the application of a statute in a specific case will set a legal precedent for subsequent judicial rulings on it, whereby judicial rulings themselves start to form recursive text/paratext chains. Explicit commentary on the role of punctuation in these hermeneutic processes is therefore especially valuable.

In early modern legal documents, punctuation of all sorts is conceptually moved from a textual to paratextual status. This view is sometimes justified on an erroneous claim that punctuation was never historically used in English statutes, and sometimes on the paradoxical grounds that legal punctuation is fully redundant, and hence not part of the primary text, since it can be supplied by any competent reader/hearer from the very wording of the statute in question (Mellinkoff 1963, 159–170). Thus, for example, an authoritative legal handbook summarizes the role of punctuation in British law as follows:

> The British statutes, on the original rolls of parliament, are not punctuated at all, and although more or less marks of punctuation appear in the printed transcripts of the acts of parliament, they are not inserted by authority and are not regarded as an essential part of the law. (Black 1896, 185)

These assumptions (whatever their historical accuracy) carry direct implications for the hermeneutic status of any punctuation that does happen to stray into a statute. It is stipulated that:

> The punctuation marks in the published copies of an act are not allowed to control, enlarge, or restrict the plain and evident meaning of the legislature as disclosed by the language employed.

Furthermore, it is not just the reading of the act by a judge that is thus constrained. The assumptions also dictate that a statute must be initially drafted in such a way that there is the least possible mismatch between the intended meaning of the author of the statute and the "plain and evident" meaning of its wording: for example, where punctuation might standardly be used to resolve a possible ambiguity as to whether a relative clause is understood as restrictive or non-restrictive, the statute must be deliberately arranged syntactically so as to preclude the ambiguity arising. In effect, the wording of the statute should ideally be "self-punctuating."

The way that quotation is punctuated in the Western tradition makes an instructive counterpoint to that of legal punctuation, since there is a broad movement in its *mise-en-page* which is in the opposite direction, starting with marginal marks and gradually becoming a structural part of the primary text. For present purposes we will here focus only on quotation in the narrow sense of the marking of direct speech. Quotation in its larger sense includes a vast span of paratextual elements, including *intra*-textual cross-referencing, such as the marking of scriptural echoes between old and new testaments in the Christian tradition, and *inter*-textual cross-referencing giving links to texts other than the primary one which indicate sources for or commentary on it. The central case of direct speech is of particular interest since it flags a point in a text where there is a change of voice to one belonging to someone other than the main author of the primary text. In effect, punctuation of direct speech thus marks both a paratextual and a textual boundary at the same time.

The gradual evolution of quotation marks in the Western tradition is explored in detail, with ample illustration from both manuscript and print, in Malcolm Parkes's splendid volume *Pause and Effect* (1992).[54] One institutional motivation for such marks was where a religious work made verbatim reference to a biblical passage, when in a medieval scriptorium closer supervision might be required to ensure the integrity of the biblical text. The origin of what emerged as the modern quotation mark was a wedge-shaped symbol known as a "diple," the shape of which is still visible in the modern French version, guillemets "« »." The diple was placed in the margin of the manuscript to indicate the line of text where the quotation began, in much the same way that an image of a pointing finger or "manicule" was also used. The diple was subsequently often doubled and also repeated on each relevant line of text, either outside or immediately inside the edge of the text block. The symbols were subsequently moved into the body of the text to mark the precise points at which a quotation started and ended, in parallel to the way that pairs of parentheses are used to bracket off a passage. These various developments were standardized only gradually, with all of the variations in marginal and textual positioning surviving into the era of print. But it is noteworthy that an anonymous treatise on punctuation published in London in 1680 still affirms, contrary to the actual trend in usage, that the inverted commas used to mark a quotation "is always in the Margin."[55] By the end of the following century, however, the marking of direct speech was firmly anchored in the main text, as in modern usage.

There is a further quirk in eighteenth-century practice not noted by Parkes but relevant to our present concerns. In the epistolary novels of the period, it is not uncommon to come across cases such as the following, from Tobias Smollett's *Humphry Clinker*,[56] (see figure 8.2):

I don't pretend to be a judge of those matters; (said he) but I understand that warts are often caused by the distemper [. . .]. (Smollett 1771, 31)

Here the verb "saying" indicating the original voice of the quoted material, "said he," is placed in parentheses, this unit being thus nested within the boundaries of the two outer quotation marks. This is interesting from a syntactic as well as a pragmatic point of view. Direct quotation—speaking in a voice other than one's own—is a speech act of a paratextual sort, whereby the "cited" material is not asserted by the speaker but is "exhibited" or "shown."

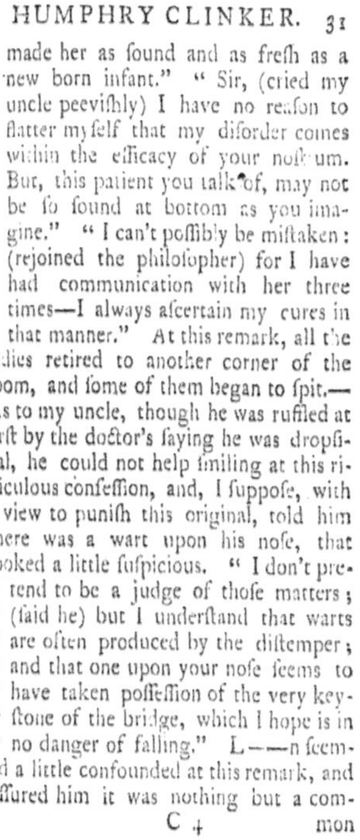

Figure 8.2 The Expedition of Humphry Clinker.

On strictly syntactic grounds, one must take the verb "said" in this example as the matrix verb of the construction as a whole, taking the quoted material as its direct object. But this matrix verb has, in syntactic terminology, been "dislocated" or "fragmented," so that it is no longer in immediate syntactic construction with its direct object and has floated to a parenthetical position within it. The grammatical status of the "nested" bracketed element in this example, reflecting its pragmatic function, is thus in fact well represented by the manner in which it is punctuated.

This kind of syntactic fragmentation looks messy within a generative framework, within which other pragmatic phenomena associated with topicalization and focus can be comfortably analyzed. But one can readily find grammatical parallels elsewhere, notably in what is known as conversational "repair work" (Geluykens 1989, 1994), where misunderstanding about what has been said triggers explicit discussion of what the words uttered were intended to convey. As Geluykens's data shows, such repair work can be initiated either by the addressee, asking for clarification, or by the speaker, anticipating a possible misunderstanding and forestalling it.[57] More recently, the phenomenon of metalinguistic "self-glossing" (equivalent to what Geluykens would term self-initiated repair work) has been identified and analyzed by Jacqueline Authier-Revuz and a network of Francophone researchers working in the same framework. A substantial review of this literature, which appears to have been largely overlooked in Anglophone linguistic circles, both British and American, is beyond the scope of the present chapter.[58] But it is worth observing that this excellent Francophone research has itself made only scant reference to well-studied traditions of written glossing and indeed has tended to promote a mistaken view that the phenomena being discussed are not just characteristic of spoken rather than written language, but intrinsic to it.

There is copious room for further study of punctuation along the lines this suggests, exploring the interplay between text and paratext from an empirical and comparative point of view. The interplay is one that manifestly works in both directions, resulting in what we would like to call the "paratextual paradox" from a codicological perspective, paratext is essentially *marginal* to the primary text, while from a pragmatic perspective, paratext *frames* the primary text and commands our reading of it, in ways to be further explored in the following section.

MARGINS, FRAMES, AND HORIZONS

Our aim in this study has been to rearticulate perspectives on glossing in the medieval and early modern periods in terms of modern pragmatic theory. The notion of the margin has been pivotal throughout this discussion, as a codicological feature of page layout which correlates with the situational context of speech which is the central focus of pragmatic theory. We conclude with a short reflection on the idea of the margin as a *frame*, both in the art historical and the cognitive sense. We suggest that this usefully connects our discussion with a number of philosophical ideas concerning the role of frames and horizons in human cognition in ways that corroborate and further extend the pragmatic line we have been developing.

The most straightforward way of applying this idea is to see paratextual elements as the frame in which the text is presented and to focus immediately on paratext. But it is worthwhile starting out by thinking about the text itself, and the sorts of texts for which a culture deems a frame to be necessary or desirable. Although the process of glossing can apply to language in any form, whether written or spoken—as the data from "self-glossing" in conversational speech demonstrate—an accumulation of glosses on a specific text serves to identify it as being culturally special in some way, be it legal, religious or literary. It is then tempting to search for a functional characteristic that is common to such primary texts. They need not necessarily be written, since non-literate cultures have oral means for transmitting laws and belief systems from generation to generation; nor need they necessarily be linked to cultural institutions, which in the case of law and religion is often the case, if examples ranging from literary works to proverb systems are to be included in this category. A simple definition that would distinguish primary texts from everyday conversational utterances is that they are culturally transmitted and are intended to be read more than once, which in turn leads us to think of the frame as essentially a relational notion.

Let us here revisit the observation by Holtz from which we started out, namely that there is a fundamental distinction in *kind* between text and gloss. What surrounds and demarcates a primary text is not so much a textual fringe or indeed anything strictly textual at all: it is the empty margin itself.[59] As Genette himself explain:

> More than a boundary or a sealed border, the paratext is, rather, a threshold [. . .] It is an "undefined zone" between the inside and the outside, a zone without any hard and fast boundary on either the inward side (turned toward the text) or the outward side. (Genette 1997, 2, 1987, 8)

Several metaphors have been used in the preceding discussion to identify relevant features of the relation between text and paratext which connect paratext with genres such as the catechism, where the activity of glossing is inculcated. And Genette himself immediately goes on to talk about the threshold as a place of activity along the same sort of lines:

> Indeed this fringe [. . .] constitutes a zone between text and off-text, a zone not only of transition but also of transaction: a privileged place of a pragmatics and a strategy, of an influence on the public, an influence that—whether well or poorly understood and achieved—is at the service of a better reception for the text and a more pertinent reading of it. (Genette 1997, 2)

While our scaffolding metaphor works well for the glossing activity itself, we also need a metaphor for the margin, the zone in which the activity takes place. The one that suggests itself is that of the frame, both in the physical sense of a picture frame and also in the cognitive sense of a horizon associated with a given viewpoint.

The picture frame, and its relation to the image which it surrounds, allows us to tap into a rich art-historical literature, giving us a fresh way of thinking about the relation between text and paratext. For anyone newly venturing into this topic, a good starting point is a short essay by the Spanish philosopher José Ortega y Gasset, translated as *Meditations on the frame* (1990). His simple central point is that any picture necessarily has a frame, and he proceeds to spell out the reasons why. The argument derives from the basic principle of Gestalt Theory: a picture *needs* a frame in the sense that there can be no such thing as a picture without a fringe (to redeploy Genette's term) which distinguishes it from the wall it hangs upon (its *Hintergrund*):

> A picture without a frame has the air about it of a naked, despoiled man. Its contents seem to spill out over the four sides of the canvas and dissolve into the atmosphere. (Ortega y Gasset 1990, 187)

This argument works in both directions. A picture is always "framed," since even a picture which lacks a physical frame nevertheless has a fringe where a physical frame would be if it had one, and that fringe *is* its frame. Conversely, if you put a frame around any object you happen to pick up—an *objet trouvé*—you thereby make it into a piece of art, in the same way that putting a margin round any random piece of text can make it a *poème trouvé*. In both cases, the very framing invites, or even demands (in the case of conceptual art), a paratextual reaction on the part of the viewer or reader.

Those who wish to pursue art-historical ideas about the frame in greater detail are referred to a monograph by Ernst Gombrich (1979) devoted entirely to this topic—an extended footnote, as it were, to his classic *Art and illusion* (1960), and taking the same cognitive approach. One avenue that Gombrich explores, further to the just-mentioned distinction between framed and unframed pictures, is the "visibility" of the frame where a picture indeed has one. The oddity is that a physical picture frame is very often cognitively invisible: people who have seen the Mona Lisa will usually be able to give a rough description of the posture of the figure, and also of the room where it was hanging, while having a mental blank as regards what the frame itself was like. The exception, Gombrich argues, is when the frame is somehow inappropriate for the kind of picture it surrounds.

> [W]hen a frame is appropriate we simply don't see it, because it seamlessly conveys to us the mode by which we should encounter what it frames. It is mainly when it is inappropriate (imagine a Titian framed in Perspex) that we are suddenly aware that there is indeed a frame. (Gombrich 1979, 15)

There are of course exceptions and limiting cases which immediately spring to mind, and Gombrich devotes a whole volume to discussing these: frames are in fact typically multiple (since a frame itself has inside and outside edges which themselves call for framing); elements of the picture can protrude across one edge of the frame (e.g., the toe of a figure in a medieval portrait) thereby drawing attention to the frame; and the frame may be "authorial" (rather than provided by someone other than the painter) and be constructed in such a way as to be an integral part of the painting as a whole. But such considerations do not undermine but reinforce the interest of Gombrich's central point of view.

Gombrich's ideas about the cognitive effects of the picture frame have a clear and immediate relevance to our understanding of the relation between text and paratext, and the framing function of the (empty) margin itself. The resonances are not just metaphorical ones: the parallel between the physical picture frame and the margin in book design is a direct one, and there is opportunity for the cognitive aspects of the margin to be explored further in the study of glossing.

There is a large relevant literature on framing and margins in literary theory, some of it clear and illuminating,[60] and some of it of a postmodernist nature that can generate more heat than light.[61] But it is worth drawing attention to the fact that the notion of a frame is widely used in linguistic (as distinct from literary) theory in a radically different sense than is intended here. In discourse analysis, for example, it has been used for elements *within* the structure of the text (e.g., for utterances which serve to provide the interpretative context for a following one); and elsewhere it is used (in a sense which originates in sociology) to mean the same as the "script" which guides and gives overall structure to conversational exchange (Goffman 1974; Tannen 1993). In both cases, the notion is applied to aspects of the structure of the discourse itself, and not to an empty margin that surrounds it. In terms of the art-historical parallel, this is the equivalent of focussing on aspects of the picture itself, rather than on those of the physical or cognitive frame.

Oddly, perhaps, it is not obvious how the parallel between picture framing and the marginal framing of primary texts can be usefully articulated in terms of pragmatic theory. The pragmatic equivalent of the picture frame or the empty margin would be (to use terms introduced above) the zone between cognitive shortfall and cognitive overshoot: the immediately relevant context. But in Relevance Theory the notion of "context" is not a primary one; it is a secondary category constructed in terms of the Relevance Principles. Nevertheless, the idea of an immediately relevant context, one associated with both speaker's and hearer's points of view and manifesting joint attention (Tomasello and Rakoczy 2003), is one that can be constructed in the spirit of Relevance Theory and has the critical property, like that of the picture frame, of being recursive.[62] The precursors for such a notion can be found in the literature of phenomenology, anchored in the terms "horizon," "margin," and "field" as deployed in a cognitive sense by Edmund Husserl, William James, Aron Gurwitsch, and others.[63]

The pragmatics of the frame—the zone which intervenes between text and paratext, and which separates them hierarchically (Holtz 1977, 257) and metalinguistically—remains to be worked out in detail with respect to glossing. Thus, within the medieval Western tradition, alongside the monastic industries concerned with marginal glossing, we find further examples ranging from emblem books, with image and paratext juxtaposed,[64] to religious relics which are framed by their labels (Smith 2018). Cultures vary with respect to which kinds of texts become framed as primary texts and which kinds of objects other than texts are similarly framed and invite paratextual glossing. Glossing is remarkably ubiquitous throughout the world, and it is good to be reminded we all do it slightly differently (Whitman 2011).

NOTES

1. For an authoritative survey of the origins of the Christian hermeneutic tradition, see Barton (2019), who also provides a critical overview of recent developments since the publication of the pioneering work by Smalley (1941, 1952). For a more linguistically oriented survey of modern perspectives, see Thiselton (1992, 179–203).

2. This biblical/legal parallel was signposted by Smalley by the addition, in the second edition of her just-mentioned work, of an excursus on the glossing of legal texts by Hermann Kantorowicz (1952). See Maclean (1992) on the hermeneutics of legal interpretation in the classical and medieval periods, and Mellinkoff (1963) on the history of language and the law more generally. For a comparative perspective, see Russell (1998, 2008, 2018) on legal glosses and glossaries in Old Irish.

3. On the role of interpretation in the medieval medical tradition, see Maclean (2002); on the equally important but largely neglected medical dimension in the early

modern philosophy of language, see the discussion of Locke's thought in Romanell (1984). See further, Harrison (2002) on the way in which the tradition relating to the interpretation of the book of scripture informed and underpinned the scientific interpretation of the book of nature in the early modern period.

4. The classic study in the case of English, Jones (1953) places the relevant period in the sixteenth and seventeenth centuries.

5. For larger-scale studies of Old Irish glosses, see Hofman (1996), Cinato (2015), Blom (2017). On glossing in the older Germanic languages, see Meritt (1945), Rousseau (1978), and the recent collections of articles in Bergmann and Stricker (2009) and Teeuwen and van Renswoude (2017). On Latin glosses and glossaries, see Holtz (1981) and Lindsay (1996).

6. The relation between glossing and the genre of catechism and dialogue, on which see Burke (1989), Weijers (2013), Cameron and Gaul (2017), is one that remains to be fully explored.

7. On the typology of glosses, see Holtz (1977), Hunt (1991, vol. I, 19–55), Moran (2015), Blom (2017, 2018).

8. Study of such phenomena was launched by a study of Persian usage by Gershevitch (1979), who coined the term "alloglottography" for cases where a text is written in a language other than the one in which it is intended to be read. For alternative analyses of the Chinese/Korean case, see King (2015) and Robert (2016).

9. This chapter was jointly drafted primarily by the first-named author as a speculative think piece to complement the more empirically illustrated presentation in the second-named author's inaugural lecture at Marburg (Blom 2018). It is the outcome of their discussions about paratextual paraphernalia over many years, bringing together their respective expertise in the early modern (Cram 1989, 1994, 2003) and the medieval (Blom 2009, 2011, 2013a, 2013b, 2016, 2017) periods.

10. Genette's ideas were developed in a trilogy of books, *Introduction à l'architexte* (1979), *Palimpsestes* (1982), and *Seuils* (1987), all of which appeared in English translation soon after their publication. The term "paratext" is associated with a number of other key terms, notably "intertextuality," several of which have subsequently passed into common academic currency, often being used without technical precision. For a recent and exemplary application of the notion of paratext in a medieval context, with a clear introductory exposition of Genette's ideas, see Crawford (2019). For a lively and accessible introduction for the general reader, see Duncan and Smyth (2020).

11. A point made by Watson (2010, 2) in a short but insightful article that is recommended as a bon-bouche introduction for anyone unfamiliar with the notion of paratext.

12. The expression "naked text" is taken here from Genette (1987, 7 and passim) but echoes a long-standing Western tradition of referring to rhetorical decoration as the "vestment" of thought (cf. Cicero's lines "Reconditas exquisitasque sententias/ mollis et pellucens vestiebat oratio." *Brutus*: 79, 274).

13. To use a linguistic terminology, the paratextual element is here the "marked" pole of the dichotomy, and the textual element is the "unmarked" one.

14. Genette, *Seuils*, 1987, 11; trans. *Paratexts* 1997, 5. In Genette's usage, *peri*-textual elements are located inside the book (e.g., title, footnotes, index); *epi*-textual

elements are located outside the book (e.g., letters, diaries, and other associated documents).

15. This is arguably an explanation for Genette's above-mentioned blind-spot as regards the specific category of "gloss."

16. The classic listing comprises: "titre, sous-titre, intertitres; préfaces, postfaces, avertissements, avant-propos, etc.; *notes marginales*, infrapaginales, terminales; épigraphes; illustrations; prière d'insérer, bande, jaquette, et bien d'autre types de signaux accessoires, autographes ou allographes, qui procurent au texte un entourage (variable) et parfois un commentaire, officiel ou officieux." (Genette 1982, 9; emphasis added)

17. See Teeuwen (2017) on Carolingian annotation, and other case studies in the same volume.

18. On women's property in the medieval and early modern period, see Erickson (1993, 26, 174–186). We are grateful to Anne Laurence for this reference.

19. On the Latin tradition, see the discussion at the outset above; on the Hebrew tradition, see the articles by Grafton, Beit-Arié, and Olszowy-Schlanger in Boxel and Arndt (2009), and those in Vidro et al. (2014).

20. This danger is a constant preoccupation in Wycliffite biblical scholarship, on which see the various studies in Hudson (2015) and Solopova (2017).

21. A case in point are marginalia in a fifteenth-century copy of Cicero's *De officiis* (Brasenose College, MS Oxford VII), where the scribe has used a four-letter English expletive (the f-word) in comments directed at the abbot (Wilson 1993). These would not strictly qualify as paratext in the sense under discussion but are nevertheless of some relevance to his activities as a scribe.

22. The same recursive looping occurs when an "established" gloss becomes seen as misleading or wrong; a correction to the first gloss does not simply replace it but rather piggy-backs on it.

23. For a detailed discussion of the notion of "literal" in the context of the traditional four levels of biblical interpretation, see Wyclif's *De veritate Sanctae Scripturae*, accessible in a "condensed" English translation with a helpful introduction by Levy (Wyclif 2001, 86–118). A contemporary summary of Wyclif's views on these issues, in surprisingly lucid Middle English, can be found in the General Prologue to the Wycliffite version of the Bible, penned after his death by John Purvey (1550, chaps. 12–15).

24. Kuczynski (2019) is a book-length study of a glossed Wycliffite psalter, which has a very useful general introduction. On the theory and practice of theory of Wycliffite glossing, see Kuczynski (2017).

25. It is worth noting that Justinian specifically prohibited any commentary on statutes (Maclean 1992, 50–59), even though the implementation of the statutes in question would of course have required judicial interpretation of them.

26. This echoes, of course, the "double contrast" between text and commentary in the discussion by Cinato (2015, 188; cited above).

27. The early modern terms for such a work would be a *Primer*, a *Janua*, a *Rudiments*, a *Delectus*, etc.

28. "Im jar 1515 des mandages na dem witten sondage . . . kam ik Johannes Oldecop to Wyttenberge. . . . Und umme de tit hof an doctor Martinus Luther epistolas Pauli ad Romanos to lesende. Der doctor hadde dar up bi Johan Grunenberg dem bokdrucker bestellet, dat de epistula Pauli, de rige ein wiet von der andern gedrucket wart, umme Gloserens willen." (Oldekop 1891, 45)

29. A copy of St Paul's epistle to the Romans in the named 1515 printed edition, with interlinear and marginal notes by a certain Sigismund Reichenbach, is preserved on the Anhaltische Landesbücherei (VD 16, b 5019) and is accessible online. Cf. also Koch (2014) on a copy in Dessau. For a study comparing the text of Luther's lectures and the notes made by his pupils, see Schmidt-Lauber (1994).

30. "Die Meister veranlassten die Drucklegung kurzer antiker Texte, über die sie lesen wollten. Die Druckausgaben konnten von den Studenten um einen geringen Preis erworben und wärend der Vorlesungen benutzt werden." (Altmann 1990, 158)

31. On the use of such "text-books" in school teaching, see Grafton (1981), Powitz (1981), Henkel (2009), and Altmann (1990).

32. The same claim is made by Job Everadt some decades later in a promotional verse for his new system of shorthand: "Reader in two words to descrie,/This Arts *exceeding Excellencie*;/Hereby *as much more* write may bee,/In *Margent*, as in *Page* you see:/And what *at large*, takes up *A D A Y*;/May in *An Houre* be writ *this way*." (Everardt 1658, sig B recto)

33. Macaulay (1747). See Underhill (2005) on the popular use of shorthand in early Methodism.

34. See King-Hele's biography (1999, 11–13), where a specimen is given of the shorthand notes taken by Erasmus Darwin at George Baker's medical lectures at Cambridge in 1752.

35. Hamilton published various classical texts formatted with interlining and provided a defense of the "Hamiltonian Method" shortly before his death (Hamilton 1829), in reply to an attack from a competitor (Santagnello 1827).

36. The gradual emergence of the concept of the title is a classic chicken and egg issue: catalogues of texts cannot serve any useful purposes if books don't have titles, but titles don't serve any necessary purposes unless there is a need for them for cataloguing purposes (assuming the paratextual tool of the catalog) or for cross-reference between one text and another (assuming the systematic use of intertextual annotation).

37. Other relevant terms for paratextual tools listed by Bailey include *Concordance, Elenchus, Gnomon, Index*, q.v.

38. The principle of Relevance in Sperber and Wilson's framework is a generalization of Grice's third principle of *Relation*: its status and operation are radically different, but the differences do not affect the present discussion. The classic presentation of Relevance Theory is Sperber and Wilson (1985; revised 1995). For a briefer programmatic outline, which develops the central ideas for a general audience rather than a specialist linguistic one, see Sperber and Wilson (1985/6). For an introduction in the form of a university textbook, see Clark (2013). For a recent summary and survey aimed at a general rather than specialized readership, see Wilson (2018).

39. The interface between semantics and pragmatics continues to be a central and controversial issue in pragmatic theory generally: see Huang (2014). For a general discussion which is not linked specifically either to Neo-Gricean theory or Relevance Theory, see Jaszczolt (2002).

40. This framework is a radical departure from a Chomskyan one which defines the proper object of linguistics as being "competence" (a speaker's knowledge of the rules of language) as distinct from "performance" (a speaker's use of language in particular contexts). This point need not concern us for present purposes.

41. We are grateful to Franck Cinato for having drawn our attention to this study.

42. In technical terms, sentence-meaning is primarily but not *exclusively* the object of semantic inquiry, and speaker-meaning is primarily but not *exclusively* the object of pragmatic inquiry.

43. Sperber and Wilson put forward their theory as a radical departure from what they call the "code" model of human communication. The pivotal arguments for this position were first put forward in their pioneering work (Sperber and Wilson 1985, 1–38); for a compact summary and replies from other specialists in the field, see Sperber and Wilson 1987.

44. Fuller details of this decree, and documentation of the subsequent debate, can be found in Chilton and Cram (2018): see especially pages 407–415. Our discussion here is necessarily truncated.

45. A representative example of a speculative grammar is that of Thomas of Erfurt, of which there is an edition and translation by Bursill-Hall (1972); this includes one of the best available short introductions for the non-specialist reader. On the larger context of medieval theories of the Eucharist, see Adams (2010).

46. On the parallel between medieval biblical hermeneutics and modern pragmatics, see Brungs and Goubier (2009), Goubier and Pouscoulous (2011), and Goubier (2013a, 2013b).

47. On this debate, see Courtenay (1984), Ghosh (2002, chap. 1), and Valente (2004).

48. The classic book on metaphors (Lakoff and Johnson 1980) launched a veritable metaphor industry in higher education, based on a doctrine that metaphor is the single central organizing principle in the semantics of language. The doctrine is readily (and usefully) exemplified, and indeed, if *everything* is metaphorical, it cannot be falsified. For a comprehensive survey of the various current theories of metaphor, see Kohl (2017).

49. Recanati (2003) is a monograph devoted to this issue. For a shorter programmatic discussion, see his earlier article, delightfully titled "The alleged priority of literal interpretation" (Recanati 1995).

50. On the term "literal" in biblical hermeneutics, see Dahan (2009, chap. 5) and Barton (2019, chap.15). On the issue of literal meaning in a Wycliffite context, where it is debated in detail and at length, see the analysis in Minnis (1975).

51. See Robertson (1969, 331–332) on the explicit references to "glossing" in the Friar's and the Summoner's tales and the larger section "Chaucer's Exegetes" (317–336) on the role of biblical interpretation as a critical part of the background to the Canterbury Tales more generally.

52. For an exemplary study, see Jolly (2016), and on English catechisms Green (1996). On the larger medieval "culture of disputation," see the contributions in

Novikoff (2013). On the Carolingian cultures of dialogue, see De Jong and van Renswoude (2017). For an edition and discussion of an Old Irish legal dialogue (on the then important topic of bee keeping), see Charles-Edwards and Kelly (1983). On the early modern interplay between the European catechism and the indigenous Mexican tradition, with an edition of a Nahua pictorial catechism, see Boone et al. (2017).

53. For an accessible general account of legal punctuation, see Mellinkoff (1963, 159–170); see further Black (1896, 185–189), Watson (2012), and Butt (2013, 288–296). See Marcin (1977) for an account of the legally controversial execution of Sir Roger Casement, who was famously "hung on a comma."

54. See especially Parkes (1992, 58–61). On the history of the marking of quotation see also Catach (1968, 299–301), Marnette (2006), and Palmer (1985, 2010). On the marking of quotation more generally, see Cappelen and Lepore (2007), Finnegan (2011), Mair (2018), and Rée (1990, 1991).

55. "This Note is used is som Books, when any thing is quoted from another Author, as you will find by observation; and it is always placed in the Margin" (Anon, *A treatise of stops*, 1680, 18).

56. This example is of larger interest, since in addition to the parenthetical verb of saying, it shows the repetition of quotation marks on multiple lines inside the edge of the text block.

57. In Geluykens (1988) a strong case is made that conversational repair work is the historical origin of the various types of clefting syntactic construction known as left- and right-dislocation.

58. The theoretic framework is set out in detail in Authier-Revuz (1994, 1995) and has been developed and applied by her and by others in a large number of more specific studies. See Julia (2001) for an accessible and empirically documented survey; Offord (2003) gives a useful discussion of the typology of the various categories of self-glossing in a review of this work.

59. Put more carefully: the relation between text and paratext is metalinguistic. A gloss is not a continuation of the primary text to which it attaches, it is a comment upon it; if it suggests an extension to the primary text, it must do so by means of direct quotation, which is a syntactic means for straddling a metalinguistic boundary (Cram 1978; Cappelen and Lepore 2007).

60. See, for example, the collections of studies in Wolf and Bernhart (2006) and Jansen (2014).

61. Derrida (1987) would fall into this category, but his ideas on the relation between speech and writing (1978) and his discussion of the cognitive margin/horizon (cf. Derrida 1982) are here of immediate relevance and importance.

62. Such an approach is developed in Cram (forthcoming).

63. As Embree notes, in a discussion of Gurwitsch's work on "marginal consciousness" (1985): "Relevancy is something that occurs within the field of consciousness. Gurwitsch acknowledges that the notion of *field* comes from Gestalt theory, [. . .] and also from William James, who held that the total field is structured into a focus and a margin." (Embree 2004, 3206)

64. See the webpages for emblem book projects at the Universities of Glasgow, Penn State, and Utrecht.

REFERENCES

Ahlqvist, Anders. 1983. *The Early Irish Linguist: An Edition of the Canonical Part of the Auraicept na n-éces*. Helsinki: Societas Scientiarum Fennica.

Altmann, Ursula. 1990. "Klassiker-Ausgaben für Studenten und Lateinschüler am Ende des 15. Jahrhunderts." In *Von der Wirkung des Buches: Festgabe für Horst Kunze zum 80. Geburtstag*, edited by F. Krause, 148–159. Berlin: Deutsche Staatsbibliothek.

Anon. 1680. *A Treatise of Stops, Points, or Pauses and of Notes Which Are Used in Writing and in Print*. London: Printed for the Authors Use in His School.

Authier-Revuz, Jacqueline. 1994. "L'énonciateur glosateur de ses mots: explicitation et interprétation." *Langue française* 103: 91–102.

Authier-Revuz, Jacqueline. 1995. *Ces mots qui ne vont pas de soi*. 2 vols. Paris: Larousse.

Bailey, Nathaniel. 1730. *Dictionarium Britannicum; or a more compleat universal etymological English dictionary than any extant*. London: T. Cox.

Bales, Peter. 1597. *The Arte of Brachygraphie*. London: George Shawe and Ralph Blower for Thomas Charde.

Barton, John. 2019. *A History of the Bible: The Book and Its Faiths*. London: Allen Lane.

Berger, Thomas L., and Sonia Massai. 2014. *Paratexts in English Printed Drama to 1642*. 2 vols. Cambridge: Cambridge University Press.

Bergmann, Rolf, and Stefanie Stricker, eds. 2009. *Die althochdeutsche und altsächsische Glossographie: Ein Handbuch*. 2 vols. Berlin: De Gruyter.

Black, Henry C. 1896. *Handbook on the Construction and Interpretation of the Laws*. St. Paul, Minn.: West Pub. Co.

Blom, Alderik H. 2009. "The Welsh Glosses in the Vocabularium Cornicum." *Cambrian Medieval Celtic Studies* 57: 23–40.

Blom, Alderik H. 2011. "Endlicher's Glossary." *Etudes Celtiques* 37: 159–182.

Blom, Alderik H. 2013a. "Multilingualism and the Vocabularium Cornicum." In *Multilingualism in Medieval Britain (c. 1066–1520)*, edited by A. Putter and J. Jefferson, 59–71. Turnhout: Brepols.

Blom, Alderik H. 2013b. "Compiling a Glossary on the Psalms in Eleventh-Century Tegernsee." *Beiträge zur Geschichte der deutschen Sprache und Literatur* 135(4): 475–514.

Blom, Alderik H. 2016. "Function and Transmission of Latin and Irish Glosses: The Psalter of St Caimín." In *Adapting Texts and Styles in a Celtic Context: Interdisciplinary Perspectives on Processes of Literary Transfer in the Middle Ages. Studies in Honour of Erich Poppe*, edited by A. Harlos and N. Harlos, 195–214. Münster: Nodus Publikationen.

Blom, Alderik H. 2017. *Glossing the Psalms: The Emergence of the Written Vernaculars in Western Europe From the Seventh to the Twelfth Centuries*. Berlin: De Gruyter.

Blom, Alderik H. 2018. *Mittelalterliche Glossen: Paläographie, Paratext und Pragmatik*. Inaugural Lecture: University of Marburg: 2nd November 2018. https://www.youtube.com/watch?v=yM_SNS3wXxU.

Boone, Elizabeth, Louise M. Burkhart, and David Tavárez. 2017. *Painted Words: Nahua Catholicism, Politics, and Memory in the Atzaqualco Pictorial Catechism.* Washington, D.C.: Dumbarton Oaks Research Library and Collection.

Boxel, Piet van, and Sabine Arndt. 2009. *Crossing Borders: Hebrew Manuscripts as a Meeting-Place of Cultures.* Oxford: Bodleian Library.

Breatnach, Liam. 1978. *Uraicecht na ríar: the poetic grades in early Irish law.* Dublin: Dublin Institute for Advanced Studies.

Brungs, Alexander, and Frédéric Goubier. 2009. "On Biblical Logicism. Wyclif, Virtus Sermonis and Equivocation." *Recherches de théologie et philosophie médiévales* 76: 199–244.

Burke, Peter. 1989. "The Renaissance Dialogue." *Renaissance Studies* 3(1): 1–12.

Butt, Peter. 2013. *Modern Legal Drafting: A Guide to Using Clearer Language.* Cambridge: Cambridge University Press.

Cameron, Averil, and Gaul Niels, eds. 2017. *Dialogues and Debates From Late Antiquity to Late Byzantium.* Milton Park, Abingdon, Oxon and New York, NY: Routledge.

Cappelen, Herman, and Ernest Lepore. 2007. *Language Turned on Itself: The Semantics and Pragmatics of Metalinguistic Discourse.* Oxford: Oxford University Press.

Catach, Nina. 1968. *L'orthographe française à l'époque de la Renaissance.* Genève: Droz.

Charles Edwards, Thomas, and Fergus Kelly, eds. 1983. *Bechbretha: An Old Irish Law-Tract on Bee-Keeping.* Dublin: Dublin Institute for Advanced Studies.

Chilton, Paul, and David Cram. 2018. "Hoc est Corpus: Deixis and the Integration of Ritual Space." In *Religion, Language, and the Human Mind*, edited by Paul Chilton and Monika Kopytowska, 407–436. Oxford: Oxford University Press.

Chomsky, Noam. 1976. *Reflections on Language.* London: Fontana/Collins.

Cinato, Franck. 2015. *Priscien glosé. L'Ars grammatica de Priscien vue à travers les gloses carolingiennes.* Turnhout: Brepols.

Clark, Billy. 2013. *Relevance Theory.* Cambridge: Cambridge University Press.

Considine, John. 2008. *Dictionaries in Early Modern Europe: Lexicography and the Making of Heritage.* Cambridge: Cambridge University Press.

Considine, John. 2017. *Small Dictionaries and Curiosity: Lexicography and Fieldwork in Post-Medieval Europe.* Oxford: Oxford University Press.

Courtenay, William J. 1984. "Force of Words and Figures of Speech: The Crisis Over *Virtus Sermonis* in the Fourteenth Century." *Franciscan Studies* 44: 107–128.

Cram, David. 1978. "The Syntax of Direct Quotation." *Cahiers de Lexicologie* 33: 41–52.

Cram, David. 1989. "Seventeenth-Century Punctuation Theory: Charles Butler's Philosophical Analysis and John Wilkins's Philosophical Critique." *Folia Linguistica Historica* 8: 309–349.

Cram, David. 1994. "Concordances of Words and Concordances of Things: A Neglected Aspect of Seventeenth-Century English Lexicography." In *Die Welt in einer Liste von Wörtern*, edited by W. Hüllen, 83–93. Tübingen: Niemeyer.

Cram, David. 2003. "The Doctrine of Sentence Distinctions in Seventeenth-Century Grammatical Theory." In *History of Linguistics 1999: Papers From ICHOLS. VIII*, edited by S. Auroux, 109–127. Amsterdam: Benjamins.

Cram, David. 2007. "Shelf Life and Time Horizons in the Historiography of Linguistics." *Historiographia Linguistica* 34 (2/3): 189–212.

Cram, David. forthcoming. *Nested Contexts: The Pragmatics of Talk, Tact and Taciturnity.*

Crawford, Matthew R. 2019. *The Eusebian Canon Tables: Ordering Textual Knowledge in Late Antiquity.* Oxford: Oxford University Press.

Crespi, Bernard, and Christopher Badcock. 2008. "Psychosis and Autism as Diametrical Disorders of the Social Brain." *Behavioral and Brain Sciences* 31: 241–320.

Dahan, Gilbert. 2009. *Lire la Bible au Moyen Âge. Essais d'herméneutique médiévale.* Genève: Droz.

De Jong, Mayke, and Irene van Renswoude. 2017. "Carolingian Cultures of Dialogue, Debate and Disputation." *Early Medieval Europe* 25(1): 6–18.

Derrida, Jacques. 1978. *Writing and Difference.* Translated by Alan Bass. London: Routledge.

Derrida, Jacques. 1982. "Signature, Event, Context." In *Margins of Philosophy*, translated with additional notes, by Alan Bass, 309–230. Brighton: Harvester.

Derrida, Jacques. 1987. *The Truth in Painting.* Translated by Geoff Bennington and Ian McLeod. Chicago and London: Chicago University Press.

Duncan, Dennis, and Adam Smyth. 2019. *Book Parts.* Oxford: Oxford University Press.

Eco, Umberto. 1992. *Interpretation and Overinterpretation.* Cambridge: Cambridge University Press.

Eco, Umberto. 2003. "Losses and Gains." In *Mouse or Rat? Translation as Negotiation*, 37–61. London: Weidenfeld and Nicholson.

Embree, Lester. 2004. "The Three Species of Relevancy in Gurwitsch." In *Gurwitsch's Relevancy for Cognitive Science*, edited by Lester Embree, 205–219. Dordrecht: Springer.

Erickson, Amy L. 1993. *Women and Property in Early Modern England.* London: Routledge.

Everardt, Job. 1658. *An Epitome of Stenographie; Or, An Abridgement and Contraction, of the Art of Short, Swift, and Secret Writing by Characters.* London: Lodowick Lloyd,

Finnegan, Ruth H. 2011. "Quotation Marks: Present, Past, and Future." In *Why Do We Quote? The Culture and History of Quotation*, 79–111. Cambridge: Open Book Publishers.

Formigatti, Camillo Alessio. 2015. "Sanskrit Annotated Manuscripts From Northern India and Nepal." Doctoral Dissertation, Hamburg University.

Geluykens, Ronald. 1988. "Five Types of Clefting In English Discourse." *Linguistics* 26(5): 823–842.

Geluykens, Ronald. 1989. "Referent-Tracking and Cooperation in Conversations: Evidence From Repair." *Chicago Linguistics Society* 25: 1–12.

Geluykens, Ronald. 1994. *The Pragmatics of Discourse Anaphora in English: Evidence From Conversational Repair.* Berlin: De Gruyter.

Genette, Gérard. 1979. *Introduction à l'architexte*. Paris: Éditions du Seuil. [English translation: *The Architext: An Introduction*. Berkeley; Oxford: University of California Press, 1992.]

Genette, Gérard. 1982. *Palimpsestes: la littérature au second degré*. Paris: Éditions du Seuil. [English Translation: *Palimpsests: literature in the second degree*. Lincoln: University of Nebraska Press, 1997.]

Genette, Gérard. 1987. *Seuils*. Paris: Éditions du Seuil. [English Translation: *Paratexts: thresholds of interpretation*. Cambridge: Cambridge University Press, 1997.]

Gershevitch, Ilya. 1979. "The Alloglottography of Old Persian." *Transactions of the Philological Society* 1979: 114–190.

Ghosh, Kantik. 2002. *The Wycliffite Heresy: Authority and the Interpretation of Texts*. Cambridge: Cambridge University Press.

Goffman, Erving. 1974. *Frame Analysis: An Essay on the Organization of Experience*. London: Harper and Row.

Gombrich, Ernst H. 1960. *Art and Illusion: A Study in the Psychology of Pictorial Representation*. London: Phaidon Press.

Gombrich, Ernst H. 1979. *The Sense of Order: A Study in the Psychology of Decorative Art*. Ithaca: Cornell University Press.

Goubier, Frédéric. 2013a. "*Dire* et *vouloir dire* dans la logique médiévale: Quelques jalons pour situer une frontière." *Methodos: Savoirs et textes* 14. http://journals.openedition.org/methodos/3790.

Goubier, Frédéric. 2013b. "Les propriétés du discours sont-elles réductibles à celles des mots? Sémantique de l'impropre chez John Wyclif et John Kenningham." *Beiträge zur Geschichte der Sprachwissenschaft* 23(2): 173–198.

Goubier, Frédéric, and Irène Rosier-Catach. 2020. "The *Trivium* in the 12th Century." In *A Companion to Twelfth-Century Schools*, edited by Cédric Giraud, 141–179. Leiden/Boston: Brill.

Goubier, Frédéric, and Nausicaa Pouscoulous. 2011. "*Virtus sermonis* and the Semantics-Pragmatics Distinction." *Vivarium* 49(1–3): 214-39.

Grafton, Anthony. 1981. "Teacher, Text and Pupil in the Renaissance Class-Room: A Case Study From a Parisian College." *History of Universities* 1: 37.

Green, Ian M. 1996. *The Christian's ABC: Catechisms and Catechizing in England c. 1530–1740*. Oxford: Clarendon Press.

Grice, H. Paul. 1957. "Meaning." *Philosophical Review* 67: 377–388.

Grice, H. Paul. 1975. "Logic and Conversation." In *Syntax and Semantics, Vol. 3: Speech Acts*, edited by P. Cole and J. Morgan, 43–58. New York: Academic Press.

Gurwitsch, Aron. 1985. *Marginal Consciousness*. Athens, CH: Ohio University Press.

Hamilton, James. 1829. *The History, Principles, Practice and Results of the Hamiltonian System for the Last Twelve Years*. Manchester: T. Sowler.

Harrison, Peter. 2002. *The Bible, Protestantism, and the Rise of Early-Modern Science*. Cambridge and New York: Cambridge University Press.

Henkel, Nikolaus. 1988. *Deutsche Übersetzungen lateinischer Schultexte: Ihre Verbreitung und Funktion im Mittelalter und in der frühen Neuzeit*. München: Artemis Verlag.

Henkel, Nikolaus. 2009. "Glossierung und Texterschließung. Zur Funktion lateinischer und volkssprachiger Glossen im Schulunterricht." In *Die althochdeutsche und altsächsische Glossographie*, edited by R. Bergmann and S. Stricker, Vol. 1, 468–496. Berlin and New York: De Gruyter.

Hofman, Rijcklof. 1996. *The Sankt Gallen Priscian commentary*. 2 Vols. Münster: Nodus.

Holtz, Louis. 1977. "La typologie des manuscrits grammaticaux latins." *Revue d'Histoire des Textes* 7: 247–269.

Holtz, Louis. 1981. *Donat et la tradition de l'enseignement grammatical: étude sur l'Ars Donati et sa diffusion (IVe-IXe siècle) et édition critique*. Paris: Centre national de la recherche scientifique.

Huang, Yan. 2014. *Pragmatics*. Second Edition. Oxford: Oxford University Press.

Hudson, Anne, ed. 2015. *Doctors in English: A study of the Wycliffite Gospel Commentaries*. Liverpool: Liverpool University Press.

Hunt, Tony. 1991. *Teaching and Learning Latin in Thirteenth-Century England*. 3 Vols. Cambridge: Brewer.

Jansen, Laura, ed. 2014. *The Roman Paratext: Frame, Texts, Readers*. Cambridge: Cambridge University Press.

Jaszczolt, Kasia. 2002. *Semantics and Pragmatics: Meaning in Language and Discourse*. London: Longman.

Jolly, Karen Louise. 2016. "The Process of Glossing and Glossing as Process: Scholarship and Education in Durham, Cathedral Library, MS A.iv.19." In *The Old English Gloss to the Lindisfarne Gospel: Language, Author and Context*, edited by Julia Fernández Cuesta and Sara María Pons-Sanz. Berlin: De Gruyter.

Jones, Richard Foster. 1953. *The Triumph of the English Language: A Survey of Opinions Concerning the Vernacular From the Introduction of Printing to the Restoration*. London: Oxford University Press.

Josselson, Ruthellen. 2004. "The Hermeneutics of Faith and the Hermeneutics of Suspicion." *Narrative Inquiry* 14(1): 1–28.

Julia, Catherine. 2001. *Fixer le sens! La sémantique spontanée des gloses de spécification du sens*. Paris: Presses Sorbonne Nouvelle.

Kantorowicz, Hermann. 1964. "The Development of the Gloss to the Justinian and the Canon Law." *The Second and Subsequent Editions of Smalley* 1952: 52–55.

King, Ross. 2015. "Ditching 'Diglossia': Describing Ecologies of the Spoken and Inscribed in Pre-Modern Korea." *Sungkyun Journal of East Asian Studies* 15(1): 1–19.

King-Hele, Desmond. 1999. *Erasmus Darwin: A Life of Unequalled Achievement*. London: Giles de la Mare.

Koch, Ernst. 2014. "Aufzeichnungen zu Luthers Auslegung des Römerbriefs: Die Handschrift in Dessau." In *Meilensteine der Reformation; Schlüsseldokumente der frühen Wirksamkeit Martin Luthers*, edited by Irene Dingel and Henning P. Jürgens, 56–59. Gütersloh: Gütersloher Verlagshaus.

Kohl, Katrin. 2007. *Metapher*. Stuttgart: Verlag J.B. Metzle.

Kuczynski, Michael P. 2017. "Glossing and Glosses." In *The Wycliffite Bible: Origin, History and Interpretation*, edited by Elizabeth Solopova, 346–367. Leiden: Brill.

Kuczynski, Michael P. 2019. *A Glossed Wycliffite Psalter: Oxford, Bodleian Library MS Bodley 554*. Oxford: Oxford University Press.
Lakoff, George, and Mark Johnson. 1980. *Metaphors We Live By*. Chicago: University of Chicago Press.
Lejeune, Philippe. 1975. *Le pacte autobiographique*. Paris: Éditions du Seuil.
Lindsay, Wallace Martin. 1996. *Studies in Early Mediaeval Latin Glossaries*. Aldershot: Ashgate.
Locke, John. 1693. *Some Thoughts Concerning Education*. London: A. and J. Churchill.
Luther, Martin, ed. 1515. *Diui Pauli apostoli ad Romanos epistola*. Wittenberg: Ioan: Grunenberg. Apud Augustinianos.
Macaulay, Aulay. 1747. *Polygraphy or Shorthand*. London: For the Author.
Maclean, Ian. 1992. *Interpretation and Meaning in the Renaissance: The Case of Law*. Cambridge: Cambridge University Press.
Maclean, Ian. 2002. *Logic, Signs and Nature in the Renaissance: The Case of Learned Medicine*. Cambridge: Cambridge University Press.
Maier, Emar. 2018. "Quotation, Demonstration, and Attraction in Sign Language Role Shift." *Theoretical Linguistics* 44(3): 265–276.
Marcin, Raymond B. 1977. "Punctuation and the Interpretation of Statutes." *Connecticut Law Review* 9(2): 227–245.
Marnette, Sophie. 2006. "The Marking Of Reported Discourse In Medieval French Manuscripts." *Langue française* 149: 31–47.
McGilchrist, Iain. 2010. *The Master and His Emissary: The Divided Brain and the Making of the Western World*. New Haven and London: Yale University Press.
Mellinkoff, David. 1963. *The Language of the Law*. Boston: Little, Brown and Co.
Meritt, Herbert. 1945. *Old English glosses*. New York: Modern Language Association.
Minnis, Alastair. 1975. "'Authorial Intention' and 'Literal Sense' in the Exegetical Theories of Richard Fitzralph and John Wyclif. An Essay in the Medieval History of Biblical Hermeneutics." *Proceedings of the Royal Irish Academy. Section C: Archaeology, Celtic Studies, History, Linguistics, Literature* 75: 1–31.
Moran, Pádraic. 2015. "Language Interaction in the St Gall Priscian." *Peritia* 26: 113–142.
Moran, Pádraic. 2019. *De origine Scoticae linguae (O'Mulcrony's Glossary): An Early Irish Linguistic Tract, Edited With a Related Glossary*. Turnhout: Brepols.
Moran, Pádraic, and John Whitman. 2022. "Glossing and Reading in Western Europe and East Asia: A Comparative Case Study." *Speculum* 97: 112–139.
Novikoff, Alex J., ed. 2013. *The Medieval Culture of Disputation: Pedagogy, Practice, and Performance*. Philadelphia: University of Pennsylvania Press.
Ó Cuív, Brian. 1965. "Linguistic Terminology in the Mediaeval Irish Bardic Tracts." *Transactions of the Philological Society* 64(1): 141–164.
Ó Cuív, Brian. 1973. *The Linguistic Training of the Mediaeval Irish Poet*. Dublin: Institute for Advanced Studies.
Offord, Malcolm. 2003. "Review of Julia, *Fixer le sens!* 1991." *Journal of French Languages Studies* 13: 146–147.

Oldekop, Johann. 1891. *Chronik des Johann Oldecop*, edited by Karl Euling. Tübingen: Lit. Verein.

Ortega y Gasset, José. 1990. "Meditations on the Frame." *Perspecta* 26: 185–190.

Palmer, Nigel. 1985. "Zur Vortragsweise der Wien-Münchener Evangelienübersetzung." *Zeitschrift für deutsches Altertum und deutsche Literatur* 114(2): 95–118.

Palmer, Nigel. 2010. "Simul cantemus, simul pausemus: Zur mittelalterlichen Zisterzienser-interpunktion." In *Lesevorgänge. Prozesse des Erkennens in mittelalterlichen Texten, Bildern und Handschriften*, edited by E. C. Lutz, 483–569. Zurich: Chronos.

Parkes, Malcom B. 1992. *Pause and Effect: An Introduction to the History of Punctuation in the West*. Aldershot: Scolar Press.

Plucknett, Theodore F. T. 1922. *Statues and Their Interpretation in the First Half of the Fourteenth Century*. Cambridge: Cambridge University Press.

Plucknett, Theodore F. T. 1956. "The Problem of Interpretation." In *A Concise History of the Common Law*. 5th edition. Boston: Little, Brown.

Pollock, Sheldon. 2000. "Cosmopolitan and Vernacular in History." *Public Culture* 12(3): 591–625.

Pollock, Sheldon. 2006. *The Language of the Gods in the World of Men: Sanskrit, Culture, and Power in Premodern India*. Berkeley, Los Angeles and London: University of California Press.

Powitz, Gerhardt. 1981. "Text und Kommentar im Buch des 15. Jahrhunderts." In *Buch und Text im 15. Jahrhundert*, edited by L. Hellinga and H. Härte, 135–145. Hamburg: Hauswedell.

Purvey, John. 1550. *The true copye of a prolog wrytten about two C. yeres paste by Iohn Wycklife [. . .] the originall whereof is founde written in an olde English Bible bitwixt the olde Testament and the Newe*. London: Robert Crowley.

Recanati, François. 1995. "The Alleged Priority of Literal Interpretation." *Cognitive Science* 19: 207–232.

Recanati, François. 2003. *Literal Meaning*. Cambridge: Cambridge University Press.

Rée, Jonathan. 1990. "Funny Voices: Stories, Punctuation, and Personal Identity." *New Literary History* 21(4): 1039–1058.

Rée, Jonathan. 1991. "Les mots des autres." In *Le langage comme défi*, edited by Henri Meschonnic, 259–267. Paris: Presses Universitaires de Vincennes.

Robert, Jean-Noël. 2006. "Hieroglossia: A Proposal." *Nanzan Institute for Religion and Culture Bulletin* 30: 25–48. Nagoya: Nanzan University.

Robertson, Durant W., Jr. 1969. *Preface to Chaucer: Studies in Medieval Perspective*. Princeton: Princeton University Press.

Romanell, Patrick. 1984. *John Locke and Medicine: A New Key to Locke*. Buffalo, NY: Prometheus Books.

Rouse, Richard, and Mary Rouse. 1990. "Concordances et index." In *Mise en page et mise en texte du livre manuscrit*, edited by J. Vezin and H.-J. Martin, 219–228. Paris: Promodis.

Rousseau, A. 1978. "Réflections sur la nature et la function des gloses et des traductions en vieux-haut-allemand." In *Littérature et société au moyen au moyen âge:*

Actes du colloque des 5 et 6 mai 1978, edited by Danielle Buschinger, 353–370. Paris: H. Champion.

Russell, Paul. 1998. "Laws, Glossaries and Legal Glossaries." *Zeitschrift für celtische Philologie* 51: 85–115.

Russell, Paul. 2008. *'Read It in a Glossary': Glossaries and Learned Discourse in Medieval Ireland.* Cambridge: Hughes Hall and Department of Anglo-Saxon, Norse Celtic.

Russell, Paul. 2018. "The Language and Registers of Law in Medieval Ireland and Wales." In *Law and Language in the Middle Ages*, edited by J. Benham, M. McHaffie, and H. Vogt, 83–103. Leiden: Brill.

Santagnello, M. 1827. *An Impartial Examination of the Hamiltonian System of Teaching Languages, to Which Are Appended a Few Hints Relative to the Real Method of Teaching Living Languages.* London: John Souter.

Sauer, Hans. 2009. "Glosses, Glossaries and Dictionaries in the Medieval Period." In *The Oxford History of English Lexicography*, edited by A. P. Cowie, Vol. 1, 17–40. Oxford: Clarendon Press.

Schiegg, Markus. 2016. "How To Do Things With Glosses: Illocutionary Forces in the Margins of Medieval Manuscripts." *Journal of Historical Pragmatics* 17(1): 55–78.

Schmidt-Lauber, Gabriele. 1994. *Luthers Vorlesung über den Römerbrief 1515/16. Ein Vergleich zwischen Luthers Manuskript und den studentischen Nachschriften.* Köln: Böhlau.

Searle, John R. 1969. *Speech Acts: An Essay in the Philosophy of Language.* Cambridge: Cambridge University Press.

Sharpe, Richard. 2005. *Titulus: Identifying Medieval Latin Texts: An Evidence-Based Approach.* Turnhout: Brepols.

Smalley, Beryl. 1941 [1952]. *The Study of the Bible in the Middle Ages.* Oxford: Clarendon Press. (2nd revised and enlarged edition, Oxford: Blackwell, 1952.)

Smith, Julia. 2018. *Relics and the Insular World, c. 600–c. 800.* (Kathleen Hughes Memorial Lectures, 15). Cambridge: Department of Anglo-Saxon, Norse and Celtic.

Smollett, Tobias G. 1771. *The Expedition of Humphry Clinker*, Vol. 1. London: W. Johnston.

Sperber, Dan, and Deirdre Wilson. 1985/6. "Loose Talk." *Proceedings of the Aristotelian Society* (New Series) 6: 153–171.

Sperber, Dan, and Deirdre Wilson. 1987. "Précis of *Relevance*." *The Behavioral and Brain Sciences* 10(4): 697–701.

Sperber, Dan, and Deirdre Wilson. 1995 [1985]. *Relevance: Communication and Cognition.* 2nd edition. Oxford: Blackwell.

Sperber, Dan, Fabrice Clement, Christophe Heintz, Olivier Mascaro, Hugo Mercier, Gloria Origgi, and Deirdre Wilson. 2010. "Epistemic Vigilance." *Mind and Language* 25(4): 359–393.

Teeuwen, Mariken. 2017. "Voices From the Edge: Anotating Books in the Carolingian Period." In *The Annotated Book in Then Early Middle Ages: Practices of Reading and Writing*, edited by M. Teeuwen and I. van Renswoude, 13–36. Turnhout: Brepols.

Thiselton, Anthony C. 1992. "The Hermeneutics of Enquiry: From the Reformation to Modern Theory." In *New Horizons in Hermeneutics*, 179–203. London: HarperCollins.

Thiselton, Anthony C. 2009. *Hermeneutics: An Introduction.* Grand Rapids, MI; Cambridge, UK: Eerdmans.

Tomasello, Michael, and Hannes Rakoczy. 2003. "What Makes Human Cognition Unique? From Individual to Shared to Collective Intentionality." *Mind and Language* 18: 121–147.

Tubb, Gary A., and Emery R. Boose. 2007. *Scholastic Sanskrit: A Handbook for Students.* New York: Columbia University Press.

Underhill, Timothy. 2015. "John Byrom and the Contexts of Charles Wesley's Shorthand." *Wesley and Methodist Studies* 7(1): 27–53.

Valente, Luisa. 2004. "Virtus significationis, violentia usus. Porretan Views on Theological Hermeneutics." In *Medieval Theories on Assertive and Non-Assertive Language*, edited by Alfonso Maierù and Luisa Valente, 163–184. Florence: Leo L. Olschki.

Vidro, Nadia, Irene E. Zweip, and Judith Olszowy-Schlanger, eds. 2014. *A Universal Art: Hebrew Grammar Across Disciplines and Faiths.* Leiden: Brill.

Walton, Roberto J. 2003. "On the Manifold Senses of Horizonedness: The Theories of E. Husserl and A. Gurwitsch." *Husserl Studies* 19: 1–24.

Watson, Alex. 2010. "Thirteen Ways of Glossing 'To a Haggis': Disputing the Borders of Robert Burns' Paratexts." *International Journal of Scottish Literature* 6: 1–24.

Watson, Cecelia. 2012. "Points of Contention; Rethinking the Past, Present, and Future of Punctuation." *Critical Inquiry* 38(3): 649–672.

Weijers, Olga. 2013. *In Search of the Truth: A History of Disputation Techniques From Antiquity to Early Modern Times.* Turnhout: Brepols.

Whitman, John. 2011. "The Ubiquity of the Gloss." *Scripta* 3: 95–121.

Whitman, John. in press. "Gloss to Lexicon East and West: A Comparison of the Relationship Between Glossing and Lexicography in Medieval East Asia and Europe, With a Translation of the Preface to the Shinsen jikyō (新撰字鏡)."

Whitman, John, and Franck Cinato, eds. 2014. *Lecture vernaculaire des textes classiques chinois/Reading Classical Texts in the Vernacular.* (Dossiers Histoire Épistémologie Langage 7). http//dossierhel.hypotheses.org/dossiers-hel7-sommaire.

Wieland, Gernot R. 1983. *The Latin Glosses on Arator and Prudentius in Cambridge University Library MS Gg. 5. 35.* Toronto: Pontifical Institute of Mediaeval Studies.

Wieland, Gernot R. 1985. "The Glossed Manuscript: Classbook or Library Book?" *Anglo-Saxon England* 14: 153–173.

Wilson, Deirdre. 2018. "Relevance Theory and Literary Interpretation." In *Reading Beyond the Code: Literature and Relevance Theory*, edited by T. Cave and D. Wilson, 185–204. Oxford: Oxford University Press.

Wilson, Edward. 1993. "A Damned Fin Abbott: The Earliest English Example of a Four-Letter Word." *Notes and Queries* 40(1): 29–34.

Wilson, Thomas. 1563. *The Rule of Reasone. Conteinyng the Arte of Logicke, Set Forth in Englishe.* London: Ihon Kingston.

Wolf, Werner. 2006. "Introduction: Frames, Framings and Framing Borders in Literature and Other Media." In *Framing Borders in Literature and Other Media*, edited by W. Wolf and W. Bernhart, 1–40. Amsterdam and New York: Rodopi.

Wyclif, John. 2001. *On the Truth of Holy Scripture*. Translated by I. C. Levy. Kalamazoo: Medieval Institute Publications.

9

A Revised Typology for the St Gall Priscian Glosses

Pádraic Moran

Manuscripts with interlinear and marginal glosses, especially in very large numbers, can present a daunting interpretive challenge. Glosses are by nature disconnected units. Individual glosses may vary considerably in form, and glosses of similar form may fulfill a wide variety of different functions, sometimes overlapping. Determining the functions of individual glosses is not always an easy task, and finding patterns of overall coherence within a body of glosses is often more difficult again.

A general typology of glosses that would be applicable to many different types of glossed manuscripts would be a valuable aid to research. Such a typology would not only help us to consider all of the possible functions of individual glosses, but it would also allow us to assess the overall profile of a collection of glosses, by examining the proportions of glosses dedicated to different functions and thereby determining what were the priorities of the glossators.

A common typology would also allow us to clarify, in a measurable way, how glossators of the same primary text in different manuscripts approached their task differently, how different primary texts might have attracted distinct methods of glossing, or perhaps how different genres of text were read and studied differently. Such comparison need not be local in scope. If a typology were sufficiently generalizable, we could hope to make a meaningful comparison between glossing practices in different regions and cultures, and across different time periods.

The ground-breaking work on gloss typology is Gernot Wieland's book-length study (Wieland 1983) of glosses on the Latin poetry of Arator and Prudentius in Cambridge, University Library, MS Gg.5.35, a manuscript from mid-eleventh-century Canterbury. Wieland's work made several important contributions. In the first place, it highlighted the importance of studying the entirety of glosses in a collection and not merely the selection of interest for vernacular linguistics. Second, it treated the symbol annotations which provide information on syntactical relationships as glosses in their own right, on a par with verbal glosses. And third, Wieland's work, although a case study on an individual manuscript, explicitly aimed at providing a typology that was generalizable to other gloss collections.[1]

Wieland's typology was further elaborated in Rijcklof Hofman's study of glosses on the Latin grammarian Priscian in St Gall, Stiftsbibliothek, MS 904.[2] The manuscript was written during 850–851 by Irish scribes and is generally held to have originated in Ireland.[3] There are about 10,016 interlinear and marginal verbal glosses, the majority of which are written in Latin, but approximately a third contain Old Irish or a mixture of the two languages.[4] In addition to these verbal glosses, the main glossator also wrote about c. 3,379 groups of symbol glosses. The first half of the collection (Priscian, books 1–5) was published in Hofman 1996.[5] More recently, his full transcription has been published online (Bauer et al. 2017).[6] The availability of a digital edition now enables us to interrogate the corpus more efficiently than was possible in print.

This study offers a detailed analysis of Hofman's typology, elaborating on the very brief outline provided in his edition. The analysis takes into account both theory and praxis. It investigates Hofman's application, in practice, of the typology to the c. 13,395 glosses in the corpus, supported by quantitative data derived from the digital edition. In parallel, the study reviews the internal structure of the typology, with some observations on consistency and redundancy. The structural analysis further incorporates insights from two recent studies of gloss typologies (Cinato 2015; Blom 2017). (The former is particularly relevant since it also concerns glosses on Priscian, including those in the present manuscript.)

By seeking to make refinements to Hofman's typology, in terms of both its structure and its application, the study has two broader objectives. Fundamentally, it aims to sharpen our understanding of the functional distribution of glosses within the St Gall corpus. But furthermore, it seeks to present a revised typology that would be both robust and flexible enough to be applicable in the future to other collections of glosses. This is the main comparative aspect of this study: a general typological framework would offer the potential to make detailed and measurable comparisons between large collections of glosses in different manuscripts, potentially also in different cultural traditions.

The possibility of applying Wieland's typology for Latin glosses to East Asian glosses was first explored in Whitman 2011. Moran and Whitman (2022) take this application further, in a comparative case study between the St Gall Priscian glosses and those on the eighth-century Japanese manuscript *Saidaiji-bon Konkōmyō saishō ōkyō* 西大寺本金光明最勝王経. The latter study argues that, despite obvious differences between the respective manuscripts and traditions, Western and Eastern glossing systems are directly comparable at a structural level. That is, of course, not to say that the respective systems are identical. But the application of a common typology allows similarities and differences to be identified with more precision, opening the way for a more granular cultural comparison, as well as the possibility of finding new interpretations where approaches from one scholarly tradition might be transferred profitably to another.

The validity of any such comparative exploration to some extent stands or falls on the robustness of the common typology used for the comparison. Since Hofman's typology has not previously been subjected to a detailed critical analysis, the present study aims to identify where there might be room for improvement.

OVERVIEW OF HOFMAN'S TYPOLOGY

Hofman presented his typology in the introduction to his edition (1996: i 83–93). His descriptions of categories were for the most part minimal, referring to Wieland (1983) for further discussion. Hofman's structure is also much more elaborate than Wieland's, employing hierarchical, numbered referencing for 75 distinct subtypes. The individual types are each given a short, one-line description and a single illustrative example, without commentary. As a result, their precise delineations are not always clear, and sometimes need to be recovered from a study of their application in the edition. This study will review the application of the typology in detail, sometimes aiming to recover unstated assumptions and in other places offering some correctives.

We should bear in mind here the inherent difficulty of applying, in a consistent way, as many as 75 categories to such a vast number of glosses. It should also be remembered that only the first half of the gloss collection was ever revised for print publication, which may explain some inconsistencies in the second half in particular.[7] Moreover, the focus of Hofman's application of his typology was providing interpretation for individual glosses. Assigning one or more type numbers to each gloss was a very economical way for the editor to signal its function(s), thereby reducing the amount of repetition that the commentary would otherwise contain. Hofman did not comment on the distribution patterns of types throughout the body of glosses overall, partly no doubt because the second half of the collection was yet to be published. In any case, assembling statistical information with the technology available at that time would have been extremely laborious. Now, thanks to the availability of a digital corpus, we can quantify information and observe overall patterns much more effectively.

Hofman adopted Wieland's five broad typological groups, listed in table 9.1 with the number of glosses assigned to each group and their proportions within the collection as a whole.[8]

Hofman allowed for glosses to be assigned to more than one type, and the resulting overlap is the reason that percentages add up to more than 100%.[9] Groups 4 and 5 (syntax and explanatory glosses) are of similar size and are by far the largest groups. About 73% of all glosses fall into either or both of these categories.

Cinato (2015: 210–253, 430–434) elaborated a very detailed classification system for glosses, broader in scope than that offered by Wieland/Hofman. His schema is oriented along three major dimensions: form, meaning, and actors (*forme, sens, acteurs*). The first (F) is concerned with aspects of glosses external to their meaning. Its primary distinction is along the lines of linguistic complexity, ranging from graphical signs without intrinsic meaning (F1) to word groups of increasing syntactic complexity: morpheme (F2), syntagma (F3), proposition (F4).[10] As subcategories of F, he distinguishes aspects related to scribal activity: concerning the location of a gloss on the manuscript page (P), the place (L, *lieu*), and time (T) of writing, relative to that of the main text. Cinato's second dimension (S, *sens*) considers the internal meaning of the glosses themselves, in relation to the primary text. Here, he adopted the Wieland–Hofman typology in essence, with some modifications. His final dimension (A, *acteurs*) distinguishes different working methods followed by glossators and further takes into account their potential goals (B, *buts*).

Cinato's multifaceted system provides a very comprehensive framework for analyzing glosses, taking many interrelated aspects into account. For the present purpose of analyzing Hofman's typology, his remarks on categories of meaning (S) are most relevant. He followed the five major groups elaborated by Wieland (designated S1–S5) but introduced two additional groups to include critical annotations (*ecdotiques*) and "socio-historical notes." I return to these distinctions in the discussion below.

Blom's book-length study (2017; see the detailed review by Cinato 2022) of glosses on the Psalms surveys 13 manuscripts with glosses in Old

Table 9.1 Count of Glosses in Hofman's Five Main Typological Groups

1	Glosses on prosody	582	4%
2	Lexical glosses	2821	21%
3	Glosses on morphology/Grammatical glosses	1429	11%
4	Glosses on syntax	4819	36%
5	Explanatory glosses, elucidating the content of the text	4949	37%

Source: Bauer et al. (2017).

Irish and several Germanic languages (including Old English, Old High German, and Old Saxon). Blom proposed a typology (2017: 26–35, 295) that followed Cinato in first separating form from other aspects of glosses. He focused on three formal categories: script, "formal type" (i.e., written manifestation, ranging from abstract signs to isolated letters, to long commentary; cf. Cinato's category F), and location on the page (cf. Cinato's category P). The other aspect of Blom's typology was function, which he reduced to three categories, according to the syntactic relationship of the gloss to the primary text. Substitution glosses effectively replace the lemma in the primary text, providing a direct synonym or translation (SUB1), or a broader semantic interpretation (SUB2), or a syntactically looser paraphrase (SUB3). Supplement glosses add content in order to clarify the primary text's morphology or syntax, either supplying (SUP1) or supplementing (SUP2) a constituent. Finally, commentary glosses provide new information, whether lexical or etymological (COM1), relating to morphology or syntax (COM2), text-critical information (COM3), or other commentaries (COM4).

Blom's study is important because it is explicitly comparative in orientation. It is significant, then, that his typological scheme differs from that created by Wieland and subsequently adopted by Hofman and endorsed by Cinato. The economy of Blom's alternative typology is certainly an advantage, since fewer categories make it easier to apply in practice. On the other hand, a simpler typology may lack granularity, since it offers fewer distinctions on the level of detail. Furthermore, there is a possibility of overgeneralization. Blom's studies are built around a selection of examples that illustrate his typology. Since this approach is not intended to be exhaustive, it remains to be seen what a complete study of each of the sources would reveal about the relative distribution of categories, and whether further distinctions might then prove useful.

How does Blom's focus on "functional aspects of glossing" relate to the Wieland–Hofman model? Function may be understood in various ways. In its broadest conception, the function of glosses might be regarded as generally hermeneutic: they provide information on the text (by means of clarifications) and its context (with supplementary content). The Wieland–Hofman typology focuses on the internal linguistic functions of the primary text that the glosses intend to clarify (prosody, lexis, morphology, syntax; the fifth category is essentially miscellaneous). Blom defines function narrowly, referring to the "possible relations [of a gloss] with regard to its principal text" (Blom 2017: 29). This approach focuses instead on the relationship between the gloss and the primary text, that is, not *what* it clarifies, but *how* it does so. I label this the "relational function," as opposed to the "explanatory function" prioritized in Wieland–Hofman.

In what follows, I provide both quantitative and qualitative analysis for each of Hofman's major groups, in turn, taking into account observations from Cinato and Blom in places.

Glosses on Prosody

The term "prosody" as used here covers its traditional sense, the study of versification, and in particular meter, as well as its modern linguistic sense, referring to suprasegmental phonological features (specifically vowel length). Its subtypes are shown in table 9.2.

For types 11 and 12, the functional objective is the same: to indicate the length of syllables. Hofman's descriptions suggest a distinction mainly of form: the former are diacritical marks (length marks), the latter verbal descriptions (taking "glosses" to mean verbal glosses). In their application, however, this is only partly true: while type 11 uses only length marks, type 12 uses sometimes verbal glosses (e.g., *producta/longus* "long," *correpta/brevis* "short") or sometimes length marks equally.[11] Another distinction regards context: however, although the description of type 11 limited it to "poetic quotations" in Priscian, both types may be found applied both to citations and to Priscian's own discussion.

Despite its description, type 13 generally does not contain "elaborate comment," but rather miscellaneous information. In fact, only 57 of 192 glosses contain any verbal comment at all. The majority involve mostly distinguishing metrical feet in citations through the use of symbols. (The glosses in this category would presumably be designated COM4 in Blom's typology.)

Lexical Glosses

Hofman (1996: i 84) explains the types in this group as serving to "explain the many rare and obscure words Priscian uses (mostly in his examples)" and their broader purpose as "obviously to increase the vocabulary of the readers." The subtypes within this group are shown in table 9.3.

Table 9.2 Subtypes of Glosses on Prosody

11	Length mark indicating syllable length in poetic quotations[1]	270	2%
12	Glosses on the length of syllables	137	1%
13	Elaborate comment on meter	192	1%

[1]The total of category 11 here includes 222 glosses with the type number 111, occurring in the second half of the corpus from book 8 on, at which point type 11 is no longer found. Since type 111 is not mentioned in Hofman's introduction, I take it to be identical with 11, assuming that the inconsistency would have been removed had the second half been revised for print.
Source: Bauer et al. (2017).

Table 9.3 Subtypes of Lexical Glosses

211	Translations into Old Irish	1539	12%
212	Synonyms	497	4%
213	Negated antonyms	8	0%
214	Hyponym defined by a hypernym with *differentia specifica*	91	1%
215	Definition given by an entire sentence	83	1%
221	Greek glosses and glosses over Greek words	335	3%
222	Use of different prefixes	5	0%
223	Adjectives glossed with a noun in the genitive (or another case)	5	0%
23	*Differentiae*	67	1%
24	Further derivations in a gloss	14	0%
25	Glosses showing the original form of the word	371	3%

Source: Bauer et al. (2017).

Most of these glosses correspond to substitution glosses in Blom's relational typology, though types 215, 24, and 25 would qualify instead as commentary glosses (COM1).

Hofman's numbering suggests an implicit hierarchical structure within this group. The rationale for subgroupings is not made explicit, however. The numbering of types 211–215 suggests they are to be regarded as a group (notionally 21), and 221–223 similarly (22), though it is difficult to identify what the unifying factors are in each case.

Of the 11 types, 211 "translations into Old Irish" is particularly significant in terms of number (12% of the total of glosses). Three others (212, 221, 25) are present in significant numbers, while the remaining types are relatively few. In any revised version of the typology, there would seem to be little benefit in retaining types for which there are as few as five or eight representative examples. Consideration could be given to amalgamating types with fewer than 1% of the glosses, possibly into a category of miscellaneous lexical explanations.

The definition for type 211 is based on both function ("translation"; cf. Blom's SUB1) and specific language ("Old Irish"). Since the vast majority of these translations are one-word synonyms, the category overlaps functionally with 212 "synonyms," which Hofman reserves instead for Latin synonyms on Latin words. Along with type 221 "Greek glosses and glosses over Greek words," type 211 is the only type that restricts its definition by reference to the language of the glosses.[12] This is by no means to suggest that all of the glosses containing Old Irish belong in this category: in fact, almost every category of verbal gloss includes some glosses in the vernacular.[13] It would therefore seem useful to separate function and language entirely and merge most of type 211 into type 212, collecting synonyms together.

A similar distinction between function and language may be made regarding type 221 "Greek glosses and glosses over Greek words." Here, the designation is based on language, not function. This is a hybrid category split almost evenly between glosses containing Greek words (165 glosses) and glosses over Greek words (170 glosses). Like type 211, the former marks a choice of language within the gloss itself; the latter is based on the nature of the lemma in the primary text (cf. type 11 above).[14] Also like types 211 and 212, most of these glosses supply synonyms. Therefore, from a functional perspective, all three categories could be grouped together, with language specificity as a separate consideration.

Regarding the overall characterization of this group, Hofman's assertion that these glosses explain "rare and obscure words" could also be reconsidered. While Priscian, being a grammarian, does indeed discuss many rare and recondite terms, very many lexical glosses also occur on words that are relatively commonplace. For example, the single word receiving the highest frequency of lexical glosses is *significatio* meaning "meaning," glossed with Latin *intellectus* or Irish *cíall, folad, inne,* or *intliucht* 22 times. The word itself is not rare or obscure, but the glosses rather draw attention to its use in a specific technical sense. In other cases, the purpose of lexical glosses is not to explain the meaning of a difficult word, but rather to disambiguate between homonyms. A common example is Latin *quod*, which may be the conjunction "because," in which case it is sometimes glossed with an Irish equivalent, *ol* "because," or else the neuter relative pronoun, sometimes glossed in Irish *a n-í sin* "the aforementioned thing" and similarly.[15] In these cases, the categorization "lexical" is still valid, since the glosses are concerned with the basic meaning of individual words, but the glosses seek to clarify a difficulty not inherent in the word itself, but rather arising from its context.

Glosses on Morphology/Grammatical Glosses

After glosses on prosody, this group is the next smallest in the number of associated glosses. Although Hofman labeled the group "Morphological glosses" in his initial overview (Hofman 1996: i 84), he afterward used the looser description "Grammatical glosses" (following Wieland). Hofman (1996: i 85) remarked that "the most frequently occurring types explain ambiguous inflected forms, such as endings used to express two case-forms."[16] These are further divided according to the traditional parts of speech in Latin (uniting the verb and participle into one category) (see table 9.4).

It is clear that glosses on the pronoun and, to a lesser extent, on the noun are by far the most important types, while, at the other end of the scale, glosses on the preposition and interjections are quite rare. These two largest

Table 9.4 Subtypes of Glosses on Morphology/Grammatical Glosses

31	Grammatical glosses on the noun	364	3%
32	Grammatical glosses on the pronoun	679	5%
33	Grammatical glosses on the verb and the participle	95	1%
34	Grammatical glosses on the adverb	116	1%
35	Grammatical glosses on the conjunction	75	1%
36	Grammatical glosses on the preposition	21	0%
37	Grammatical glosses on the interjection	10	0%

Source: Bauer et al. (2017).

Table 9.5 Subtypes of Glosses on Nouns

311	Glosses on case forms:	(228)	(2%)
3111	Glosses on case: nominative	25	0%
3112	Glosses on case: vocative	24	0%
3113	Glosses on case: genitive	38	0%
3114	Glosses on case: dative	38	0%
3115	Glosses on case: accusative	49	0%
3116	Glosses on case: ablative	54	0%
312	Glosses on number	16	0%
313	Glosses on gender and various other morphological points	120	1%

Source: Bauer et al. (2017).

groups each have a number of subtypes. Taking the noun first, its subtypes are given in table 9.5.

The type descriptions might warrant some clarification. Glosses are assigned to these types not simply because of their occurrence on words in the named grammatical categories, but rather because they disambiguate words in those categories where some confusion is possible (as signaled by Hofman in his introduction). For that reason, they might be more helpfully labeled "Glosses *clarifying* case forms," and so on. As meta-linguistic glosses, they would correspond to Blom's COM2.

The next-largest category of grammatical glosses is 32 "grammatical glosses on the pronoun." Hofman here (1996: i 86) cites Wieland directly (1983: 48): these glosses "provide the nouns for which pronouns and pronominal adverbs substitute, thereby literally showing them to stand *pro nomine*." These mostly therefore correspond to Blom's relational function SUB1, even though their explanatory function is quite different from the SUB1 lexical glosses considered above. This category is further divided as in table 9.6.

Hofman remarks (1996: i 86) that within this group "glosses on relative pronouns [sc. 322] significantly outnumber glosses on other pronouns," for the reasons that Latin relative pronouns are often ambiguous in form (though arguably not more so than other pronouns), are also often identical in form to

Table 9.6 Subtypes of Glosses on Pronouns

321	Glosses on pronouns in general	17	0%
322	Glosses on relative pronouns:[1]	(127)	1%
3221	Rel. pronoun glossed by its antecedent	38	0%
3222	Rel. pronoun glossed by the gloss above the antecedent	7	0%
3223	Rel. pronoun glossed by an interpretation or lexical equivalent of the antecedent	36	0%
3224	Rel. pronoun without identifiable antecedent	0 (!)	0%
323	Other pronouns:	(581)	(4%)
3231	Interchangeability of demonstrative pronouns or Old Irish glosses solving ambiguity	3	0%
3232	Glosses over pronouns referring to a concept in the preceding/following line/paragraph	495	4%
3233	Glosses that differ in case from the pronoun and can substitute it	83	1%

[1] The edition (both print and online versions) contains four further categories within subgroup 322 that are not listed or explained in the typology outlined in the print edition. These are 3225 (1 gloss), 3226 (41), 3227 (5), 3228 (1). The three types with a very small number of glosses may well have originated as typographical errors. Type 3226, however, has a significant number of glosses. It is striking that nearly half of these involve the Latin word *ius* (16 glosses) or its Irish equivalent *dliged* (3), both here meaning "grammatical rule." Perhaps these were intended for the type 3224 "rel. pronoun without identifiable antecedent," which otherwise has no glosses at all. (The example supplied for 3224 in the introduction (Hofman 1996: i 87) is in fact assigned number 3226 in the edition.)

Source: Bauer et al. (2017).

various adverbs and conjunctions, and speakers of Old Irish did not have a native equivalent to the Latin relative pronoun, and so needed particular help on this point (see also Draak 1967: 19; Lambert 1981). However, the count of glosses in each type does not support this impression. There are 127 glosses on the relative pronouns, whereas subtype 323 "other pronouns" has 581. Of these "other pronouns," the predominant categories are deictic pronouns *hic haec hoc* "this" (175 glosses) and *ille illa illud* "that" (45), the anaphoric pronoun *is ea id* "he, she, it" (144 glosses), and *idem eadem idem* "the same" (36).[17]

With the subcategory of relative pronouns, the two main subtypes are 3221 "rel. pronoun glossed by its antecedent" and 3223 "rel. pronoun glossed by an interpretation or lexical equivalent of the antecedent." The first facilitates substitution. By showing the antecedent of a relative pronoun, a reader has the option of substituting the pronoun with its referent and thereby adapting the primary text while maintaining its grammatical cohesion. The second combines glosses that have two different functions. The first of these replicates the substitution function of the previous type, except here the antecedent is not explicit in the primary text, but rather inferred by the glossator. This can be distinguished from other glosses in type 3223 that offer supplementary interpretative comment (e.g., 198a9 n *quod: .i. anaithfoilsigud sin* "that is their re-demonstration"). These, by contrast, stand in a disruptive relationship to the primary text and must have been read as though in parenthesis.

By far the most frequent type with the group "grammatical glosses" is 3232 "glosses over pronouns referring to a concept in the preceding/following line/paragraph," under "other pronouns." This could be subdivided along similar lines, since it contains glosses offering substitutions, facilitating continuous readings, as well as supplementary glosses, offering parenthetical explanations. Of the 495 glosses in this type, 244 (49%) comprise one word only, nearly all of which have a grammatical agreement with the glossed lemma, indicating that these are substitution glosses. The remainder provides explanations of varying complexity, up to 16 words in length.

All of these pronouns share the quality of being anaphoric/cataphoric, that is, they either refer back to a previous referent or anticipate one to follow. Type 3232 includes 22 glosses on forms of the word *supradictus* "above-mentioned," which, though not a pronoun at all, is coherent here if we take anaphora, rather than word class, as the fundamental characteristic of this group.

The two major categories discussed above—glosses on nouns and glosses on pronouns—are unified by their focus on a single part of speech. Their functions, however, are quite different. The former provides meta-linguistic information on the forms of the lemmata and as such can clearly be described as morphological glosses, since they clarify aspects of morphology. The latter, however, explains the relationships of lemmata to other words. The relationship between words is generally regarded as pertaining to syntax, and there would be a case for re-assigning these types to that group.

The remaining groups (34 adverbs, 35 conjunctions, 36 prepositions, 37 interjections) are internally undifferentiated. Only the first two are represented in significant numbers. Sometimes the function is disambiguation, for the adverb either by meta-linguistic labeling (6a14 u *Postremo: adverbium*) or—more frequently—by Irish substitution (5b11 f, etc. *tam: .i. emith*). The latter is exceptionally common for conjunctions: 73 out of 75 glosses are expressed in Old Irish.[18]

Glosses on Syntax

This large group is divided into two subtypes, distinguished according to the form of the glosses: symbols or words. The former is significantly larger, as shown in table 9.7.

Symbol glosses (categorized as SUP2 in Blom) have only relatively recently been subjected to scholarly examination. A short, ground-breaking initial study, focused on the St Gall Priscian glosses, was published by Maartje Draak in 1957, followed by a longer article in 1967. Fred Robinson extended the inquiry to Anglo-Saxon manuscripts in 1973 (see also O'Neill 1992), and Michael Korhammer published a wide-ranging survey in 1980.[19]

Table 9.7 Subtypes of Glosses on Syntax

| 41 | Syntactical glosses using symbols | 3287 | 25% |
| 42 | Syntactical glosses using words | 1552 | 11% |

Source: Bauer et al. (2017).

Robinson (1973: 468) and Korhammer (1980: 23, 32) suggested that a system of symbol glosses for clarifying the syntax of Latin sentences originated in Ireland, given its widespread proliferation in Insular circles and its early attestation in the Irish manuscripts.[20] Hofman's very painstaking transcription of all of the symbol glosses in the St Gall Priscian now gives us the opportunity to study this system more exhaustively than was possible before.

In his introduction, Hofman followed both Robinson (1973) and Wieland (1983) in adopting the term "symbol glosses" instead of the earlier "construe marks" (used by Draak; cf. Korhammer's *Konstruktionshilfen*) emphasizing that, despite their scholarly neglect, these symbols should be regarded as having importance equal to verbal glosses. He also noted that not all of these glosses "construe" syntax, but rather "belong more to the domain of logic" (1996: i 88).[21]

The major group 41 "syntactical glosses using symbols" contains altogether 11 distinct subtypes (see table 9.8).

Korhammer made a fundamental distinction between sequence glosses and correlating glosses: the former encode a re-arrangement of words in the primary text and the latter signal some direct relationship between words without indicating any priority. Of the former type (413), there are just three examples in the St Gall Priscian manuscript.[22] The first instance is the most elaborate. It uses Latin letters *a–k* to indicate a new reading sequence for

Table 9.8 Subtypes of Group 41 "Syntactical Glosses Using Symbols"

4111	Symbols correlating adjectives/prepositions with substantives	494	4%
4112	Symbols correlating a genitive in apposition with a substantive	50	0%
4121	Symbols correlating a rel. pronoun with its antecedent	530	4%
4122	Symbols correlating other pronouns with nouns	261	2%
4123	Symbols correlating verbal forms, verbs, subjects, etc.	146	1%
413	Glosses establishing word order with the help of different symbols	3	0%
4141	Symbols clarifying the skeletal structure of a sentence	686	5%
4142	Symbols correlating two sentences	465	4%
4143	Symbols supplying word(s) omitted by the author	451	3%
4144	Symbols correlating theoretical explanation with examples	338	3%
4145	Various other uses	28	0%

Source: Bauer et al. (2017).

the start of a difficult sentence at the opening of Priscian's work (p. 1a2–9; Hertz ii 1.1–3): *cum omnis eloquentiae doctrinam et omne studiorum genus sapientiae luce praefulgens a Graecorum fontibus deriuatum Latinos proprio sermone inuenio celebrasse.*[23] The second example occurs on p. 23b9–11 (Hertz iii 48.23):

> inuenio/.a\ *tamen* in uah | et ah et oh · inte*r*iectionib*us*/f\ te*r*minale*m*/d\ uideri/c\ | syllabae\e/ h\.b/.
> "I find, however, in the interjections *uah* and *ah* and *oh* that the final of the syllable seems to be *h*."[24]

The skeletal word order indicated here would be: *inuenio h uideri terminalem syllabae interiectionibus* "I find that *h* seems to be the final of the syllable in interjections." The glosses effectively bring the direct object (*h*, referring to the letter) forward to follow the main verb and reorganize the infinitive clause following, bringing the infinitive verb (*uideri*) to the front and its object (*terminalem*) directly after. The sentence is short and not especially difficult, so it is hard to see the motivation for using sequence glosses here. One detail is striking, however: this is the second time only that Priscian expressed an idea by fronting the sentence with the verb *inuenio*, and both examples have sequence glosses. Since the first example is indeed challenging, the second may have been prompted simply by imitation.

The third example occurs on p. 71b22–27 (Hertz ii 173.11–14), where there are several layers of glossing combined:

> *quod*/d\ *enim* dicas singula|ris[25] nu*m*eri adue*r*bium\e/ *uel quod* pluralis[26] c*um*/f\ simi|llite*r*[27] om*n*e adue*r*bium tam singulari|bus q*uam* pluralibus ue*r*bis adiungi-tu*r* etiam/b\ | numerale quencunq*ue*\c/ nu*m*erum signi|ficet\a/
> "Indeed, which adverb would you say is of singular number or which of plural? Since every adverb is joined in a similar way to both singular and plural verbs, the [verbal] number can also indicate whatever number [the adverb has]."

In addition to the glosses indicated above, correlating symbol glosses link the conjunction *cum* with the dependent verb *adiungitur*, marking the limits of a clause, and *enim* and *significet* are similarly linked, outlining the larger sense unit. Other correlating symbol glosses link *numerum* and its qualifier *quencunque*, and *etiam* with *numerale*. The fact that only 6 out of 24 words have a sequence gloss leaves the intended order for the remaining words open to interpretation. However, integrating all of the sequences and correlating glosses, one possible reading is as follows (using underscores here to indicate words linked by correlating glosses): *significet_enim etiam_numerale quencunque_numerum quod aduerbium dicas singular numeri uel quod pluralis cum adiungitur similiter omne aduerbium tam singularis quam pluralibus uerbis* "Indeed the [verbal] number can also indicate whatever [adverbial] number—which adverb you might say is of singular number or which of plural—since every adverb is joined in a similar way to both singular and plural verbs." Note that the syntactic word order of the first clause is clearly Verb-Subject-Object, a feature of the Irish vernacular. If nothing else, this passage illustrates the complexity of glossing practice, showing several layers of glosses with varying form and function interacting.

Turning to correlating symbol glosses, these typically occur in pairs (77%), although sometimes also in groups of three (16%) or occasionally four (5%).[28] Hofman's transcription indicates a very wide repertoire of forms for symbol glosses—some 78 altogether—although a very small number predominate in practice. Indeed, the top four most frequently occurring forms account for 87% of all occurrences: <"> (1,342 occurrences, 41% of all symbols), <.-> (672, 21%), <:> (462, 14%), <.,> (214, 7%).[29] Each of these symbols is found in every one of the subtypes of symbol glosses, as indicated in table 9.9.

The table makes it clear that symbols do not have inherent functions. Instead, their function must be inferred from the context. That being said, some looser patterns of usage can be observed. The table lists the number of different symbols used in each type. In general, we can observe that the 414 types are characterized by a greater diversity of usage than 411. For example, type 4111 "symbols correlating adjectives/prepositions with substantives" contains 494 glosses, elaborated with 16 distinct symbols. Type 4121 "symbols correlating a rel. pronoun with its antecedent" is of comparative size (530 glosses) and has a similar range of symbols (19). On the other hand, type 4142 "symbols correlating two sentences" has only slightly fewer glosses (465) but is elaborated with as many as 45 different symbols. The most common symbol form in the manuscript (<">) accounts for 59% of the glosses in type 4111 and 45% of glosses in type 4121, but only 27% of those in 4142. This means that a reader confronted with the symbol <"> might, on the basis of experience, consider first the possibility that the symbol correlated an adjective or preposition with a substantive, before exploring other interpretations afterward. The same reader encountering a rare symbol, however, might presuppose another function (e.g., correlating sentences), knowing that more unusual symbols were less likely to represent the function of type 4111.

We can make some further observations about the two broad categories of symbol glosses, 411 and 414, in turn. Although neither group is explicitly defined in Hofman, the former appears to focus on relationships between individual words and therefore pertains to syntax. Some of these types appear to share a function with types in group 3 "grammatical glosses" and are distinguished principally by form. For example type 4121 "symbols correlating

Table 9.9 Distribution of Symbols According to Gloss Type

Type:	4111	4112	4121	4122	4123	4141	4142	4143	4144	4145
=	291	26	236	100	76	241	127	168	126	12
.-	51	6	130	67	17	142	118	110	67	4
.:	72	8	75	34	15	124	48	64	39	1
.,	40	5	32	13	13	58	27	38	8	2
Total of glosses:	494	50	530	261	146	686	465	451	338	28
Distinct symbols:	16	9	19	28	17	39	45	33	41	12

Source: Bauer et al. (2017).

a rel. pronoun with its antecedent" would seem to correspond in function with 3221 "rel. pronoun glossed by its antecedent," although it is notable that symbol glosses are clearly by far the preferred way to identify an antecedent: type 4121 has 530 glosses compared to just 38 in type 3221. A similar overlap of function occurs between 4122 "symbols correlating other pronouns with nouns" and 3232 "glosses over pronouns referring to a concept in the preceding/following line/paragraph." Glosses in both types are concerned to find the anaphoric reference of the pronouns *is, hic, ille,* and *idem* especially. In this case, however, the frequency pattern is reversed: symbols are used in 146 cases (type 4122), but words in 495 (type 3232).

Moving to the 414 subgroup, type 4141 "symbols clarifying the skeletal structure of a sentence" is easily the largest of all types of symbol glosses (686 glosses). The term "skeletal structure" may be traced to Robinson (1973: 460) and later Wieland (1983: 104). It suggests the articulation of a complex structure, but in practice 77% of glosses in this type comprise two symbols only. These, therefore, in effect, mark just the boundaries of clauses. The second element is nearly always a verb (which is sentence final in standard Latin word order), the first is usually a conjunction. A wide variety of conjunctions are marked. Sometimes they stand at the head of a dependent clause: for example, *cum* (44 glosses), *ut* (16), *ne* (9). Sometimes they introduce parallel clauses: for example, *et* (27), *sed* (21), *nam* (17), *quamvis* (16), *igitur* (15), *nec* (11), *vel* (11), *unde* (10), *quomodo* (9), *quoque* (9), and so on. And sometimes the gloss occurs on second-position discourse markers: for example, *enim* (29), *autem* (19), *vero* (15). In the last case, the symbol glosses have been transferred from the clause boundary proper to second-position constituents. Take, for example, the glossed sentence on p. 4b25–27 sentence (Hertz ii 8.21–2): *mutae autem/'''\ a se incipientes et in e uocalem desinentes, exceptis q et k, quarum altera in u, altera in a finitur, sua conficiunt nomina\'''/.* "Mute consonants, moreover, form their [letter] names beginning with [the sound] itself and ending with the vowel *e*, except for *q* and *k*, one of which has an ending in *u*, the other in *a*." The starting boundary of the clause is *mutae*, but the gloss occurs instead on the second element, *autem*. This has two advantages. A reader encountering a symbol gloss on *mutae* might look for a matching symbol on some correlating word with a grammatical agreement. However, since *autem* is indeclinable, and therefore has no grammatical agreement, this gloss must signal a different function. Second, *autem*, as a discourse marker, signals to the reader that the text is moving on to a new idea; the corresponding symbol gloss marks the extent of that idea in the manuscript.

Type 4142 "symbols correlating two sentences" stretches the designation "gloss on syntax," since one sentence is normally the largest linguistic structure to which syntactic analysis can be applied (Horrocks 2011: 118). The correlation might therefore be better regarded as one concerning discourse units. Glosses in type 4142 show an inverted pattern of application compared to type 4141. In type 4141, glosses mark boundaries of clauses with a first symbol very often on a conjunction or discourse marker and the second usually on the following verb at the end of the clause.[30] In type 4142, however, glosses bridge two sentences by placing a first symbol on a word that can fall into many categories and the second usually on a discourse marker in the following sentence. The first word therefore appears to be a focalized topic. The lemmata in type 4142 are found in a narrower range than for 4141: the most common, accounting for almost two-thirds of the glosses in this type are: *enim* (113), *nam* (53), *unde* (41), *tamen* (29), *igitur* (18), *quamvis* (11), *nisi* (10), *quod* (9), and *sed* (9). These glosses help to articulate the structure of the discourse, indicating where Priscian introduces new ideas and highlighting the discourse markers that define how these ideas stand in relation to those already asserted.

Of all the types discussed so far, type 4144 "symbols correlating theoretical explanation with examples" may well be the most specific to the content of the St Gall manuscript. Priscian's text is a technical work, elaborating a vast number of rules relating to the Latin language. Priscian very often mentions individual words with noteworthy grammatical properties and then provides literary citations as illustrations. The symbol glosses "correlating theoretical explanation with examples" have a double function: not only do they show readers where to find illustrations for a particular word, but they also clarify which word in the citation is the focus of the example. Here again, the label "syntax glosses" is inaccurate. These words do not have any syntactic relationship. As for the previous type, these symbols highlight words that help to articulate the author's discourse.

The major group "glosses on syntax" is divided along formal lines into "syntactic glosses using symbols" (41) and "syntactic glosses using words" (42). The major function of the latter subgroup is suppletion (corresponding to Blom's supplement glosses category) (see table 9.10).

Explanatory Glosses

The final group is described as "explanatory glosses, elucidating the content of the text" in Hofman's initial overview (1996: i 84), but afterward referred to as "commentary glosses" (1996: i 92), following Wieland. These glosses provide commentary (generally other than linguistic commentary) on the text itself as well as its content.[31] This is the largest constituent group overall (marginally larger than glosses on syntax). The breakdown of constituent subtypes and their frequency of occurrence is as shown in table 9.11.

The types in this group might be organized into three main subgroups: (1) glosses concerned with the establishment and organization of the text itself

Table 9.10 Subtypes of Group 42 "Syntactical Glosses Using Words"

421	Glosses identifying a speaker or an example	89	1%
422	Suppletive glosses:	(1039)	(8%)
4221	Suppletive nouns/pronouns in the nominative	263	2%
4222	Suppletive nouns/pronouns in the genitive	92	1%
4223	Suppletive nouns/pronouns in the dative	6	0%
4224	Suppletive nouns/pronouns in the accusative	45	0%
4225	Suppletive nouns/pronouns in the vocative	0 (!)	0%
4226	Suppletive adverbial adjuncts	148	1%
4227	Suppletive adjectives and adjectival clauses	49	0%
4228	Suppletive verbs and short clauses	399	3%
4229	Suppletive conjunctions or prepositions	37	0%
423	Glosses modifying adjectives	398	3%
424	*Adit* glosses	14	0%

Source: Bauer et al. (2017).

Table 9.11 Subtypes of Explanatory Glosses

51	Glosses decoding figures of speech	40	0%
52	Glosses summarizing content	952	7%
53	Cross-references	221	2%
541	(Elaborate) comment on the main text	884	7%
542	*Quia* glosses	80	0%
543	Glosses elucidating the main text	1523	11%
55	Etymological glosses	35	0%
56	Encyclopedic glosses:	(616)	(5%)
561	Geographical names	200	2%
562	Unusual objects	2	0%
563	Proper names	128	1%
57	Source glosses:	(343)	3%
571	Grammatical sources identified/Priscian confronted with other sources	116	1%
572	Glosses revealing an acquaintance with Latin authors or Roman mythology	227	2%
58	Glosses giving variant readings	300	2%
59	Glosses giving information about the socio-historical context	209	2%

(critical annotations), (2) glosses that interpret the text by internal reference to the text itself (intra-textual reference), and (3) glosses that interpret the text by reference to external sources (extra-textual reference). We might also consider a fourth group: (4) those that do not engage with the text at all. The last more or less overlaps with the final type 59 "glosses giving information about the socio-historical context." The "socio-historical context" intended here is that of the glossators and copyists. These include pen tests, scribes' names, prayers, records of time, remarks on the process of writing, and so on.[32] Strictly speaking, however, these are not explanatory glosses.[33]

The first subgroup proposed above, critical annotations, would include 58 "glosses giving variant readings" and 53 "cross-references."[34] The description of type 52 "glosses summarizing content" is misleading. Of the 952 glosses here, nearly all are critical signs in the margin drawing attention to some feature in the main text. Almost three-quarters (686 glosses) are marginal glosses noting the letter *V* against a citation of Virgil in the text. There are 60 other marginal glosses (nearly all in a later hand) marking *V*, presumably for *versus*, against other authors. Other glosses in this type include a series of numbers, articulating a succession of points in Priscian; *greca* for references to Greek deemed noteworthy; and *exceptio(nes)* to mark where Priscian gives exceptions to grammatical rules. Since no summaries are offered here, the type might better be described as "glosses highlighting content."

The second proposed subgroup, intra-textual reference, would include types 51 "glosses decoding figures of speech" and 542 "*quia* glosses," the latter effectively summarizing content.[35] Hofman (1996: i 93) explains type 543 "glosses elucidating the main text" as the comment that "can be traced back to the immediate content." The third subgroup, extra-textual reference, would include 57 "source glosses" and 56 "encyclopedic glosses."[36] Type 541 "(elaborate) comment on the main text" belongs here too, since Hofman (1996: i 92) defines its contents as "adding information which cannot be derived from the context" and containing "glosses which display originality on the part of the glossator, deviating from the facts and statements which can be found in Priscian or other Roman grammarians."

Type 563 is designated as "proper names," even though these are in fact nearly all hypernym glosses (matching the description for the lexical type 214).[37] Glosses that designate nouns as proper names are instead found in type 566 (with 287 glosses), not included at all in Hofman's elaboration of types.[38] In any case, this is a grammatical categorization, many probably inferred from context as much as drawing on external knowledge, and they might therefore be categorized rather as morphological glosses (e.g., under type 313).

CONCLUSIONS

The typology that Hofman developed for his edition of the St Gall Priscian glosses, building on and refining that first set out by Wieland, was remarkably granular in its 75 individual types. The larger divisions are very clear and useful, including the fundamental divide between glosses that focus on language and its literal meaning (groups 1–4) and glosses that provide other types of commentary (group 5). In the former, the division along linguistic categories (prosody, lexicon, morphology, syntax) is clear-cut and has the advantage of being applicable to glossed texts in any language. Although Hofman uses both "morphological glosses" and the looser designation "grammatical glosses" for the same category (the latter following Wieland), it seems preferable to retain the former. The treatment of symbols as glosses on the same standing as verbal glosses is also well-supported by their frequency of use and complexity of function.

In its application, Hofman's typology functioned as a very economical method of commentary to individual glosses in his edition. The type numbers allow a reader, after referring to the introduction of his edition, to form a quick understanding of the nature and function of a particular gloss. Rather than assess individual glosses, however, this study has taken advantage of the digital edition to evaluate broader patterns in the application of the typology.

The quantitative part of this study has shown the precise distribution of glosses within each of the 75 types. In doing so, it has revealed a number of types that have associated glosses in very small numbers (or, rarely, none at all). There are 13 types, for example, with 10 glosses or fewer.[39] In the interests of economy, therefore, the overall number of categories could potentially be reduced, by conflating some lesser-used types and perhaps abandoning others. This would bring the advantage of making future applications of the typology to other gloss collections easier. And by removing categories with fine grades of distinction, the likelihood of inconsistent application from person to person would also be reduced. Furthermore, more broadly defined categories would allow for more meaningful comparisons between different collections of glosses. In the revised scheme presented below, I have chosen to conflate types with a representation of less than 1% of the total number of glosses.

The qualitative analysis identified a number of issues where some improvement could be made to the typology. These include:

1) Consolidation of overlapping explanatory function. In some cases, distinctions in the definitions of two categories were not consistently followed in practice (e.g., 11 and 12). Such categories could therefore be conflated.
2) Clarification of type descriptions. Some categories could be redefined to reflect their application in practice: for example, type 13 "elaborate comment," really "miscellaneous comment on meter" (since comment is often very spare); type 25 "glosses showing the original form of the word," really "etymological glosses" (equivalent to type 55); type 52 "glosses summarizing content," really "glosses highlighting content."
3) Distinction between function and language. For example, the lexical types 211, 212, and 211 mainly provide synonyms, with the distinction

being one of language (Irish, Latin, Greek). If we take an explanatory function as the defining factor in the typology, these types would be united into a single category. The language of glosses could be distinguished by different means, particularly in the context of a digital edition.

4) Distinction between function and category of lemma. The types within group 3 are organized by the part of speech of the lemma, but these split into two groups that exhibit quite different functions (both explanatory and relational). Glosses on the noun clarify its morphological categories (with a commentary relational function), but glosses on the pronoun provide information on syntactic relationships (with a substitutional relational function). Giving priority to function, most of the pronoun group would be therefore reassigned to group 4 "syntax glosses."

5) Distinction between function of gloss and form (reflecting the observations of both Cinato and Blom). Again, assuming the precedence of function, some types might be grouped together, regardless of their form: for example, 3221 and 4121, both glosses identifying the antecedents of relative pronouns.

6) Clarifications to the definition and organization of subgroupings. Not all subgroups are explicitly defined, and in some cases (e.g., group 5) they could be reorganized into clearer hierarchies. This would help future editors to locate types within the hierarchy and would reduce the risk of inconsistent application.

Taking these reflections into account, I have proposed a revised version of Hofman's typology below. It retains the four basic linguistic categories but adds a fifth for discourse glosses (see discussion above under syntax glosses). It aims to make explicit the description of each second-tier subgroup, allowing also for a miscellaneous category with each group to reduce the number of rarely found types at this level.[40] This two-tier typology is intended to be a minimal elaboration. It would be further expanded to three, four, or even further subdivisions, by adopting or modifying the categories already developed by Hofman, or introducing new categories relevant to a specific corpus (see table 9.12).

Any typology is a construction, based on observation and interpretation, and not a record of fact. For that reason, no typology will perfectly meet all requirements and expectations. It is possible that every editor will feel inclined to adapt a given typology to the specifics of their own glossed material and the particular research questions they have in mind, and perhaps no two editors will agree completely on a common approach. If at least the top-level categories outlined by Wieland and Hofman (and augmented here

Table 9.12 Proposed Revised Typology for the St Gall Priscian Glosses

1	**Glosses on prosody**	(599)	(4%)
11	Glosses on syllable length (= 11, 12)	407	3%
12	Other comment on meter (= 13)	192	1%
2	**Lexical glosses**	(3143)	(23%)
21	Synonyms (= 211, 212, part of 221)	2371	18%
22	Etymological glosses (25, 55)	406	3%
23	Other lexical glosses (213–215, 222, 223, 23, 24, 563)	273	3%
3	**Glosses on morphology**	1070	(8%)
31	Morphology of the noun (31, 556)	650	5%
32	Morphology of other parts of speech (remaining types)	420	3%
4	**Glosses on syntax**	4182	(31%)
41	Glosses marking boundaries (4141)	685	5%
42	Glosses marking correlation (4111, 4112, 4121–4123)	951	7%
43	Suppletion (322, 4121, 4143, 422)	2499	19%
44	Glosses establishing word order (413, 424)	18	0%
45	Other syntax glosses	28	0%
5	**Discourse glosses**	1387	(10%)
51	Glosses articulating the linear structure (3232, 4142)	960	7%
52	Other discourse glosses (4144, 421)	427	3%
6	**Commentary glosses**	4789	(36%)
61	Critical annotations (58, 53, 52)[1]	1473	11%
62	Intra-textual reference (51, 542, 543)	1643	12%
63	Extra-textual reference (57, 56, 541, excluding 563)	1429	11%
64	Non-textual comment (59)	209	2%

[1] I have maintained categories 61 and 64 with "Commentary glosses" here, though they can be easily seen to correspond to Cinato's S6 (= Blom, COM3) and S7.
Source: Pádraic Moran.

with the proposed category of discourse glosses) can be accepted as universal, then we have some potential to make meaningful comparisons between a variety of different collections. If these second-level categories are adopted, then the comparison will be more fine-grained. The specific numbering or other referencing system used is unimportant.

NOTES

1. Wieland 1983: 2: "The resulting categories have validity not only for Gg.5.35 but practically for all other manuscripts containing Latin glosses."

2. Priscian's text is edited in Hertz 1855–1859 (hereafter Hertz).

3. For a manuscript description and discussion of the place of origin, see Hofman 1996: i 12–31; see also Hofman 2000: 260–262; Dumville 1997: 23–27, 34–36, 51–52.

4. This figure is the total of glosses in the digital edition discussed below, expanding on the figure of 9,412 cited in Hofman 1996: i 8. About 90% of the glosses were written in one hand distinct from those of the primary text, apparently directly after the writing of the primary text. The remainder were added afterward in up to ten different hands.

5. An older edition of the Old Irish glosses is Stokes and Strachan (1901–3), II xx–xxiii, 49–224.

6. This edition supersedes the version originally launched by Moran in 2010.

7. For example, inconsistencies in the punctuation and word spacing in Old Irish words (according to different methods of normalization).

8. All percentages are rounded to the nearest whole number. See Moran 2015: 217 for a breakdown by book of Priscian.

9. 11,476 glosses (86%) are assigned to one type only, 1,866 (14%) to two types, and 51 (<1%) to three. Only one gloss (103a20 l) has four types and one other (95a37 m) has five. (References are those of the digital edition, comprising manuscript page, column, and line number, followed by a letter or letters designating an individual gloss in that column.)

10. Approximate to word, phrase, and sentence.

11. Length marks in type 12 occur mainly in the second half, from book 7, and may therefore have potentially been subject to revision as well.

12. I ignore here type 3231 "interchangeability of demonstrative pronouns or Old Irish glosses solving ambiguity," to which just three glosses are assigned, all of which are also designated 211.

13. In the lexical group, for example, c. 35% of glosses in types 214 and 215 contain Irish and likewise 63% for type 23. Old Irish is found in the other major groups too: see Moran 2015: 127.

14. Of the 170 glosses over Greek words, 73 are symbol glosses, overlapping with type 4144 (see below).

15. These glosses therefore also serve to clarify the morphological category (see next group). For similar examples see Moran 2018: 4–5.

16. The remark that glosses in this group "are intended to facilitate the reading of Priscian's text: they guide the reader through his sentences" (Hofman 1996: i 85) is less helpful, since it may potentially be applied to all of the glosses groups 1–4, if not to the entire corpus.

17. The individual forms most frequently glossed are *hoc* (80 glosses), *ea* (38), *haec* (31).

18. According to Hofman, 46 of them also fall into category 211.

19. Other studies include Lemoine 1994 (on Breton manuscripts), Reynolds 1990, O'Neill 1992, Cinato 2020.

20. Indeed the earliest witness to the system, not noted by Robinson or Korhammer, is the early- to mid-seventh century Irish gospel manuscript known as Usserianus Primus (see Ó Néill 1998; 2020), which contains dry-point symbol and other glosses. This is also the oldest-known Irish glossed manuscript, indicating that symbol glosses were present from the very beginning of the (known) Irish glossing tradition.

21. Hofman did not identify which glosses or types of glosses he was referring to and, despite his distinction, retained all of them within category of syntactical glosses, presumably following Wieland. See discussion below on what I label discourse glosses. A smaller number of symbol glosses are also lexical in function; see further below.

22. Two examples at pp. 1a2 and 23b7 are mislabelled type 4132. A type 4131 at p. 2b1 is an error, probably for 4112.

23. "Since I find that the Latins celebrated in their own language the teaching of all eloquence and that every type of study shining forth with the light of wisdom is derived from Greek sources..." Re-arranged as: *cum inuenio Latinos celebrasse proprio sermone doctrinam omnis eloquentiae et omne studiorum genus praefulgens luce sapientiae a Graecorum fontibus deriuatum.* For detailed discussion on this example, see Moran and Whitman 2022.

24. Priscian here modifies his prior assertion that *h* is not found in syllable-final position and goes on to explain the inconsistency by suggesting that these interjections might be shortenings of original longer forms *uaha, aha, oho.* (Hertz in his edition suppressed the example *oh* and subsequent *oho*.)

25. Glossed (71b22 u): *ut semel singulatim* "as in *semel* [once], *singulatim* [singly]." This gloss seems to offer examples of adverbs that are singular by definition, so misunderstanding Priscian's point that adverbs can be determined as singular from context (depending on the number of the associated verb).

26. Glossed (71b23 w) *ut pluraliter* "as in *pluraliter* [in the plural]" (possibly motivated by the same misunderstanding discussed in the previous note).

27. Glossed (71b23 x), summarizing the point that follows [type 532 "elucidating," but really 52 "summarizing"]: *.i. issí indobriather chétna ad/chomaltar fris/na briathra hua/thati ⁊ hilddai.,* "i.e. it is the same adverb that is joined to the singular and plural verbs."

28. The largest groups are a group of eight symbol glosses at 204a14–18, nine at 192a40–b1, and two interlaced groups of ten symbol glosses at 10b7–14.

29. Other common symbols are: <..-> (78, 2%), <.> (68, 2%), <:-> (54, 2%), </.> (49, 2%), <...> (35, 1%), <;> (32, 1%). Hofman's transcription <"> could equally be <..>. Draak 1957: 274 (and 1967: 116) suggested that more elaborate signs are used when the space between symbols is larger.

30. On discourse markers, see Kroon 1998; 2011.

31. Cinato (2015: 218, 227) observes that explanatory glosses sometimes fulfill the same function as lexical or grammatical glosses, the main distinction being the mode of expression: while the former are invariably sentences (in his scheme, category F4), the latter are normally single words or short phrases (his categories F2 and F3).

32. See Stokes and Strachan 1901–3: ii, pp. xx–xxiii for a collection.

33. Hence Cinato separated them into category S7 (*notes socio-historiques*).

34. Corresponding roughly with Cinato's category S6 "critical annotations" (*ecdotiques/annotations critiques*).

35. Not all of the glosses contain Latin *quia* "because." About half instead use the Irish equivalents (*h*)*úare, ar,* or *arindí.*

36. I have listed both intra- and extra-textual types by what seems to me to be order of increasing complexity.

37. For example, 68b25 k *ilex: nomen arboris* "name of a tree," 68b32 q *carex: nomen féiuir* "name of a grass," 69b17" h *git: .i. nomen etha* "name of a grain," etc.
38. 32b32 tt *pithias: proprium* "proper noun," 34a6 l *dioné: mulier* "a woman," 34b5 d *[ar]gia: proprium mulieris* "proper noun/name of a woman."
39. Types 213, 222, 223, 3222, 3224, 3231, 332, 334, 37, 413, 4223, 4225, 562.
40. The exception is the new type 44 "glossing establishing word order," which is retained as a second-tier type, despite having just 18 glosses. This seems worth retaining at this level because of its clear distinction from other types and its importance in the field of glossing scholarship: see discussion above and references there.

REFERENCES

Bauer, Bernhard, Rijcklof Hofman, Pádraic Moran. 2017. *St Gall Priscian Glosses*, version 2.0 <www.stgallpriscian.ie> [accessed 23 November 2019].

Blom, Alderik. 2017. *Glossing the Psalms: The Emergence of the Written Vernaculars in Western Europe From the Seventh to the Twelfth Centuries*. Berlin: De Gruyter.

Cinato, Franck. 2015. *Priscien glosé. L'Ars grammatica de Priscien vue à travers les gloses carolingiennes*. Studia Artistarum 41. Turnhout: Brepols.

Cinato, Franck. 2020. 'La diffusion des signes de construction syntaxique entre la France et l'Angleterre'. In Charlotte Denoël and Francesco Siri (eds), *France et Angleterre: manuscrits médiévaux entre 700 et 1200*. Turnhout: Brepols, pp. 333–361.

Cinato, Franck. «"Gloser les Psaumes". À propos d'un livre récent d'Alderik Blom», Le Moyen Âge 128/3-4 (2022).

Clackson, James, ed. 2011. *A Companion to the Latin Language*. Oxford: Wiley-Blackwell.

Draak, Maartje. 1957. 'Construe Marks in Hiberno-Latin Manuscripts'. *Mededelingen der Koninklijke Nederlandse Akademie van Wetenschappen* 20/10: 261–282.

Draak, Maartje. 1967. 'The Higher Teaching of Latin in Ninth-Century Ireland'. *Mededelingen der Koninklijke Nederlandse Akademie van Wetenschappen* 30/4: 107–144.

Dumville, David N. 1997. *Three Men in a Boat: Scribe, Language, and Culture in the Church of Viking-Age Europe*. Cambridge: Cambridge University Press.

Hertz, Martin. 1855–1859. 'Prisciani grammatici Caesariensis Institutionum grammaticarum libri XVIII'. In Heinrich Keil (ed.), *Grammatici latini*, 6 vols. Leipzig: Teubner, 1855–1880, ii 1–597, iii 384.

Hofman, Rijcklof. 1996. *The Sankt Gall Priscian Commentary. Part 1*. 2 vols. Münster: Nodus.

Hofman, Rijcklof. 2000. 'The Irish Tradition of Priscian'. In Mario de Nonno, Paolo de Paolis, and Louis Holtz (eds), *Manuscripts and Tradition of Grammatical Texts From Antiquity to the Renaissance*, 2 vols. Cassino: Edizioni dell'Università, pp. 257–288.

Horrocks, Geoffrey. 2011. 'Latin Syntax'. In Clackson 2011, pp. 118–143.

Korhammer, Michael. 1980. 'Mittelalterliche Konstruktionshilfen und Altenglische Wortstellung'. *Scriptorium* 34/1: 18–58.

Kroon, Caroline. 1998. 'A Framework for the Description of Latin Discourse Markers'. *Journal of Pragmatics* 30/2: 205–223.

Kroon, Caroline. 2011. 'Latin Particles and the Grammar of Discourse.' In Clackson 2001, pp. 176–195.

Lambert, Pierre-Yves. 1981. 'La traduction du pronom relatif latin dans les gloses en vieil-irlandais'. *Études Celtiques* 18: 121–139. DOI: 10.3406/ecelt.1981.1679.

Lemoine, Louis. 1994. 'Signes de construction syntaxique dans les manuscrits bretons du haut Moyen Âge'. *Archivum latinitatis medii aevi* 52: 77–108.

Moran, Pádraic. 2015. 'Language Interaction in the St Gall Priscian'. *Peritia* 26: 113–142.

Moran, Pádraic, and John Whitman. 2022. 'Glossing and Reading in Western Europe and East Asia: A Comparative Case Study'. *Speculum* 97: 112–139.

Ó Néill, Pádraig [O'Neill, Patrick]. 1998. 'The Earliest Dry-Point Glosses in Codex Usserianus Primus'. In Toby Barnard, Dáibhí Ó. Cróinín, and Katharine Simms (eds), *'A Miracle of Learning': Studies in Manuscripts and Irish Learning. Essays in Honour of William O'Sullivan*. Aldershot: Ashgate, pp. 1–28.

O'Neill, Patrick. 1992. 'Syntactical Glosses in the Lambeth Psalter and the Reading of the Old English Interlinear Translation as Sentences'. *Scriptorium* 46/2: 250–256.

O'Neill, Patrick. 2020. 'The Earliest Evidence for Construing in the West: The *Codex Usserianus Primus* and the Cambridge, Trinity College, Pauline Epistles'. In Yoko Wada (ed.), *Trends in Eastern and Western Literature, Medieval and Modern*. Osaka: Kansai University Institute of Oriental and Occidental Studies, pp. 1–41.

Reynolds, Suzanne. 1990. '*Ad Auctorum Expositionem*: Syntactic Theory and Interpretative Practice in the Twelfth Century'. *Histoire Épistémologie Langage* 12/2: 31–51.

Robinson, Fred C. 1973. 'Syntactical Glosses in Latin manuscripts of Anglo-Saxon Provenance'. *Speculum* 48: 443–475.

Stokes, Whitley, and John Strachan. 1901–1903. *Thesaurus Palaeohibernicus: A Collection of Old-Irish Glosses, Scholia, Prose and Verse*. 2 vols. Cambridge: Cambridge University Press.

Whitman, John. 2011. 'The Ubiquity of the Gloss'. *Scripta* 3: 95–121.

Wieland, Gernot. 1983. *The Latin Glosses on Arator and Prudentius in Cambridge University Library MS Gg. 5. 35*. Toronto: Pontifical Institute of Mediaeval Studies.

10

Glossing Practices in 1850–1911 Descriptions of Languages with Complex Verbal Morphology

Aimée Lahaussois

INTRODUCTION

Kiranti (Eastern Nepal) and Algonquian (North America) languages share, with quite a few other languages around the world, the feature of marking two arguments on transitive verbs. An example is given in (1), in which the verb marks both the subject and the object through a single suffix on the verb:

(1) phoka-ka ŋjak-tɨtsi   ʔe (Thulung, Kiranti group, Sino-Tibetan)

    ash-INSTR cover-3SG>3DU.PST HEARSAY
    "He/She covered them both with ash."

Even in the absence of explicit noun phrases expressing the arguments, as is the case in (1), the verb suffix *-tɨtsi* indicates that the verb is marked for a third person singular subject and a third person dual object. The gloss "3SG>3DU.PST" signals this by the use of a ">" representing the argument to the left of the arrow "acting on" the argument to the right. The person and number of the two arguments are glossed with a combination of numbers (1, 2, or 3 for the person) and letters (SG, DU, or PL for the number).[1] In the case of the suffix *-tɨtsi* in (1), the formative is a portmanteau marking a combination of person, number, role, and past tense for both arguments. The glosses in (1) are generally interpretable for contemporary linguists, as they make use of a standardized glossing system, the establishment of which dates to the 1980s (Lehmann 1982) and which makes it possible to code formatives for the arguments they express.

The main question I wish to address in this chapter is what glossing and annotation[2] for complex, multiple-argument verbal morphology looked like before the establishment of current standardized practices. Generally, as will be seen, linguists used the lexical forms of personal pronouns of English for this type of glossing, something which is problematic for second person arguments, as English "you" has been neutralized with respect to nominative/accusative case and a singular/plural distinction.[3] This makes second person argument glosses interesting, in terms of the techniques which linguists resorted to in order to produce glosses capable of coding all relevant features. I will explore this topic through a sampling of grammatical descriptions of Kiranti and Algonquian languages from the period 1850 to 1911.

The organization of this chapter will be as follows: In the following section I will lay out preliminary concepts that are relevant to the study of annotated textual materials, before describing current glossing practices and providing a brief history of their standardization. I will then describe data annotation practices in the grammatical descriptions in the corpus. This will be followed by an exploration of some of the trends that can be observed over this time period, before I present my conclusions.

PRELIMINARIES

The Corpus

The corpus used for this study is based on a sampling of Kiranti and Algonquian grammatical descriptions from 1850 to 1911. The descriptions I have used are listed here, with complete references in the bibliography.

Kiranti descriptions:

Grammars of Vayu and Bahing, published in the *Journal of the Asiatic Society of Bengal* (Hodgson 1857, 1858)
Kiranti language sketches in the *Linguistic Survey of India Vol.III.1* (Grierson 1909)

Algonquian descriptions:

Grammar of Ochipwe (Baraga 1850)
Description of the Chippewa verb (Schoolcraft 1855)
Grammar and Dictionary of the Blackfoot (Tims 1889)
Algonquian (Fox), in Boas's *Handbook of American Indian Languages*, (Jones, rev. Michelson 1911)

The corpus includes all known materials presenting new data on Kiranti during this period: although other sources do exist, they are compilations of word lists and phrases (such as Hunter 1868; Campbell 1874) that are based on data collected by Hodgson, and as such they bring nothing new in terms of general annotation and analysis. Hodgson was a prolific researcher on the languages of Nepal and produced detailed sketches of both Vayu (now Hayu) and Bahing, in addition to collecting vocabulary lists and phrases in many other Kiranti languages. Additionally, Hodgson's work is interesting in that he visibly adapts the presentation of data over the course of the sketches of Vayu and Bahing, in order to better suit the languages (see Lahaussois 2020, 202).

The end date on the selected corpus is 1911, in order to include sketches from two large-scale linguistic surveys: Grierson's *Linguistic Survey of India* (the volume on Tibeto-Burman languages of the Himalayas was published in 1909, as part of a series published over the period of 1894–1928), and Boas's *Handbook of American Indian Languages* (published in three volumes, in 1911, 1922, and 1933), which features a sketch of Fox in Volume 1.

There is considerably more material on Algonquian than on Kiranti in the chosen period, and I have attempted not to overwhelm the corpus with Algonquian, in the interest of keeping a balance between the two. I thus consider only three descriptions prior to the 1911 description of Fox: descriptions of Chippewa/Ojibwe (1850 and 1855), and of Blackfoot (1889), providing what I feel to be representative coverage of the 1850–1911 period.

Description of Current Glossing Practices

Current practices in presenting and annotating linguistic data most commonly make use of a three-tiered system, as illustrated in (1). In this system, the three lines, or tiers as they are often called, contain distinct types of data. These are typically referred to as the transcription tier, for the top-most line, where the linguistic data is provided in transcribed form (this can be in a phonetic alphabet or a local orthographic system, among other possibilities); the glossing tier, for the middle line, composed of lexical items, often in combination with abbreviations for grammatical terms, corresponding to the various elements that make up the transcription tier; and the translation tier, for the bottom-most line, usually a free translation of the overall meaning of the transcription tier into the metalanguage of description.

This standardization of annotation practices is largely a result of work by Christian Lehmann (1982),[4] later formalized into the *Leipzig Glossing Rules* by Balthasar Bickel, Bernard Comrie, and Martin Haspelmath. The *Leipzig Glossing Rules*,[5] the presentation document of which bears the subtitle "Conventions for interlinear morpheme-by-morpheme glosses," lay out ten rules for the presentation of linguistic data in interlinear form and propose a list of 80-odd abbreviations for grammatical glosses. The rules have been widely adopted in the presentation of field data in descriptive grammars and articles and in work on linguistic typology and are the required format for data presentation in a large number of linguistics journals in those subfields.

We now turn to the topic of interest, which is how arguments are glossed in languages which mark both subject and object on the verb, and specifically, how this is carried out by contemporary linguists. We need to bear in mind that there are two types of argument marking that potentially need to be glossed in these languages: free noun phrases, which can include personal pronouns, often with case marking to indicate the roles of the arguments; and indexes, which indicate through inflectional material the nature and role of up to two transitive arguments on the verb. Our focus is on the latter.

As far as indexes are concerned, they are often translated using grammatical glosses, which most often identify person/number/clusivity through abbreviations, such as the following: "2SG" for second singular, "1PI" for first person plural inclusive, "3DU" for third person dual, and so on. These can be combined with letters indicating argument role—some examples found in the literature are "A" for actor, "U" for undergoer, "O" for object, "P" for patient—or, if a single portmanteau is used to index a two-argument scenario, with symbols indicating the relationship between arguments: "X/Y," "X-->Y," and "X>Y" (the latter can be seen in (1)) are examples of symbols that are used to indicate that X "acts on" Y, or that X is the subject (or agent) and Y is the object (or patient).[6] Grammarians must of course clarify any idiosyncratic abbreviations and symbols in their grammars but the existence of standard abbreviations and practices greatly facilitates understanding.

Examples (2) and (3), from Kiranti and Algonquian respectively, illustrate the use of glosses that make explicit the argument roles of the scenarios:

(2) Belhare (Bickel 1999, 38)

    cama   m-pak-yakt-u-naŋa   ta-hatt-he-ŋ
    food   3nsA-serve-IPFV-3U-ERG   reach-TELIC-PT-1sA
    "I arrived there when they were dealing out the food."

(3) Arapaho (Cowell and Moss 2008, 89)

    eti-niiteheiw-e3en   nii3oxoeyei-nehk
    IC.FUT-help(TA)-1S/2S   fence(AI)-2S.SUBJ
    "I'll help you when you fix the fence." [E:30.9]

In (2), the glosses "3nsA" and "3U" are given respectively for the prefix and one suffix of the verb "serve," with "A" indicating that "3ns" (third person non-singular) is the actor and "U" indicating that 3 is the undergoer. The second verb, "reach," has a single argument glossed with "A" indicating a first person singular actor. In (3), the first verb, "help," takes a suffix which is glossed "1S/2S," indicating a first person singular actor and a second person singular undergoer, with the symbol "/" used to signal the actor on the left-hand side and the undergoer on the right-hand side. The second verb, "fence," has a suffix glossed "2S.SUBJ," indicating that the subject of the intransitive verb is a second person singular. Additionally, in the glosses in (3), the verbs are given lexical glosses accompanied by codes in parentheses: "TA" indicates a "transitive animate" verb (a transitive verb with an animate object), and "AI" indicates an "animate intransitive" verb (an intransitive verb with an animate subject), providing helpful information (in a form familiar to Algonquian scholars) about the verb's expected arguments.

Note that neither (2) nor (3) involves any free pronouns as arguments: (2) has an object argument "food" for the first of its two verbs (which is indexed on the verb as "3U," as a third person(-like) undergoer), and in (3), the arguments are only present through verb indexation. As far as the glossing of free pronominal arguments is concerned, some contemporary linguists use lexical glosses for these (reserving grammatical glosses for indexes; this follows Lehmann's Rule 4 "An L1 lexeme is glossed by L2 lexemes"),[7] while some use the same alphanumeric abbreviations for free pronouns as for pronominal indexes.

In addition to glossing techniques such as those seen in (2) and (3) above, another feature of contemporary grammatical descriptions of multiple-argument indexing languages is that they contain explicitly laid out verbal paradigms, with clear identification of the two arguments of transitive verbs. Argument glosses are thus accompanied by an additional apparatus, beyond glosses, which ensures that a reader has access to a supplementary key to interpreting verb forms found in examples in the description.[8]

Terminology

This section discusses some terminology that is relevant to the study of our corpus, namely the various types of translations that can accompany annotated data. I will refer to the language being described in the grammars as the *object language* and the language used to write the description as the *metalanguage*.

To better account for the kinds of translation-based material that accompanies transcriptions, it is useful to set up a continuum of translation which extends from the most free to the least free. The "most free" end of the continuum is characterized by translations that operate at the sentence level, and sometimes encompass even larger units, and are primarily concerned with conveying the narrative content of the unit in question. The "least free" end of the continuum is characterized by translations with a focus on the word level, and sometimes even smaller units. As a result of this focus on word units, the least free translations highlight the syntax of the object language, and when focusing on smaller units yet (which is possible when the words in the transcription are segmented, thereby opening access to the translation of sub-word entities), they provide information about morphology as well. In contemporary terms, the least free end of the continuum results in the use of glosses: lexical glosses are used to render lexical items (this is often the case in word-for-word translations), while grammatical glosses are often used to render sub-word level material (often in morpheme-for-morpheme translations). These two extreme ends of the continuum can be labeled "free translation" (see, for example, Bow et al. 2003, 2) and "gloss translation." The latter term is borrowed from Nida (1964, 159), for whom it is "designed to permit the reader to identify himself as fully as possible with a person in the source-language context"; see Lahaussois (2016) for more discussion of Nida's use of the term. In my usage, a gloss translation is a translation made up of glosses, which are by definition word- or sub-word-based. Interestingly, these definitions place "literal translation" not at the "least free" extreme of the continuum, but in the middle: a literal translation is generally one which renders the content of the object language into the metalanguage according to the original word order of the former, but a number of additional characteristics can be identified. Literal translations are, significantly, intended to be readable in the metalanguage. As such they do not usually delve into material at the sub-word level (while they may reproduce formative order, such as "house-in," it is rarer for them to provide a sub-word level translation of verb forms), with the result that they do not feature segmentation marks. Additionally, they often respect punctuation and typographic conventions of the metalanguage, capitalizing the first letter of the sentence. Gloss translations, on the other hand, are primarily focused on the conveyance of the morphosyntactic features of the object language. They frequently feature segmentation marks and generally do not contain any punctuation or capitalization. Figure 10.1 places the translation types on the proposed continuum.

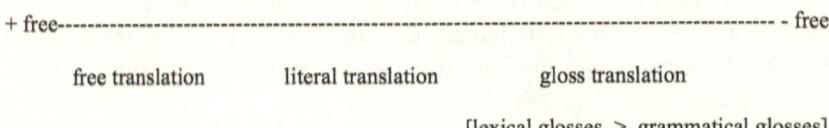

Figure 10.1 The Continuum from "Most Free" to "Least Free" Translation Types.

Figure 10.1 specifies a hierarchy of the types of gloss that make up a gloss translation, suggesting that lexical glosses are more free than grammatical. Lexical glosses, unsurprisingly, make use of lexical items from the metalanguage in order to provide word-for-word or morpheme-for-morpheme[9] translations of the object language. Grammatical glosses, on the other hand, are used to convey (morpho-)syntactic information and in contemporary practice often receive standardized abbreviations and set typography (small caps), in order to set them apart. An example of a grammatical gloss can be seen in "INSTR" in the first word of the glossing tier in (1), indicating that -*ka* marks the instrumental case in the sentence in question.[10] Even if not all contemporary linguists adopt identical practices in terms of assigning lexical or grammatical glosses to various formatives in the object language, annotations in the contemporary presentation of data will almost invariably include a combination of both types of glosses.[11]

But such was not always the case. Across the corpus explored herein, there is nothing that would be considered a grammatical gloss by current standards.[12] This is in part because, over a large part of the corpus, there is very little that can be considered any kind of a gloss: as will be described in the section "Annotation Practices Found in the Corpus," in the initial texts of the corpus, transcriptions are accompanied by free translations of the material, with no detail as to how individual words (or segments of words, in the rare cases where segmentation is used) are to be interpreted. Only in the last two texts of the corpus do we see a double translation accompanying transcriptions, one of which is free, and the other which switches between literal translation and gloss translation. I will argue here that some of the lexical glosses we find in these translations are precursors to grammatical glosses, as they fully convey all of the morphosyntactic features of the formatives in question and do so in such a way that standard English lexemes cannot.

The relationship between the types of translations accompanying data of course depends on a number of factors, an important one being the typological proximity between the object language and the metalanguage: if they are close, the distance between free and literal translation will be greatly reduced (see, e.g., Nida and Taber 1982, 5–6; Schultze-Berndt 2006).

ANNOTATION PRACTICES FOUND IN THE CORPUS

The data presented here are in chronological order, grammar by grammar, allowing the reader to see the evolution in practices across the time period.

In examining the descriptions, I was interested in particular in the following questions:

a) What kind of annotation (free translation, literal translation, and gloss translation) accompanies transcribed data?
b) Is segmentation present in the transcribed data? In the annotation? If so, what is it used for?
c) Given that all the languages in the corpus encode both subject and object arguments on verbs, how are verbal paradigms presented to account for this feature?
d) What systems of annotation are used to identify the arguments for the different forms in the paradigms?
e) In particular, how are different types of second person arguments distinguished for role and number?
f) What kind of translation accompanies material such as imperative forms, the English forms of which do not explicitly state the subject?
g) Is there a difference between the presentation of data in paradigms and examples in terms of annotation?

The following descriptions present the information based on a close reading of the grammars in the corpus with respect to these questions. Note however that the material is presented in the order in which it appears in the grammars, rather than in that of the questions above.

A Theoretical and Practical Grammar of the Otchipwe Language, by Baraga (1850)

In Baraga's description of verbal paradigms, we find minimal annotation. This is intentional, as "[t]his will save many a line in this book" (Baraga 1850, 102). Baraga specifies further that "[i]n the paradigms of these Conjugations,

PRESENT TENSE.

Nind ikit, I say,
kid ikit,
ikito,   ⎧ one says,
ikitom,   ⎨ (on dit,*)
nind ikitomin, ⎩ or they say,
kid ikitom,
ikitowag,

Figure 10.2   Paradigm for the Present Tense of the Verb "Say."

PRESENT TENSE.—*Kid ákos na ?—Kawin nind ákosissi ; ninidjanissag ákosiwag, ningá gaie ákosi.* Art thou sick? I am not sick; my children are sick, and my mother is sick.

Figure 10.3 Example of the Free Translation (with Archaic Pronouns) that Accompanies Verb Form Examples.

we express the English verb only at the first person singular in every tense, and the others will again be supplied by you" (*ibid.*, 102). This results in a paradigm like that in figure 10.2.

Intransitive and transitive paradigms for each conjugation class are followed by exemplification with sentences including verbs from that conjugation. The sentences are translated freely, making use of archaic pronouns for second person disambiguation, as in figure 10.3. Note however that archaic pronouns are only used for singular reference and that only "you" is used for both subject and object roles for second person plurals.

Paradigms involving objects other than third person referents are presented in a distinct section, with the labels "first case: I . . . thee" and "second case: thou . . . me." These paradigms are accompanied by full translations of the different forms, as seen in figure 10.4, as the ordering of arguments is not self-explanatory.

Imperative forms are also given special treatment: the forms are translated using subject pronouns, in parentheses, to clarify the nature of the argument, turning an otherwise free translation into a literal one, as seen in figure 10.5.

The description can be said to be characterized by the use of free translation, accompanying largely unsegmented transcriptions. The archaic pronouns "thou" and "thee" are used consistently to refer to a second singular pronoun, with "you" for both subject and object roles of the second person plural. In situations where it significantly enhances understanding of the forms, as in the case of imperatives, translations look more literal, identifying the subject argument, but putting it in parentheses.

Chippewa Language, by Schoolcraft (1855)

Schoolcraft's description focuses exclusively on the verb in Chippewa (another name for Ojibwe) and is thus made up of a very large number of verbal

*Ki wábam*in, I see thee,
*ki wábam*igo,* we see thee,
*ki wábam*ig, he sees thee,†
*ki wábam*igog, they see thee,
*ki wábam*ininim, I see you,
*ki wábam*igom, we see you,
*ki wábam*igowa, he sees you,
*ki wábam*igowag, they see you,

Figure 10.4 First Paradigm with a Speech Act Participant Object.

232   Aimée Lahaussois

$$\left.\begin{array}{l}\textit{Nóndawishin,}\\ \textit{nondawishikan,}\end{array}\right\} \text{hear me (thou,)}$$

　　　　　　nondawishig, hear me (you,)
　　　nin ga-nondag, let him hear me,
　　　nin ga-nondagog, let them hear me,
　　　　　　nondawishinam, hear us (thou,)
　　　　　　nondawishinam, hear us (you,)
　　　nin ga-nondagonan, let him hear us,
　　　nin ga-nondagonanig, let them hear us,

Figure 10.5   Imperative Paradigm Involving Speech Act Participant Objects.

paradigms. As with Baraga's description, the main paradigms vary for subject only, with transitive paradigms presented with a third singular object, probably reflecting a Latin model of verb paradigm presentation (see Lahaussois 2018, 138). Again, like Baraga, distinct paradigms are provided for forms with non-third singular object arguments, in separate sections of the grammar.

As the same organization of paradigms is used throughout the book, Schoolcraft dispenses with the translation of most forms, as is seen in figure 10.6. The paradigm is presented in two columns, with singular (subject) forms on the left, plural on the right, and with the rows identified by numbers representing person: 1 for first person (divided, in the plural, into exclusive and inclusive), 2 for second person, 3 for third person, and 4 for third person possessive forms. The forms are followed by a translation, a full sentence for the first person singular "I see him or her," and just the subject pronoun for other verb forms.

As can be seen in figure 10.6, the transcription is segmented into word-like entities. It is not clear what they are meant to represent: they are possibly morphemes or syllables.

In the section of the grammar presenting paradigms for "Inverse transition," in which the arguments are a third singular subject and varying objects, the number codes (1–4) now refer to the person of the object. In this case, the first two singular forms are accompanied by free translations, presumably in order to establish the pattern, before reverting to listing only the object pronoun associated with each form, as can be seen in figure 10.7.

In yet another section, labeled "Transitions between First and Second Persons" (*ibid.*, 373 ff.), Schoolcraft presents verb forms involving first and

	Singular.			*Plural.*	
1 Ne wau bu mau'.	....	I see him or her.	1 Ne wau bu mau naun	....	We; Ex.
2 Ge " " "	....	Thou.	1 Ge " " " "	....	We; In.
3 O " " maun	....	He.	2 " " " " wau	....	You.
4 " " " mau ni	....	His.	3 O " " " waun	....	They.
			4 " " " " ni	....	Theirs.

Figure 10.6   Present Indicative Paradigm for the Verb "See."

```
1 Ne wau bu meg............... He sees me.      1 Ne wau bu me go naun............. Us; Ex.
2 Ge   "    "    ............... He sees thee.   1 Ge   "    "    "    ............. Us; In.
3 O    "  me goon.......... Him.                 2 "    "    "    wau................. You.
4 "    "  me goo ne........ His.                 3 O    "    "    waun................ Them.
                                                 4 "    "    "    ne................... Theirs.
```

Figure 10.7   Inverse Present Indicative Paradigm for "See."

second person arguments only. The forms are accompanied by free translations and again make use of the archaic pronoun forms "thou" and "thee" in order to distinguish singular from plural and subject from object.

As in Baraga, the translations accompanying imperative forms, unlike those in the rest of the description, are not free translations: they include the subject pronominal argument, although unlike in Baraga, the subject pronoun is not in parentheses here, as seen in figure 10.8.

The intent is clearly to clarify the nature of the subject argument, and this not only pushes the translation into a more literal style but makes the use of the archaic pronouns necessary, as is evidenced by an additional distinction in the plural pronoun forms: whereas other paradigms in the grammar distinguish "thou" and "thee" for the singular, they use only "you" for the plural; here, "ye" emerges to make clear that it is a subject plural pronoun. Together with the parenthetical comment "(This is not an interrogation)," this suggests the author felt a need to provide additional explanations about the argument structure of the form.

Grammar of Vayu, by Hodgson (1857)

The grammar of Vayu begins with a presentation of nominal morphology, with declensional paradigms for pronouns and nouns, making use of grammatical abbreviations for the various cases encountered ("N," "G," "D Ac,"

```
Present Tense.  Wau bum...................... See thou him or them.
Future   "        "  bu mau gun.................. See thou him or them, in future.
Ga goo.           "    "  gan..................... Do not see him or them.

Present Tense.  Wau bu meg ................. See ye him or them.
Future   "        "  mau gĕg ................... See ye him or them, in future.
Ga goo.           "    "  ga gon .................. See ye not him or them.
                                                   (This is not an interrogation)

Present Tense.  Wau bun dun...................... See thou it or them; things.
Future   "        "  du moo gun ............... See thou it or them, in future.
Ga goo.           "     eun gan.................... See thou it or them not.
```

Figure 10.8   Imperative Paradigm of the Verb "See."

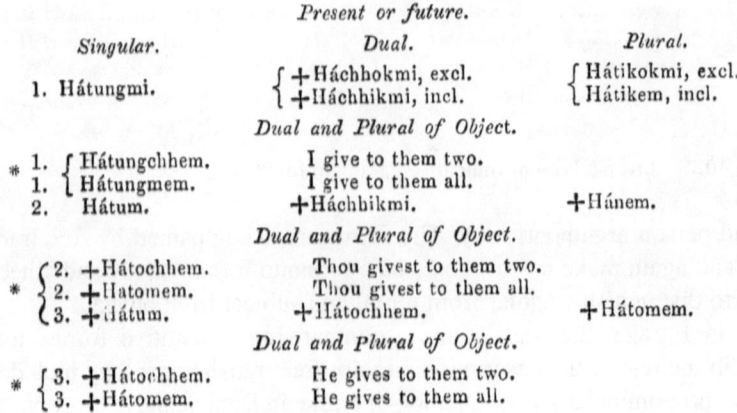

Figure 10.9 Paradigm for the Verb "Give."

"L," "Abs," "Ins," "Soc"), as well as using abbreviations to distinguish feminine from masculine terms ("f." vs. "m.") and inclusive from exclusive pronouns ("incl." vs. "excl."). Second person pronouns are only translated in the genitive forms ("thy," "thine") in these declensions, all other forms being left untranslated and coded by their position within the paradigms.

Verb paradigms for intransitive verbs are not accompanied by translations, as they are organized in a clear order, with labels "1," "2," "3" (for person) and "singular," "dual," "plural" (for number). This analytical presentation becomes more difficult to maintain without adding translations for transitive verbs. While forms involving a third person singular object are not translated (they are presumed to be obvious from the arrangement of the paradigm), free translations are provided for forms involving dual and plural objects, as seen in figure 10.9.

As with the Ojibwe/Chippewa grammars above, imperative forms cannot easily be provided with free translations in English, as the latter does not

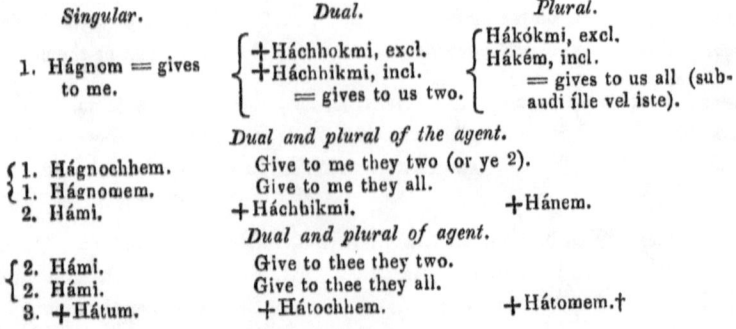

Figure 10.10 A "Passive" Paradigm from Vayu.

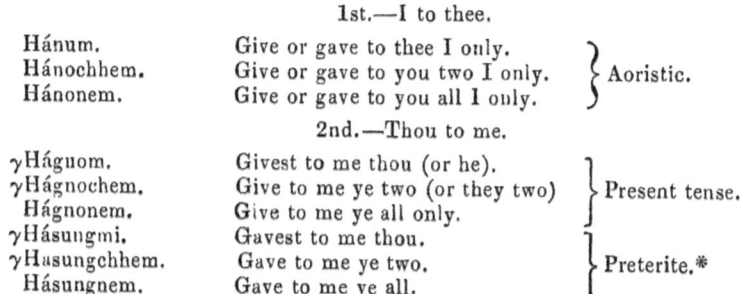

Figure 10.11 A Paradigm with First and Second Persons as Both Subject and Object.

accommodate the subject pronoun. As a result, imperative paradigms are accompanied by literal translations within these grammars. Similarly, inverse paradigms (labeled "passive" by Hodgson) are given a literal rather than a free translation, as seen in figure 10.10, but with the additional factor that the verb root is the first element in the translations, even though these are not imperative forms.

While the above word order may leave the reader wondering whether Hodgson has ordered the arguments according to a person hierarchy (such as first>second>third), keeping the arguments higher in this hierarchy closer to the verb or to the front of the utterance, this is revealed not to be the case in the paradigm in figure 10.11, which shows verb forms involving only first and second person arguments.

The translation here again runs the danger of being misinterpreted as an imperative form, even though it clearly is not, based on the labels above the paradigms. Nor does the translation provided appear to respect the order of the morphemes within the Vayu form: while the verb stem is indeed the initial morpheme, when contrasting *Hánochhem* ("Give to you two I only") and *Hágnochem* ("Give to me ye two"), it becomes clear that the second dual is coded by the "chem" segment, and that the order of morphemes is not the same as that in the translation. This suggests that while the translation is not free, it also cannot be considered a gloss translation, as it does not follow the order of formatives in the verb form.

This pattern is repeated throughout the grammar: translations, when provided, are usually free, unless they involve imperative forms or inverse forms ("passive," involving a first or second person object, or "special forms," involving only first and second person arguments), in which case they are literal translations, insofar as they show unusual word order.

Archaic pronouns are used consistently, with not only a role opposition in the second singular pronouns, but also in the second plural ("ye" for subject, "you" for object). This presents a contrast with the two Ojibwe descriptions, which have "you" for both the subject and object plural argument, except in very specific circumstances (namely the translation of imperative forms). A specimen text presented at the end of the Vayu grammar (*ibid.*, 483 ff.) consists of a transcription followed by the translation, as a separate block. Within the translation, which is free, instances of what is clearly referring to a second person singular are translated with "you," rather than "thou," suggesting that the archaic pronouns found within the grammatical description were there for the specific purpose of glossing the full set of features of the pronoun.

Grammar of Bahing, by Hodgson (1858)

The sketch of Bahing grammar by Hodgson was published in volume 27 of the *Journal of the Asiatic Society of Bengal*, in the volume immediately following the one containing his grammar of Vayu. As a result, the description is at times of an elliptical nature, presumably based on the assumption that readers will be familiar with the Vayu sketch and carry over what they know of the latter language to their understanding of the Bahing presentation.

As an example, the presentation of verb forms is very succinct. Figure 10.12 shows the first transitive paradigm to be presented: After initial forms which lay out the pattern, using translations to make clear what the numerical system is (the number corresponds not to the person, but to the number of the object), this schematic presentation makes it possible to do away with translations for the presented forms.

When presenting "special" inverse forms, involving first and second person pronouns as the sole arguments, translations are provided, free in form and making use of archaic pronouns for disambiguation. This can be seen in figure 10.13.

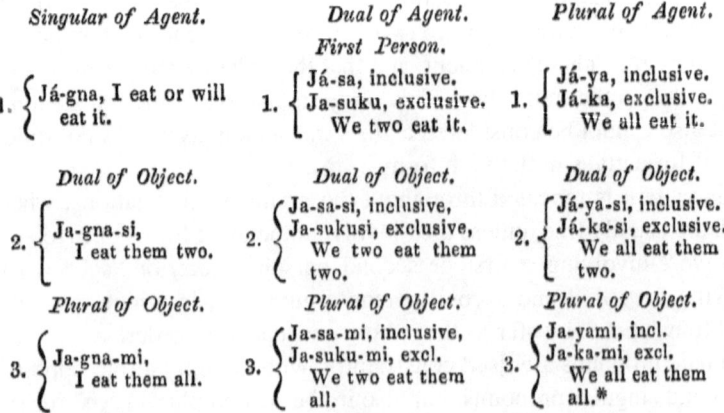

Figure 10.12 Number-Coded Verb Forms for Bahing.

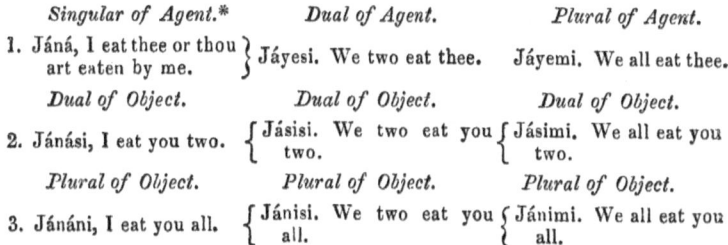

Figure 10.13 Paradigm with only Speech Act Participant Arguments.

There is thus a transition in the presentation of special form paradigms from the Vayu to the Bahing grammars: where the former used literal translations for special forms, the latter uses free translations. This presumably results from Hodgson's confidence in the ability of the paradigm presentation system he has devised to convey the nature of the arguments in question.[13]

Like the Vayu grammar, the Bahing sketch ends with a text specimen: again, this is transcribed as a block of text, with no segmentation; the translation follows, also as a block, in natural English. There are no analytical notes linking the transcription with the translation. As with the Vayu specimen, second singular forms are rendered as "you" in the translation, making it quite clear that the archaic forms used within the grammar are chosen for the purposes of providing extra clarification on the nature of the forms.

Grammar and Dictionary of the Blackfoot, by Tims (1889)

This grammar differs from those seen so far through the pervasive use made of segmentation in the transcribed material. The grammar describes in detail the functions of certain morphemes, and the segmentation thus matches the analytical presentation of the grammar.

The section on pronouns (Tims 1889, 6 ff.) presents a paradigm of personal pronouns in two columns, for singular and plural number, and three rows, for the three persons (with first plural separated in two, for inclusive and exclusive forms). The 2sg form is glossed as "you"; yet when presenting the paradigm of possessive pronouns, the 2sg form is given as "thy." In exemplifying the use of pronouns in sentences, a second singular is translated as "you," while the second plural pronoun is "ye." The use of archaic pronouns in this grammar is thus characterized by inconsistency: a contrast is always maintained in translations between 2sg and 2pl, but this is sometimes through the pair "you" vs "ye" (ibid, 7), "thou" vs "you" (*ibid.*, 26–27), "thou" vs "ye" (*ibid.*, 63), and "you" followed by a parenthetical indication ("you" for 2sg, "you (plu)" for 2pl; *ibid.*, 8). Only very rarely does the same translation "you"

Nit'-ŭk-o-mĭm-mok, *he loves me.*
Kit'-ŭk-o-mĭm-mok, *he loves you.*
Ot'-ŭk-o-mĭm-mok-ai-e, } *he loves him.*
Ŭk-o-mĭm-mi-u-ai-e,
Nit'-ŭk-o-mĭm-mok-in-an, *he loves us.*
Kit'-ŭk-o-mĭm-mok-o-an, *he loves you.*
Ot'-ŭk-o-mĭm-mok-o-ai-au-ai-e, } *he loves them.*
Ŭk-o-mĭm'-mi-u-ax,

Figure 10.14 An Inverse Paradigm.

refer to different arguments within the same paradigms, yet this situation too is found, as in figure 10.14. Note, however, that the positions of forms in paradigms do, in essence, clarify the nature of the argument.

In the inverse paradigm on the following page, shown in figure 10.15, we find "you" for both singular and plural arguments, but accompanied by parenthetical material for clarification.

While the seemingly inconsistent use in this grammar might be considered to be a move away from the establishment of a system, it is also possible to interpret the data in a different way: even when using the archaic pronouns inconsistently, from one part of the grammar to another, in order to clarify the number of the pronouns in question, Tims always manages to code the difference between the two. The fact that he makes use of different systems makes an all the more convincing case for the idea that he sees archaic pronouns as a tool to achieve his descriptive purposes.

In terms of translation types, the translations accompanying the transcriptions of data are all free, apart from presentations of imperative paradigms, where we find formulations that highlight the subject argument ("love thou it," "love ye it"; *ibid.* 53–54), resulting in a literal translation.

Among the grammars we have seen thus far in the corpus, the Blackfoot grammar stands out in a few ways: it does not apply archaic pronouns in a consistent way, but the way it does so suggests a transition toward using them as part of a toolset that resembles grammatical glossing. Additionally, and this is new in the chronological exploration of our corpus, segmentation is pervasive in this grammar, and, while the translations are mostly free (barring those of imperative forms) and cannot thus be used for the identification

Kit-ŭk'-o-mĭm-mo, *I love you.*
Kit-ŭk'-o-mĭm-mo-pu-au, *I love you (plu.).*
Kit-ŭk'-o-mĭm-mo-pin-an, *we love you (sing. and plu.).*

Figure 10.15 An Inverse Paradigm with Non-Archaic Second Person Pronouns.

of individual formatives, the content of the grammar does make it possible to explore the permutations that accompany the use of one formative vs. another.

Kiranti Language Sketches in G.A. Grierson's Linguistic Survey of India Vol.III.1 (1909)

In the *Linguistic Survey of India* (henceforth *LSI*), the Kiranti languages are grouped together within what Grierson labels the "complex pronominalized languages," on account of the object indexing on verbs. Even from the introduction to this language group, it is clear that the annotation of data differs from that seen in earlier grammars in the corpus: it often contains three annotation levels, with two translation tiers accompanying the transcription, one that resembles a literal translation, conveying the word order and in some cases the morpheme order of the original, while another is a free translation, conveying the content. They are in a horizontal sequence, rather than the vertical alignment found in contemporary practices. An example is from Khambu (Grierson 1909, 237), presented thus: "khodo-pikā, him-said, he said to him." Another, from Vayu (*ibid.*, 387), features a second singular subject archaic pronoun but notably only in the gloss translation: "gō gōn-hā mut-ping-ku-m, I thee-by to-stay gave, you made me stay."

This practice is not used systematically, and in many cases, a single translation line accompanies the transcription, but its appearance in this material represents a turning point in annotation practices within our corpus. As with the Tims material on Blackfoot, we find segmentation in the Kiranti *LSI* materials, and, additionally, the sense that there is an attempt to translate individual formatives. Furthermore, the use of archaic pronouns in only one of the translation lines, suggesting that they are seen as part of a technical apparatus.

The addition of the extra translation level is also found in the text specimens that accompany the *LSI* sketches. The Vayu text specimen (*ibid.*, 395) is identified as having been collected by Hodgson and is indeed the same story that was found at the end of the 1857 Hodgson article discussed above. In this case, however, it has been provided with an interlinear translation (along with the free translation following, in a block of text, as before). The translation partly resembles a literal translation—it has capitalization and punctuation, and respects the word order of the object language while remaining mostly readable—and in some places, resembles a gloss translation, in providing glosses for the segments within some of the word units.[14] The fact that the specimen text is also accompanied by a free translation frees up this interlinear translation to be less readable, in terms of narrative content, something which is reinforced by the segmented words.

One issue with segmentation at this time is that the same marks (hyphens) are used both to separate formatives and to group together compound words, sometimes in the same word. While a word (on the second line of transcription in figure 10.16) like *dāvo-be*, translated "language-in" resembles a gloss translation, with two formatives in the transcribed word each translated in the order in which they occur, a different principle is operating in the translation of *hāthā-bong* (on the third line of transcription in figure 10.16), translated "how-much-up-to." Only by reading the sketch grammar does one learn that *hāthā* corresponds to "how much" and *bong* to "up to," a fact which cannot be discerned from the four hyphenated segments that make up the translation, which cannot be matched to the two hyphenated segments in the transcription without additional information.[15]

Another feature of this text specimen is the use of archaic pronouns, as seen in the seventh and eighth lines of the transcription of figure 10.16. The phrase *gon-hā* is rendered as "thee-by," with a matching number of segments across the transcription and translation making it possible to see the translation as a gloss translation. The use of the archaic pronoun here, which is not taken up in the corresponding free translation (*ibid.*, 398), suggests that it is chosen as a compact translation conveying all the features of the object language formative, in other words, as a gloss. This remains a lexical gloss, in that a lexical item is used, but unlike the corresponding modern English pronoun "you," "thee" additionally carries the features of singular number and of object argument role, matching the level of featural detail conveyed by a grammatical gloss.

Algonquian (Fox), by William Jones, Revised by Truman Michelson (1911), in *Handbook of American Indian Languages*

The final text in our corpus, in chronological terms, is a sketch grammar from the first volume of Boas's *Handbook of American Indian languages*. The text was written by William Jones, and later revised by Truman Michelson. The

Ang	ming	Pāchya	nom.	Ang	thōko	Vāyu	nōmi.	Khāsa-khāta
My	*name*	*Pāchya*	*is.*	*My*	*tribe*	*Vāyu*	*is.*	*Khas*
Hāyu	it-ke-m.	Ung-ki	dāvo-be	Vāyu	is-chi-ke-m.			Gō jek-ta
Hāyu	*call-us.*	*Our*	*language-in*	*Vāyu*	*call-ourself-we.*			*I old*
dum-sung-mi.		Hāthā-bong		dum-sung-mi	g-hā		mā	se-ng-mi.
became-I.		*How-much-up-to*		*became-I*	*me-by*		*not*	*know-I.*
Lē-gōt-kulup		chhuyung		wani-khen.				Dhankuta-mu
Foot-hands-entire		*three*		*top-from.*				*Dhankuta-of*
khakchhing-puchhum-chup-vi-khāta				pōgu-ha	hā-ta	vik		pā-chi-kok-mi.
soldiers				*Rāja-by*	*given*	*field*		*cultivate-for-us-we.*

Figure 10.16 Text Specimen from Vayu Sketch Grammar in the LSI.

translations which accompany the presentation of examples include a single translation line, which is free; occasionally, component morphemes are listed as well, in which case they are accompanied by translations. The following reproduces the presentation of an example verb form: "kīcitcāgipyānitc after all had arrived (*kīci-* and *pyä-* initial stems; *-nitc* for *-nitc*[i] 3d person plural, animate)" (Jones 1911, 771).

Like Tims's 1889 grammar, the translations used in conjunction with the second person arguments are not consistent: when examples of verbs including second person arguments appear in the grammar (Jones 1911, 790), they are translated variously as "thou," "thee," "you," even though all three refer to the same formative *-n-*, this inconsistency suggesting that the translation is not chosen for the specific purpose of highlighting features of the argument.

The first verbal paradigm is presented in a table with clearly labeled columns and rows, with object pronouns down the first column and subject pronouns across the top row (*ibid.*, 817). The headers of the rows and columns are pronouns, indicating the argument in question. The pronouns are archaic, except for the particularity of using "ye" used for both subject and object. The role is nonetheless clear from other contrasts: "me" vs. "I," "us" vs. "we," and so on. In the example verb forms that follow the paradigm, archaic pronouns are maintained, for clarity.[16]

When the imperative paradigm is presented (*ibid.*, 826), the same archaic pronouns are used as labels on the rows and columns. Illustrative verb forms are accompanied by translations that include subject pronouns, as seen in all other descriptions in our corpus, thus conveying information that the free English translation cannot.

Through the rest of the grammar, translations of arguments in examples alternate between modern and archaic pronouns for the second person: "I am sleeping, you are sleeping, he sleeps" (*ibid.*, 839), "I did not come, thou didst not come, he did not come" (*ibid.*, 840). It seems, exceptions aside, that archaic pronouns are used when necessary for the purposes of disambiguation, and modern pronouns are used when the ordering of examples (e.g., into a paradigm of first sg, second sg, third sg) renders the interpretation obvious. As for the type of translation, it is usually free, together with a few translated formatives that are relevant to the sentence, thus taking on a gloss-like role.

The text specimen provided at the end of the grammatical sketch is presented in two tiers: a transcription, based on word divisions in Fox, without segmentation, and a line that provides translations for each of these words, rather than for their constituent parts, and resembling, based on the punctuation, the lack of segmentation and readability, a literal translation.

Ample grammatical notes are provided through footnotes below the text (figure 10.17 shows practically every word receiving a footnote). The text is followed by a free translation, presented in a single block.

Ḯnip¹³   acawaiyᵉ⁴   negutenw¹⁵   ä'pepōg¹⁶   ä·A·skime'pug¹⁷
It is said   long ago   it was once   when it was   when first it had
                                          winter   snowed

ä·A·skānwĭg¹⁸ neswi⁹ neniwʌg¹¹⁰ ăcīcāwātc¹¹¹ māmaiyᵃ¹² kegiceyäpᵃ.¹³
while the first three   men   they went to early   in the morning.
snow was on   hunt for game

Apʌtä'kĭg¹¹⁴   ä'pe'kwisasʌga'k¹¹⁵   ma'kwʌn¹¹⁶   ä'pītci'kawănitc¹.¹⁷
On the hillside where it was thick   bear   he went in making a
                 with growth   trail.

Figure 10.17   Text Specimen with Interlinear Translation.

This sketch, together with the *LSI* text specimen, is thus the second instance of a text being accompanied by a double translation, and we can presumably consider that this period of the 1910s marks a turning point in the presentation of textual material, accompanied with a double translational apparatus, focusing on the one hand on the narrative content, and on the other on the morphosyntactic characteristics of the material.

DISCUSSION

The presentation of the corpus in the previous section addressed in detail how the descriptions fared with respect to a number of questions. These questions are grouped here into the following topics: the nature of the annotation (free translation, literal translation, glosses) accompanying transcribed data and the number of types being used concurrently; the means of conveying various features of arguments that cannot be expressed using English pronouns; the presentation of verbal data; the presence and use of segmentation. In this section, I will discuss the evolving trends pertaining to these topics, with respect to the annotation of materials across the corpus.

Nature of Annotation and Number of Annotation Types

All of the grammars in our corpus make ample use of free translations to accompany texts and examples, although there are some specific instances where literal translations are found: the presentation of imperative forms, which include an additional subject pronoun, in order to clarify the argument. This results in a translation that does not match the English but instead conveys a feature of the object language and is therefore considered literal. Additionally, in the first of Hodgson's two grammars (but not in the second, on Bahing), so-called passive paradigms (involving speech act participant object argument) were accompanied by literal translations.

We must however note that the Hodgson descriptions, which are followed by a text specimen, reveal an interesting phenomenon with respect to translation types: while the free translations within the grammar consistently use archaic pronouns, the free translation which accompanies the text specimen at the end of the grammar does not. As such, it would be wise to make a distinction between the two types of free translation: the one within the grammar is free, reflecting natural word order for English, but it makes use of a translational apparatus that adds featural distinctions that modern English cannot make, in the form of archaic pronouns. The free translation of the text specimen is free without restrictions, focused solely on the narrative content of the text.

Only in the last two descriptions, in other words 1909 and 1911, do we see the precursors of a contemporary annotation system emerging, with a second translation tier appearing: one which is variously a literal translation (in the 1911 Fox description) or a gloss translation (in the 1909 Kiranti descriptions), and a free translation. In the text specimens that accompany these two descriptions, the literal/gloss translation is interlinear, whereas the free translation occurs as a separate block, following the text.

Expression of Pronominal Features through Archaic Pronouns

All the descriptions in the corpus make use of archaic pronouns in order to distinguish number and role where modern English no longer can. There are nonetheless some trends that emerge on a chronological scale. The first two grammars in our corpus use the "thou"/"thee" opposition consistently, but generally use "you" for both subject and object plural arguments (the exception is Schoolcraft, who uses "ye" for a second person plural subject, but only in imperative forms). The next two grammars, both by Hodgson, use "thou"/"thee" and "ye"/"you" consistently throughout the descriptions. Tims's Blackfoot grammar is very inconsistent in its use of archaic pronouns but respects the principle of distinguishing number and role by using various opposing pairs, as discussed above. The last two grammars, which are those with double-translation tiers, only use archaic pronouns in the more literal of the translations, and not entirely consistently (notably, Jones uses "thou" or "thee" for the singular but "ye" for both roles for the plural), with modern pronouns in the free translations.

It is only in the texts that show an opposition between types of translation that one can truly evaluate the role of these archaic pronouns, in other words in the Hodgson texts (for which text specimens used modern pronouns, while the rest of the description's free translations used archaic pronouns), and the Grierson and Jones texts, in which archaic pronouns were found in the literal/gloss translations, and modern pronouns in the free. We require a contrast in pronoun use within a grammar in order to evaluate the use of the pronouns because it signals that the grammarians are making a conscious decision when selecting archaic pronouns. While the archaic pronouns are still lexical items, they are no longer in common use in the metalanguage at the time of the corpus, and their use is intended to convey additional features. This is precisely what a grammatical gloss does: it conveys, through the use of specialized terminology (and nowadays, standardized abbreviations for that terminology), morphosyntactic features of the object language that lexical glosses alone cannot convey. In this sense, the use of archaic pronouns, especially in situations where they are limited to literal or gloss translations, can be considered a step toward the development of a widespread system of grammatical glosses.

The Presentation of Verbal Data

Verbal paradigms were presented in sections in the initial texts within the corpus, through Tims's 1889 grammar, with separate paradigms for forms involving speech act participants as objects (labeled "inverse," "passive," "special" in the various grammars). As for the last two grammars, Grierson does not use paradigms, but rather a description of the affixal material which expresses subject role and object role. Only in the Jones grammar do we see all the forms captured together in a single paradigm, of a type I have called "matrix paradigms" (Lahaussois 2019). Note that this is the paradigm form adopted most frequently in contemporary Algonquian and Kiranti grammars.

The Use of Segmentation

In the early materials in the corpus, segmentation of transcriptions is mostly used for derivational morphology.[17] It becomes more prevalent in later descriptions (Tims, Grierson), where it is used to segment words into formatives. It is not present in the transcriptions of the last description in the corpus (Jones), but this is countered by the fact that translations of the material are followed by reproduced formatives, with hyphens, along with an analysis of their meaning. What we see across the corpus is an increased attention to the analysis of sub-word units, which goes hand in hand with annotational tools in order to express this analysis, such as the development of grammatical glosses.

CONCLUSION

The study of a sample of Kiranti and Algonquian grammars from the period 1850 to 1911 suggests a number of paths to pursue in exploring the development of glossing in the nineteenth- and early twentieth-century grammars. Two of these paths are the development of grammatical glosses, in addition to lexical glosses, and the reorganization of annotation schemes to include an additional level of translation and/or analysis.

As seen in the presentation of the corpus and the discussion, where the five earliest descriptions have a transcription accompanied by a single (free) translation, the two descriptions produced after 1900 associate two types of translation with the transcription: one is a word-for-word or morpheme-for-morpheme translation, interlinearized in the text specimen presentations, while the other is a free translation.

The periodicity for the development of three-"tiered" annotation matches what has been proposed by Lehmann (2004), according to whom Fincke (1909) is "one of the first linguistic publications that illustrate the working of a language with a sizable text provided with a free translation and an I[nterlinear] M[orphemic] G[lossing]" (Lehmann 2004, 1837). I have sought here to present a picture of what immediately precedes this period, looking for the seeds that resulted in the interlinear double-translation tiers that emerge in the early 1900s.

I have suggested here that the description of languages marking subjects and objects on verbs, as with the Kiranti and Algonquian groups, may have led to the (maintenance of) use of archaic pronouns, which were useful in distinguishing second person arguments for number and role. These archaic pronouns, which made it possible to code additional linguistic features, appear to be an important part of the apparatus that marked a transition from literal translations to gloss translations using both lexical and grammatical glosses. The increasing awareness of the need for a fine-grained analysis not only of the words but of the formatives of the transcribed data led to an extension of this new type of translation to other formatives, and eventually to a full glossing system such as the current *Leipzig Glossing Rules*.

NOTES

1. Note that Kiranti languages also have a clusivity distinction, with distinct pronouns and suffixes for inclusive vs. exclusive non-singular arguments. This is only relevant for first person arguments.

2. The terms are used interchangeably here. Note that the term "glossing" is in fact polysemous, as it can be used to refer to the entire practice of annotating linguistic materials ("glossed texts," in contemporary linguistics, refer to the entire three-tiered annotation discussed in section "Description of Current Glossing Practices"), as well as to the practice of translating individual formatives in the object language, which constitutes only a part of the process of annotating materials.

3. The pronouns "thou," "thee," "ye," "you" of Early Modern English, which I label "archaic" herein, spoken 1500–1700 (Raumolin-Brunberg 2006), express, respectively, the functions of singular subject, plural subject, singular object, plural object.

4. See also Christian Lehmann's website, where he explains in depth his methodology of interlinearization, which has evolved since the 1982 publication: https://

www.christianlehmann.eu/ling/ling_meth/ling_description/representations/gloss/index.php

5. https://www.eva.mpg.de/lingua/pdf/Glossing-Rules.pdf.

6. See Lahaussois 2020 for discussion of the use of subject vs agent and object vs patient in Kiranti grammars.

7. For the complete list of rules, see https://www.christianlehmann.eu/ling/ling_meth/ling_description/representations/gloss/index.php?open=rules

8. For the evolution of the presentation of transitive paradigms in Kiranti languages from 1850 to the present, see Lahaussois (2020).

9. An example of morpheme-for-morpheme translation using lexical glosses might be glossing *phoka-ka* in (1) as "ash-with," translating the instrumental case marker with a lexical item.

10. The glosses 3SG>3DU.PST (third singular agent and third dual patient in the past) and HS (hearsay marker) are also grammatical glosses; "ash" and "cover" are lexical glosses.

11. Note that this appears to be a post-Lehmann (1982) phenomenon. In some materials from the 1970s, transcriptions are accompanied by exclusively lexical glosses (Lahaussois 2016).

12. The exceptions are the abbreviations used for inclusive and exclusive first person pronouns, but these cannot be considered glosses as they are not used to translate a formative, but rather added onto lexical translations in order to specify them further. See, for example, figure 10.6.

13. The change in systems may also indicate Hodgson's increasing familiarity with the structure of these languages; an analogy to this can be found in work by contemporary descriptive linguists, many of whom describe initially providing interlinear glosses for all their data, and eventually becoming familiar enough with the language that their corpus is made up of only transcription + free translation.

14. For more information on glossing in additional language sketches from the Linguistic Survey of India, and its precursors, see Lahaussois (2021).

15. A matching number of segments in the transcription and glossing tiers is one of the important principles of the Leipzig Glossing Rules: a translation can only be considered a gloss when it is clear what (minimal) formative it corresponds to.

16. Nonetheless, in a few examples, p. 825, we find "you (sing.)" and "you (pl.)," within the free translation of the verb form ("you (sing.) would have come back to life"), among examples with "thou" as the subject and "thee" as the object.

17. An outlier to the use of hyphens is Schoolcraft's description, which seems to segment according to syllable.

REFERENCES

Baraga, Frederick. 1850. *A Theoretical and Practical Grammar of the Otchipwe Language, the Language Spoken by the Chippewa Indians; Which Is Also Spoken by the Algonquin, Otawa and Potawatami Indians, With Little Difference.* Detroit: Jabez Fox.

Bickel, Balthasar. 1999. "From Ergativus Absolutus to Topic Marking in Kiranti: A Typological Perspective." *Proceedings of the Annual Meeting of the Berkeley Linguistics Society* 25: 38–49.

Bow, C., B. Hughes, and S. Bird. 2003. "Towards a General Model of Interlinear Text." *Proceedings of EMELD Workshop*, 1–47. http://emeld.org/workshop/2003/bowbadenbird-paper.pdf.

Campbell, George. 1874. *Specimens of Languages of India, Including Those of the Aboriginal Tribes of Bengal, the Central Provinces, and the Eastern Frontier.* Calcutta: Bengal Secretariat Press.

Comrie, Bernard, Martin Haspelmath, and Balthasar Bickel. 2008. *The Leipzig Glossing Rules: Conventions for Interlinear Morpheme-by-Morpheme Glosses.* Department of Linguistics of the Max Planck Institute for Evolutionary Anthropology and The Department of Linguistics of the University of Leipzig. https://www.eva.mpg.de/lingua/resources/glossing-rules.php. Retrieved July 10, 2020.

Cowell, Andrew, and Alonzo Sr. Moss. 2008. *The Arapaho Language.* Boulder: University Press of Colorado.

Finck, Franz Nikolaus. 1909. *Die Haupttypen Des Sprachbaus.* Leipzig: B. G. Teubner.

Grierson, G. A., ed. 1909. *Linguistic Survey of India, Tibeto-Burman Family: General Introduction, Specimen of the Tibetan Dialects, The Himalayan Dialects, and the North Assam Group.* Vol. 3.1. 11 Vols. Delhi, Varanasi, Patna: Motilal Banarsidass.

Hodgson, Brian H. 1857. "Comparative Vocabulary of the Languages of the Broken Tribes of Nepal [Vocabulary and Grammar of the Vayu Tribe]." *Journal of the Asiatic Society of Bengal* 26: 317–522 [372–485].

———. 1858. "Comparative Vocabulary of the Languages of the Broken Tribes of Nepal (Continued From Vol 26) [Grammar of the Bahing Tribe]." *Journal of the Asiatic Society of Bengal* 27: 393–456 [393–442].

Hunter, W. W. 1868. *A Comparative Dictionary of the Languages of India and High Asia with a Dissertation, Based on the Hodgson Lists, Official Records, and MSS.* London: Trübner and Co.

Jones, William, and Truman Michelson. 1911. "Algonquian (Fox)." In *Handbook of American Indian Languages*, edited by Franz Boas, 1: 735–874. Smithsonian Institution Bureau of American Ethnology, Bulletin 40. Washington: Government Printing Office.

Lahaussois, Aimée. 2016. "The Translation Tier in Interlinear Glossed Text: Changing Practices in the Description of Endangered Languages." In *Translation as Innovation: Bridging the Sciences and the Humanities*, edited by Patricia M. Phillips-Batoma and Florence Xiangyun Zhang, 261–278. Victoria, TX: Dalkey Archive Press.

———. 2018. "Examining Approaches to Describing Complex Verbal Morphology for an Unwritten Language." In *Histoire Des Langues et Histoire Des Représentations Linguistiques*, edited by Bernard Colombat, Bernard Combettes, Valérie Raby, and Gilles Siouffi. Paris: Honoré Champion.

———. 2020. "The Shapes of Verbal Paradigms in Kiranti Languages." *Faits de Langues* 50(2): 71–93.

———. 2021. "Glossing in the Linguistic Survey of India: Some Insights into Early 20th Century Practices." *Historiographia Linguistica* 48(1): 25–59.

Lehmann, Christian. 1982. "Directions for Interlinear Morphemic Translations." *Folia Linguistica* 16: 199–224.

———. 2004. "Interlinear Morphemic Glossing." In *Morphologie. Ein Internationales Handbuch Zur Flexion Und Wortbildung*, edited by Geert Booij, Christian Lehmann, Joachim Mugdan, and Stavros Skopeteas, 1834–1857. Handbücher Der Sprach- Und Kommunikationswissenschaft, 17/2. Berlin and New York: W. de Gruyter.

Nida, Eugene. 1964. *Towards a Science of Translating*. Leiden: E. J. Brill.

Nida, Eugene, and Charles Taber. 1982. *The Theory and Practice of Translation*. Helps for Translators, VIII. Leiden: E. J. Brill.

Raumolin-Brunberg, Helena. 2006. "Leaders of Linguistic Change in Early Modern England." In *Corpus-Based Studies of Diachronic English*, edited by Matti Rissanen and Roberta Facchinetti, 115–134. Bern: Peter Lang.

Schoolcraft, Henry R. 1855. "Chippewa Language." In *Historical and Statistical Information Respecting the History, Condition and Prospects of the Indian Tribes of the United States*, edited by Henry R. Schoolcraft, 297–388. Philadelphia: Lippencott.

Schultze-Berndt, Eva. 2006. "Linguistic Annotation." In *Essentials of Language Documentation*, edited by Jost Gippert, Nikolaus Himmelmann, and Ulrike Mosel. Berlin and New York: Mouton de Gruyter.

Tims, John William. 1889. *Grammar and Dictionary of the Blackfoot Language in the Dominion of Canada: For the Use of Missionaries, School-Teachers, and Others*. London: Society for Promoting Christian Knowledge.

Index

abbreviation, 144–45
accentuation, 144
ākṣepasamādhāna (answering of objections), 28–29, 31
algonquian, 223–27, 240, 244–45
alignment, 95, 103–4
alloglottography, 181n8
Amazonidum, 35
Analects, The (of Confucius), 51–52, 64
anatomy, 117–19, 129
annotation tier, 225, 229, 239, 241, 243, 245
Anselme of Laon, 19
anvayamukhī (commentary), 28, 36
apapāṭhaḥ, 32
aphorisms, 124–25, 129
archaic pronouns, 231, 233, 235–45
Aristotle, 114, 121–25; *Metaphysics*, 122–23; *Physics*, 123
ars medicine, 124
article, definite, 142, 144, 148
Asia, East, 17
Audax (grammarian), 32
Auraicept na nÉces, 113–31
Auroux, Sylvain, 37–38, 41
Authier-Revuz, Jacqueline, 176
autonymy (autonymic processes, practices), 31–32

Badb, 99
Bailey, Nathaniel, 166–67
Bede, 97
bhāṣya (commentary), 28
black. *See* gloss
Blom, Alderik, 201
Book of Ballymote, the, 128
Brāhmī, 31
Breton, Old, 16. *See also* gloss
Buddhism, 13

Cabinet Library, 84, *84*
Calvin, John, 168
cano (verbe), 34
Carmen Saliarium, 42n8
catechism, 164, 168, 172, 184n52
category labels. *See* glossing, labels
causality, 122–23, 125
Celtic (language family), 16. *See also* gloss
Chaucer, Geoffrey, 170
Chinese: Buddhist texts, Chinese-translated, 92n4; character(s), 87, 89, 92n1; character dictionary, 85; Classical (language), 12, 13; Classical text(s), 83, 92, 92n1; compounds, 54–56, 69; notes, 92n2; secular texts, 91
Cinato, Frank, 11, 200

Classical Chinese. *See* Literary Sinitic
Code-switching, 95, 99–101, 103
Collectio, 95, 103
colored pencil, 143–44
commentary: as distinct from glossary and dictionary, 165. *See also anvayamukhī* (commentary); *bhāṣya* (commentary); *kathaṃbhūtinī* (commentary); Sanskrit; *vyākhyāna* (commentary)
compendium. *See Kunten, goi shūsei*
complex verbal morphology, 223–24, 239
construction: of the verb *exsolvo*, 42. *See also ordo* (construction); *anvayamukhī* (commentary); *vākyayojanā* (construing the sentences)
copula, 53, 66. See also Japanese clitics
Council of Trent, 168
cryptography, 142
Cyrillus glossary. *See* Pseudo-Cyrillus glossary

Daibirushana-kyō sho, 85, *85*, 86, 92n3
Dainichi-kyō sho. *See Daibirushana-kyō sho*
Damascus, John of, 124–25
Danai, 36
Daniel of Lérins, 20
Desbordes, Françoise, 40
Devanagari, 31
dictionary. *See* Japanese; Chinese
diglossia, 38, 41
Diomedes (grammarian), 27, 29–34, 40, 42
discretio, 33
Dì zāng shí lún jīng, 90, 93n6. *See also Jizō jūrin-kyō*
Domingo de Santo Tomas, 21
Donatus (grammarian), 114
Draak, Maartje, 207–8
Durchschuss. *See* inter-lining (German 'Durchschuss')

Eco, Umberto, 170
education, 121–22, 125, 130

emendatio (emendation), 29–32
enarratio (interpretation), 29–34, 36–37, 40
epi-text. *See* paratext
essence, 119–23, 128–29
etargaire, 120–21
Etymology, 35, 39, 97–98, 117. *See also* Isidore; *scinderatio phonorum*
Eucharistic formula, 167
Eusebius, 103–4; *Chronicon*, 103–4
exegesis, 115, 120, 125
exquisitio, 29, 34

fǎnqiè spellings, 56, 71, 79n4
free translation, 225–43, 245
fudokuji. *See* unread characters (*fudokuji*)

Gaius *Institutiones*, 41n4
Geluykens, Ronald, 176
Genette, Gérard, 155–57, 177–78
German, Old High, 16
gloss. *See* inter-lining (German 'Durchschuss'); Japanese; kana; *kunten*; lemma; Martianus Capella; Middle Chinese; *okototen*; paratext; phonogram glosses; Prudentius; seuil; *vārttika*; *vṛtti*: black, 91; Breton, 143; Carolingian, 11, 13; Celtic, 143, 148; commentary, 201; cross-references, 215; definition of, 10; dry-point, 139–48; durability of, 11; explanatory, 213–14; function (relational/explanatory), 201; grammatical, 139–48, 204–5, 226–29, 238, 240, 244–45; Greek, 203–4, 217, 219, 220; inversion. *See re-ten* (inversion glosses); Japanese, 141, 143–44, 147–48; Japanese kunten, 92n2; *kana*, 50, 53–54, 57–59, 69–70, 75, 86, 91; *katakana*, 84; Korean, 141, 143–44; Latin, 141, 144, 146–48, 197–221; lexical, 202–3, 225, 227–29, 240, 244–45; morphemic, 48, 63–67, 76–78; morphology, 204–5; Old

English, 141, 143–44, 147–48, 201; Old French, 143; Old High German, 139–48, 201; Old Irish, 141, 143, 147–48, 198, 201, 203, 206–7, 219; Old Saxon, 143–44, 201; Old Slavic, 143; prosody, 202; reading, 11; substitution (subtype of), 11, 201, 203; summarizing content, 215; symbol, 198, 202, 207–13, 219, 220; syntactic, 19, 140, 214; syntax, 207–8; tiers of, 12; transcription, 12; translation, 12, 228–30, 235, 239, 240, 243–45; trilineal, 12; typology of, 9; unstable, 11; variant readings, 215; vermillion, 85; vermillion *kana*, 86; vernacular Japanese, 87; white, 91; white ink, 89–91
Glossa ordinaria, 19
Glossaries, 9, 16, 95–98. See Pseudo-Cyrillus glossary
glossarium, 20
glossators, 12–13, 15, 19, 88, 92. See also *kunten*
glossing, 12; comparative research on, 47–48, 76; interlinear, 225–26, 239, 242–43, 245; Japanese traditions, 47–56, 79nn2–3. See also kanbun kundoku; Korean traditions, 47–48, 75–76, 79nn2–3. See also *kugyŏl*; *kunten*, 13, 15, 17–19; labels, 48, 64–68, 70–71, 76–78; medieval practices of, 11–13; order of, 91; polysemy of, 12; process, 92; software for, 18; standardization of, 15–16; systematicity of, 15–16; textual, 10–13; typological, 15; Vietnamese traditions, 47–48; white ink, 89. See *kugyŏl*; Leipzig Glossing Rules; legal texts
glossulis (*poeticis*), 29, 34, 42
gōfu (compound bars), 56, 70, 79n3
Gombrich, Ernst, 178–80
Graeca collecta, 96
grammar: fonctions of g., 29–30; missionary, 21. See also *grammatica*; Pāṇini (grammarian)

grammarians 10, 13, 15–16; Greek, 10. See Audax; Diomedes (grammarian); Donatus (grammarian); Pāṇini (grammarian); Papias (grammarian); Priscian (grammarian); Scaurus, Terentius (grammarian); Servius (grammarian); Victorinus, Maximus (grammarian)
grammatica, 29–30, 32, 42, 113; *practica*, 15; *speculativa*, 15
grammatical: incongruence, 142, 145. See also gloss
grammatisation, 27, 38
Grice, Paul, 166
Grubier, Frédéric, 169
Grunenberg, Johannes, 163
gugyeol. See *kugyŏl*
Gupta, 31, 41n3
Gurwitsch, Aron, 180
Gù Yìn, 88

Hadrian, 32
Hakaseke-ten, 15
hakuten, 19
Hamilton, James, 164
Hàn shū: *Hàn shū gǔjīn jíyì*, 88; *Hàn shū jí zhù*, 88; *Hàn shū xūn zuǎn*, 88; *Hàn shū Yáng Xióng Zhuàn*, 87–91
Hayashi Gahō, 84
Heian jidai no kanbun kundokugo ni tsukite no kenkyū, 90
hendoku. See word, order inversion (*hendoku*)
Hermeneumata, 96–97
hiragana, 53–54, 58–59. See also *kana*
hodoku. See supplemented readings (*hodoku*)
Hofman, Ricjklof, 198–221
Holtz, Louis, 159, 177, 180
Hrabanus Maurus, 97
Husserl, Edmund, 180

idoku. See reading, alternate (*idoku*)
incongruence. See grammatical
index: as a paratextual tool, 164

indexation. *See* object indexation; subject indexation
interlinear: version, 144, 147–48. *See also* glossing
inter-lining (German 'Durchschuss'): blank lines inserted for later glossing, 163–64
intertextuality, 181n10
inversion marks, 19, 92n1; *kaeriten*, 84. *See also yeokdokjeom* (inversion glosses); *re-ten* (inversion glosses)
Irish, Old, 16
Irvine, Martin, 10, 20, 30, 32–34, 42
Isidore (of Seville), 97–98; *Etymologiae*, 97
iti, 31–32, 35
iudicium (criticism), 29, 31–32

James, William, 180
Japan, 15
Japanese: auxiliary verbs, 51, 65, 67; classical Japanese literature, 90; clitics, 66 (*see also* copula); compounds, 56, 67; Early Middle Japanese, 50, 54, 72–74; *kō-otsu* distinction, 72; labial lenition, 72–73; Late Middle Japanese, 54, 72–74; lexical strata, 70; Middle Japanese, 83, 90; Modern Japanese, 73–74; monophthongization, 72; mora nasal, 72, 74; mora obstruent, 74; nasal codas, 72, 74; Old Japanese, 72–73, 90; Old Japanese dictionary, 92n2; Old Japanese materials, 91; particles, 49, 52–55, 59, 65–66; phonemicization thereof, 71–74; post-consonantal glides, 73–74; union segments, 80n8; verbal suffixes, 49, 51–53, 59, 65–67. *See also* gloss; *kunten*; languages; reading
JapanKnowledge Lib, 87
jato (abbreviated Chinese character glosses), 75
jeomto (dot glosses), 75

Jizō jūrin-kyō, 90. *See also Dì zāng shí lún jīng*
John Scottus Eriugena, 97
Jōyō kanji, 89–90, 93n5

kadanten (paragraph marks), 56, 70
kaeriten. *See* inversion marks; word; order inversion
kana, 50, 56–57; literature, 90; *man'yōgana*, 53–54; spellings, 72, 74. *See also* gloss
kanbun kundoku, 11, 13, 48–64, 67–71, 75–76, 79nn1–2
Kanchiin-bon Ruiju myōgishō. *See Ruiju myōgishō*
kanji. *See Jōyō* kanji
kara, 32
karigane-ten (inversion glosses). *See re-ten* (inversion glosses)
kārikā (mnemonic stance), 28
karmani, 32
Kasuga, Masaji (1878–1962), 59–63, 67
katakana, 53–55, 58–59. *See* gloss
kathaṃbhūtinī (commentary), 28, 36
Kegon-gyō (Avataṃsaka sūtra), 50, 79n2
Kegon kanjōki (Huìyuǎn's Commentary on the Avataṃsaka sutra). *See index of Manuscripts* Daitōkyū Kinen Bunko MS
Kiranti, 223–26, 239, 243–45
Kojiki, 90; Account of Ancient Matters, 50, 79n1; *Kojiki* song, 90
Konkōmyō saishōō-kyō (Golden Light Sutra). *See index of Manuscripts* Saidaiji MS
Korean. *See* gloss
Korhammer, Michael, 207–8
Kosukegawa, Teiji, 14
Kotenpon no kokugogakuteki kenkyū, *Kōzanji-bon*, 85, *85*
kugyŏl, 13, 17–18
kun (訓 Chinese *xùn*), 11
kunten: an expression exclusive to kunten materials, 90; glossators,

88; glosses, 83–84, 87, 89–91, 92nn1–2; glosses on Buddhist texts, 91; glossing, *87–88*, 91; goi shūsei, 83, 85–86, 89–90; materials, 83, 87, 90, 92n1, 92n3; tool, 91. *See also* glossing; Japanese; *Kunten, goi shūsei*
kuntengogaku (gloss linguistics), 57–62
kun yomi, 11
Kyoto National Museum, 84, *84*, 85, *86*, *87*, 88, *88*, *89*

Lactantius, 97
Lahaussois, Aimée, 16
languages: endangered, 13; Japanese, 87; Latin, 15, 27–42; undescribed, 21. *See also* gloss; Japanese
Latin. *See* languages
law, 116, 120, 125–26, 128–29
lectio (reading), 29–33, 37, 39–40; *discontinuata* (disjointed reading), 20
legal texts: glossing of, 153, 162, 172; punctuation of, 173–74; text of statutes ideally self-punctuating, 174
Lehmann, Christian, 15, 223, 225, 227
Leipzig Glossing Rules, 16, 63–64, 76, 225, 245
lemma, 10, 11; gloss pairing, 10, 13
lexical: substitution, 10. *See also* gloss
literacy, 121, 123, 129
literal meaning: early modern senses of the term, 169–70; sense of the term in the Wycliffite tradition, 184n50
literal translation, 228–31, 233, 235, 237–39, 241–44
Literary Sinitic: annotations, 56, 70–71; compounds. *See* Chinese characters, compounds; particles, 51–52
litterae significativae, 144
Liú Xiàobiāo, 84
Liú Yìqìng, 84
Locke, John, 164
logic, 114
Lombard, Pierre, 19

Luther, Martin, 162

man'yōgana. *See* kana
Man'yōshū, 90
Martianus Capella, 95–103; *De nuptiis Philologiae et Mercurii*, 96, 99–101, 103; Oldest Gloss Tradition, 96, 100–101, 103
McNamee, Kathleen, 13
medicine, 113–31
memoria, 103–4
Mesopotamian: clay tablets, 9
metadata, 18
Middle Ages, 14, 16
Middle Chinese, 55, 64, 71, 75, 79n4; tone marks (*shōten*), 55–56, 70–71
mise-en-page, 164, 168, 173
misinterpretation, 91
mistake (scribe's), 146
Morohashi's Dai *Kanwa Jiten*, 85, 88
morphology, 16. *See* complex verbal morphology
morphosyntactic glosses. *See* okototen
mūla (root text), 28, 32, 36
mythographers, the, 97

Naikaku bunko. *See* cabinet library
Nakada Norio, 90
nāma, 34
Neo-Gricean theory. *See* Grice, Paul
Network for the study of glossing, 47
New Account of Tales of the World. *See Shìshuō xīnshū*
New Corrected *Taishō Tripitaka* text database, 85, 92n4
Nihon kokugo daijiten, 86–87, 89
Nihon shoki (Chronicles of Japan), 50, 79n1, 87
nineteenth century, 244
null morphemes, 65–66, 77
Nyāyakośa, 28

object indexation, 223, 226–27, 230–36, 239, 241, 243–45
officia, 27, 29–32

okiji. See unread characters (*fudokuji*)
okototen, 19, 54–55, 57–59, 67–70, 75; vermillion, 84, 86
Oldecop, Johannes, 163, 178
ontology, 114, 119, 123
ordo (construction), 29, 36, 39
Ōya Tōru (1851–1928), 57–59

padaccheda (word divison), 28–29, 31, 33, 39
padapāṭha, 31
padārthokti (meaning of the word), 28–29, 31, 34, 37, 39
Pāṇini (grammarian), 28, 35
Papias (grammarian), 17
papyrus scrolls (*volumina*), 18
paradigm. *See* verbal paradigm
Pārameśvaratantra, 41n3
paraphernalia, 157
Paraśārapurāṇa, 28
paratext, 153–80; coining of term paratext by Genette, 155–56; Genette's paratextual categories, 182n16; glosses as paratextual elements, 156; paratext as "frame" to a primary text, 176–80; the "paratextual paradox," 176; peri-text and epi-text distinguished, 156, 159; recursive nesting of paratextual elements, 160, 175–76
parchment books (*codices*), 18
Parkes, Malcolm, 174–75
partes orationis, 21
part of speech, 145
pāṭha, 31–32
paṭhati, 32
peri-text. *See* paratext
philosophy, 117, 119–25
phonemicization, 48, 63–67, 69. *See also* Japanese, phonemicization thereof
phonogram glosses. *See* gloss
photographic image, 91
Pierre le Vénérable, 20
poetry, 115–17, 119–20, 125–30

Porphyry, 114, 123
pragmatics, 153–80; relation between semantics and pragmatics, *166*; sentence-meaning *versus* speaker-meaning, 166
prārthayadhvam, 32
Priscian (Priscianus Caesariensis, grammarian), 11, 39, 99, 101, 197–221. *See also Index of manuscripts* St. Gallen, Stiftsbibliothek, Cod. Sang. 904
pronouns. *See* archaic pronouns
prosodic mark, 144
Prudentius, 95–96, 101, 103; *Psychomachia*, 95, 101, 103; Weitz glosses, 101
Psalms, 200, 221
Pseudo-Cyrillus glossary, 97
punctuation, 33, 50, 54–56, 70, 84, 92n1, 172–76. *See also* legal texts

Quechua, 21
Quintilian, 42n8

reading: aid, 144; alternate (*idoku*), 53, 59, 69–70; everyday, 91; iterated (*saidoku*), 51–52, 68; Japanese, 89, 91; standard, 89; supplemented (*hodoku*), 49, 52–53, 70; vernacular, 11, 49, 52, 57, 63, 70, 75, 93n5. *See also* gloss; *kugyŏl*; *kanbun kundoku*; *lectio*
Relevance Theory, 166–71, 180, 183n38
Remigius of Auxerre, 97
Renaissance, 12, 21
re-ten (inversion glosses), 55, 67
Robinson, Fred, 207–8
Rosier-Catach, Irène, 169
Ruiju myōgishō, 92n2; *Kanchiin-bon Ruiju myōgishō*, 83, 85, 88, 92n2; *Zushoryō-bon Ruiju myōgishō*, 83, 92n2

śabda, 32

Index

sacred languages (*tres lingae sacrae*), 38
saidoku. *See* iterated readings (*saidoku*)
sandhi, 31, 37
Sanskrit, 18, 27–41, 154, 160; Commentaries, 27–37, 39
SAT. *See* New Corrected *Taishō Tripitaka* text database
Scaurus, Terentius (grammarian), 32–33
Scholica graecarum glossarum, 97
scinderatio phonorum (etymology), 35
script, 31, 40; *scriptio continua*, 31–32, 37
scriptorium, 146
Searle, John, 167
segmentation, 228–30, 237–42, 244
self-interpreting texts, 158, 161
Servius (grammarian), 34–36, 97
seuil (threshold): gloss as "threshold" to text, 157. *See also* Genette, Gérard; paratext
Sharpe, Richard, 164
Shìshuō xīnshū, 84, *84*, *86*, 86
shorthand, 163
Shōsōin-bon, 90
Sidham, 31
significatio, 33–34, 39
Sino-Japanese, 49, 53, 56, 67, 70, 72, 74; compounds, 56, 67; t-codas, 74; velar nasal, 74
Smollett, Tobias, 175
Sperber, Dan. *See* Relevance Theory
standardization, 224–25
Statius, 99; *Thebaid*, 99
Stilo, Aelius, 42n8
stylus, 79nn2–3, 143–46, 148
subject indexation, 223, 226–27, 230–33, 235–36, 238–39, 241–45
symbol. *See* gloss

Táin Bó Cúailnge, 99
Taishō Tripitaka. *See* New Corrected *Taishō Tripitaka* text database
Teeuwen, Mariken, 10
teni(w)oha, 15

textbook, early modern sense of, 162–64
text transposition. *See* reading, vernacular
textual information, 91
Tironian notes, 102
Tisiphone, 99
Tōdaiji library, 90
Tōji Kongōzō, 85, *85*, 86
tone marks. *See* Middle Chinese, tone marks
transitive arguments, 223–24, 226–27, 230–33, 235–38, 241–43, 245
translation, 19, 49–50, 52–54, 56, 63. *See* free translation; gloss, translation; literal translation
triads, 119
Tsukishima Hiroshi, 83, 85, *85*, 86, 89, 90
two-lines-in-one annotations (*warichū*), 71
typology, 104, 197–218

unread characters (*fudokuji*), 52, 59, 69
Usserianus Primus, 143

vākyayojanā (construing the sentences), 28–29, 31, 35, 37, 39
Varro, Marcus Terentius, 27, 29–30, 32, 40
vārttika, 28
verbal paradigm, 227, 230–36, 238, 241–42
vermillion. *See* gloss, *okototen*
vernacular. *See* gloss; reading
Victorinus, Maximus (grammarian), 30, 32, 42n5
vigraha, 29, 31, 34–35, 37, 39
vikriyanta, 32
Virgil, 34, 36, 95, 101–3
viśeṣa, 34
Voegelin, Charles and Florence, 15
vṛtti (gloss), 28
Vulcanius (Bonaventure De Smet), 20
vyākhyāna (commentary), 28–29

wax tablet, 143
white. *See* gloss; glossing
Wieland, Gernot, 197–221
Wilson, Deirdre. *See* Relevance Theory
(w)okototen. *See okototen*
word: formation, 145; order inversion (*hendoku*), 49–51, 54, 57, 59, 67–68, 75, 79n2; separation, 144. *See also padaccheda*; *padārthokti*; Word-Pairing
word-Pairing, 95–99, 103
Wyclif, John: Wycliffite commentary tradition, 160–61, 182n23

Xylographs, 18

Yán Shīgǔ, 88
Yáo Chá, 88
yeokdokjeom (inversion glosses), 75
yodhāḥ, 35
Yoshizawa, Yoshinori (1876–1954), 57–59
yudhyanta, 35

Zushoryō-bon Ruiju myōgishō. *See Ruiju myōgishō*
Zwingli, Ulrich, 168

Index of Manuscripts

Berlin, Staatsbibliothek zu Berlin, Preussischer Kulturbesitz, MS Hamilton 542, 147
Brussels, Bibliothèque Royale, lat. 9968–72, 101

Cambridge, Corpus Christi College, MS 153, 99–101
Cambridge, Corpus Christi College, MS 330, 99
Cambridge, University Library, Gg.5.35, 197
Cambridge, University Library, MS Add.1049.1, 41n3
Cologne, Dombibliothek, MS 81, 101

Daitōkyū Kinen Bunko MS, 50, 54, 79n2
Dublin, National Library of Ireland, MS G3, 116
Dublin, Royal Irish Academy, MS 23 N 29, 126
Dublin, Royal Irish Academy, MS 23 P 12 ('The Book of Ballymote'), 128
Dublin, Royal Irish Academy, MS 24 B 3, 126

Dublin, Trinity College Library, MS 55 (Usserianus Primus), 143
Dublin, Trinity College Library, MS 1318 (H 2. 16), 120

Edinburgh, National Library of Scotland Advocates' MS 72. 1. 2, 119, 122

Kyoto, Kozanji, Second Division 117 (Daibirushana-kyō sho), 85
Kyoto, Kyoto National Museum, B First 1113 (Hàn shū Yáng Xióng Zhuàn), 87–91
Kyoto, Kyoto National Museum, B First 549 (Shìshuō xīnshū), 84–86

London, British Library, MS Arundel 333, 122
London, British Library, MS Egerton 88, 120, 128

Munich, Bayerische Staatsbibliothek, Clm 4542, 145, 147
Munich, Bayerische Staatsbibliothek, Clm 4614, 147

Orléans, Médiathèque municipale, Ms. 191, 103
Oxford, Bodleian Library, Auct. F. 2. 8, 102
Oxford, Sackler Library, Papyrology Rooms P. Oxy. 2103, 41n4

Saidaiji, Saidaiji-bon Konkōmyō saishō ōkyō, 59–60, 69–70, 199
St. Gallen, Stiftsbibliothek, Cod. Sang. 904, 99, 101, 147, 197–221

About the Editors

Franck Cinato is currently researcher at the CNRS *History of Linguistic Theories* (HTL, UMR 7597) research group. He earned his BA and MA at the University of Montreal (Québec, Canada) and his PhD at École Pratique des Hautes Études (Paris, Sorbonne) in 2010. He occupied during the four years project *Europanea Regia* (2008–2012) a part-time position at the Bibliothèque Nationale de France in the Manuscripts department. He works on Early Middle Ages' glosses and glossaries and has developed an expertise in Carolingian books. He published studies and a monography focusing on the Carolingian reception of the sixth-century Priscian's grammar (*Priscien glosé*, 2015). He has also assisted Anne Grondeux in the new digital edition of the *Liber glossarum*, which is the foundational seventh-century work in European lexicography.

Aimée Lahaussois is a linguist at the CNRS *Histoire des théories linguistiques* research group, who received her training at the University of California, Berkeley. She has carried out descriptive work on languages of the Kiranti subgroup (Tibeto-Burman, Nepal) for the past 20 years, contributing data from these languages to typological studies. Among her interests are the history and epistemology of language description and the emergence of practices currently used for data collection and analysis of poorly described languages.

John B. Whitman is a professor of linguistics at Cornell University and the Department of Crosslinguistic Studies at the National Institute for Japanese Language and Linguistics (NINJAL) in Tokyo. He has served as chair of Linguistics at Cornell and Director of the East Asia Program. He works on historical/comparative linguistics, language typology, and syntactic theory, with a primary focus on the languages of East Asia. He has published on the diachronic syntax, phonology, and morphology of Japanese, modern Japanese syntax, Korean syntax, and the diachronic syntax of Chinese. His current research focus is on the principles of syntactic change. Recent publications include "Postpositions vs. prepositions in Mandarin Chinese: The articulation of disharmony" (with Redouane Djamouri and Waltraud Paul), 2013, in Theresa Biberauer (ed.) *Theoretical Approaches to Disharmonic Word Order*, Oxford, and "The diachronic consequences of the RTR analysis of Tungusic vowel harmony" (with Andrew Joseph), 2013, in Umut Özge (ed.) *Proceedings of the 8th Workshop on Altaic Formal Linguistics*. Cambridge, Massachusetts: *MIT Working Papers in Linguistics*. Books include *Proto-Japanese* (co-edited with Bjarke Frellesvig, John Benjamins, 2008).

About the Contributors

Alderik H. Blom is a professor of Celtic in the Department of Comparative Indo-European Philology at the University of Marburg/Philipps-Universität Marburg, Germany. His research interests include the study of early medieval manuscripts in Latin, Celtic, and Germanic languages (producing, for example, *Glossing the Psalms: The Emergence of the Written Vernaculars in Western Europe from the Seventh to the Twelfth Centuries*, De Gruyter, 2017). Other interests include the study of Continental Celtic and the history of nineteenth-century philology and textual criticism as it developed within the context of romantic nationalism in the Netherlands/Frisia, Germany, Britain, Russia, and the Scandinavian countries.

Andreas Nievergelt is a professor at the University of Zurich in German linguistics. He works as a scientific research assistant at the University of Bonn and in the Abbey Library of St Gall. He lectures and researches in the field of historical linguistics mainly in the areas of Old High German, Old Saxon, and Old English glossography.

David Cram is an emeritus fellow of Jesus College, Oxford, formerly a university lecturer in General Linguistics specializing in semantics and pragmatics. His research has been primarily on the history of ideas about language, with special reference to the seventeenth century. His book-length publications include two critical editions, both jointly with Jaap Maat: *George Dalgarno on universal language*: *The Art of Signs and the unpublished papers* (2001) and *John Wallis on teaching language to a boy born deaf: the Popham Notebook and associated texts* (2017).

About the Contributors

Deborah Hayden is an associate professor in the Department of Early Irish at Maynooth University. Her research interests and publications range widely across various aspects of medieval Irish, Welsh, and Latin language and literature, with a particular focus on the history of linguistic ideas and education, vernacular legal texts, Irish-language medical manuscripts, and late-medieval scribal culture.

Matthew Zisk is an associate professor of theoretical linguistics at Tohoku University Graduate School of International Cultural Studies. His primary fields of research include Japanese linguistics, historical linguistics, language contact, and translation. He is the principal investigator of the JSPS Kakenhi project, *Development of a Multilingual Dictionary of Japanese Linguistics Terminology and a Glossing Standard for Japonic Languages* (2019–2023). Recent publications include *Japanese Linguistics* (Asakura Shoten, 2019), coauthored with Mark Irwin of Yamagata University.

Pádraic Moran is a lecturer in Classics at the University of Galway. His research is focused on education and scholarship in Antiquity and the Early Middle Ages, including the grammatical and rhetorical traditions; glosses, glossaries, and commentaries; and knowledge of Greek and Hebrew in the Early Medieval West. Recent publications include *De Origine Scoticae Linguae (O'Mulconry's Glossary): An early Irish linguistic tract, edited with a related glossary, Irsan* (CCCM, Lexica Latina Medii Aevi 7).

Sinéad O'Sullivan is a reader in medieval history at Queen's University Belfast. Her research focuses on early medieval glosses and their importance. She has published two books on the reception of Late Antique authors: the first on Prudentius (Brill), the second on Martianus Capella in the series Corpus Christianorum Continuatio Mediaevalis (Brepols). Recent research interests include the reception of Virgil in the Carolingian age and the practice of collectio. Her current project, focusing on glosses on the Psalms, investigates glosses for insight into crafting knowledge in the Carolingian world.

Teiji Kosukegawa received his M.A. from Hokkaido University in 1986, worked as an assistant professor there from 1987 to 1993, then taught Japanese linguistics at the University of Toyama from 1993 to 2022, and is currently a professor emeritus at the University of Toyama. His fields of research are mainly Japanese linguistics, with special attention to vernacular reading of Classical Chinese text in Sinosphere (China, Japan, Korea, and Vietnam). He is the co-author of the bibliography for volumes 1, 5, 6, 7, 9, 11, and 12 of the *Tōyō Bunko Zenpon Sōsho* [Reproduction series of good books held by the Tōyō Bunko] (Bensei Shuppan, 2014-2015).

www.ingramcontent.com/pod-product-compliance
Lightning Source LLC
Chambersburg PA
CBHW021350300426
44114CB00012B/1161